CHINA IN WORLD POLITICS

BY J. P. JAIN

Documentary Study of the Warsaw Pact

China Pakistan and Bangladesh

India and Disarmament : Nehru Era

Nuclear India
(in two volumes)

Soviet Policy Towards Pakistan and Bangladesh

After Mao What ? Army Party and Group Rivalries in China

China in World Politics
A Study of Sino-British Relations, 1949-1975

CHINA
IN
WORLD POLITICS

A Study of Sino-British Relations
1949-1975

by

J. P. Jain

RADIANT PUBLISHERS

First Published 1976 by
Radiant Publishers
E-155, Kalkaji, New Delhi-110019

Printed in India by
Dhawan Printing Works
26-A Mayapuri, New Delhi-110027

Preface

In spite of its disclaimer about becoming a super Power, China is determined to have "an independent and relatively comprehensive industrial and economic system" by 1980 and to accomplish the "comprehensive modernization of agriculture, industry, national defence and science and technology" by the end of this century. Evidently, China aspires to attain super Power status through diplomacy and through serious efforts to transform itself into "a powerful modern socialist country" by placing its economy in the "front ranks of the world." Peking is already an important factor in world politics and is likely to play an even greater role in international affairs in the years to come. However, its future role in the world would depend, to a great extent, on internal conditions—the stability at home and the character of its leadership. The domestic politics of China is discussed in the author's book, *After Mao What? Army Party and Group Rivalries in China.* The present work deals with the emergence of China as a factor in world politics and its role in international affairs. The book also examines the course of Sino-British relations in its proper perspective, keeping in view the changing world situation, the internal compulsions and the external constraints. It discusses in detail the various moves and counter-moves on the diplomatic chessboard, the strains and stresses in their relations and prospects for the future.

In the post World War II period, Britain and China, owing to their weak economic and military position, were not capable of influencing the course of international events to the extent of either the USA or the USSR. Circumstances compelled them to align themselves with the two rival groupings (into which the world was divided) under the leadership of the two super Powers. They, nevertheless, retained a certain degree of manoeuvrability in world affairs. In recent years, the complexion of international relations has changed substantially with the emergence of Sino-Soviet confrontation, super Power *detente* and Sino-US *rapprochement*.

As a result of the British entry into the European Economic Community (EEC), the "special relationship" between Britain and the United States, which had persisted for over two decades, has come to an end. Moreover, Vice-Premier Teng Hsiao-ping has now emphatically stated that the so-called socialist camp no longer existed and that China belonged to the Third World countries. Thus, Peking looks forward to rig up a broad united front comprising Third World (the developing countries in Asia, Africa and Latin America) and Second World countries (the industrialized developed societies of Europe and other regions) under its leadership and against the hegemonistic policies of the First World—the two super Powers. The anti-Sovietism, which has now become the linchpin of Chinese foreign policy, in a way, inhibits Peking's freedom of action just as its pro-Soviet stance hampered the pursuit of an independent policy in the late 1940s and 1950s. However, at the same time, this anti-Sovietism opens up new vistas in China's relations with Western countries.

The book analyses in depth the problem (which has all along remained a riddle for most China watchers) of China not responding favourably to the recognition accorded by one of the principal Western Powers in the early 1950s. The study seeks to clarify that problem and various other aspects of Chinese foreign policy—the syndrome of Sino-Soviet relations; Peking's role during the Korean crisis, the Indo-China conflict and the Formosan Straits crises; the attitude of China towards developments in Southeast Asia, Western Europe and Hong Kong; the question of China's representation in the UN; and trade relations with capitalist countries. The study also focuses attention on the changed Chinese perception of Britain and other West European countries. Peking no longer regards Britain a camp follower or a subservient ally of the USA, but considers it a useful member of a grouping (EEC) that can play a significant role in opposing the hegemony of the two super Powers.

The present work is a thoroughly revised and updated version of the author's thesis, for which he was the first to be awarded a Ph. D. degree in the Chinese Studies Division of the Centre for East Asian Studies of the Indian School of International Studies (now part of Jawaharlal Nehru University). The author has made full use of the material available in the Chinese language.

The views expressed in this study are entirely the personal views of the author and are not to be attributed to any institution, organization or body. I thank my son Rajendra for his help in editing the manuscript and other members of my family for their unfailing cooperation and assistance of various kinds.

New Delhi   J.P. Jain

Contents

Preface   *v*

I   *Historical Background*   1

BRITISH PREDOMINANCE IN CHINA   2
RIVALRY OF OTHER POWERS   3
"OPEN DOOR" IN CHINA   5
COLLABORATION OF CHINESE NATIONALISM WITH
    THE SOVIET UNION   6
WORLD WAR II   12
TREATY OF 1943   12
TRADE PROSPECTS AFTER THE WAR   15
CHINESE CIVIL WAR, 1945-49   16
BRITISH ATTITUDE   16
ECONOMIC COMPETITION WITH THE UNITED STATES   19
STRAINED RELATIONS WITH THE KUOMINTANG   22

II *British Recognition and Peking's Reaction*   24

ASSUMPTIONS BEHIND BRITISH RECOGNITION   24
CHINESE RESPONSE   29
SOVIET ATTITUDE   37
BRITISH MANOEUVRES   41
RELATIONS AT CHARGE D'AFFAIRES LEVEL   43
CULTURAL REVOLUTION   44
FULL DIPLOMATIC RELATIONS   45

III *The Korean Question*   48

STRATEGIC IMPORTANCE OF KOREA   48
OUTBREAK OF THE KOREAN WAR   49
BRITISH REACTION   50
CHINESE INTERVENTION   54
BRITISH POLICY AFTER CHINESE INVERVENTION   56
QUEST FOR A CEASEFIRE   59
EFFORTS TO REACH A POLITICAL SETTLEMENT   69

IMPACT OF THE KOREAN WAR ON SINO-BRITISH
    RELATIONS   71
RECENT DEVELOPMENTS IN KOREA   73

IV   *Taiwan and the Offshore Islands*   82

STRATEGIC IMPORTANCE OF FORMOSA AND THE
    PESCADORES   83
HISTORICAL BACKGROUND   83
LEGAL ASPECTS OF THE PROBLEM   84
BRITISH VIEW   85
CHINESE STAND   89
POLITICAL ASPECTS OF THE PROBLEM   92
BRITISH ATTITUDE   93
CHINESE STAND   98
THE FIRST TAIWAN STRAITS CRISIS, 1954-55   103
THE SECOND TAIWAN STRAITS CRISIS, 1958   106
SINO-US RAPPROCHEMENT AND CHANGE IN BRITISH
    ATTITUDE ON FORMOSA   109

V   *Southeast Asia*   112

BRITISH STAKE IN MALAYA   113
MILITARY UPRISING   113
CALCUTTA CONFERENCE OF ASIAN COMMUNIST
    PARTIES, 1948   115
CHINESE ATTITUDE   116
BRITISH RECOGNITION OF CHINA AND ITS IMPACT
    ON MALAYA   118
CHANGE IN TACTICS OF COMMUNIST INSURGENTS   121
INDEPENDENCE AND AFTER   123
BRITISH INTERESTS IN OTHER COUNTRIES OF SOUTH-
    EAST ASIA   123
WAR IN INDO-CHINA   125
CHINA'S ROLE IN THE INDO-CHINA WAR   126
BRITISH ATTITUDE   130
THE GENEVA CONFERENCE   133
AFTER GENEVA   135
DEVELOPMENTS IN LAOS   135
UNIFICATION OF VIETNAM   139
FORMATION OF A DEFENCE ORGANIZATION IN SOUTH-
    EAST ASIA   140

EDEN'S LOCARNO IDEA   140
BRITAIN JOINS SEATO   143
CHINESE REACTION   145
VIETNAM CONFLICT IN THE 1960s   146
BRITISH PROPOSALS   149
CHINESE REACTION   151
RECENT DEVELOPMENTS, 1970-75   154

VI   *Hong Kong*   158

HISTORICAL PERSPECTIVE   159
KOWLOON CITY INCIDENT OF 1948   162
TRADE WITH NATIONALIST CHINA   163
COMMUNIST TAKEOVER IN CHINA AND AFTER   164
TRADE WITH COMMUNIST CHINA   165
THE KOREAN WAR AND EMBARGO   167
UTILITY OF HONG KONG FOR CHINA   170
CHINESE ATTITUDE   172
KOWLOON RIOTS, 1956   174
CULTURAL REVOLUTION   176
CHINESE REPRESENTATION IN HONG KONG   181
THE FUTURE OF HONG KONG   182

VII   *Chinese Representation in the UN*   184

BRITISH ABSTENTION IN THE SECURITY COUNCIL   185
THE KOREAN WAR   187
CHINESE INTERVENTION IN KOREA AND BRITISH
    REACTION   192
BRITISH POLICY AFTER THE KOREAN ARMISTICE   195
INDO-CHINA CONFLICT   197
PEKING'S BID FOR ADMISSION IN THE UN, 1955   200
BRITISH RESERVATIONS CONTINUED, 1956-60   203
TOWARDS A "TWO-CHINA" SOLUTION, 1961-70   206
PEKING'S ADMISSION IN THE UN, 1971   211

VIII   *Trade*   215

EFFECT OF KOREAN WAR   216
PROBLEMS OF BRITISH ENTERPRISES IN CHINA   217
REPRESENTATIONS AND PROTESTS   219
TRADE WITH CHINA   225
THE EMBARGO AND ITS RELAXATION   230

CHINESE REACTION TO BRITISH POLICY ON TRADE
CONTROLS   238
PROBLEM OF SUPPLYING STRATEGIC GOODS TO CHINA   240
SINO-SOVIET RIFT AND CHINA'S TRADE RELATIONS
WITH THE WEST   242
RECENT DEVELOPMENTS AND OUTLOOK FOR THE
FUTURE   245

IX   *Conclusion*   249

Abbreviations used in Notes   267

Notes   269

Appendices

1   SINO-BRITISH COMMUNIQUE ON EXCHANGE OF
AMBASSADORS, 13 MARCH 1972   338
2   TRADE BETWEEN CHINA AND HONG KONG,
1946-74   339
3   TRADE BETWEEN CHINA AND BRITAIN, 1938
AND 1946-74   340

Bibliography   341

Index   361

CHAPTER ONE

Historical Background

Potentially China represents "the largest market of the world."[1]
As a strong naval and leading industrial Power, Britain could
not possibly ignore it. Therefore, after methods of persuasion
failed, it decided to use force to "open up" China. Thus, China
was compelled to sign the Treaty of Nanking (1842), by which
five Chinese ports were opened to trade. London also obtained
Hong Kong "as a place of residence and commerce for British
subjects," where their persons may be safe and their property
secure against "the arbitrary caprice either of the Government
at Peking, or its local authorities at the sea-ports."[2]

Furthermore, by the Treaty of 1842, China agreed to levy
"a fair and regular tariff."[3] In that connection, Sir John
Pratt observes :

> The Treaty tariff...which dated back to the arrangements
> made immediately after the Treaty of Nanking in 1842,
> was one of the major grievances of the [Chinese] nationalists
> of the twentieth century. By agreeing in general terms that
> she would levy only moderate duties on the foreign trade
> and by translating moderate duties into specific rates and
> granting most-favoured nation rights in all the treaties
> negotiated with foreign powers, China almost inadvertently
> surrendered her tariff autonomy and in twentieth century
> she found that she had no power to alter the tariff rates—
> which aimed at a general average of five per cent—without
> first negotiating separately with nineteen different treaty
> powers and obtaining the consent of each.[4]

The treaty Powers were not expected to accede to the Chinese
demand on the recovery of tariff autonomy—a move detrimental to their own interests. Since Britain occupied a
dominant position in the China market and paid almost two-

thirds of the customs revenue by 1898, it was most unwilling to grant any concession to China on that score.[5] However, the restriction on China not to raise its customs duty by more than 5 per cent when other countries, the United States for instance, levied duties at the rate of several hundred per cent, was clearly unjust and indefensible.

Rapid industrialization and the need for expanding trade made Britain eager "to obtain access generally to the whole interior of the Chinese Empire as well as to the cities on the coast"[6] by extending the orbit of foreign rights in China. The joint Anglo-French military campaigns resulted in the conclusion of Tientsin Treaties (signed 1858, effective 1860). These treaties threw open more ports to foreign commerce; authorized British subjects "to travel, for their pleasure or for purposes of trade, to all ports of the interior"[7]; ceded Kowloon to Britain; and contained an explicit recognition of extra-territoriality— another major component of "unequal treaties" imposed on China.

British Predominance in China

The Tientsin Treaties completed the opening of China. Having led the way in war and diplomacy, Britain benefitted most from it. It chose the newly-opened, the richest and the most populous Yangtse region and the interior as its "sphere of interest or influence," where its vast commercial interests were concentrated. London jealously guarded its predominant position in China against any encroachment by any other Power. It also sought to protect its interests against internal disorders. The mechanism of a Maritime Customs Administration under a British Inspector-General was devised to safeguard and promote British commercial interests in China. Thus, Britain succeeded in establishing a predominant position in almost every branch of the Chinese economy, be it trade, banking, shipping, or railways—a position which it continued to enjoy till the beginning of the First World War. As early as 1864, over 80 per cent of China's trade was with the British Empire. All foreign banks, save one, and three-fourths of the large business houses in Shanghai were British. The British share in shipping, both in tonnage and number of vessels entered and cleared in foreign and coastal trade, was greater than that of all the other Powers combined, including China.[8] In railroad construction too, the UK had the lion's share. At the end of 1898, British concessions amounted to 2,800 miles, the Russian to 1,530, the German to 720, the Belgian to 650, the French to 420 and the American to 300 miles.[9]

Rivalry of Other Powers

Britain's near-monopoly position in the rich Yangtse valley naturally aroused the jealousy of other Powers. In the 1890s, Russia and France sought to extend their Government-owned railways northward and southward into the heart of China, meeting at Hankow on the Yangtse, and to obtain control of the Maritime Customs Administration. The British felt seriously concerned about their surreptitious attempt to exclude British industrialists and financiers from the work of railroad construction, to oust British personnel from the Customs Administration and thereby discriminate against British merchants in matters of trade. The Franco-Russian "plot"[10] for the "joint domination of China," John Pratt observes, was "a direct assault on the position built up by England during the previous one hundred and fifty years" and aimed at driving the "British interests off the map" of China.[11]

Britain's response to the Franco-Russian "plot" was prompt and vigorous. With no support whatsoever from other Powers, it foiled "the plot by insisting that the railways to be built in the wealthiest and most populous provinces of China should be built, not as foreign government railways, but as commercial enterprises, and that a fair proportion of the capital required for such enterprises should be obtained from British sources."[12] As a result, Britain acquired two of the three big foreign loans and secured the greatest mileage of railroad concessions. As a counterpoise to German, French and Russian seizures of Kiao-chou, Kuang-chou and Port Arthur respectively, the UK secured two leased territories, *viz.* Weihaiwei and Kowloon. To insure against any seizure of ports on the Yangtse by hostile Powers, London obtained "a definite assurance that China will never alienate any territory in the Provinces adjoining the Yangtse to any other power whether under loan, mortgage or any other designation."[13] Moreover, without consulting the Chinese Government, Britain concluded, on 28 April 1899, an agreement with Russia, by which Russia accepted the Yangtse valley as the exclusive province of the British for the purpose of railroad-building in return for a similar undertaking on the part of Britain as regards the north of the Great Wall.[14] In this way, Britain sought to preserve its position of primacy in the Yangtse valley.

Having seized Kiao-chou, and thereby acquiring a sphere of influence in Shantung province, Germany also felt tempted towards the rich Yangtse Valley. Posing as China's friend, it tried to wrest a promise from the latter that it would not "grant to any Power special advantages of a political, military, maritime, or economic nature, nor to allow the occupation of any other points commanding the river either below or above Shanghai." Commenting on this somewhat ingenuous attempt to tie British hands in a district where its interests were overwhelming, Lord Landsdowne remarked : "We shall not pay regard to any pledges given by the Chinese Government or Viceroys by which their and our freedom as regards the maintenance of order and protection of our interests in the Yangtse region would be limited."[15]

Since it was becoming increasingly difficult for it to check a combination of two or more rival Powers, London deemed it necessary to abandon its splendid isolation by concluding an alliance with Japan. While London considered the Anglo-Japanese Treaty of 1902 an "insurance against a general war,"[16] designed to serve its interests in East Asia by maintaining a proper balance of power, the Japanese used it "to good purpose in the Manchurian war and the Treaty of Portsmouth."[17]

The preoccupation of European Powers in World War I afforded another opportunity for Japan to push its designs against China. Thus, in 1915 Tokyo presented its Twenty-one Demands, the practical effect of which was "to reduce China to the status of a vassal."[18] Since these demands seriously affected British interests in China, London pressurized Japan to withdraw Group V of the Twenty-one Demands, that demanded political rights throughout China.[19] During World

War I, Japan also acquired German rights in Shantung province and in the Pacific. Thus, after World War I, Japan was in a much stronger position to threaten British interests in the rich Yangtse basin. London, therefore, terminated the alliance with its erstwhile ally and began to act in concert with the United States in order to check Japan's rising power and to uphold the "open door" policy in China.[20]

"Open Door" in China

The "Open Door" policy, and its corollary, the integrity of China and equal opportunity for all in the ordinary operations of commerce, was essentially a British idea which the American Government pursued most vigorously because it stood to gain the most from it. Before Secretary of State Hay wrote his famous Open Door Notes to the European Powers on 6 September 1899, the British House of Commons had passed a resolution (1 March 1898) "that it is of vital importance for British commerce and influence that the independence of Chinese territory be maintained."[21] Even Hay's Open Door Notes had much to do with British advice and suggestion. Needless to say, British interest in the "Open Door" policy was dictated by its self-interest and cannot, in any way, be construed as altruistic. "In its origin," observes J.K. Fairbank, "the Open Door was an Anglo-American defensive measure in power politics, without much thought for the interests of the Chinese state."[22]

As stated earlier, Britain seized Weihaiwei and Kowloon in 1898 in order to safeguard its commercial interests and to maintain a proper balance in China. Nevertheless, because of its predominance in the China market, London had the highest stake in the maintenance of the "Open Door" policy and the territorial integrity of China. In this context. J.K. Fairbank observes :

> Britain's relation to the Open Door is clearly visible in the trade statistics. In 1898 British shipping carried two-thirds of the tonnage in China's ports and paid two-thirds of the Customs revenue. To defend this commercial empire against imperialist encroachment by other powers Britain

followed at first a policy of taking compensation....But no
amount of success in a partition of China could benefit
British interests when they already dominated the trade of
the whole country. Concessions and spheres could only
reduce her area of trade.[23]

Anarchy or internal disorders were also detrimental to British
commercial interests. Therefore, Britain could not possibly
remain inactive in the face of the "Taiping" and "Boxer"
rebellions.

Superior naval and economic power enabled Britain to play
a decisive role in determining the outcome of a conflict between
two or more warring factions within China. It could deploy
its troops in the Yangtse and on the coast. It could give loans
and remit the money collected through customs tariff to any
Chinese authority of its choice.[24] Britain did not bother to
look into the credentials of a person—whether he was a king,
a usurper of the throne or a warlord—or the character of a
regime, be it a republic, a monarchy or a dictatorship. London
rendered support to all those who were found helpful in the
furtherance of its interests and were amenable to its influence.
Thus, it supported the Manchu dynasty against the "Taipings,"
Yuan Shih-kai against Sun Yat-sen's republicans, and Chiang
Kai-shek against the communists. What Lord Palmerston
had said in 1848 in regard to British policy towards foreign
Powers was equally applicable to the British attitude towards
the various groups or factions in a foreign land. Lord Palmerston
had stated : "It is a narrow policy to suppose that this country or that is to be marked out as the eternal ally or the
perpetual enemy of England. We have no eternal allies and
no perpetual enemies. Our interests are perpetual and eternal
and those interests it is our duty to follow."[25]

Collaboration of Chinese Nationalism with the Soviet Union

The ruthlessness, high-handedness and unscrupulousness with
which Britain pursued its "perpetual and eternal interests" in
China made other Powers jealous of its privileged position.
Russia, in particular, felt balked and thwarted by the UK[26] at
every stage while the Chinese nationalists held Britain res-

ponsible for all their woes. Consequently, the two came together and singled out Britain as their common enemy. On 30 May 1925, a crowd of 10,000 demonstrated in the International Settlement of Shanghai. The crowd was fired upon under orders from British police officials. Twelve persons were killed and nearly 20 wounded. The Shanghai incident gave rise to bitter anti-British strikes and led to a boycott of British goods, which lasted for nearly 18 months and thereby threatened the ruin of British trade in China. Ronald Farquharson observes :

> The first real blow to British prestige in China happened in 1926 when...the British concessional territory in Hankow was limply handed over with no resistance at all...the apparent myth of British strength and infallibility has been exploded for the first time. That was the beginning of the end of British prestige throughout China.[27]

The anti-British movement of 1925-27 cannot simply be dismissed as a product of a Comintern conspiracy to bring about "world revolution." The spirit of nationalism—the struggle against "unequal treaties"—was the primary motivating force behind it, although Soviet assistance in arms and expert advice, training and money, was undoubtedly found useful by nationalist leaders like Sun Yat-sen and Chiang Kai-shek.[28] The Soviet renunciation of extra-territorial privileges in China also created a good impression upon the masses.[29]

Until the mid 1920s the British paid little or no heed to the Chinese nationalist movement,[30] which was steadily gaining momentum after the Boxer rebellion. The Chinese felt humiliated by the occupation of Peking by foreign troops in 1900 and the imposition of a huge and crushing indemnity by the Boxer Protocol of 1901. Japan's victory over Russia in 1904-5 exploded the myth of Western invincibility and gave a fillip to nationalist sentiments. The failure of the 1911 revolution (partly because of the support received by Yuan Shih-kai from foreign Powers) was in itself sufficient cause of irritation to the nationalists. What enraged them further was "even greater encroachment on China's sovereign rights than the privileges sanctioned by the treaties."[31]

The first revolutionary outburst of nationalist feeling

occurred on 4 May 1919, when nearly 3,000 students in Peking demonstrated against the Allied decision at the Paris Peace Conference to transfer all the German rights in Shantung to Japan. This was followed by a strike of over 70,000 workers in Shanghai from 5 to 11 June 1919, which not only affected Japanese-owned textile mills but American, British and French enterprises as well.[32]

From its very inception, the "May 4th Movement" was exposed to such influences as world trade unionism and the socialist and anarchist philosophies which exalted the proletariat.[33] The Soviet Union exploited the just grievances of the Chinese people with the two-fold objective : firstly, to restore its prestige and influence in the Far East, which had reached a low level after the October Revolution; and secondly, to weaken the capitalist Powers, who were persistently interfering in its internal affairs. While announcing the abrogation of unequal treaties and special privileges obtained by Czarist Russia, Karakhan spoke of making common cause with the Chinese people in their attempt to "escape the evil fate of being a second India and Korea as has been planned for her at the Paris Peace Conference."[34]

The Western Powers seemed to have learnt no lesson at all from the first upsurge of Chinese nationalism. At the Washington Conference of 1921-22, they endeavoured to settle only a few minor grievances of the Chinese people.[35] The major Chinese demands remained practically untouched. Russian comments on the Washington Conference, from which it had been excluded, could hardly be favourable. In fact, as early as August 1921, the Executive Committee of the Communist International (Comintern) considered the forthcoming Washington Conference as representing "only an attempt to reconcile the interests of the great Anglo-Saxon imperialist robbers at the expense of the weaker robber, Japan, of China and of Soviet Russia." It, therefore, called upon "the masses in China, Korea and Eastern Siberia to adhere more closely to Soviet Russia, the only state in the world willing to render assistance upon a basis of equality and of fraternal help to the peoples of the Orient who are being menaced by world imperialism."[36] The "united front" between the Soviet Union and Sun Yat-sen was aimed at achieving "not only agitational but also organizational results."[37]

The Chinese Communist Party (CCP) was established in 1921, *i.e.* during the period between the May 4th Movement and the Shanghai incident of 30 May 1925. The working class movement also gained momentum during that period. The first Manifesto, issued by the CCP on 10 June 1922, gave pride of place, among its "most immediate demands," to the "revision of the system of tariffs forcibly imposed on China by world capitalism; abolition of consular jurisdiction (extra-territoriality) and of the entire system of privileges for foreigners..."[38] The Second National Labour Congress, attended by 281 delegates representing 166 trade unions and 540,000 organized workers, was convened under the leadership of the CCP and the auspices of the four largest trade unions of China "on the eve of an impending nation-wide anti-imperialist storm"[39] of May 1925. Two days before the Shanghai incident (30 May 1925), the Central Committee of the CCP decided to link "the economic struggle of the working class...with the daily growing anti-imperialist movement" and turn it "into a clear-cut political struggle."[40] The outburst of anti-foreign feelings, which could hardly be considered "sudden and unexpected,"[41] posed a serious threat to British interests in China. Chinese nationalism, controlled and fed by communism, it was believed, was directed "not merely at the unequal treaties, but all the Western interests in China."[42]

In these circumstances, Britain realized the gravity of the situation. It recognized that vague promises of doubtful validity, that usually postponed action to some future date,[43] would not be of much help now. It took note of the "growth of a powerful nationalist movement" in China. The objective of the Washington Conference, it was stated, was "to relax—not to tighten—foreign control" on China. The British memorandum of December 1926 called upon the Powers concerned to "modify their traditional attitude of rigid insistence on the strict letter of treaty rights." It proposed that the Washington Treaty Powers should declare their readiness "to negotiate on treaty revision" and "to recognize her [China's] right to the enjoyment of tariff autonomy." It further stated :

The Cantonese did, in fact, seize the Washington surtaxes

by levying, in defiance of the treaties, certain additional taxes on the foreign trade of the port. His Majesty's Government have with much reluctance joined in the protest against the new taxes for the sake of maintaining solidarity with the Powers, but they are not satisfied that this is the right policy for the present situation....His Majesty's Government therefore strongly urge that the Powers should now authorize the immediate levy of the Washington surtaxes unconditionally throughout China. They hope that this may provide a basis for regularizing the position at Canton.

The Memorandum rejected the argument that "in strict logic it would amount to condoning the breach of treaty" by stating that it did not take sufficient account of "the realities of the situation." "The basic facts of the present situation," it categorically asserted, "are that the treaties are now admittedly in many respects out of date." The immediate unconditional grant of the Washington surtaxes was "the first step" towards the implementation of the new policy,[44] which the British Government intended to adopt towards China in the future.

On 25 January 1927, the Chinese authorities (both in the North and the South) were told that Britain would be willing to recognize modern Chinese Law Courts and would no longer insist on the presence of a British official. London also agreed to apply the prevalent modern Chinese civil and commercial codes in British courts in China.

In his speech at Birmingham two days later, Austin Chamberlain declared :

We are prepared to go farther than this as soon as all the Chinese codes and judicial administrations are ready. As regards taxation, we are prepared to make British subjects liable to pay regular Chinese taxation, provided that it does not involve discrimination against British subjects or British goods. This would include taxation levied under a national tariff, as and when such tariff law is promulgated....We are thinking of our relations with China for the next 100 years.

He justified the despatch of British troops to China as a precautionary measure to protect the large British community residing in Shanghai and "the immense interests which British enterprise has built up in that city." At the same time, he stated : "His Majesty's Government will not be deflected from their policy of patient conciliation." After the 1927 rupture between the Kuomintang and Russian advisers, Austin Chamberlain observed :

> We stand by this policy of peaceful conciliation. We cannot permit ourselves to be deprived by forceful action of our treaty rights, but we are ready at any moment in a generous spirit to negotiate...to adjust the old treaties to the new position...we have no territorial ambitions....We are ready to negotiate...for the gradual surrender of the special rights and privileges which under those treaties we enjoy in China.[45]

In pursuance of its "new policy," Britain signed a number of agreements with China providing for the restitution of British concessions at Hankow, Kiukiang, Chinkiang, Amoy and Weihaiwei. In September 1930, it also agreed to remit its share of the Indemnity of 1901. The Chinese Government, in turn, undertook to devote "the greater part of the said indemnity funds...in rehabilitating and building railways and in other production enterprises in China." However, it was made obligatory that all orders for materials required for the purpose had to be placed in the UK.[46] The recovery of tariff autonomy in 1930, *i.e.* after a lapse of nearly 88 years, was the major gain for China. A year later, the salt administration was also handed over to the Chinese.

The "policy of patient conciliation" and what, at one time, seemed to be a "gradual surrender of special rights" was a very statesmanlike act on the part of the British Government since it enabled Britain to recover its lost prestige in China.

The rupture between the Kuomintang and the Comintern in 1927 was followed by the weakening of the Chinese Communists and the deterioration of relations between Nationalist China and the Soviet Union. Friction reached its climax in 1929 when the Chinese police raided a Soviet consulate in Harbin and Moscow despatched its troops to assert its treaty rights in the Chinese Eastern Railway. Diplomatic relations between the two countries were also severed.

The policy of "patient conciliation" and "gradual surrender of special rights" enabled Britain to recover its lost prestige.

But London did not continue for long that "right and wise course"[47] of action. It reverted to its shortsighted and selfish policy of preserving and promoting its selfish interests under whatever special rights it continued to enjoy. Britain followed this course of action partly due to Japanese aggression in Manchuria[48] and partly due to the fact that, from 1931 onwards, the Conservative Party was in power in Britain. In these circumstances, Chiang Kai-shek's efforts to recover the special rights still enjoyed by foreigners[49] had no chance of success. The concerned Powers were reluctant to surrender their special privileges which shielded their persons and enterprises against Chinese laws and taxes and thereby enabled them to maximize profits. Extra-territoriality—the keystone of unequal treaties— persisted and rights of foreign Powers to station troops and warships in China and navigate its inland waters remained intact.

World War II

In October 1942, London and Washington announced their decision to enter into negotiations with China in order to relinquish extra-territorial rights. By that time, it might be recalled, Japan had embarked upon a course of action that sought to wipe out British interests in the Yangtse and threa- tened the British Empire in the Far East. When the Treaty of 11 January 1943 (surrendering extra-territorial rights) was signed almost all the concessions the UK had in China were under Japanese occupation. In fact, British rights had become "more of a liability, by the odium they evoked, than an asset for the protection they provided."[50]

Treaty of 1943

Britain's primary objective in initialling the Treaty of 1943 was to raise the sagging morale of the Chinese army in its struggle against the Japanese invaders, and thereby seek to save its Indian Empire. London was aware of Japan's "covert peace approaches to Chungking."[51] With a view to secure the active cooperation of China in the War, Japan began to relinquish its concessional rights to the Nanking Government. Any compromise between Chiang Kai-shek and Tokyo would have been fatal to British interests in Asia. It would have freed nearly a million Japanese soldiers for attack on British possessions. Britain and the United States, therefore, felt an added urgency to prevent Chiang Kai-shek from coming to terms with Japan. While Tokyo could, at best, promise China only *status quo ante* 1937, the Western Powers had no difficulty in promising Chiang all that China had lost to Japan since 1894. Thus, the Cairo Conference of December 1943 declared :

> Japan, after her defeat, was to be stripped not only of everything that she had seized since 1931, but also of territories which had long been recognized by international treaties as being hers : Formosa, the Pescadores, Korea, and the ex-German islands in the Pacific.[52]

The Western Powers gave both moral and material support to China because they considered "her fight" to be "our fight."[53]

The Treaty of 1943 was signed by Britain in the hope that it would put Sino-British relations "on a status of absolute equality," and thereby mark "the beginning of a new and happy chapter of close collaboration between the two countries."[54] However, when British merchants found themselves helpless against harsh and discriminating Chinese laws at the end of the War, many Britons began to speak of the 1943 Treaty as "a bad treaty written in haste, if not in panic."[55]

Instead of resolving outstanding issues between the two countries, the Treaty of 1943 gave birth to many fresh problems. The Chinese felt dissatisfied because the Treaty did not cancel the lease of the Kowloon territories on the mainland. Therefore, they reserved the right to reopen the question for discussion with the British government at a later stage.[56] Under Article 4 of the Treaty, the Chinese Government took over the administration and control of International Settlements and Concessions. It also undertook "the assumption and discharge of the official obligations and liabilities of those Settlements and Concessions and for the recognition and protection of all legitimate rights therein." Article 6 of the Treaty ensured for

British subjects the right "to travel, reside and carry on commerce" throughout the whole country and protected them, in matters of justice and taxation, against discrimination, even *vis-a-vis* its own nationals. Under Article 8, the United Kingdom and China agreed to "enter into negotiations for the conclusion of a comprehensive modern treaty or treaties of friendship, commerce, navigation and consular rights upon the request of either of them or in any case within six months after the cessation of the hostilities..."[57] Subsequently, all these issues and treaty provisions became the subject of much wrangling and a source of friction between the two countries.

During World War II, the Japanese Government had seized considerable property belonging to British subjects. When the War came to an end, the Chinese authorities took over those properties. Under Article 4 of the 1943 Treaty, the Chinese Government was obliged to return these properties to their rightful owners. However, it could not implement that provision mainly because the mandate of the Central Government of China was not obeyed by subordinates. The British Government made several representations. Eventually, most of the more important properties were returned. Nevertheless, there was considerable delay in removing the inconveniences of British employees in the former International Settlement. There were also difficulties in determining the liabilities undertaken by the Chinese Government under the 1943 Treaty. Since this issue entailed a burden on the British exchequer, Foreign Secretary Bevin promised to "follow the matter up personally in a vigorous manner." He asserted : "In the meantime these former employees are receiving from the British Government up to £40 a month per person, which we shall call upon the Chinese Government to settle in the final adjustment."[58]

The Chinese Government also paid scant attention to Article 6 of the Treaty. Yielding to nationalist pressures for the exclusion of foreign flag vessels from the inland waterway and coastal trade, China decided to forbid British and all foreign ships from trading on their coast and rivers. This resulted in a general stagnation of shipping. Since China did not have enough ships of its own, it had to conclude an agreement with Britain in October 1945. However, nationalist sentiments "proved too strong once again, and in July 1946, the agreement was terminated."[59]   The Chinese discriminated against foreign businessmen and commercial houses in matters of taxation as well.   In the case of insurance companies, for instance, while Chinese firms paid a business tax of 4 per cent per annum on its capital, foreign firms were required to pay "35 times as much as Chinese firms."[60]   In September 1945, tariff rates were revised and the rates of duty were fixed between 20 and 30 per cent.   While certain types of machinery, tools and other goods needed for reconstruction were lightly taxed, nearly 80% import duty was imposed on luxury goods.[61]

The Treaty of 1943 had envisaged the conclusion of a Sino-British Commercial Treaty.   Both the British and the US Government approached the Chinese Government in the matter at about the same time.[62]   The United States succeeded in signing a Commercial Treaty in November 1946.[63]   But negotiations with Britain were at first postponed till the Chinese Government had signed an agreement with the United States. Thereafter, differences proved irreconcilable and the talks finally broke down in October 1947.

Trade Prospects after the War

At the end of War, Britain had hoped for a considerable expansion of trade with China.   As early as March 1943, Lord Listowel remarked :

> We are witnessing a gradually developing industrial revolution in China, a most useful symptom of immediate progress in an agricultural community....There will be a demand immediately after the war for skilled technicians, for machinery, for machine-tools, and also, of course, for the means of building a vast network of roads and railways that will open up the immense territories of China. These demands can only be satisfied if Britain and the United States are prepared to participate in the framing of plans for the economic future of China. Nothing could be more advantageous in the long run to manufacturing and exporting countries like our own than an increase in the purchasing power of the inhabitants of these densely populated Asiatic areas. They form the greatest potential market in

the world.   Here we have a possible factor in the maintenance of employment in the older industrial nations.[64]

In view of the industrialization programme envisaged by the
Chinese Nationalist Government[65] and the removal of two
rivals, Japan and Germany, British hopes of increased trade
with China did not appear to be wholly unjustified.   However,
"the most fantastic inflation...economic strain...interruption of
communication..." seemed to destroy all such hopes.   While
the official spokesman of the British Government failed to
criticize the Chiang Kai-shek administration for the unhappy
situation,[66] non-official opinion openly blamed the Kuomintang
regime for the state of strained relations between the two
countries.   Commenting on the steadily deteriorating economic
conditions and the steep rise in living costs, *The Times*
correspondent remarked :

> These conditions are due mainly to the Civil War...but also
> to the Government's economic policy, which is strangling
> what little trade is still possible.   The policy is supposedly
> necessitated by the Government's desperate need of foreign
> exchange for financing the war.[67]

Chinese Civil War, 1945-49

As long as the Civil War raged on, China could not execute its
industrialization programme because expenditure on arms
exhausted the national treasury and impeded economic recovery.
During 1945, military expenditure accounted for 80 to 85 per
cent of the national budget.[68]   According to the statement of
the Finance Minister, Government expenditure increased by
450 per cent in 1947 over the previous year owing to the
increased cost of the Civil War.   This, in itself, was "sufficiently
alarming to China's friends abroad."[69]   Mounting administrative costs and the loss of large territories (nearly one-third of
the whole) made it even more difficult for the Kuomintang
regime to overcome its steadily growing economic difficulties.

British Attitude

The diversion of scarce resources to unproductive purposes

prevented the Chinese Government from having a balanced budget and created the problem of unfavourable balance of payments in its foreign trade.[70] The first led to inflation,[71] which in turn resulted in the reduction of the purchasing power of the masses. The second affected the Government's capacity to import capital goods, so badly needed for the industrialization of the country. Thus, the Civil War had a damaging effect on Sino-British trade and consequently London desired its early end. However, intervention by the USA and/or the USSR, far from easing the situation, was more likely to further aggravate the problem. Intervention by either country was likely to prolong, rather than shorten, the Chinese Civil War.[72] Moreover, it would have resulted in the escalation of the conflict into a wider war,[73] which was also harmful to British interests.

The year 1948 saw neither an end to the afflictions of the Chinese people nor the disappearance of the danger of a general war breaking out. In this connection, *The Times* editorial remarked :

> At a time when the split between communist and anti-communist forces is everywhere becoming identified with rivalry between groups of nations headed respectively by the Soviet Union and by the United States, there is a risk that the Kuomintang-Communist feud, which is essentially domestic to China, may invite intervention by rival international groups.[74]

Britain realized that "closed economic blocs" often result in the exploitation of weaker nations by the stronger members of the blocs. Therefore, in view of its weak position after World War II, Britain desired to see "a free and integrated economy in Europe" and prevent the split of Europe into economic or political blocs.[75] Britain also endeavoured to keep China away from bloc politics. Thus, *The Times* laid stress on the "special features"[76] of Chinese Communism and considered the conflict between communist and anti-communist forces in China "altogether different from the cleavage in Europe."[77] After the Czechoslovak *coup* in February 1948, Washington revised its policy towards China, particularly in regard to the second part of the Moscow Declaration of December 1945 that recognized the need of a coalition government in China.[78] However, there seemed no change whatsoever in the British attitude towards China.

British adherence to the Moscow Declaration was almost total.[79] Their attitude to the "non-interference" clause as also to the second part of the Moscow Declaration had to be viewed in relation to two other propositions contained in that Declaration, *viz.* a "United China" and "a cessation of civil strife." In the circumstances, foreign intervention was not conducive to either of them. F.C. Jones observes :

> In view of the growing tenseness in their relations [US and USSR] it is doubtful whether the U.S.S.R. would stand by and see the Kuomintang, which it thinks to be on American leading strings, defeat the Communists, at least to an extent which would bring all Manchuria under the control of Nanking. Nor may America be willing to acquiesce in a Communist victory, which she would fear might bring all China north of the Yellow River, or perhaps the Yangtze, into the orbit of the U.S.S.R.[80]

Thus, foreign intervention would have either resulted in the indefinite prolongation of the Civil War, or in the partition of China into two states under the nominal control of the Kuomintang and the Communists, but actually dominated by the USA and the USSR respectively. Britain never desired to see a partitioned China. In the conditions obtaining in the post-1945 period, a partitioned China was even more harmful to British interests than in the 1890s, when London could hope to keep a substantial portion of rich Chinese territory within its own sphere of influence. In the changed power situation of the 1940s, Britiain faced the prospect of altogether washing its hands off from China.

In view of what has been stated above, the most desirable thing from the British point of view was a united China, be it under the Kuomintang or the Communists, which was neither subservient to the USA nor to the USSR.[81] The Chinese Communists could hope to defy or act independently of the Kremlin only if they became the masters of the whole of China and the Civil War was brought to an early end. In its editorial of 12 February 1948, *The Times* observed:

Since it is not to her [Russia's] interest that a strong and independent China, possibly unfriendly to her own ambitions should grow up in the near future, she looks upon the Chinese Communists as a valuable check upon the national aspirations of President Chiang Kai-shek and the Kuomintang. If they should replace the Kuomintang in control of China, she would find them a formidable obstacle to her ambitions in the Far East. But if they should succeed in expelling the Government forces from Manchuria, and in turning that rich territory into a State separate from the rest of China, they would be hard put to it to preserve their characteristic ideas in face of the pressure which the Soviet Union could then exert upon them.

A Communist-controlled united China seemed better than a Kuomintang-dominated unified China. Britain had no illusion in regard to Chiang Kai-shek's claims about being the champion of Western political democracy and Chinese national independence.[82] In fact, the Kuomintang which had received billions of dollars of aid from Washington,[83] in addition to considerable help in equipment, training and transportation of its armies and expert advice from American military advisers, was expected to be less independent of foreign control than the Communists who had received practically little or no direct help, military or economic, from the Russians ever since 1927.[84] Some British observers regarded the change to communism in China as a transfer from a corrupt to an efficient state capitalism.

Economic Competition with the United States

Britain also could not ignore the fact that the United States had emerged as a serious economic rival to Britain in the Chinese market. From 1911 to 1930, China's total gross trade increased by 133%, its trade with the USA grew by 328%, and with the Japanese Empire by 234%, but with the British Empire (excluding Hong Kong) it increased only by 82.3%.[85] The USA was the chief beneficiary of the anti-British agitation of the 1920s. World War II eliminated two principal competitors, *viz.* Japan and Germany. Therefore, the British Trade Mission, which visited China in 1946, expressed the hope that "an expansion of United Kingdom exports to China to fill part of the gap left by Germany and Japan should be possible and might be more or less permanent."[86]   But America seemed to destroy all such hopes.   A comparison of 1936 and 1946 trade figures reveals that while Britain's share in the import trade of China declined from 11.7% in 1936 to 4.59% in 1946, that of the USA rose appreciably from 19.66% to 57.16% (this excluded United Nations Relief and Rehabilitation Association—UNRRA—supplies).   If one takes into account UNRRA supplies, which amounted to CN $399,231 millions in 1946, the American "predominance in the import trade of China" was almost complete.   It was recognized that even after the termination of the programme of UNRRA supplies in June 1947, its adverse effect on British commercial imports into China would "inevitably persist for a time."   The United States threatened the British near-monopoly position even in those fields in which it had all along occupied a prominent place. For instance, in shipping Britain enjoyed first position in 1937 with 42% but in 1946 it accounted for only 10%.   The USA, which was far below China (36%) and Japan (11%) in 1937, accounted for 36% of the total tonnage in 1946.   In civil aviation, the USA held the "dominant position."   Nearly all aircraft and equipment used by the Chinese were of American manufacture, and American standardised interchangeable parts were stocked.   "The Chinese Corporations would therefore have found difficulty in introducing British aircraft on the routes operating in 1946...."[87]

As regards the power plant market, the British Trade Mission Report noted the leading position of the UK in the pre-war period and remarked :

> Capital participation determines the destination of orders, and between 1932 and 1937 the growing effect of American and Japanese capital participation was making it increasingly difficult for Britain to maintain her position in power plant business and allied equipment.   The position after war is even more difficult.

The British Report referred to the extensive technical training facilities, that were made available to Chinese students by the USA and observed: "Familiarity with and knowledge of the products of the country where they study usually leads them to prefer those products afterwards in their own country."[88] The American threat to British trade with China, the Report of the British Mission warned, was not a transitory phase but a long-term one.

The British Trade Mission's observation that "there is plenty of scope for both United States and United Kingdom trade with China" was probably designed to avoid giving offence to America. However, the British Mission felt seriously concerned about American competition. It stated :

> Trade in China has always been very closely linked with credit, and as the U.S.A. is at the present time the only country in a position to extend large credits, a high proportion of China's requirements of capital goods must, if these are to be satisfied within a calculable period, inevitably be purchased in the United States....Thus United States commercial and, more particularly, financial activities in China have a noticeable effect on British activities there.

Although the loan of $500 million, authorized by the US Congress to strengthen General Marshall's hands in his efforts to reconcile differences between the contending political factions in China, was withheld, the possibility of American lending in the future could not be ruled out. Such loans, the British Trade Mission warned, would adversely affect Sino-British trade.[89] In these circumstances, it was not at all surprising that when aid to Chiang Kai-shek was discussed in the USA in the beginning of 1948, British comments were hardly favourable. American aid to Chiang, *The Times* observed, was in "tacit opposition to the Marshall plan"[90] because it impeded European recovery by competing for scarce commodities and destroyed the European aid programme by a Chinese diversion.

As compared to Britain, the USA was in a better position in so far as trade with China was concerned because of its capacity to advance loans and also because of the Commercial Treaty it had concluded with China. Britain could not possibly hope to compete with such a formidable rival, particularly so long as the US-dominated corrupt Chiang regime remained in power. The Chinese market offered one of the most hopeful adjuncts to the post-war recovery of British industry. But the Kuomintang government was deliberately making it impossible for Britain to trade with China. It closed the Yangtse to foreign shipping, instituted trade controls and preferred to deal with the USA. After 1945, British relations with the Kuomintang had continued to deteriorate. London was disappointed with the implementation of the 1943 Treaty and frustrated in its hopes of a brisk trade with China. Furthermore, in the beginning of 1948, there was a violent outburst of anti-British agitation over the death of a Kowloon hawker. On 16 January 1948, the rioters looted and burnt the British Consulate-General's office at Shameen (Canton) and nearby British property. *The Times* blamed Chinese authorities for the incident by stating that the "instruction to all Canton newspapers was issued by the local Kuomintang."[91] The Chinese Government expressed regret over the incident. It also offered to give protection to British subjects in the future and punish the offenders. However, attempts to secure compensation for damage, estimated at about £300,000, and an inquiry into the incident proved unproductive despite prolonged negotiations.[92]

Strained Relations with the Kuomintang

British relations with the Chiang Kai-shek regime reached its lowest level in 1949. In June 1949, Chiang ordered the closure of ports and endeavoured to enforce that decision. This step directly affected current, as well as future, trade relations between Britain and China. The British Government, therefore, made "the strongest representations"[93] to the Nationalist Government and asserted its right "to give naval protection to British merchantmen outside Chinese territorial waters." London also warned Chiang that "attempts to enforce the closure order by attacks on unarmed merchantmen" would be regarded "illegitimate and unfriendly even if such attacks are made inside territorial waters."[94] Failure to break the "blockade" on the high seas would have been considered by the Chinese Communists as tacit support of the Kuomintang regime. Active naval protection to British vessels inside Chinese territorial waters, on the other hand, invited Communist complaints about "imperialism."

For obvious reasons, of all the Powers only Britain reacted

strongly to the Nationalist "blockade" of Chinese ports, which were controlled by the Communists. The US State Department too had protested against the illegality of the "blockade," but on 23 December 1949 it solemnly warned captains of American vessels against making any attempts to call into Shanghai waters. Moscow's aloofness in the matter[95] might be attributed to two factors: in the first place, its trade with China was mostly through a land route and, therefore, it remained unaffected by the "blockade"; secondly, Moscow had everything to gain by the deterioration in China's relations with Western Powers.

The "blockade" of Chinese ports was harmful to British interests for several reasons. Firstly, it hurt Britain economically at a time when it was eagerly looking for an expansion of its foreign trade. Secondly, it aggravated the economic position of British businessmen in both Shanghai and Hong Kong. Thirdly, the "blockade" accentuated the hardships of the Chinese people and increased discontent within China, which not only undermined trade prospects but also strengthened the hands of extremists in Chinese politics, thereby accelerating the trend toward a state-controlled economy and alignment with the Soviet Union. Furthermore, it weakened the position of nationalists within the Chinese Communist Party and undermined their will to counteract pro-Russian leanings. A doctrinaire approach to socio-economic problems could prove harmful to British investments in China, while alignment with Moscow and the adoption of a revolutionary line in foreign affairs was likely to threaten the security of British possessions in the Far East. All these considerations contributed largely to British anxiety in regard to the Nationalist blockade of Chinese ports and to their desire to come to terms, and even "cooperate,"[96] with the Communist rulers of China. The British recognition of Communist China facilitated the task of the Royal Navy to deal more effectively with Nationalist warships since Britain thereby gained "a stronger juridical position for breaking the blockade of Shanghai."[97] It might be recalled that British investments in China were, for the most part, concentrated in that city and almost all the head offices of British firms were also located there.

CHAPTER TWO

British Recognition and Peking's Reaction

Britain recognized the People's Republic of China on 6 January 1950 but the latter seemed in no hurry to establish diplomatic relations with the former. During 1950-54, therefore, London maintained only "the facade of normal relations with Peking, while the reality was that relations were negligible."[1] Throughout this period, the British *charge d'affaires* in Peking was treated strictly as *Ying-kuo t'an-p'an t'ai-piao* (the British Government's Negotiating Representative) for the establishment of diplomatic relations and was not accorded diplomatic rights and status. Thus, for nearly four years, he was uneasily perched in Peking with an indeterminate status and there was no Chinese diplomatic representation in London at all. The British *charge d'affaires* was for the first time received by Chou En-lai, Premier and Foreign Minister of China, only on 8 July 1954 when he was permitted to present his letter of appointment. In accordance with the agreement, reached at Geneva on 17 June 1954, a Chinese *charge d'affaires* arrived in London on 27 October 1954. In 1962, Britain sought to initiate discussions with the Chinese Government with a view to raise diplomatic relations to ambassadorial level. However, the British proposal was rejected by Peking. Relations at the ambassadorial level were established only in March 1972.

Assumptions behind British Recognition

In according recognition to the communist regime in

China, the British Government proceeded from three main
assumptions. Firstly, Britain accepted the Chinese revolution
as an accomplished fact, an irreversible decision—a decision
arrived at in China by the Chinese themselves.[2] Military
intervention for the purpose of safeguarding British interests
was out of the question and, indeed, a dangerous course to
follow. It was also beyond Britain's capacity. Secondly,
Britain proceeded from the assumption that there were certain
significant differences between Chinese Communism and
Soviet Communism. Chinese Communism differed from
Russian Communism not only in the circumstances of its
growth and development but, to a certain extent, in its content
as well. The Chinese agrarian law, observed *Pravda* on 23
September 1950, "preserves the private ownership of land and
grants the landlord the right to buy or sell freely and to rent
the land."[3] In the Soviet Union, on the other hand, private
enterprise was not allowed to exist in any form. China's
industrial policy, which gave entrepreneurs the right "to
dismiss workers if this is necessitated by the demands of production, provided ten-days notice is given before dismissal,"[4]
was also not in conformity with the Soviet practice. Moreover, Peking tolerated national *bourgeoisie* within limits and
for reasons of its own.[5] In these circumstances, the Kremlin
was not quite sure about the ultimate direction of the Chinese
revolution.

To the Russians, the People's Democratic Dictatorship of
Mao did not appear to be the same as "the Leninist theory
of the dictatorship of the proletariat...a theory obligatory to all
countries." In the words of a Soviet writer, the path to
socialism in China was not "proceeding against a background
of fierce class struggle."[6] In fact, the concept of class struggle
seemed to be superseded by slogans that took into account "both
public and private interests" and benefitted both labour and
capital.[7] In this context, *Pravda* remarked :

It is impossible to ignore the disparity between the people's
democracy in China and the people's democracy in the
countries of central and southeastern Europe....The regime
of the people's democracy in the countries of central and
southeastern Europe is exercising the functions of the

dictatorship of the proletariat in the struggle to lay the foundations of socialism. At the present stage, the Chinese People's Democracy is not a type of proletarian dictatorship. Socialist construction is not yet regarded as the immediate task of China.[8]

Mao clearly distinguished the two stages of the Chinese revolution : its present phase, *i.e.* the first stage, was a "bourgeois-democratic revolution."[9] The second stage of Communism was relegated to the distant future and made conditional upon the creation of "a flourishing national economy and culture" and the "approval of the entire country."[10]

In the beginning of 1950, therefore, there appeared only the remotest possibility of Communism, as understood in the Soviet Union, being applied in China. Moreover, Chinese Communism was in a fluid and uncertain state and it was difficult to forecast whether it would lead to "communising the bourgeoisie" or to "bourgeoising communism."[11] Since the outcome of the Chinese revolution had an important bearing on British interests in China and far reaching international repercussions, Britain could not be expected to sit idle and let Moscow manipulate the situation to its advantage.

The continuance of differences between Chinese and Russian Communism was a matter of concern for Stalin. As late as January 1952, he regarded Chinese departures from the Russian practice as "dangerous dogmatism" and "criminal stupidity" that would lead to the "restoration of capitalism."[12] Besides ideological differences, there were reasons to believe that Mao would not permit his country's national interests to become subservient to those of the USSR. The Soviet dictator remarked :

> The deviation toward nationalism is an adaptation of the internationalist policy of the working class to the nationalistic policy of the bourgeoisie....The deviation toward nationalism reflects the attempts of one's 'own' national bourgeoisie to restore capitalism.[13]

Pospelov, the editor of *Pravda*, warned the countries of "new democracy" and "people's democracy" against any deviation "toward nationalism of any sort" in the most explicit terms. He declared : "Only by participating in the united democratic anti-imperialist camp headed by the Soviet Union" and only by "devotion to the Leninist principles of proletarian internationalism and implacability toward nationalism of any sort" can any country of people's democracy or new democracy hope to preserve its "national liberty and independence." "Nationalism, as the ideology of the bourgeoisie," he added, "is the enemy of Marxism."[14]

The third assumption behind the British move to recognize Communist China was that it was "something quite different from an ordinary Soviet satellite."[15] Soviet control over Mao could neither be considered "certain and absolute"[16] nor could the alliance between the two Powers deemed to be "permanent."[17] It was believed that China might, perhaps, succumb to Soviet pressures in the short run because of its weakness and special circumstances but it seemed quite unlikely that it would ever become a satellite of Russia. The size, population, geographical location, racial composition and long memories of the past—all militated against the idea of Mao becoming a stooge of Moscow. Oliver Frank, British Ambassador to the United States, observed :

> In the long run it is far from certain that the nationalism of China can be made to serve the interests of aggressive Russian imperialism....Great efforts are being made by Russia to treat China now as though she was a free, equal and independent power, but if Russia is going to get what she wants out of China, she may in the end be compelled to reduce China, like the countries of Eastern Europe, to the status of a satellite. If they ever try, Chinese nationalism will resist the foreigner's efforts to control China as it always has in the past. If that happens, provided the door has not been finally closed from our side, China, like Yugoslavia, might well be ready to enter into relations with the western world.[18]

Proceeding from the above-mentioned three assumptions, Britain came to the conclusion that it was both possible and necessary to cultivate normal diplomatic and friendly relations with China. It was believed that in order to safeguard its territorial integrity against Soviet encroachments and to cater to the well-being of its people by concentrating its energies on economic rehabilitation and industrialisation, China would be interested in establishing close relations, both commercial and political, with Britain. On the other hand, a China dominated and controlled by the Kremlin was likely to be concerned with "aggravating the general crisis in capitalism and the crisis in the colonial system of imperialism."[19]   A Soviet-dominated China might even contemplate confiscating British investments in China, valued at about £250 million,[20] and embark on an invasion of Hong Kong.

The cultivation of friendly relations with Peking was also considered necessary by Britain for reasons of trade and defence. Trade with China had always occupied a pride of place in British policy towards East Asia. In view of its economic difficulties in the post-1945 period and the dollar gap, Britain was particularly keen to develop trade relations with Peking. The complementary nature of Sino-British trade offered a way out for Britain to escape from economic dependence on the United States and provided a hope for the future, when aid under the Marshall Plan would come to an end. Moreover, Britain, like France, was well aware of the fact that Soviet control and domination of the eastern half of Europe threatened the security of Western Europe. Therefore, London felt deeply concerned about the defence and security of its homeland. Friendly relations with China would not only relieve Britain of the burden and anxiety of looking to the security of its possessions and interests in the East Asian area but would also enable it to concentrate its forces and energies in other vital areas nearer home. And if somehow London succeeded in bringing about, and accentuating, the Sino-Soviet rift, then it would have simultaneously reduced Soviet pressures in Western Europe and Chinese pressures on Hong Kong and Southeast Asia

In view of what has been stated above, London was "anxious to maintain reasonable relations"[21] with China and eager "to prevent Communist China from becoming a whole-hearted satellite of the Soviet Union."[22] Of the three factors —trade, Hong Kong and dissociation of China from Russia— that were largely responsible for British recognition of China, the last one was considered more important than others.[23]

Trade and Hong Kong were important partly because they helped in the achievement of the main objective. Trade facilitated economic recovery and the building of the necessary industrial strength which would enable Peking to withstand Soviet pressure. Hong Kong was compared with "West Berlin" in its effect on communist Asia and considered "the show case, the shop window of our democratic way of life... the best answer to all the anti-British and anti-American propaganda put out by Moscow or Peking."[24]

Britain was, thus, playing for time and Titoism. Recognition was the prerequisite to develop commercial, political and cultural contacts with the Chinese people. Since military intervention was ruled out, the maintenance of contacts was the only other way whereby Britain could hope to influence internal developments within China and to prevent an enduring Sino-Soviet alliance. In the absence of military power and economic strength, Britain could only rely upon its diplomatic skill and patience. Obviously, the odds were against it but the game had to be played partly because the stakes were high and partly because, even if it did not succeed, Britain stood to lose nothing by trying. Success or failure depended not only on how Britain played its cards (including the support it might get from America), but also on how well the Russians played theirs.

Chinese Response

While the guidelines of British policy to recognize China are, thus, quite clear, the Chinese attitude towards Britain has remained a knotty problem for commentators and experts on China. For instance, C. P. Fitzerald observes : "Peking's conduct has been puzzling to friends, gratifying to opponents, and mystifying to many of the Chinese people themselves."[25] Though Fitzerald does not claim to give any "direct and wholly convincing answer to this riddle,"[26] he, nevertheless, attempts to indicate the lines on which the mystery can be unravelled. Unfortunately, he appears to be groping in the dark. Far from clarifying the issue, he rather confuses it all the more. He not only exaggerates the "considerable benefits" accruing to China

by the exchange of ambassadors with Britain, but also under-
estimates the importance which Britain's severance of all its
connections with the Chiang Kai-shek regime in Formosa
had for China. He seems to belittle the importance Peking
attached to gaining admission into the UN and of obtaining
Chinese assets, especially the 71 aircraft lying in Hong Kong,
which would have facilitated its task of breaking the Kuomintang blockade of the Chinese coast.[27] Thus, he overestimates
the significance of the British gesture (which was devoid of
any content) of good-will towards China. His answer to
China's refusal to exchange diplomatic representatives with
Britain is an answer based on considerations of prestige alone.
The haughtiness, ignorance and foolishness of the Chinese
leaders, he says, was just a repetition of the old Chinese
imperial practice.[28]

Michael Lindsay, the author of *China and the Cold War*,
concedes his inability to give any "definite answer" to the
problem without having "access to Chinese government records
and power to cross-examine the responsible Chinese leaders."[29]
However, he examines two hypotheses to explain the Chinese
behaviour. According to the first, *i. e.* the "official British
view," the Chinese leadership, in refusing to establish diplomatic relations, was acting rationally but with bad faith :
Peking's intention being to seize British business assets in
China without paying any compensation. Chinese statements
about improving Sino-British relations are dubbed as a purely
propagandist device to embarrass the British Government and
weaken Anglo-American co-operation. However, Lindsay
states :

> The weakness of this hypothesis is that it does not provide
> an adequate rational motive for Chinese behaviour.
> Chinese policy has harmed Chinese as well as British
> interests, and, if the Chinese government really wants to
> embarrass the British government and produce a split
> between Britain and America, it could probably work for
> these ends more effectively with normal diplomatic relations
> than without them.

Lindsay's second hypothesis is based on the belief that
Chinese policy was determined by emotional rather than

rational considerations. Consequently, it reflected Chinese resentment against British policy towards China in the past. The attitude of sacrificing real advantages in the present and the future in order to repay past grudges reflects a rather infantile state of mind, which, he feels, "exists in China." "This theory," Lindsay states, "gives a *possible* explanation of the causes which have produced Chinese policy." But he does not seem quite satisfied with a theory that "does not show Chinese policy to be reasonable." He, therefore, comes to a conclusion not dissimilar to that of Fitzerald. Like the latter, he also feels that Chinese policy might "almost be described as returning to the traditions of Chien-lung,"[30] the Emperor of China who refused to receive an ambassador from King George III unless the envoy agreed to perform a ceremony indicating acknowledgement of Chinese suzerainty.

A careful study of the programme and policies enunciated by Chinese leaders, both before and after the establishment of People's Republic in October 1949, leads one to the conclusion that despite all their ideological passions, they were pragmatists. They displayed a cool and calm attitude in examining the problems they confronted and proceeded with tact, caution and moderation to tackle them. Caution and moderation, in both domestic and foreign affairs, was all the more necessary in the immediate aftermath of the establishment of the communist regime. Hence, the Chinese leaders were not impatient to abolish private property, nationalize commerce, collectivize land or to embark on an invasion of Hong Kong.

Writing in *Hsueh-hsi*, soon after the establishment of the People's Republic, Ko Pai-nien observed : "The major task of the diplomatic policy of the People's Republic of China lies in the consolidation of the victory which the Chinese people have now won."[31] This was no easy task. The communist leadership of China inherited a backward, war-devastated and stagnant economy, with industry occupying only 10 per cent of total production. In the peculiar circumstances obtaining in China (lack of industrialization and insufficient development of capitalism), it is not surprising that Mao initially favoured a mixed economy or the policy of simultaneous development of both "capitalistic and socialistic factors."[32] It was, indeed, noteworthy that "even under a Communist regime, half of

China's textile mills, half her coal mines, and almost all her steam-powered coastal shipping" were "still foreign owned." Foreign investment in these holdings was estimated to be of the order of $3 billion, nearly half of which was British.[33]

Sheer necessity of self-preservation dictated that the Communists should wipe out the remnants of the Kuomintang (estimated to be about one million by the end of 1949[34]) and tackle the food problem, which had defied solution by all Chinese governments.[35] However, these problems could only be solved with the whole-hearted cooperation and support of all classes. Any deterioration in economic conditions would have caused dissatisfaction among the masses, which could be easily exploited by the Kuomintang remnants. This threatened the existence of the infant People's Republic. In the summer of 1950, partly due to the bombardment of Shanghai by Kuomintang planes (6 February 1950) and partly because of government policies, a number of factories and shops closed down and the unemployment problem became acute.[36] The new rulers of China rightly assigned the highest priority to the demands of production. Land reforms, by way of distributing land in individual plots, gave millions of Chinese a personal stake in the new order and released the peasants' productive energies. Much emphasis was also laid on increasing industrial output. Lack of capital, technical know-how and equipment compelled Peking authorities to utilise the services of private capitalists, who were given every encouragement in the form of government loans and tax exemptions. All the energy and attention of the Chinese leaders, Liu Shao-chi stated on 14 June 1950, was geared to "the achievement of democracy, industrialization, independence, unification and prosperity in our country."[37] These objectives were sought to be achieved by "New Democracy"—the basic tenet of their policy in the domestic field. This concept not only tolerated the existence of various classes "in China today," but also recognized "the impelling need to seek and win unity among the four classes"[38]—the workers, peasants, petty *bourgeoisie* and national capitalists. This was considered essential for eliminating Kuomintang remnants from the mainland and for developing national economy. It was also considered necessary for winning the support of the masses against possible attempts by foreign Powers to undermine China's territorial integrity and sovereignty.

Thus, the Maoist leadership had to tackle urgent and pressing problems at home. The international situation at the time of the establishment of the People's Republic was no less menacing. The polarization of the world into two rival blocs, the onset of the Cold War and continued American support of the Taiwan regime were all matters of serious concern to Peking. Mao personally referred to these problems in his speech at the Preparatory Committee Meeting of the Chinese People's Political Consultative Conference on 15 June 1949.[39]

In proclaiming the "lean-to-one-side" policy on 1 July 1949, Mao took into account several factors : the presence of enemies, both within and outside the country ; the existence of a long frontier with the Soviet Union ; the delicate international situation ; the political, economic and military weakness of China ; the hostility of the USA ; and above all, Stalin's policy that "those who are not with us are against us." In these circumstances, the adoption of a neutral stance by China was considered risky. What the Soviet attitude would have been in case Mao had adopted a neutral posture can be visualized from an article on Titoism apearing in the Cominform journal. The article stated that the struggle against "the Yugoslav hirelings of Anglo-American imperialism" could not be defensive. It must be offensive, and it must be waged with increasing force.[40] Therefore, Moscow would not have tolerated any Titoist leaning on the part of Mao. Even if Stalin did not contemplate military intervention to dislodge Mao from power, he could have easily taken steps "to detach Manchuria —in common with other border areas—so as to acquire buffer regions for the protection of the growing industries of Soviet Russia."[41] The loss of Manchuria, which was indispensable to China for reasons of national unity, economic recovery and industrialization,[42] was fraught with the gravest consequences for the Mao regime. A pro-Soviet policy was, thus, considered necessary in the interest of national security, national unity and national prosperity. It was not merely a question of doctrine.[43]

Whether or not "New Democracy" and the "lean-to-one-side" policy—the two fundamental policies of the Mao regime —were reconcilable or not, is beside the point. The fact

remains that they were eminently suited to the conditions then
obtaining in China and helped Peking in facing the three main
dangers confronting the nascent People's Republic, *viz.* deterioration in economic conditions, an attack by Kuomintang in
collusion with the USA, and intervention by the Soviet Union.
Peking seems to have calculated that Britain could prove useful
in facing all these dangers. Therefore, it was in Chinese
interests to cultivate normal, friendly relations with Britain.
In fact, there are reasons to believe that Mao was moving in
that direction even before the establishment of the People's
Republic. China had nothing whatsoever to fear from Britain
because the latter was considerably weak, both economically
and militarily, and, unlike the USA, it was not associated either
with the Kuomintang or with Japan. Peking, therefore, stood
to lose nothing by establishing normal, diplomatic relations
with Britain. Instead, it stood to gain everything by cultivating relations with London. The development of trade relations
with Britain, the utilization of British shipping companies and
the facilities afforded by Hong Kong were very important from
the point of view of economic rehabilitation and industrialization of China.

Besides economic compulsions, political considerations also
demanded that Peking cultivate relations with London. In
the event of American military intervention, Britain could be
useful to China. The British and American attitudes differed
on many issues. The United States, for instance, withdrew
its consular personnel in China whereas Britain retained them.
The US Department of State warned American shipping companies against sending their vessels into Shanghai. Britain, on
the other hand, provided naval protection for British merchantmen on international waters. "And just a little while
ago," Wang Min-chih observed in an article in *World Culture*
on 1 January 1950, "the court in Hong Kong dismissed the
claim of Chennault to the property of the two Chinese aviation
corporations."[44] Peking also took note of the fact that British
interests did not coincide with America's "foster Japan policy"
since the economic resurgence of Japan under American aid
was likely to have a deleterious effect on the textile industry of
Lancashire. Moreover, British recognition of China was
likely to influence other members of the Commonwealth,

accentuate Anglo-American contradictions and thus "isolate the United States diplomatically and affect her Far Eastern policy."[45] Since China stood to gain by exploiting these contradictions, Peking did not rule out the possibility of making use of them.[46]

Accomodation with Britain and the establishment of normal relations with London was also necessary as a precautionary measure against the possibility of the USSR either exerting too much pressure on China or contemplating any interference in its internal affairs. For obvious reasons, this point was never publicly stated. However, it could not be completely dismissed as a matter of no consequence. In case of Soviet high-handedness, as Tito's example amply demonstrated, it was only natural for Peking to look towards the West for trade, credits and even diplomatic support. In that eventuality, London might well have served as a bridge between Peking and Washington. Isolation from the Western world would have meant subservience to the Soviet Union and slackened the country's industrial progress. There appeared a close resemblance between Mao's view that he did not oppose capitalism as such but only "the imperialist system and its conspiratorial plots against the Chinese people"[47] and the British view that they were not opposed to communism as such but to the exploitation thereof as a tool by Russian imperialism. Thus, for reasons of both national security and national prosperity, Peking considered *rapprochement* with Britain desirable.

As early as June 1948, democratic personages like Marshal Li Chi-sen of the Kuomintang Revolutionary Committee, Shen Chun-ju and Chang Po-chun of the China Democratic League, and Ma Shu-lun addressed a letter to the British-China Campaign Committee. The letter stated :

At this critical moment, your request that your Government must adopt a China policy different from that of America is helpful both to reduce the general danger to world peace and to restore the British fame in the Far East ; and consistent with the independent and self-controlled policy beneficial to the two great peoples of China and Britain alike. We fully agree to your positive proposals that economic and cultural relations be established between Britain and Liberated China.[48]

In March 1949, S.K. Li, writing in *China Digest*, used moderate language in discussing "the Communist charge against the British in Hong Kong and Malaya of being brutal and undemocratic towards the overseas Chinese."[49] Both Mao's speech of 15 June 1949 and the Common Programme (adopted on 29 September 1949) emphasized the need for the restoration and development of commercial relations with all countries of the world. Severance of ties with the Kuomintang was the only pre-condition laid down for the establishment of diplomatic relations.[50] Mao also sent his greetings to the Britain-China Conference, that opened in London on 3 December 1949 to promote trade relations between Britain and New China and to urge British recognition of the People's Government. He observed : "My warmest greetings to the convocation of the Britain-China Conference. Chinese people welcome all efforts to strengthen friendship between the peoples of China and Britain."[51]

Wang Min-chih welcomed "the establishment of relations with the United Kingdom and the British Commonwealth nations." He expressed the belief that "there is a good chance for the development of peaceful trade between China and Britain" and endeavoured to remove misgivings in British minds. He stated : "China is prepared to live in harmony with all her neighbours, for she harbours no aggressive intentions....China permits British merchants to pursue *bonafide* trade and to acquire legitimate profit therefrom."[52] Since Britain met the pre-conditions stipulated in the Common Programme, *viz.* that diplomatic relations would be established on the basis of equality, mutual benefit and mutual respect for territory and sovereignty *provided* foreign governments severed relations with the Kuomintang,[53] the first Chinese reaction to the British recognition was quite favourable. This was apparent from China's reply to the British note of recognition and the fact that British barracks in Peking were exempted from requisition.[54] In his reply dated 9 January 1950, Chou En-lai expressed his willingness "to establish diplomatic relations" with Britain. He accepted Hutchinson as *charge d' affaires ad interim* and offered to provide him all the necessary facilities regarding the shifting of his staff and archives from Nanking to Peking.[55] If Peking desired to "talk" about the problem of the establishment of diplomatic relations with Britain, there was nothing unusual about it. China had followed an exactly similar course with India. Chou En-lai's reply to Bevin, therefore, was in no way less friendlier than his reply to Prime Minister Nehru.[56] In his note of 9 January 1950 to Bevin, Chou made no mention of "negotiations on preliminary and procedural questions" as a condition precedent to the establishment of diplomatic relations. This condition was stipulated only on 28 January 1950.[57] Ssu Mu's article in *World Culture* (13 January 1950) considered British recognition "a matter of great significance" to China. British recognition, he said, enhanced the international prestige of the Peking regime, marked the divergence of views between the USA and Britain and signified "the failure of the imperialist dream to restore China to her old colonial status." The American diehards like Knowland, Connolly and others, Ssu Mu pointed out, had castigated the British act of recognition as "betrayal" and had threatened Britain with reduction of aid under the Marshall Plan. Ssu Mu distinguished between "an imperialist nation," such as Britain, and China's ally, the Soviet Union, and expressed the view that "the British action" would not lead China "to deviate from the path of 'leaning to one side'." However, he did not rule out the possibility of establishing "diplomatic relations with capitalistic countries on the basis of equality, mutual benefit, and respect for each other's territorial sovereignty."[58]

Soviet Attitude

It was only after Britain abstained on the question of Peking's admission in the UN Security Council on 13 January 1950, that Hsiao Chien spoke of "complications" arising in relations between Britain, "an anti-communist nation," and "New China led by the Communist Party."[59] Moreover, Peking began to insist on negotiations on preliminary and procedural questions concerning the establishment of diplomatic relations between China and Britain after Chou En-lai's visit to the Soviet Union. In order to understand this shift in the Chinese attitude towards Britain, it is necessary to take into account the

Soviet views in the matter and the play of power politics in the world.

The Soviet Union, it might be recalled, wished that the economic crisis in capitalist countries should worsen. Moscow also had high expectations about the Chinese revolution reaching "a desperate battle with imperialism shaking the very foundation of imperialism throughout the world."[60] The Kremlin, therefore, disliked the development of fruitful trade contacts and close political relations between China and Britain. Diplomatic intercourse with the Western Powers was bound to make for Peking's independence and correspondingly affect its amenability to Soviet influence. Moscow, therefore, viewed with serious concern the Western Powers' dominant position in China's foreign trade,[61] and Britain's friendly overtures towards Peking. The Soviet Union recognized its own inability to meet all the requirements of machinery, tools and raw materials, needed by China for its industrialization and calculated risks involved in taking recourse to such high-handed methods as the use of force or direct intervention in China. In these circumstances, any wrong step on the part of the Soviet Union would not only have driven Mao to rely heavily on the support of the *bourgeoisie* and other non-communist elements at home, but would have also compelled Peking to cultivate closer relations with the Western nations. Tito's example had vividly demonstrated that the exigencies of the political situation could often bring together people of the most diverse aims and views.

Had China been a satellite of the Soviet Union (which obviously was not the case) the Kremlin might not have been so much perturbed about the establishment of diplomatic relations between China and Britain. In fact, as Fitzerald suggests, Moscow might have even asked Peking "to welcome" British recognition so that "the unity of the democracies would be impaired and the case of the Left-wing European critics of America greatly strengthened." Had China been a satellite of the Soviet Union, the latter might have regarded the establishment of diplomatic relations between China and Britain beneficial to the communist cause because it would have ensured the presence of Chinese Communist consuls in Malaya. Since Fitzerald believes that Peking's total alignment with the

USSR "logically followed from the victory of the Communist Party in the civil war," he refuses to accept the view that the establishment of diplomatic relations between Britain and China could, in any way, be prejudicial to Russian interests. "If that is so," he observes, "it would have been best...to prevent the exchange of ambassadors with India also."[62] The analogy of India, however, is not relevant because New Delhi was in no position to compete, as Britain could, with the USSR in either the cultural, economic or political field and could not possibly act as a bridge between Peking and Washington. India had no counterpart of the British Council or the *Tass* in China and was hardly in a position to supply the capital goods required by China. Besides, India followed a logical and consistent policy both as regards Chinese representation in the UN and in its dealings with the Chiang Kai-shek regime in Formosa. India could not be described either as an imperialist country or a Western Power in league with the United States.

Chinese hostility towards the USA was, to a certain extent, the direct consequence of the communist victory in the Civil War. Therefore, there appeared little or no possibility of an early Sino-US *rapprochement*. But the same could not be said of Sino-British relations because Britain had not taken any side in the Civil War. Accordingly, it was not quite easy for Moscow to discredit London in Chinese eyes. Any reference to the past, though of some help, was not quite safe partly because it was a two-edged weapon. In these circumstances, Moscow was on the look-out for a suitable opportunity so that it could accomplish its purpose of preventing the normalization of Sino-British relations, which was considered only a step towards Sino-Western *detente*.

Realizing that the British Government might not be ready "at the immediate moment of recognition...to admit a new Chinese representative" in the UN Security Council, the Soviet Government, Bevin observed, tried "to force us to implement what they regarded as the consequence"[63] of the British decision to recognize China. The manner in which the Soviet Government brought the question of Chinese representation in the UN Security Council in January 1950 and handled it (the Soviet delegate insisted that the Security Council take a decision and vote then and there[64] and staged a walk-out from the

Council after the vote) indicated that behind the diplomatic move there was a definite political purpose, *viz.* to discredit Britain in Chinese eyes and to convince Peking of British duplicity and hostility.

Soon after the Security Council voting, in which Britain had abstained, a Soviet commentary in *Izvestia* drew a sharp contrast between "the principled and consistent position of the Soviet Union" and the stand taken by the "double-dealing English parasites." The Soviet commentator pointed out that the main purpose of the Commonwealth Conference of Foreign Ministers (held in Ceylon from 9 to 14 January 1950), was to organize an "anti-communist front in South-eastern Asia."[65] Apparently, the Soviet commentator was trying to impress upon his Chinese friends that Britain, like the USA, was no less hostile to their interests and that the two Western Powers were working hand in glove against Peking. The Soviet walk-out was a calculated move aimed against Britain as well as China. After this exposure of British insincerity, if Peking still felt inclined to come to terms with Britain, Stalin could justifiably feel irritated. Mao's recognition of the Vietminh regime of Ho Chi-minh shattered all hopes of an early recognition of China by France and made Paris reluctant to support Peking's case for admission in the UN.

Subtle pressure exerted upon Peking by Moscow might not have worked had Britain not hesitated in supporting China's case for a seat in the UN and in handing over the 71 aircraft stationed in Hong Kong. A combination of all these factors led to the hardening of the Chinese attitude towards the establishment of diplomatic relations with Britain. Peking began to insist on the fulfilment of certain pre-conditions before it could establish normal relations with London. Its right to represent China in the UN and its right to its national properties and assets, especially the 71 aircraft in Hong Kong, were two important issues on which China saw "inconsistency between words and deeds" of the British Government and officially sought clarifications.[66] Other matters, *e.g.* restrictions on Chinese immigration into Hong Kong, action against Chinese Communists and imposition of a ban on Chinese books and other publications in Malaya, were later added to the list of grievances in the Chinese press.[67] However, they were not officially treated as obstacles to the establishment of diplomatic relations.

British Manoeuvres

Hostility towards China, Bevin remarked, signified throwing "away our position in the Far East for ever."[68] Britain, therefore, could not think of deviating from the path of seeking a *modus vivendi* with Peking. Accordingly, London endeavoured to assure Peking that it would vote for its admission into the UN as and when there were enough other favourable votes to give the required majority of seven in the Security Council.[69] On 23 February 1950, the Hong Kong Supreme Court adjudged that the 71 aircraft were the property of the Chinese People's Government and that it would be a violation of the rights of a foreign sovereign Power to make an order directing that the property in its possession and control should be delivered over to a receiver appointed by the Court.[70] Consequently, the airplanes were free to fly away to China. In fact, on 15 March 1950, 5,777 cases of valuable aircraft spares and parts, including engines, valued at about $3 million were shipped from Hong Hong in a British steamer to Tsingtao in North China.[71]

However, despite these assurances London continued to abstain on the question of Chinese representation in the various UN organs.[72] Moreover, Britain did not allow a single aircraft to leave Hong Kong for China. This contradiction in words and deeds might have been partly due to American pressure and partly due to Britain's own desire to ensure that China took the next step by establishing diplomatic relations with it. However, this half-hearted British attitude failed to satisfy China. As a reprisal against the damage caused to 7 of the 71 aircraft detained in Hong Kong and in order to exert pressure on London, Peking requisitioned the British barracks in April 1950. However, Britain was still reluctant to give up its bargaining points. The Chinese note of 8 May 1950, therefore, rejected all explanations offered by Britain on 17 March 1950 as unsatisfactory. It demanded further clarifications of the British stand as regards the question of Chinese representation in the UN and its property rights in Hong Kong.

In response to China's stiffening attitude, Britain issued an Order in Council (10 May 1950) whereby the British Government expressly decreed the detention of the aircraft in Hong Kong and prevented their flight to Peking. This greatly displeased Chinese leaders who considered it "an extremely unfriendly attitude towards the People's Republic of China."[73]

Anglo-Chinese talks on the establishment of diplomatic relations, that officially began on 2 March 1950, dragged on. Britain's reply to Chinese inquiries (contained in their note of 8 May 1950) was given by the British *charge d' affaires* in Peking on 17 June 1950. In the meantime, the failure of crops and the "critical phase" of the economy induced Peking to assuage the fears of private enterprises at home. It took "concrete measures to readjust industry and commerce and the relations between public and private enterprises."[74] China also began to think of increasing its trade with Hong Kong,[75] as well as with "capitalist countries."[76] It was even prepared to welcome foreign credits and investments from "certain capitalistic countries"[77] in order to industrialize the country. Thus, Britain and China seemed to be moving in the direction of closer economic relations. In these circumstances, the establishment of diplomatic relations seemed only a matter of time. Relations between China and Britain could perhaps have been normalized had the Korean War not broken out or had Peking succeeded in occupying Taiwan.

Before China and Britain could reach an agreement about the exchange of ambassadors, the Korean War broke out. Subsequently, Britain voted in favour of Peking at the Fifth Session of the UN General Assembly. This was evidently a tactical move[78] designed to forestall the Chinese entry into the Korean War. After the Chinese intervention, Britain openly supported Washington in condemning Peking for its aggression in Korea. It also voted against China's admission in the UN and in favour of the imposition of an embargo on the shipment of strategic goods to Peking. As a result, Sino-British relations were put under heavy strain. Peking, in turn, imposed restrictions on British firms in China while London reacted by handing over the 71 airplanes, detained in Hong Kong, to American interests.

Relations at charge d' affaires *Level*

It was only after the Korean armistice that at a dinner party given by Foreign Secretary Eden to Chou En-lai, during their stay in Geneva for the Conference on Indo-China in 1954, it was agreed that diplomatic relations should be established between Britain and China at the level of *charge d' affaires*. Thus, "partial diplomatic relations" were established between the two countries.[79] Relations at the ambassadorial level could not be established because of British participation in the SEATO (formed just after the Geneva Conference) and because of London's continued opposition to Chinese entry in the UN. These created "new obstacles to improvement of Sino-British relations,"[80] which still required "normalization."[81]

In its attempt to establish relations with China at ambassadorial level, Britain endeavoured to rectify some of the Chinese complaints. For instance, in May 1957 it took the initiative in bringing trade restrictions with China at par with other Communist countries of Europe and in August 1958 it played an important role in the relaxation of the embargo. In December 1961, Britain sold six Viscount planes to China and, for the first time since February 1951, voted in favour of China's admission into the UN. London watched with keen interest the developing Sino-Soviet rift, the growing Chinese desire to reduce its economic dependence on Communist countries, and the possibilities of increased Sino-British trade. Although the British stand over Vietnam was considered subservient to that of Washington, the British Trade Minister visited China in 1964 and the Chinese Trade Minister returned that visit in 1965.

An interesting development of the widening Sino-Soviet rift was the establishment of the "Society for Anglo-Chinese Understanding" by confirmed sinophils. It represented a splinter movement from the British-China Friendship Association, which pro-Peking elements believed had come under the influence of the pro-Soviet British Communist Party. The new Society, which included well-known academicians and public figures of Britain, was supported, if not actually inspired, by the People's Republic of China. This was evident from the fact that Peking welcomed the establishment of the new organisation and, in October 1965, extended an invitation to a delegation of the Society to visit China for several weeks at its expense. On his return, a member of the delegation, Hugh Trevor-Roper, Professor of Modern History, Oxford University, in an article entitled "All's So Smugly Right in Red China," remarked that the danger of aggression from China "is, at present, remote" and that claims "to conquer the world are mere rhetoric."

Cultural Revolution

During the period of the "Great Proletarian Cultural Revolution," Sino-British relations were at a low ebb. In August 1967, the British Mission in Peking was burnt and its staff, including the Head of the Mission (Donald Hopson) were manhandled by the Red Guards. The staff of the Chinese Mission in London also staged a pitched battle with police outside their Embassy. Before the British Mission was burnt, a 48-hour ultimatum was given to London to rescind a ban on three pro-Peking newspapers in Hong Kong. British diplomatic radio facilities were destroyed and Peking detained a number of British subjects, including Anthony Grey—the Reuters correspondent. The British retaliated by imposing restrictions on the movements of Chinese nationals (making their exit from the UK subject to control by exit *visa*) and on the Chinese diplomatic and other staff (restricting their travel from 35 to only five miles from Marble Arch with effect from 22 August 1967) and denying them the facility to use Chinese transmitters in London. These developments constituted the subject matter of the three British notes dated 18, 23 and 24 August 1967 and of two Chinese notes of 24 August (described as "the most urgent and strongest protest") and 27 August 1967. The Chinese protest note of 27 August was also labelled as "the strongest protest" lodged with "immense indignation" against what it called "extremely serious political provocation against the great Chinese people." The redoubling of efforts on the part of the British Government in "persecuting Chinese patriotic countrymen in Hong Kong by Fascist atrocities," the imposition of "unreasonable restrictions" on the exit from and travel in Britain of Chinese personnel and the suspension of the use of Chinese diplomatic radio transmitters were said to hinder the normal, diplomatic and business activities of the office of the Chinese *charge d' affaires* and other Chinese organizations in Britain. The note warned of "grave consequences" if the above-mentioned "unreasonable restrictions" were not removed forthwith.

As disturbances within China spilled across the border into Hong Kong, the latter also witnessed communist-inspired demonstrations, strikes and even violent riots leading to large-scale arrests. By mid-1971, over 30 prisoners were still serving sentences in Hong Kong jails for their part in the 1967 riots. However, neither London nor Peking lost sight of the realities of the situation so as to contemplate a rupture in their relations. The British Government was particularly keen to keep open its channel of communication with the Chinese and to maintain normal diplomatic relations with Peking. When tension was at its height, the British Foreign Office issued a statement declaring that Her Majesty's Government had no wish to exacerbate the already unhappy relations between themselves and the People's Republic of China. "They are willing," it said, "at any time to discuss with the Chinese Government, on a rational and businesslike basis, the mutual relaxation of all these restrictions and the return to conditions between them and the Chinese Government conducive to the proper conduct of international affairs." A Foreign Office Official remarked : "To have no link with Peking would make things more difficult on Hong Kong. If you remove Donald Hopson and his staff how can the Chinese demonstrate they can be beastly to the British except by taking over Hong Kong." The Chinese, on their part, were not prepared to lose $700 million a year in convertible currency earnings on account of trade, besides remittances, if they expelled the British from Hong Kong.

Full Diplomatic Relations

In the post-Cultural Revolution period, Peking established full diplomatic relations with Canada and Italy after they agreed to take note of Peking's position that Taiwan was an inalienable part of China. This raised hopes that Sino-British relations would soon be upgraded. However, things did not seem to move further. In November 1970 there was, for the first time, a simple majority (51 to 49 with 25 abstentions) in the UN General Assembly in favour of Peking's admission and Taiwan's expulsion from the world organization. Britain supported that resolution, but it also continued to vote in favour of the US draft resolution which declared that the question of Chinese representation was an important question requiring two-thirds majority. Peking disliked Britain's dual approach in the matter and also the presence of a British consul in Taiwan.

In March 1971, Chou En-lai received the British *charge d'affaires*, John Denson, and apologised to him for the burning of the British Mission. He also agreed to reimburse the cost of its restoration. This indicated that Peking was interested in improving Sino-British relations. With the establishment of full diplomatic relations between China and an increasing number of West European, Asian and African countries, it was becoming all the more galling to London to see its relations frozen at the *charge d' affaires* level. In the wake of Kissinger's secret trip to Peking and the July 1971 announcement about President Nixon's forthcoming visit to China, Peking's chances of being admitted into the UN in the fall of 1971 considerably increased. In these circumstances, Britain decided to reverse its position (followed since 1961) of supporting the US draft resolution requiring two-thirds majority for Peking's admission in the UN. Accordingly, London voted against the American draft in October 1971. This move as well as Britain's anti-Soviet posture (in 1971 London expelled 105 Soviet diplomats on charges of espionage) greatly impressed Peking. Britain's entry into the European Common Market (EEC) was, likewise, viewed in Peking as a welcome trend in British foreign policy. The emergence of a powerful, unified and an enlarged grouping in West Europe—an independent "European Europe"—was considered a new and important step, which could be of use in resisting super Power domination and preserving a proper balance in the world. Consequently, Peking abandoned its earlier misgivings about Britain being subservient to American control and having a special relationship with Washington.

It was against this background that Anglo-Chinese discussions about the exchange of ambassadors were resumed in early

1971. They were successfully concluded in March 1972 when an agreement was reached to raise the level of diplomatic representation from *charge d' affaires* to ambassador level with effect from 13 March 1972. In the Joint Communique of the two Governments, Britain conceded the Chinese demand that Taiwan was a province of the People's Republic of China and that the latter was the sole legal government of China. Accordingly, the British Government agreed to remove their official representation in Taiwan on 13 March 1972. After the withdrawal of the British consulate from Taiwan, the task of looking after British interests in Taiwan was entrusted to the Australians.

Within a few months of the agreement to establish full diplomatic relations at ambassadorial level, the British Parliamentary Under-Secretary for Foreign and Commonwealth Affairs, Anthony Royle, visited China. This was followed by the first-ever visit of a British Foreign Secretary (Alec Douglas-Home) to the People's Republic of China. Thus, contacts at the highest levels were established. Most of the British nationals, arrested during the Cultural Revolution, were released in 1972. In an interview published on 14 October 1972 in *The Times* (which was allowed to have a resident correspondent in Peking with every kind of assistance being offered to him), Premier Chou En-lai regretted that full diplomatic relations between China and Britain were not established earlier. He expressed the belief that relations between the two countries would improve in the years to come. At the end of his visit to China, Sir Alec Douglas-Home also expressed similar feelings as regards the development of Sino-British relations in the future. He observed : "The ice in our relationship has been broken. Now the water is warm and we can swim in it together."

CHAPTER THREE

The Korean Question

Strategic Importance of Korea

The Korean peninsula, about 85,000 square miles in area, occupies a position of great strategic importance in East Asia. Its boundaries with Manchuria, the Ruhr of China, run along the Yalu and Tumen river for nearly 600 miles and China depends for some of its electric power on facilities located on the Korean side of the frontier. For these reasons, "the independent existence or destruction of Korea" has always been regarded as "closely related to China's security."[1] The Soviet Union too has a common frontier with Korea for 11 miles and Vladivostok—the major Soviet port in the Pacific—is about 100 miles from it. The peninsula of Korea is also dangerously close to Japan. It "thrusts itself, like a menacing dagger, from the continent towards the vital parts of Japan."[2] Thus, the three Powers most directly interested in Korea had been Japan, China and the USSR, and each one had endeavoured to dominate it. However, one country's control was considered a threat to the security of others. The Western Powers' interest in Korea had, for the most part, been indirect; their primary concern being to maintain a balance of power in the West Pacific—a region of vital concern to them. They were more interested in China, Japan, and Hong Kong than in Korea. Lt. General A. C. Wedemeyer, in his "Report on Korea" submitted to the US President in September 1947, considered South Korea to be militarily indefensible. However, he deemed it to be a major US interest "to deny to the Soviet Union direct or indirect control of all Korea and prevent her free use of the entire nation as a military base of operations, including the ice-free ports in South Korea." Wedemeyer, therefore, recommended that "the United States Government provide as early as practicable moral, advisory, and material support to China and South Korea...."[3]   With the establishment of the People's Republic of China in 1949, it became increasingly difficult for the Western Powers to contemplate bolstering China against the USSR and to defend Korea in order to ensure stability in the West Pacific region.

Outbreak of the Korean War

The Western Powers faced an uphill task in defending South Korea[4] against the North Koreans in June 1950. The decision of the US Government and that of other Western Powers[5] to assist South Korea was taken not so much for the sake of Korea as such as for the "vital stake in the issues involved" in that aggression[6] and its "implications for peace throughout the world."[7] If the aggression in Korea was allowed to go unchecked, it was believed, it would have marked the beginning of the end of the UN[8] and might well have been "an open invitation to new acts of aggression elsewhere,"[9] thereby ushering in a world war.   Besides, the success of Communist Powers in Korea most directly impinged on the security interests of Japan[10] and consequently, threatened peace and stability in the Pacific.[11] Furthermore, the Western Powers could not be expected to remain indifferent to its probable effects on China. In fact, they were visibly concerned about "the continued inroads of Soviet power into Manchuria under the cloak of the Korean aggression."[12] If "Russia added Korea to the Primorsk," not only would the shores of Japan "be dominated by a great European power" but "Manchuria would be almost completely encircled by Russian territory."[13] Thereafter, it was believed that China would either be an obedient satellite or a subordinate and dependent partner of the USSR. It would no longer be "a great Pacific nation,"[14] which could play an important part in ensuring peace and stability in the Pacific.[15]

The Western Powers regarded the Kremlin to be the villain of the piece in the Korean War.[16] They felt that the prospect of Moscow becoming more powerful would hardly appeal to Peking and that China stood to gain nothing by a communist victory in Korea. They assumed that China was too pre-occupied with internal problems to think of intervening in the Korean War,[17] even though Stalin would have desired Peking's participation in the War. However, in view of the proximity of UN forces to the Yalu river, China could not be sure that the UN forces would not cross that river and enter into Chinese territory. Concern for its security was the primary consideration behind Peking's decision to intervene in the Korean War. Stalin welcomed it since a certain degree of Chinese blood-letting, in both human and economic resources, would widen the gulf between China and the Western Powers and compel Peking into greater dependence on Moscow.

British Reaction

When the Korean War broke out, Britain was passing through a critical economic phase. It was, therefore, hardly in a position to bear the double burden of both recovery and rearmament. While presenting the Government proposals to the House of Commons to lengthen the period of full time national service from 18 months to two years and increase the defence expenditure to £3600 millions, Premier Attlee conceded that those proposals were "distasteful and disappointing to all of us." But he considered them necessary "to meet the growing dangers to world peace of which the war in Korea is example."[18] Britain was greatly perturbed by its military weakness in the world, particularly in West Europe. From the British point of view, Korea, though the scene of actual hostilities, was "not the main point of trouble." "The centre, the seat, the real source of anxiety," Lord Chancellor Jowitt remarked, "of course rests in Europe" and it was idle, he said, to pretend that the situation there was easy.[19] West Europe was the nearest to the British Isles and, consequently, enjoyed the highest priority in British strategy.[20]

From the very beginning of the Korean crisis, London endeavoured to limit the hostilities to Korea itself,[21] minimize the risks and prevent the diversion of the Western Powers' resources from West Europe to the far distant Korean peninsula.[22] Any other course of action was regarded "strategically foolish."[23]

Defence of the homeland and anxiety to save the "civilization of Europe" was considered more important than the need to protect the relatively small British economic interests in China and Hong Kong. Churchill, therefore, counselled that the British should avoid "by every means in their power becoming entangled inextricably in a war with China....For it is in Europe that the world cause will be decided...it is there that the mortal danger lies."[24]

Any involvement in war with China entailed serious risks for Britain. Economically, it meant upsetting economic recovery at home, reduction in trade and endangering its investments in China. Politically, it would have resulted in the reduction of its influence in the whole of Asia and led to the abandonment of its policy of detaching China from Russia. Militarily, it would have jeopardized its more vital security interests in the Middle East and West Europe. Therefore, London exerted itself to localize the conflict in Korea and to avoid war with China.

For the above-mentioned reasons, London, while supporting the United States action in Korea, had its own reservations as regards US armed neutralization of Formosa. Britain recognized the "dangerous possibilities"[25] inherent in that decision. However, since Washington also undertook to prevent any raids on the Chinese mainland by Kuomintang troops, Britain refrained from publicly criticizing Washington's decision. Apparently, London seemed convinced of the arguments advanced by America and felt satisfied by the latter's decision to politely refuse Chinese nationalist contributions to the Korean War.[26] Britain also deemed it imprudent to openly endorse the US decision in regard to Formosa. Such an action would have been inconsistent with British recognition of China and contrary to its policy of seeking a *modus vivendi* with Peking. Thus, London adopted a middle course : it dissociated itself from the US decision as regards the defence of Formosa and justified its support of the UN action in Korea.[27]

As long as the military situation in Korea remained critical, the war aims of the Western Powers were modest. The Security Council resolutions of 25 June and 27 June 1950 merely called upon "the authorities of North Korea to withdraw forthwith their armed forces to the 38th Parallel." The efforts of the

British Ambassador in Moscow, David Kelly, were similarly directed towards returning to the *status quo ante* by "the cessation of hostilities and the withdrawal of the North Korean forces beyond the 38th parallel."[28]   Since the military situation was favourable to North Korean forces, the Kremlin was not inclined to accept proposals seeking to maintain the *status quo.* However, as UN troops gained an upper hand in the Korean War, after the successful landing of American troops at Inchon on 15 September 1950, the Western Powers re-appraised their war aims in the light of new conditions. Accordingly, the UN objectives in Korea were redefined as not only "to repel the armed attack," but to unify Korea as well.[29]

The eight-Power resolution, which authorised UN operations north of the 38th parallel, was "originally drafted by His Majesty's Government" and was submitted on 29 September 1950 to the Political Committee of the General Assembly.[30] Though Britain was aware that the movement of UN troops (consisting mostly of American contingents) close to Chinese and Soviet borders would be resented by Peking as well as Moscow,[31] it still seemed to rule out any possibility of China becoming involved in the Korean War. That was probably the reason why London, in presenting the eight-Power resolution in the UN, did not deem it necessary to insert any clause therein providing for specific and definite guarantees as regards the inviolability of the frontiers of Korea's neighbours.[32] Vague and general assurances were no doubt given by the spokesmen of the Western Powers[33] but such assurances and the declaration that the authority of the Republic of Korea would be limited only to South Korea,[34] could hardly assuage Chinese fears of Western intentions in Korea. Confident of their victory in Korea,[35] the Western Powers did not wish to leave Korea divided and, for that matter, unstable after expending so much of sweat, blood and treasure.[36] A divided Korea was considered neither a satisfactory nor a permanent solution of the problem.[37] Hence, they did not want to miss the opportunity of unifying Korea. If the crossing of the 38th parallel involved certain risks, so did the other alternative of abandoning the objective of unifying Korea, which would have provided "the aggressors in the North time and opportunity to reform their defence," and thereby enabled them to launch their attacks again.[38]

In sponsoring the eight-Power resolution on the crossing of the 38th parallel and describing it as "an initiative for peace,"[39] Britain seemed to be guided by the following considerations : Firstly, London believed that China stood to gain nothing by engaging in mortal combat with the highly modernized UN forces in Korea. Secondly, it was felt that the achievement of UN objectives in Korea would not, in any way, adversely affect Peking's national interests. Thirdly, Britain assumed that Peking would not like to jeopardize its chances of becoming a member of the UN by intervening in the Korean War.[40] Fourthly, the British calculated that since the solution of the Taiwan problem to Peking's satisfaction, to a great extent, depended on the goodwill of the Western Powers, China would hesitate to adopt a course of action likely to antagonize the West. The decision to postpone the consideration of the Chinese complaint regarding "an armed invasion of the island of Taiwan (Formosa)"[41] clearly indicated that the Western Powers were anxious to keep alive the hope of settling the problem of Formosa in Peking's favour. Fifthly, the victory of UN forces in Korea would have enhanced the Western Powers' prestige in the world and ensured a satisfactory balance of power in East Asia. The establishment of a unified Korea, under the auspices of the United Nations, strengthened their position *vis-a-vis* both China and Russia. Finally, it was believed that if the task of unifying Korea was accomplished with lightening speed, Peking might find no time to intervene, even if it so desired.

Conscious of Chinese susceptibilities as regards "the armies of imperialism" arriving on the Manchurian frontier, many Britishers suggested that Korea be declared a "neutral buffer state under permanent United Nations military protection, the great powers undertaking not to maintain bases or garrisons of any sort there."[42] This suggestion could have served some useful purpose as a long-term solution of the problem, but it was hardly of any immediate significance. Before a gendarmerie under the UN Command, drawn from the smaller Powers, could be found, the predominance of US troops in the UN forces, that were to stay till the accomplishment of the UN objectives in Korea, had to be maintained.[43]

Another proposal, mooted in London to allay Chinese fears,

was that UN troops stop at the "line of the waist in Korea" and leave a no-man's land to the north.[44] This proposal, if accepted, would have meant the occupation of over a third of North Korea, including its capital (Pyongyang), but it would have left a substantial buffer region to the north. It was believed that this might allay Chinese fears about the proximity of American troops to its borders and assure a continuous supply of electricity from North Korean power stations. It would have, at the same time, provided a better defensive position for the UN forces.[45] Acting on the advice of their Chief of Staff, the British Government forwarded this suggestion (*i. e.* halting at the Korean waistline) to the US Government and asked Washington to seriously consider it. However, it seems that London subsequently abandoned it for fear of betraying the political objectives of a unified Korea. It is also possible that since such a move would have been interpreted by the Chinese and other Asians as a sign of weakness, Washington rejected it. Britain was in a much weaker position in 1950 than it was during the Second World War.[46] The Supreme Commander of UN troops in Korea was solely responsible to the American Chiefs of Staff in military matters. Therefore, the question whether the UN forces ought to advance toward the Chinese border or not was never submitted before the UN for decision. However, as the UN troops launched their last offensive towards the northern border of Korea, the British Government became "gravely concerned" about it since it was felt that UN forces might be "running their heads into trouble."[47]

Chinese Intervention

As compared to the Soviet Union, which exercised considerable influence in North Korea, Peking had no diplomatic presence in Pyongyang when the war in Korea broke out.[48] China did not have very close relations with the North Korean Government in the late 1940s either. [49] Moreover, the Chinese authorities laid emphasis on economic reconstruction and unification of the country. They had also carried out demobilization of their troops and reduced military expenditure.

For all these reasons, there appeared little or no possibility of China seeking to instigate or pressurize the North Korean government to invade South Korea.[50]

However, being a close neighbour of Korea, China could hardly remain indifferent to what was happening in close proximity to its borders. The prospect of the Soviet Union becoming more powerful (as a result of the North Korean victory), particularly in the very sensitive area of Manchuria, was hardly appealing to Peking. But there was nothing it could do in the matter. It could hardly restrain its predominant partner. Besides, such a step on Peking's part was likely to be interpreted in Moscow as betrayal of the cause of communism. On the other hand, devoid of even diplomatic contacts with the West, Peking could not but view with serious concern the prospects of US forces coming close to the Chinese frontier. It is pertinent to recall that Japan was then under US occupation and Chiang Kai-shek had close rapport with Washington. Even if China did not face "an imminent invasion of Chinese soil by the United Nations troops," the establishment of United Korea, "whose Government was likely to be as hostile to China, and as closely bound to the United States, as that of Syngman Rhee," [51] posed a serious threat to Chinese security.

In his cable to the United Nations on 20 August 1950, Premier Chou En-lai expressed his country's concern about the "solution of the Korean question." That question, he observed, "must be and can be settled peacefully."[52] At the same time, China began to accuse the Western Powers of encroaching upon its territorial waters and violating its air space.[53] Peking also lodged a protest with the US Government against the alleged bombing of Chinese villages and the slaughter of Chinese people.[54] While announcing the release of battle-trained Koreans from the People's Liberation Army of China on 22 September 1950, the spokesman of the Chinese Foreign Ministry supported them "in joining in the defence of their motherland." He condemned "the criminal acts of American imperialist aggressors against Korea and their plot of extending the war."[55] On 24 September 1950, Chou En-lai drew attention to the repeated violations of Chinese territory by US armed forces. He warned UN Member States that if they continued to remain "deaf and dumb to these aggressive crimes" of the United States, "they shall not escape a share in the responsibility for lighting up the war flames in the East." The peace-loving peoples all over the world, he observed, "definitely will not stand in face of this with folded arms."[56] This was perhaps an indirect reference about China's intention to intervene in the Korean War—a disguised hint to Britain and other countries to exert themselves to stop the war and restrain Washington. The clearest warning about the impending Chinese intervention in Korea was given by Chou En-lai on 30 September 1950 when he stated that the Chinese people would not "supinely tolerate seeing their neighbours being savagely invaded by the imperialists."[57]

Greater resistance by anti-communist forces at home,[58] the impact of the North Korean defeat on Japan and neutral nations of Asia, the loss of a "buffer zone at a highly sensitive point," and the prospect of the defeated North Korean army retreating into Manchuria, thereby facilitating Soviet control over Manchuria again[59]—all seem to have influenced Peking's decision to intervene in the Korean War. However, the collapse of the North Korean resistance, the rapid advance of the UN forces under General MacArthur towards the Chinese border, and the resulting threat to Chinese security were probably the decisive factors in inducing Peking to intervene. If the Kremlin succeeded in persuading Peking to join the war effort, it was only because Chinese interests were "so directly involved in the Korean war."[60] Chou En-lai observed :

> In view of painful historical lessons and in consideration of their vital interest, the Chinese people had no choice but to volunteer assistance to Korea, fighting aggression shoulder to shoulder with the Korean people in defence of the security of their motherland. The Chinese people could not permit such a situation in which Korea could be used once again as a springboard of aggression against China.[61]

British Policy after Chinese Intervention

Even though Chinese troops in Korea were described as

"volunteers," the Western Powers (particularly Britain) felt deeply concerned about the Chinese intervention.[62] The UN Commander-in-Chief reported that "a new and fresh army now faces us, backed up by a possibility of large alien reserves, and adequate supply within easy reach to the enemy but beyond the limits of our present sphere of military action."[63] Thereafter, the Western Powers became all the more anxious to "clear away any possible misunderstanding that there may be in the minds of the Chinese" about the West having "any ulterior designs in Manchuria."[64] However, as there was no indication that the Chinese army was really committed to waging a full-scale offensive, the West did not altogether abandon the idea of uniting Korea by force. This was evident from the draft resolution introduced by six Powers, including Britain, in the UN Security Council on 10 November 1950 and Bevin's personal message to his Chinese counterpart on 22 November 1950. The draft resolution affirmed the inviolability of Chinese frontiers in the most explicit terms. But, at the same time, it called upon all States, China in particular, to immediately withdraw all their "nationals, individuals, or units which may presently be in Korea." In his attempt to clear away "misapprehension regarding the nature and purpose of the current operation of United Nations forces in Korea," Bevin told Chou En-lai :

There is...no threat to the security of China or of any other State. Believing that a free and independent Korea is in the interests of China as of all peace-loving countries, His Majesty's Government earnestly desire to prevent any extension of the conflict and deplore any action which may tend to prolong the sufferings of the Korean people. His Majesty's Government recognise that the Central People's Government of China are deeply interested in the future of their neighbour Korea and it is hoped that the presence of their representatives in New York will provide an opportunity to make it clear that the fulfilment of the United Nations aims in Korea will in no way endanger legitimate Chinese interests. It is, further, the hope of His Majesty's Government that the Central People's Government of China will accept my assurance that the United Nations entertain no hostile intent towards them, and it is our hope that the Central People's Government will take steps to cause the inviolability of the frontier to be respected.[65]

China launched a major offensive on 25 November 1950. UN forces were compelled to retreat and Western hopes of unifying Korea by force were thereby shattered. The Chinese offensive also signified that their commitment to the Korean War was total and irrevocable. It was apparent to both the British and Americans alike that

> total victory could not be won militarily within Korea, while any attempt to gain total victory by a widening of the war would inevitably involve millions of Americans, might lead to Soviet intervention and would offer no certainty of success.[66]

The strong military pressure exerted by Peking, Attlee remarked, obviously created "a new and very dangerous situation,"[67] which threatened to turn an incident in the far-off peninsula into a major war with China, if not indeed into World War III. Conscious of the weakness of the Western Powers in Europe, [68] which had first priority in British strategy, London became anxious to avoid war with China at all costs.[69] Britain began to minimize its responsibility in sponsoring the decisive resolution of 7 October 1950, which had served as General MacArthur's justification for crossing the 38th parallel. Henceforth, British diplomacy aimed not at the defeat of communism in war but rather sought an early end to the Korean conflict by a process of negotiation and accomodation with Peking.

After the Chinese intervention, UN members, whose troops were fighting in Korea, were left with three alternatives :

1. to completely withdraw from Korea in the face of defeat and surrender South Korea to the communists.

2. to meet "force with maximum counter-force" as General MacArthur desired.[70] This, in fact, meant bombing of Manchuria, blockading of China and the utilisation of Chinese nationalist forces.

3. to abandon the idea of "the conquest of North Korea by force"[71] and seek a negotiated settlement with

China presumably on the lines of *status quo ante* 25 June 1950.

The first alternative was unacceptable to the Western Powers because it signified a grievous blow to the prestige of the so-called "free world" and an enormous increase in that of the Sino-Soviet bloc, which could have "grave political and military consequences."[72] The second alternative, as MacArthur had stated, fitted in with "the conventional pattern." He argued: "If we lose the war to communism in Asia the fall of Europe is inevitable. There is no substitute for victory."[73] However, Western statesmen were not quite convinced by MacArthur's arguments. They were well aware of the risks involved and the dangers inherent in any extension of conflict leading to a general war.[74] The presence of Chinese residents in its colonies, concern for the security of Hong Kong, and its weak position in East Asia as a whole led Britain to one conclusion— *viz.* to avoid war with China, to seek accomodation with Peking and not to give up its policy of detaching China from the USSR. Therefore, London was most reluctant to support the second alternative.

For the reasons mentioned above, Britain abandoned "the idea that peace could be restored in the Far East by total military victory." The only possible alternative that London could think of was "a settlement by political negotiation" and, in this judgement, it did not believe that "there was any element of appeasement." "It was merely a conclusion dictated by the facts."[75] The goal of unifying Korea would henceforth be achieved only through negotiation and "peaceful means." Accordingly, London endeavoured to confine the conflict and to bring about the cessation of hostilities by reaching an agreement with Peking "as soon as possible."[76]

Quest for a Cease-fire

In its quest for a cease-fire in Korea and a negotiated settlement with Peking, London realized that it was not easy to find a mediator.[77] Consequently, Britain either attempted to play that role itself or sought to utilize India and other Asian States for the purpose. However, the success of these efforts at mediation depended, first of all, on creating necessary conditions, such as stabilization of the military situation, which would make both parties agreeable to a truce. The first attempt to bring the USA and China around a conference table was made when Peking was invited to attend the Security Council discussion of the special report of the UN Command in Korea. The arrival of the Chinese representative, Wu Hsiu-chuan, almost coincided with the large-scale Chinese offensive in Korea. In view of its strong position on the battlefield, Peking appeared in no mood to agree to a compromise settlement. In return for the Chinese acquiescence in the Korean cease-fire, Wu Hsiu-chuan, in his speech before the Security Council on 28 November 1950, demanded outright condemnation of the USA; the imposition of sanctions against Washington "for its criminal acts of armed aggression against the territory of China, Taiwan, and for its armed intervention in Korea" ; and the complete withdrawal of American troops from Taiwan and of all UN forces from Korea, thereby leaving the people of North and South Korea "to settle the domestic affairs of Korea themselves." In his subsequent speech on 30 November 1950, Wu Hsiu-chuan refused to participate in the discussion of the "fundamentally preposterous, so-called 'complaint of aggression on the Korean Republic' " and considered it "entirely unnecessary...to answer the questions posed by Mr. Austin on the basis of MacArthur's report."[78]

In the face of "one of the greatest military reverses in the history of American arms"[79] and the intransigence of the Chinese representative in the UN, President Truman warned that the use of atom bomb against China could not be ruled out.[80] Since the use of A-bomb would invariably have led to the widening of conflict, Premier Attlee deemed it necessary to send a telegram to President Truman wherein he expressed his anxiety about the "possible extension of the war in the Far East" and the likely effects of it on "Western European defence."[81] Under pressure from his Party,[82] Attlee personally flew to Washington to dissuade the White House from using the "dreadful weapon"[83] and becoming too deeply involved in the far distant peninsula which was not of primary concern to Britain. His visit was not altogether a failure because he pursuaded Truman to agree with him that Far Eastern developments must not be allowed to throw their global policies out of balance and that efforts to build up the defences of the Atlantic community should be intensified. As regards the use of the atom bomb, Truman reserved the right of the United States to use any weapon it liked. However, he expressed the hope that world conditions would never call for the use of A-bomb. He also assured Attlee to keep him "at all times informed of developments which might bring about a change in the situation." The two leaders further agreed "to seek an end to the hostilities by means of negotiations" and "to achieve the purposes of the United Nations in Korea by peaceful means."[84]

After thus counselling moderation in Washington, London directed its efforts towards securing Peking's consent in regard to a cease-fire agreement. Commending the draft resolution sponsored by Thirteen Asian States[85] to the Chinese Government for acceptance, the British delegate (Younger) observed :

> That government [Central People's Government] was faced with a historic decision, for it had to choose between a policy of peace and collaboration with the United Nations and a policy of isolation and aggression. It should be fully aware that the United Nations would do nothing to make its choice more difficult.[86]

The Group of Cease-fire, set up in accordance with the 13-Power Resolution, sent a message to Ambassador Wu on 16 December 1950, seeking to confer with him at his "earliest convenience" for the purpose of discussing "cease-fire arrangements." On the same day, the Group also addressed a request to Peking urging that "Ambassador Wu be instructed to stay on in New York and discuss with the Group the possibility of arranging a cease-fire."[87]

On 19 December 1950, the Group sent another message to Chou En-lai assuring him that once a cease-fire arrangement had been achieved, the negotiations visualized in the Twelve-Power Resolution "should be proceeded with at once."

In the flush of victory, Peking seemed in no mood to come to any compromise settlement. It disregarded the Asian and Middle East Countries' Appeal calling for a declaration from the Chinese and North Korean authorities that they would not move troops "south of the 38th parallel." It turned down the

Asian countries' request about instructing "General Wu to continue to remain in Lake Success for negotiations with the... 3-man illegal Committee."[88]   In his statement on 22 December 1950, Chou En-lai reiterated the Chinese stand of not making "any contact with the...illegal 'Three man Committee'." He characterized the US proposal of "cease-fire first and negotiations afterwards" as a trick to "gain a breathing space and prepare to attack again." He took Asian and Arabian nations to task for failing "to see through the whole intrigue of the United States Government" and for not seriously considering "the basic proposal of the Chinese Government concerning the peaceful settlement of the Korean problem." He also exhorted them to "free themselves from United States pressures."[89] China, he added, could accept a cease-fire only on the following conditions :

1.   All foreign troops must be withdrawn from Korea, and Korea's domestic affairs must be settled by the Korean people themselves.

2.   American forces must be withdrawn from Taiwan.

3.   The representative of the People's Republic of China must obtain a legitimate status in the United Nations.

On 2 January 1951 the Group on Cease-fire regretfully reported failure, in spite of its best efforts, not only to reach "a satisfactory cease-fire arrangement," but even "to pursue discussion" in that regard.[90]   Peking's intransigent attitude coincided with its strong military position in the Korean theatre of war. Chinese troops crossed the 38th parallel on 26 December 1950 and on 3 January 1951 the ruined city of Seoul was abandoned by UN forces. In these circumstances, it was feared that the US Government, which had already declared a state of national emergency in the country on 17 December 1950, would now push its proposal of labelling China an aggressor,[91] which, in all probability, would result in the escalation of the conflict.   London felt deeply concerned about the grim prospect of a long drawn out struggle, a war of attrition.   The British delegate, Sir Gladwyn Jebb, therefore, asked Member States of the UN to "ponder most carefully their next step and how best to manifest their unity of purpose." He recognized "the possible need to take action to uphold the purposes and principles of the Charter." However, he warned against taking any drastic measures which "might result in a real cleavage between China and the free world, entailing danger for all concerned, and not least for China." He pleaded for further consideration of the problem so that an honourable and reasonable solution could be agreed upon mutually. Such a solution, he felt, would enable Member States to live in harmony with the Peking regime which, in turn, must take into consideration "the dreadful effect on its own people of a final break with the United Nations and all that it represented." Such a rupture, Jebb pointed out, would do irreparable damage to the relations of the West with China and would not "immediately assist the United Nations forces then fighting in Korea." Jebb concluded :

> It would be wise to look well before leaping...if possible, a last effort should be made before the Committee started thinking in more drastic terms....The United Kingdom did not wish to favour firmly any particular mode of approach should another effort be made to induce the Peking regime to see reason. The Group on Cease-fire in Korea had already requested more time, and it was still possible that its efforts would result in more generally acceptable plans. Moreover, even if the principles which the Group proposed drawing up were rejected by Peking, the United Nations would do well to go on record itself as accepting them; that might be the best way to preserve the unity of the Organization in very difficult circumstances.[92]

Jebb's counsel of restraint was aimed at both Washington and Peking. The USA seemed willing to listen to the advice of its ally, but China, conscious of its military successes on the field, did not really think in terms of peace at that stage. The USA supported the Five Principles approved by the First Committee on 13 January 1951.[93] Peking, on the other hand, rejected them outright. In his reply to the Chairman of the First Committee on 17 January 1951, Chou En-lai reiterated those very points, which he had mentioned in his statement on 22 December 1950 as pre-conditions for a cease-fire in Korea.[94]

Gladwyn Jebb characterized the Chinese reply of 17 January 1951, which insisted on "prior granting of all the requests of the Peking Government," as "tantamount to a repudiation of the principles of the United Nations,"[95] while Premier Attlee considered it "most disappointing."[96]   In these circumstances, the USA concluded that the UN had exhausted all the possibilities of finding a peaceful settlement of the Korean problem. Washington, therefore, felt inclined to take steps to brand Communist China an aggressor and apply sanctions against it.[97] However, the British Government desisted from adopting a rigid attitude in the matter.   While conceding that Chou En-lai's latest communication had "rendered the negotiations more difficult,"[98] London expressed the view that Peking had not finally closed "the door to negotiations."[99]   Britain was not willing to take any "new and important decision" which entailed disaster both for China and for the United Kingdom.[100] Therefore, London did not wish to abandon the path of conciliation and of seeking a negotiated settlement with China. Attlee remarked :

> We must patiently pursue every possibility of a peaceful settlement with China....We do not believe that the time has yet come to consider further measures. To do so implies that we have abandoned hope of reaching a peaceful settlement, and this we have not done.[101]

On 20 January 1951, the British Foreign Secretary instructed His Majesty's *charge d' affaires* in Peking to secure an elucidation and clarification of certain points, especially those pertaining to a cease-fire, in the Chinese reply of 17 January 1951. The British *charge d' affaires* met the Chinese Vice-Minister of Foreign Affairs the next day.   He was told that China was prepared to agree to "a cease-fire for a limited period," as a first step towards the initiation of discussions covering the withdrawal of foreign troops, general political questions concerning Korea, Formosa, etc. *provided* China was given its rightful place in the UN *immediately.*[102]

The USA and the UK again differed in their interpretation of the latest Chinese communication.   According to the US representative to the UN, the new Chinese communication changed very little. It simply aimed at confusing the UN, dividing its members, and beclouding "the issues that are before

us."[103]   To the British, however, the "clarifications" received
from Peking represented a significant modification of the
previous Chinese position and contained "new features."[104] The
British delegate to the UN observed :

> We have got to decide whether there is a serious possibility
> of reaching any agreement with Peking....If we are misled,
> I freely admit that the consequences could be disastrous...In
> any case, we do not wish to close the door to all possibility
> of negotiations in the future...The culprit may see the light
> and that a process of persuasion may prove fruitful....We
> should not do well to consider measures which in fact pre-
> judged them....The punishment may cause wider havoc than
> the crime—that the cure may be even worse than the
> disease ?...We still would favour a further effort at clari-
> fication before deciding that the Korean question is, in fact,
> insoluble except as the result of some general extension of a
> warlike situation which we are all determined to avoid if it
> is humanly possible....The impossibility of a peaceful settle-
> ment must be proved before the General Assembly considers
> what might be the equivalent of sanctions.[105]

However, the divergence of opinion between the USA and
the UK was not allowed to produce a serious rift in their
relations. Britain agreed, though somewhat reluctantly,[106] to
have China declared an aggressor by the UN after obtaining
some modification in the language of the draft resolution tabled
by the US.[107]   Speaking on the occasion of the adoption of the
amended resolution, Gladwyn Jebb explained the British attitude in the following words :

> Now that we have established our moral position by
> condemning the Central People's Government for engaging
> in aggression, the most important thing as we see it is to
> concentrate on the problem of a peaceful settlement or, as
> I would prefer to say, on an agreed solution of the
> Korean question, rather than on the question of potential
> sanctions.[108]

The resolution of 1 February 1951 declared China to be an
aggressor in Korea and set up two parallel Committees—a Good
Offices Committee to arrange a cessation of hostilities in Korea,
and an Additional Measures Committee to consider additional

measures for meeting Chinese aggression. Chou En-lai criticized
that resolution in strong terms. The adoption of that resolution,
he stated,

> most clearly proves to the peace-loving people and nations
> of the world that the United States Government and its
> accomplices want not peace but war and that they have
> blocked the path to a peaceful settlement....The Chinese peo-
> ple will henceforth recognize all the more clearly the
> aggressive ambition of American imperialism, will be all the
> more determined to defeat the aggressor with action....The
> so-called 'good offices' organ provided for by the United
> States resolution...is not only a naked deceit, it is also an
> insult to the Chinese people. The Central People's Govern-
> ment of the People's Republic of China will pay absolutely
> no attention to such an organ.[109]

To London, however, the amended resolution seemed to offer
"the best hope in existing circumstances of obtaining a settlement by negotiation."[110] The United Kingdom voted in favour
of that resolution and, soon after its adoption, Lord Henderson,
the Parliamentary Under-Secretary of State for Foreign Affairs,
optimistically addressed "on behalf of His Majesty's Government," the following appeal to the Chinese Government :

> Co-operate with the Good Offices Committee. You have
> nothing to fear from co-operation with the United Nations.
> You will make a settlement far harder by turning your back
> on the United Nations and refusing to negotiate. You say
> you want peace in Korea. The United Nations have shown
> the way to peace. It is solely within your power to join with
> the Good Offices Committee to bring about a peaceful
> settlement in Korea.[111]

Although Attlee called it a "genuine offer for negotiations,"[112] Peking rejected it as unceremoniously as it had rejected the earlier cease-fire proposals of December 1950 and
January 1951. British attempts to bring to an early end "this
wasteful war in Korea,"[113] did not succeed primarily because
Peking still thought that it could force the UN troops into
continuous retreat. It was only after the military position of the
UN Command in Korea improved, "a series of phased offensives" launched by the Chinese and North Korean forces from

22 April 1951 onwards proved ineffective, and a military stalemate had been reached around the 38th parallel that China began to think of a negotiated settlement. The continuance of war in Korea told heavily on the Chinese economy and imposed additional burdens on its people. Moreover, it was realized that there was no point in sacrificing "so many lives so recklessly" in the face of "vastly superior hitting power" of the United Nations.[114] In these circumstances, the Communist Powers also began to think in terms of an agreed solution of the problem. On 18 May 1951, the General Assembly passed a resolution imposing an embargo against China and North Korea.[115] A month later, Jacob Malik, the Soviet representative at the UN, proposed a Korean truce. China endorsed the Soviet proposal on 1 July 1951. The British House of Commons regarded the Chinese endorsement as "the most important news following Mr. Malik's proposals."[116] Formal cease-fire talks began at Kaesong, Korea, on 10 July 1951. The venue of these talks was subsequently transferred to Panmunjon in October. These talks continued till July 1953, although they remained suspended from 8 October 1952 to 26 April 1953.

During the course of the truce talks, London sought to ensure the success of armistice negotiations. It refrained from needlessly irritating the Communist nations so as not to prejudice the cease-fire talks. Gladwyn Jebb considered the Kuomintang complaint against the Soviet Union regarding threats to the "Political Independence and Territorial Integrity of China" as one of "academic importance." He deemed it necessary to concentrate on positive proposals for allaying the current tension. Nothing, he said, would be gained by the adoption of the Nationalist Chinese draft resolution.[117]

By the end of May 1952 substantial agreement had been reached on 61 of the 63 articles in the Draft Armistice Agreement. Before the truce talks went into recess in October 1952 for six months, one more article was also agreed upon. The sole impediment to the conclusion of an armistice was disagreement over the question of the repatriation of the prisoners of war. While the UN Command was in favour of the principle of "voluntary repatriation," the Communist side insisted on "forced repatriation." Both sides were conscious of the justness of their stand, which they believed was "in conformity with

humanitarian principles and the Geneva Convention."[118]   In
order to break this *impasse*, Foreign Secretary Eden, in his
speech before the UN General Assembly on 11 November 1952,
laid down four principles, the essence of which was that "after
an armistice, a prisoner-of-war may not be either forcibly detained or forcibly repatriated."[119]   These principles were subsequently embodied in the Indian resolution, which was adopted
by the General Assembly on 3 December 1952 by 55 votes to
5.[120] Britain supported that resolution but the Soviet representative Vyshinsky and Chou En-lai were quite critical of it.

The rejection of reasonable Indian proposals for resolving
the prisoners of war issue dashed all hopes of an early armistice
in Korea, which was "the essential prelude to a political settlement of the Korean problem and other outstanding problems
in the Far East."[121]   The Western Powers, therefore, deemed
it necessary to pressurize the Communist Powers so as to compel
them to agree to an armistice.   On 2 February 1953, the newly-
elected Republican President of the USA stated that the Seventh
Fleet would no longer "be employed to shield Communist
China," since it had consistently rejected the proposals of the
UN Command for an armistice and had "recently joined with
Soviet Russia in rejecting the armistice proposal sponsored in
the United Nations by the Government of India."[122]   Although
Britain dissociated itself from the US move[123] it nonetheless
accepted American advice in regard to the tightening of shipping controls against China and North Korea.[124] After Stalin's
death, the Communist Powers seemed inclined to consider a
solution of the prisoners-of-war question "consistent with
humanitarian principles and the principles of the General
Assembly resolution."[125]   In his statement on 30 March 1953,
Chou En-lai expressed, on behalf of China and North Korea,
readiness "to take steps to eliminate the differences on this
question."   He proposed that both parties to the negotiations
should undertake to repatriate "all those prisoners of war in
their custody who insist upon repatriation and to hand over the
remaining prisoners of war to a neutral state so as to ensure a
just solution to the question of their repatriation."[126]   Consequently, the repatriation of Sick and Injured Captured Personnel was agreed upon on 11 April 1953. The Armistice
Agreement was signed on 27 July 1953 and entered into force

immediately.

Efforts to Reach a Political Settlement

It was stipulated in paragraph 60 of the Armistice Agreement that a political conference would be convened within 3 months, *i.e.* prior to 27 October 1953, "to settle through negotiation the questions of the withdrawal of all foreign forces from Korea, the peaceful settlement of the Korean question, etc." Arrangements for the Korean Peace Conference, however, proceeded very slowly. After much wrangling over the composition, place, timing and agenda of the Conference and other procedural, administrative and related problems, the question of the political future of divided Korea was eventually discussed at the Geneva Conference. The Conference held 14 plenary sessions and one restricted session over a period of seven weeks from 26 April to 15 June 1954, but no agreement could be reached.

The discussions at Geneva revealed that there were fundamental differences on the methods and steps to be adopted in achieving the unification of Korea. Although there was vague and general agreement over the words like "unification," "free elections" and "withdrawal of all foreign forces," etc., there was "no meeting of the minds."[127] Since the population of South Korea was larger than that of North Korea, the Western Powers insisted on proportional representation in the National Assembly of United Korea.[128] The Communist States, on the other hand, ruled out any imposition on North Korea of "the anti-popular South Korean regime." They categorically asserted that the national unification of Korea could only be achieved "on a democratic basis by working out at this Conference terms of agreement which will make it possible to preserve the democratic achievements of the Democratic People's Republic of Korea."[129] Both sides apparently agreed that the goal of the unification of Korea should be achieved through genuinely free elections. However, there was basic disagreement about the methods and procedures for conducting elections,[130] and "in practical terms...about the preparation and conduct of elections."[131] The Western Powers believed that "genuinely free elections in Korea" could be assured only "if the elections are placed under the control and supervision of the United Nations."[132] The Communist countries, on the other hand, believed that the Korean question, closely bound up as it was with the "after-effects of the war," did not come "within the competence of the United Nations," as Article 107 of the United Nations Charter clearly implied.[133] Moreover, the United Nations, they argued, was "one of the belligerents in the Korean War." Consequently, it did not have "the competence and moral authority" to deal with the Korean question "impartially."[134] The Communist Powers believed that free elections and the re-establishment of a united Korea were "above all, a matter for the Koreans themselves."[135] They proposed that the All-Korean Commission, which will prepare and hold free elections throughout Korea and attend to other matters pertaining to the unification of Korea, should carry on its work on "a basis of mutual agreement."[136] The effect of such a proposal, Eden remarked, would be two-fold : firstly, it would give "a veto to the Communist North-Korean minority"; and secondly, it would mean that "either that elections would never be held, or that they would not be free."[137]

At a later stage of the Conference, both sides seemed to make some concessions, particularly in regard to the supervision of elections. However, their basic attitude remainced unaltered. For instance, Chou En-lai proposed international supervision of Korean elections by a "neutral organ," but, at the same time, he reiterated that the all-Korean free elections were "a matter for the Korean people themselves." Furthermore, he stated that this "neutral organ" should simply "assist"[138] the all-Korean body which still remained the organization primarily responsible for arranging and holding of elections. Chou's suggestion, the US delegate pointed out, merely provided "the cloak of international participation in the conduct of Korean elections,"[139] but left "unaltered the functions and responsibilities of the all-Korean Commission." "It is to these," Foreign Secretary Eden remarked, "that we object so strongly."[140] Besides, the proposed Supervisory Commission, composed as it was of an equal number of Communist and non-Communist nations, was subject to veto by Communist members. It "could only have functioned in the unlikely event that the 'all-Korean Commission' was able to agree on a plan for the elections."[141]

Speaking on behalf of the Western Powers, Eden proposed that the members of the Supervisory Commission "need not necessarily be those who have taken part in the Korean war." They could "if desired be chosen from nations which did not take part in the Korean war." Moreover, in the opinion of the Western Powers, the Commission should be "truly impartial."[142] It should have "real powers,"[143] so that it could take effective decisions and implement them.

Both sides agreed in principle that all non-Korean forces should be withdrawn from Korea. However, they failed to come to any agreement on the schedule of troop withdrawals. The Communist Powers desired that all foreign troops should be withdrawn from Korea before elections were held so as to create conditions in which the Korean people could express their will "freely... in the nation-wide elections without foreign interference."[144] The Western Powers considered it unsatisfactory and a dangerous procedure. They made a distinction between the UN forces and the Chinese troops in Korea.[145] The former, they stated, should remain in Korea till the UN objective of a unified Korea was achieved by peaceful means, that is through elections. The fulfilment of this objective, they believed, would serve a two-fold purpose. Firstly, it would uphold the prestige of the UN and of the "free-world." Secondly, it would help in creating conditions of peace and stability in the region. It was suspected that the departure of UN troops from Korea, prior to the achievement of their objective, might produce "chaos or fresh hostilities"—a repetition of the events of 1949-50. The Western Powers, therefore, deemed it imprudent to withdraw UN forces from Korea before the goal of a unified Korea was achieved on the basis of free elections. The Communists, on the other hand, continued to insist on the withdrawal of foreign troops from Korea as a pre-condition to any progress on the peaceful settlement of the problem and the unification of Korea.

Impact of the Korean War on Sino-British Relations

The Korean War affected Sino-British relations in a number of ways. In the first place, hopes about the successful outcome of Anglo-Chinese talks on the early establishment of diplomatic relations were dashed to the ground. Secondly, Britain was compelled to impose an embargo on the export of strategic goods to Peking, while China was forced to depend more and more on the Soviet Union and other East European States. Sino-British trade fell perceptibly and the importance of Hong Kong declined. Moreover, British enterprises in China had to face liquidation in the wake of the Korean War and its aftermath. The Korean War was also responsible for bringing about a change in the British attitude as regards the question of Chinese representation in the UN and the restoration of Formosa to Peking. These issues are discussed in subsequent chapters.

The impact of the Korean War on Sino-British relations was, indeed, out of all proportion to the importance which Korea had, at any time, occupied in their relations. Britain sought to renew its contacts with Peking as soon as the war in Korea was over. After China embarked upon the course of planned development, Peking also seemed keen to resume fruitful contacts with Britain, especially in the economic field. The efforts of the two countries bore some fruit and, to a certain extent, helped in easing the situation created or aggravated by the Korean War. For instance, diplomatic relations between the two countries were established at *charge d' affaires* level in 1954 and trade restrictions were gradually removed. However, it was only in the wake of Nixon's visit to China and Sino-US *rapprochement* that Britain modified its stand on the question of Chinese representation in the UN and as regards the status of Formosa. As a result, full diplomatic relations at ambassadorial level were established in March 1972 and Sino-British trade is on the upswing again. Thus, most of the problems that bedevilled Sino-British relations in the wake of the Korean War, have more or less been resolved. However, there appears no easy solution of the division of Korea. In the words of Anthony Eden, the partition of Korea (roughly on the lines at which it existed before the outbreak of the Korean War on 25 June 1950) remained "the only means of reaching an acceptable *status quo* between the Communist and free world."[146]

Recent Developments in Korea

Year after year, the Korean question had been debated in the United Nations. While South Korea was invited to take part in the debate, North Korea had been excluded from participation in the debate till 1973 (when North Korea, for the first time, participated in the UN debate) on the ground that it did not accept the competence and the authority of the UN to deal with the question. The UN General Assembly adopted resolutions, which reaffirmed the UN objective of a "unified, independent and democratic Korea" through "genuinely free elections." While the greater part of the UN forces was said to have been withdrawn in accordance with the UN resolutions, "the sole objective" of the UN forces still remaining in Korea was stated to be "to preserve the peace and security of the area." The Governments concerned, it was asserted, were prepared to withdraw their remaining troops from Korea whenever such action was requested by South Korea or whenever the conditions for a lasting settlement formulated by the General Assembly had been fulfilled.[147]

The United Kingdom has consistently supported the Western Powers' position in the UN, both on the procedural question of hearing the representatives of North and South Korea as well as the substantive question relating to the achievement of UN objectives in Korea and the withdrawal of UN forces. Thus, on 29 October 1969 the British representative stated that while he believed that it would be useful to hear the representatives of both North and South Korea, no constructive purpose would be served by inviting North Korean representatives unless they accepted the competence and authority of the UN to deal with the Korean question. He criticized North Korean authorities for insisting that the UN entirely dissociate itself from the Korean question and that the United Nations Commission for the Unification and Rehabilitation of Korea (UNCURK) be dissolved.[148]

Speaking in the debate on the Korean question in the First Committee of the UN on 11 December 1968, the British representative stated that his delegation was vehemently opposed to the proposal about the withdrawal of UN troops from Korea because he did not wish to see the events of 1950

being repeated once again.[149] In his subsequent statement on
13 November 1969, the British delegate referred to North
Korean attempts at infiltration into South Korea and expressed
the view that the UN presence in Korea was still justified and
necessary. The UN, he observed, "should maintain its presence in Korea in the interests of peace and security and in
order to do everything it can to bring about a unified, independent and democratic Korea."[150]

A change in the British attitude towards the Korean question
was evident in the early 1970s when direct contacts were
established between North and South Korea. The initiation
of talks during 1971 between the Red Cross Societies of the
two parts of Korea was described by the British representative
as "the first contacts, the first negotiations that had taken
place between the two sides since the unhappy events of the
1950s and indeed since the division of the country in 1945."
These talks on humanitarian issues were later followed by the
Joint Communique, issued by North and South Korea on 4
July 1972. The Communique provided, *inter alia*, for the
following three principles on the reunification of Korea :

1. The reunification of the country should be achieved
    independently, without reliance upon outside force or
    its interference ;

2. the reunification of the country should be achieved by
    peaceful means, without recourse to the use of arms
    against the other side ; and

3. great national unity should be promoted.

The British delegate particularly referred to the first principle
mentioned above and expressed his desire that the Koreans
would be allowed to conduct the debate on Korea between
themselves. He also supported the UN General Assembly
decision to abstain from discussing the affairs of Korea in 1971
and 1972.[151]

During 1973 North Korea was admitted into the World
Health Organization (WHO) and other international organisations and granted permanent observer status in both Geneva
and New York. It was also, for the first time, allowed to
participate in the discussions on the Korean question which

were resumed in the General Assembly session in 1973. After debating the "Question of Korea," the Assembly reached a consensus whereby it decided to immediately dissolve UNCURK. It also urged both South and North Korea to continue their dialogue and widen their many-sided exchanges and cooperation in the spirit of their Joint Communique of 4 July 1972 so as to expedite the "independent peaceful reunification of the country."[152]

In his intervention in the debate on 21 November 1973, the British representative laid stress on "building upon that which unites us." All concerned, he said, were agreed on two basic points : firstly, that the division of Korea at the 38th parallel was an artificial division, and secondly, that the peaceful reunification of Korea be achieved by the efforts of the Korean people themselves. He did not think that any useful purpose could be served by reverting to the past or raking over the coals of old controversies. He also did not believe that the simultaneous membership of the two parts of Korea, in any way, precluded Korean reunification. He welcomed the establishment of contacts between the two parts of the too-long divided country in the discharge of their responsibility for seeking its reunification. In a reversal of the previous British position in the matter (that of the 1950s and the 1960s), the British representative stated that the proper role for the UN was not to take sides on the merits of the Governments of North and South Korea or on the merits of their proposals for reunification. "That would indeed constitute interference in matters which are properly the concern of the two parts of Korea and interference in the process of re-unification." Such an interference, he said, was clearly inadmissible. The modalities of reunification, he felt, should be left to the Koreans themselves. Nevertheless, the British delegate considered it an over-simplification to say that the Korean problem was purely an internal matter of Korea. The UN, he stated, still had an "important continuing role in the creation of conditions favourable to the peaceful reunification of Korea, and...a continuing responsibility for the maintenance of peace and security in the Korean peninsula." The essential role of the UN, he observed, was to avoid and prevent action which could disturb the still precarious stability between the two parts of

Korea. The Armistice Agreement of 1953, he continued, remained the corner-stone of stability and that it was essential to preserve it and the practical arrangements made under it for its continued observance and enforcement. In view of these considerations, the British delegate doubted whether the withdrawal of UN forces from South Korea would be a step in the right direction. The South Korean Government, he said, has the right to invite foreign troops to be stationed on its territory. He conceded that the use of the UN flag and the continuance in being of the UN Command was a separate matter. States, that were not members of the UN, might feel that it was a matter to be reviewed. But in that connection, the British delegate referred to two things : firstly, the Korean question was a matter for consideration by the Security Council rather than the General Assembly since the UN Command had been established by a Security Council resolution. Secondly, the UN Command was a signatory of the Armistice Agreement, the continued observance of which was essential. Before the UN Command could be abolished, adequate arrangements must be made for the continued observance of the Armistice Agreement and the continuation in force of the machinery set up under it. The British representative concluded his statement with an optimistic note about "peaceful change in conditions of stability." The maintenance of stability, he stated, was not synonymous with the maintenance of the *status quo*, but rather an essential pre-condition for bringing about peaceful change.[153]

In view of the consensus reached in 1973, the various resolutions on the subject were not put to the vote during that session. However, in 1974 the resolution co-sponsored by China, the Soviet Union and others (A/C. 1/L. 677) on the withdrawal of foreign troops stationed in South Korea under the flag of the United Nations (the presence of these troops was considered a serious obstacle in the way of promoting a dialogue between the North and the South for the independent and peaceful reunification of the country and for making the Armistice in Korea a durable peace) secured a tie vote—48 votes in favour, 48 against, and 38 abstentions in the First Committee. The other resolution, co-sponsored by the USA, Britain and others (A/C. 1/L. 676/Rev. 1), was adopted in the First Committee by 61 votes to 42, with 32 abstentions and in the General Assembly by 61 votes to 43, with 31 abstentions (A/Res. 3333 dated 17 December 1974).

The General Assembly expressed its awareness of the fact that tension in Korea had not completely disappeared and that the Armistice Agreement of 27 July 1953 still was indispensable to the maintenance of peace and security in the area. It recognised the responsibility of the UN in regard to the maintenance of peace and security in the Korean peninsula. The General Assembly reaffirmed its faith in the consensus reached in 1973 and expressed the hope that the Security Council, bearing in mind the need to ensure continued adherence to the Armistice Agreement and the full maintenance of peace and security in the area, would in due course give consideration, in consultation with the parties directly concerned, to those aspects of the Korean question "which fall within its responsibilities," including the dissolution of the UN Command in conjunction with appropriate arrangements to maintain the Armistice Agreement "which is calculated to preserve peace and security in the Korean peninsula, pending negotiations and conciliation between the two Korean Governments leading to a lasting peace between them."[154]

The Chinese delegate, Huang Hua, gave strong support to the resolution demanding the withdrawal of all foreign troops from South Korea by pointing out that the long-term stationing of American troops in South Korea and their interference in Korea's internal affairs constituted the principal obstacle to the Korean peoples' realisation of the independent and peaceful reunification of their fatherland. In order to promote the independent and peaceful reunification of Korea, he stated, "it is imperative to eliminate outside interference and have all United States troops withdrawn from South Korea." By prolonging their stay in Korea, Huang stated, the United States wished to continue their interference in the internal affairs of Korea and perpetuate the division of that country. He totally disagreed with the American view that the presence of US troops in Korea was aimed at maintaining peace and security in the Korean peninsula. The peace and security of the Korean peninsula, he stated, should be guaranteed by North and South Korea themselves and not by a super Power. He characterized the so-called UN Command in South Korea

as "nothing but a product of the United States aggression
against Korea committed under the signboard of the United
Nations in 1950." He declared earlier "resolutions" of the
Security Council on the Korean question to be "entirely illegal
and null and void" because they were in complete violation of
the Charter principle of non-interference in the domestic affairs
of any state and were adopted under the manipulation of the
United States in the abnormal circumstances in which the
People's Republic of China, a permanent member of the
Security Council, was deprived of its lawful rights in the
United Nations. The proposal to refer the question again to
the Security Council, Huang stated, was in fact an attempt to
resurrect those illegal resolutions and to delay indefinitely the
withdrawal of foreign troops from South Korea with the help
of veto power. He, therefore, asserted that the US-UK-
sponsored resolution was designed to give an excuse "for the
continued interference in the internal affairs of Korea by foreign
forces, for the perpetual division of Korea and for the preservation of the imperialist rule in South Korea."[155]

In his intervention in the debate, the British delegate
(Murray) expressed deep concern about what he called "the
provocative title" of the item "Withdrawal of All the Foreign
Troops Stationed in South Korea under the Flag of the United
Nations." He stated that he could not agree with the United
Nations' call for the withdrawal of all foreign troops from Korea,
if that included withdrawal of American forces in Korea under
the 1954 bilateral defence agreement between the USA and the
Republic of Korea. He regarded such a move as "interference
in a bilateral matter," which, he said, was "solely the business
of the two states concerned." He also expressed his opposition
to the precipitate dissolution of the UN Command before
adequate steps had been taken to safeguard the Armistice,
which, he pointed out, was signed on one side by the UN
Commander. He laid considerable stress on the need to ensure
continued adherence to the Armistice Agreement and the full
maintenance of peace and security in the area. He warned
against "a percipitate and ill-considered decision," which
would jeopardise the security of the Korean people. While
stating that he was not opposed "in principle" to the dissolution of the UN Command, the British representative observed :

"The dissolution of the United Nations Command should be, and must be, if we are to act responsibly, considered in conjunction with arrangements to maintain the Armistice Agreement." The dialogue between the two sides, Murray concluded, must proceed in an atmosphere of security. Time and peaceful conditions, he added, were needed in order to attain the generally agreed aim of the "ultimate" reunification of Korea by peaceful means.[156]

The UN decision on the withdrawal of the UN Command in Korea was prevented by a tie vote in 1974. However, sooner or later the UN Command is bound to be dissolved. South Korea has to be prepared for it and look to other measures or alternatives to ensure effective observance of the Armistice Agreement after the dissolution of the UN Command in Korea.[157] In fact, on 27 June 1975, the United States, in consultation with South Korea, notified the UN Security Council that they are willing to terminate the UN Command with effect from 1 January 1976 and to replace it by American and South Korean officers provided China and North Korea agreed to that. In the meantime, America expressed its desire to undertake measures to reduce manifestations of the UN Command, including restricted use of the UN Flag. Washington emphasized that its sole concern in this question was that all provisions of the Armistice Agreement, the basis of peace and security in the Korean peninsula for over 20 years, be maintained and preserved pending negotiations and conciliation between the South and the North of Korea leading to a lasting peace between them.[158]

In view of loss of faith in Indo-China (the fall of Cambodia and South Vietnam to the communists in March-April 1975), Washington has deemed it necessary to reaffirm in stronger words its determination to observe its treaty obligations with South Korea (evidently with the purpose of restoring its credibility with its allies and to forestall adventurism in the Korean peninsula).

Kim Il Sung, President of North Korea, seems eager to emulate the Vietnam experience for reunifying the country.[159] Since such an arduous task could not be performed without Russian or Chinese assistance, he undertook a surprise visit to China (his second since 1961) in April 1975 probably with a view to secure Peking's support.

Coming in the wake of communist successes in Indo-China, Kim's China visit was considered ominous—a matter of grave concern in South Korea[160]—and his 1950 visit to the Soviet Union (just before the outbreak of the Korean War) was recalled. What actual discussions took place between Kim and the Chinese leaders in Peking would obviously remain confidential. However, it appears that while China agreed to give economic aid and diplomatic support (both in the UN and outside it on the question of the withdrawal of foreign troops, etc.) and even recognized, perhaps for the first time, the Democratic People's Republic of Korea (DPRK) as "the sole legal state of the Korean nation," Kim failed to get encouragement from Chairman Mao as regards any military adventure against South Korea. Thus, it seems, China has pledged support only for the "peaceful reunification" of Korea. Mao's moderating influence on Kim seems to be justified on a number of counts. Firstly, Peking is well aware of the drain of resources —in men, money and material—involved in any large-scale military and economic assistance programme for underwriting a war. Secondly, Peking would not like to jeopardize Sino-US *rapprochement* and its policy of continued support for an American presence in Asia to counter the Russians. Thirdly, with Hanoi's precedent before it, China might not be interested in seeing a more powerful and more independent-minded (and for that matter less amenable to Chinese influence) Korea on its northeastern border (like Vietnam now is on its southern periphery) though both of them might be communist countries. Fourthly, Peking might feel that the Soviet Union would be the chief beneficiary if Washington becomes freshly embroiled in East Asia. In such a situation, Moscow would be at liberty to apply pressure on China and the latter would, thus, be playing into Moscow's hands. Finally, Kim's military victory in the South will greatly disillusion Japan as regards US commitment to Japan's security. This could possibly lead Japan into an ambitious programme of military armament which would hardly be in Chinese interests. In view of these considerations, China is likely to act as a restraining force on Kim and give precedence to its national interests over ideological considerations.

Disappointed with Peking, Kim might turn to Moscow for support. But Soviet leaders too would have to take into consideration the China and Japan factors and, above all, the problem of endangering *detente* with the USA. In the changed international situation, it would hardly be worthwhile to repeat the Stalinist stratagem of 1950 of embroiling China in war with the Western Powers partly because, unlike 1950, Peking now has direct links with Washington and also because the same tactics cannot work twice. Moreover, both China and the USA have learnt a lot from past experiences and, therefore, are unlikely to fall into any trap that Moscow might lay for them.

Inspite of all the constraints on the two communist Powers, the situation in the Korean peninsula might still remain tense and delicate because the possibility of Kim Il Sung stepping up North Korean infiltration and other provocative acts against South Korea cannot be completely ruled out.[161] However, it seems obvious that in the absence of substantial help either from China or the Soviet Union, Kim may have to put up with the division of Korea for a long time to come.

CHAPTER FOUR

Taiwan and the Offshore Islands

The island of Taiwan (Formosa)[1] lies in the Western Pacific Ocean between the Southern and the Eastern China seas. It is separated from the province of Fukien on the Chinese mainland by the Taiwan Straits, which is approximately 100 to 150 miles wide and forms a part of the sea approaches to the mainland ports of Amoy and Foochow. These ports lie roughly midway between Shanghai and Hong Kong. The island of Formosa is a link in a chain of islands stretching from the Aleutians to Singapore and Australia and has an area of 13,838 square miles. Of its 10 million population, nearly 2 million are mainland refugees, who came to Taiwan along with Chiang Kai-shek in December 1949, while the rest are Taiwanese.[2] Taipeh is the capital of Taiwan and the seat of the Government of the Republic of China (the Chinese nationalist regime), which, among others, is still recognized by the United States.

The Pescadores (or *Penghu* as they are called by the Chinese) Islands consist of 64 islands separated from Taiwan by the 30-mile wide Pescadores Channel. These islands cover an area of 25 square miles and have been linked administratively with Formosa ever since the 17th century. Besides Formosa and the Pescadores, there are a few other islands off the Chinese coast, such as Quemoy and Matsu, which, though part of China, continue to be occupied by the Nationalists. As compared to Formosa and the Pescadores, these offshore islands in a way belong to a somewhat different category because they are in close proximity to the Chinese mainland and have always been an integral part of China. There has never been any dispute about the legal status of the offshore islands. Besides, they are not of any great strategic importance.

Strategic Importance of Formosa and the Pescadores

Formosa and the Pescadores, situated between Japan and the Philippines, are of great strategic importance. In June 1945, US State Department officials observed: "Strategic factors greatly influenced the problem of Formosa. With the exception of Singapore, no location in the Far East occupies such a controlling position."[3] However, in view of the fact that it had not lost all hopes of establishing diplomatic relations with the Peking regime, Washington deemed it necessary to dispel doubts about its ulterior designs on Taiwan. Accordingly, it was stated that four times between 1948 and 1950, the highest military authorities of the USA concluded that Taiwan was not essential to the vital interests of America and that US military action was not justified for keeping it in friendly hands.[4] The USA also refrained from giving any military aid to the nationalist regime at a time when it needed it most.[5] It was only after the Korean War broke out that Washington decided that Formosa should not fall in communist hands and endeavoured to keep it in friendly hands.[6]

In the post-World War II period, Britain had hoped that China would be the bulwark of stability in the Far East. It, therefore, aimed at reconciliation and accomodation with Peking. Accordingly, London was reconciled to the occupation of Taiwan by the Maoist regime. However, with the outbreak of the Korean War and the prospect of a hostile China looming large on the horizon, Britain began to toe the American line on Formosa. A hostile China, closely aligned with the Soviet Union, was considered a disturbing factor for peace and stability in the Far East and a serious threat to British interests in Hong Kong and Malaya. Britain also could not possibly ignore the fruitful trade it carried on with Formosa and the prospects of increasing it further in the future.[7] These considerations apparently induced Winston Churchill to assert that he did not favour the idea of surrendering Formosa to Communist China.[8]

Historical Background

Formosa and the Pescadores were Chinese territory before they

were ceded to Japan by the Treaty of Shimoneseki of 18 April
1895. During the Second World War the Allies decided to
deprive Japan of all the islands (other than its home territories)
in the Pacific. At the Cairo Conference on 1 December 1943,
the Presidents of the United States and China and the Prime
Minister of Britain jointly declared : "All the territories Japan
has stolen from the Chinese, such as Manchuria, Formosa, and
the Pescadores, shall be restored to the Republic of China."[9]
In the Potsdam Proclamation of 26 July 1945 the Allies—the
USA, the UK and the Soviet Union—undertook to carry out
the terms of the Cairo Declaration as one of the conditions for
the Japanese Peace.[10] On 14 August 1945 the Japanese Government announced its acceptance of the Potsdam terms as a
basis for surrender. General Order No. 1 of the Japanese
Imperial Headquarters, issued pursuant to the terms of surrender, provided for the surrender of Japanese forces in China
(excluding Manchuria) and Formosa to Generalissimo Chiang
Kai-shek. Ever since the Japanese forces surrendered to Chiang
on 25 October 1945, the Chinese nationalist authorities have
been exercising control over Formosa and the Pescadores.

Legal Aspects of the Problem

In the Peace Treaty with Japan, signed at San Francisco by 49
nations (including Japan but excluding the Soviet Union and
China) on 8 September 1951,[11] (it came into force on 28 April
1952), the signatories made Japan formally renounce "all right,
title and claim to Formosa and the Pescadores." Thus, the
Peace Treaty did not transfer sovereignty over Formosa and the
Pescadores to either the People's Republic of China or the
Chinese Nationalist Government in Taipeh or to any other
authority or government, Chinese or non-Chinese. The Treaty
of Peace between the Republic of China (Taiwan) and Japan,
signed on 28 April 1952,[12] did not, in any way, alter the position in regard to the disposition of Formosa. Article II of the
Treaty simply recognized Japan's renunciation of "all right, title
and claim to Taiwan (Formosa) and Penghu (the Pescadores)"
under Article 2 of the San Francisco Peace Treaty. The Treaty
of Mutual Defence between the USA and Taipeh, signed in

December 1954, also did not change the legal status of Formosa and the Pescadores.[13]

The Cairo and Potsdam declarations were "made at a time when there was only one entity claiming to represent China."[14] Therefore, no one questioned the binding nature of these declarations and the retrocession of Formosa to China. The dispute arose only after the Nationalist regime of Chiang Kai-shek fled to Taipeh on 8 December 1949, and Peking failed to "liberate" Taiwan. The non-recognition of the People's Republic of China by the United States and the interposition of the Seventh Fleet by President Truman on 27 June 1950 (two days after the outbreak of the Korean War) to prevent either the seizure of Formosa by the communists or the invasion of mainland China by Chiang, created further complications. The binding effect of the Cairo Declaration was questioned and people began to interpret differently the nature of Chiang Kai-shek take-over of the administration of the island. The provision of the San Francisco Peace Treaty on the renunciation of all right, title and claim to Formosa and the Pescadores by Japan became the subject matter of conflicting opinions. Quincy Wright observes :

> By that instrument Japan renounced title but without specifying the recipient. This seems to mean, as both the United States and the United Kingdom have subsequently affirmed, that the formal transfer of the islands to China has not yet been effected, although both the Chiang and Mao Governments claim that it has.[15]

British View

Britain considered the Cairo Declaration to be merely "a statement of common purpose." It was not binding upon the parties to the Declaration.[16] The exercise of authority by Chiang Kai-shek over Formosa was only provisional in nature. The assumption of an interim administrative control in Formosa, at the direction of the Supreme Commander of the Allied Powers, in no way constituted the retrocession of the island to China or the transfer of sovereignty from Japan to China. *De jure* Formosa remained Japanese territory until the conclusion of the peace settlement with Japan in 1951. The British

Minister of State, Younger, remarked :

> Formosa is still *de jure* Japanese territory and there is no
> Government of Formosa as such. Following on the surren-
> der of Japan, the Chinese Government of the day assumed,
> with the consent of the remaining Allies, the provisional
> administration of the territory pending the final determina-
> tion of its status at a peace settlement. Not all the remain-
> ing Allies have recognized the Central People's Government
> as the Government of China, and for this reason, and
> because of the provisional nature of the present administra-
> tion of Formosa, it is the hope of His Majesty's Govern-
> ment that the disposal of Formosa will be decided, as has
> always been contemplated, in connection with the peace
> settlement with Japan.[17]

Speaking on the juridicial position of Formosa after the signing
of the San Francisco Peace Treaty with Japan, Foreign Secretary Eden observed on 4 February 1955 :

> The Cairo Declaration...was a statement of intention that
> Formosa should be retroceded to China after the war. This
> retrocession has, in fact, never taken place because of the
> difficulties arising from the existence of two entities claiming
> to represent China and the differences among the powers as
> to the status of these entities.... In September 1945, the
> administration of Formosa was taken over from the Japanese
> by Chinese forces at the direction of the Supreme Comman-
> der of the Allied Powers; but this was not a cession, nor did
> it in itself involve any change of sovereignty. The arrange-
> ments made with Chiang Kai-shek put him there on a basis
> of military occupation pending further arrangements and did
> not of themselves constitute the territory Chinese. Under
> the peace treaty of April 1952, Japan formally renounced all
> right, title and claim to Formosa and the Pescadores; but
> again this did not operate as a transfer to Chinese sovereign-
> ty, whether to the People's Republic of China or to the
> Chinese Nationalist authorities. Formosa and the Pesca-
> dores are, therefore, in the view of Her Majesty's Govern-
> ment, territory the *de jure* sovereignty over which is uncer-
> tain or undetermined.[18]

On 4 May 1955, R.H. Turton, Joint Under-Secretary of State
for Foreign Affairs, while commenting on the argument that
it was unnecessary for a defeated Power expressly to cede territory in order to constitute a valid transfer, stated that this argu-

ment was undoubtedly correct, but that, for sovereignty to pass
without cession or retrocession, there would have to be circumstances so strong as to constitute an implied transfer. In the
case of Formosa, he pointed out :

> The sovereignty was Japanese until 1952. The Japanese
> treaty came into force, and at that time Formosa was being
> administered by the Chinese Nationalists, to whom it was
> entrusted in 1945, as a military occupation. In 1952, we
> did not recognise the Chinese Nationalists as representing
> the Chinese State. Therefore, this military occupancy could
> not give them legal sovereignty nor, equally, could the
> Chinese People's Republic, which was not in occupation of
> Formosa, derive any rights from occupation of that terri-
> tory.[19]

On Turton's reasoning, the United States, which recognized
the Chinese Nationalists as representing the Chinese state, could
justifiably admit Chiang Kai-shek's claim to legal sovereignty
over Taiwan. But Britain could not because the Nationalist
regime did not represent the Government of China for
Britain.[20] Britain was also reluctant to support Peking's claim
because it did not have effective control of the territory in question, which, as Georg Schwarzenberger observes, "is of central
importance for purposes of both the acquisition and maintenance of title" to territory.[21] Accordingly, Britain believed that
the status of Formosa still remained to be settled by a multilateral international agreement either within or outside the
United Nations.[22]

The idea that the Taiwan question be considered by the
United Nations was first broached by President Truman on
27 June 1950. He stated :

> The determination of the future status of Formosa must
> await the restoration of security in the Pacific, a peace
> settlement with Japan, or consideration by the United
> Nations.[23]

On 25 August 1950, the US representative to the UN addressed
a letter to the UN Secretary General in which he welcomed UN
consideration of the question of Formosa.[24] Subsequently,
Washington requested that the question of Formosa be included

on the agenda of the UN General Assembly. British support in the matter was expressed in the statement of the Under-Secretary of State for Foreign Affairs, Ernest Davies. He observed :

> The main aim of His Majesty's Government is to help in securing a generally acceptable and peaceful solution of the Formosan problem.... We shall take advantage of any opportunity which may arise within the United Nations to bring about a solution.[25]

The joint statement of President Truman and Premier Attlee of 8 December 1950 declared :

> On the question of Formosa, we have noted that both Chinese claimants have insisted upon the validity of the Cairo Declaration and have expressed reluctance to have the matter considered by the United Nations. We agreed that the issues should be settled by peaceful means and in such a way as to safeguard the interests of the people of Formosa and the maintenance of peace and security in the Pacific, and that consideration of this question by the United Nations will contribute to these ends.[26]

In this statement, made after the Chinese intervention in the Korean War, the British Government, perhaps for the first time, spoke of taking into account the interests of native Formosans. This was in effect the first step in the direction of proposals like UN trusteeship of the island, plebiscite to determine the future status of Formosa, an independent Taiwan, or a neutralized Formosa. In a policy statement on 11 May 1951, Foreign Secretary Herbert Morrison observed :

> In fact, the problem of Formosa has now become an international problem in which a number of nations apart from those signatory to the Cairo and Potsdam Declarations are closely concerned. In the view of His Majesty's Government this is a question which could usefully be considered by the United Nations at the appropriate time....I think it is clearly desirable that the wishes of the inhabitants of Formosa should be taken into account.[27]

While speaking in defence of the government policy, Major Beamish, Labour M.P., pointed out that Article 73 of the UN

Charter was very much relevant to the case of Formosa. Under that article, he said, the territories detached from enemy states came under the trusteeship section, where "the principle is laid down that the interests of the inhabitants of these territories are paramount."[28] Prime Minister Churchill set the seal of official approval to the idea of a United Nations trusteeship over Formosa on 14 July 1954, when he told the Opposition Leader, Clement Attlee, that he saw no reason "why at some subsequent date Formosa should not be...placed in the custody of the United Nations." "I do not want to harm our relations with the United States," he added.[29]

Chinese Stand

For Peking, the Cairo Declaration, confirmed at Potsdam, was not a mere "statement of intentions" but it had unquestionable legal binding force.[30] When China accepted the surrender in the Taiwan area from Ando, the Japanese Governor-General and Commander in Taiwan, the island of Formosa, it is claimed, was reunited with the motherland both in law and in fact. Thus, Wu Hsiu-chuan, the Chinese representative, in his speech before the UN Security Council on 28 November 1950, asserted :

> When the Chinese Government accepted the surrender of the Japanese armed forces in Taiwan and established sovereignty over the island, Taiwan became, not only *de jure*, but also *de facto*, an inalienable part of Chinese territory. And this has been the situation as regards Taiwan since 1945. Hence, during the five post-war years from 1945 to June 27, 1950, no one ever questioned the fact that Taiwan, *de jure* and *de facto*, is an inseparable part of Chinese territory.[31]

Furthermore, it is contended that all rights that Chiang Kai-shek possessed in Taiwan from 25 October 1945 onwards have since passed to the People's Republic of China.

While Peking invokes the Cairo and Potsdam Declarations in support of its claim to Formosa, its basic argument primarily rests on conquest and annexation. Formosa, it is asserted, is Chinese territory in law, independently of the Cairo, Potsdam and San Francisco Agreements. It is so by virtue of the fact that the Treaty of Shimonoseki, which constituted the legal basis for Japanese occupation, was formally abrogated, together with other treaties with Japan, on 8 December 1941 by China when it issued a proclamation declaring war on Japan. From that date, it is claimed, China recovered its sovereign rights on Taiwan, though it did not actually exercise those rights till 25 October 1945. Thus Mei Ju-ao, former Judge of the Far East International Military Tribunal and member of the Executive Council of the Political Science and Law Association of China, in an article in the *People's Daily* of 31 January 1955, observed :

> Simultaneously with its formal proclamation of war on Japan on December 8, 1941, China solemnly declared the abrogation of all treaties between China and Japan. Since the Shimonoseki Treaty, on the basis of which Japan occupied Taiwan, was among the treaties abrogated, Japan's rule over Taiwan naturally became groundless from that day. It is true that Taiwan was in fact under Japan's occupation during the war against Japan. But legally speaking, China has every right to consider that it had recovered its sovereign rights over Taiwan as from that day....Taiwan has always been China's territory. It had been stolen by Japan for 50 years. Following the termination of the Second World War, China exercised the right conferred on it by international law as a nation victorious over Japan. On the basis of the proclamation it issued on December 8, 1941, China recovered Taiwan on October 25, 1945. This action by China is perfectly lawful. It is consistent with the terms of the Cairo Declaration and Potsdam Proclamation and Japan's instrument of surrender.[32]

The theory of conquest or annexation is, no doubt, generally recognized in international law as one of the methods of effecting transfers of sovereignty. However, in so far as China's claim to Formosa on that basis is concerned, it is pointed out that Japan's defeat was not brought about by Chinese efforts alone. In fact, Secretary of State John Foster Dulles had asserted that the defeat of Japan was brought about "principally...by the efforts and sacrifices of the United States."[33] Thus, it seems to be argued that since Japan surrendered not solely to China but to the Allied Powers as a whole, the island of Formosa could not properly be said, on that basis, to have been conquered or annexed by any one Power. In other words, China was not justified in imposing single-handed a victor's peace terms on the defeated enemy according to its wishes. In reply to such arguments it can be said that the surrender of Japanese forces in Taiwan was accepted by China with the acquiescence and consent of the Allied Powers. Moreover, the USA and Britain, if one follows that logic, were not completely justified in effecting the peace settlement with Japan in September 1951 in the absence of Soviet and Chinese concurrence. As regards the validity of Peking's assertion that the unilateral abrogation of the Treaty of Shimonoseki in 1941 restored Chinese sovereignty over Taiwan (the proclamation of the Chinese Government of 30 August 1945 stated that Formosa was a new province of China), the British Joint Under-Secretary of State for Foreign Affairs (Turton) remarked : "Unilateral declarations could not affect the legal status of Formosa."[34]

Since Peking contends that Formosa has already become a part of China, both *de facto* and *de jure*, it does not think that there is any question of sovereignty over Taiwan being in abeyance, suspense or remaining undetermined. The status of Formosa, it is stated, was decided long ago,[35] *i.e.* on 8 December 1941, when China abrogated the Treaty of Shimonoseki. The only issue that remains unresolved is the assertion of administrative control by the People's Republic over Taiwan, a Chinese province, by the extermination of the "Chiang Kai-shek traitorous clique." Whether Peking will accomplish this task by peaceful means or by resorting to force and when it will do it are entirely matters for the Chinese people to decide.[36] The Taiwan question, it is asserted, is an internal affair of China in which no other country, not even the UN, has any right to interfere.[37] The UN should only discuss and set right the Chinese complaint of American "armed aggression on Taiwan" resulting from the interposition of the Seventh Fleet and the shielding of Chiang Kai-shek by the US Navy.[38] It has no right to consider the question of Taiwan in any other way or to decide the status of Formosa.[39] Any attempt to interfere in China's internal affairs is considered violation of Article 2, paragraph 7, of the UN Charter.[40] For similar reasons, Peking has rejected trusteeship, neutralization, and independent Taiwan proposals. In his speech before the First Session of the First National People's Congress on 23 September 1954, Chou En-lai observed :

> All proposals to place Taiwan under United Nations trustee-ship or under neutral mandate, or to "neutralize" Taiwan or to create a so-called "independent Taiwan state," are attempts to carve up China's territory, enslave the Chinese people on Taiwan and legalize United States occupation of Taiwan. None of this will be tolerated by the Chinese people.[41]

There is a close similarity of views between Peking's attitude and Taipeh's stand in the matter. Like the People's Republic of China, the Nationalist administration in Taiwan believes that the validity of the Cairo Declaration was indisputable and that when Japan surrendered, China "repossessed Taiwan and Penghu and constituted them as Taiwan Province."[42]

Political Aspects of the Problem

The problem of Formosa is in reality a political problem. The British believe that it can neither be "solved merely by reference to the Cairo and Potsdam Declarations"[43] nor can any "useful purpose...be served in the circumstances of this case" by sug-gesting to the United States "joint submission of the legal aspects of the...[conflict of views as to title over Formosa]...to the International Court of Justice."[44] The Chinese too are not inclined to submit the question of Formosa to the jurisdiction of the World Court.[45] Thus, both Britain and China seem to agree, though for different reasons, that the matter cannot be resolved on a judicial plane. Until March 1972, Britain had expressed the opinion that the problem of Formosa was "an international problem in which a number of nations are con-cerned"[46] and which ought to be settled by international nego-tiation. China, on the other hand, had consistently held that it was an internal affair of China to be settled by the Chinese people themselves either peacefully or through resort to arms.

British Attitude

Before the outbreak of the Korean War both Britain and the USA regarded the question of Formosa to be an internal prob- lem of China.   They silently acquiesced in Peking's liberation of a number of islands, including Hainan.   Apparently, they were reconciled to the liquidation of the Chiang Kai-shek regime on Formosa as well.   Chiang's ouster, Britain believed, would have enabled British ships to carry on fruitful trade with China freely and without any hindrance from Kuomintang pirates. It would have also facilitated an early US recognition of the People's Republic,[47] thereby strengthening British hands in pursuing a policy of establishing friendly relations with Peking and trying to wean China away from the Soviet Union.   Thus, the British *charge d'affaires* in Peking, H. Trevelyan, in his *Memoirs*, frankly admits : "It would surely have been better if the Chinese civil war had at an early stage reached what, without the Americans, would have been its inevitable out- come." In those days, the Americans, he said, were not disposed to intervene and the capture of Taiwan by the communists at that time would not have materially sharpened the repercussions felt in Southeast Asia as a result of the Communist victory on the mainland.[48]

After the Korean War, American policy towards Taiwan underwent a distinct change.   Whatever may have been the military considerations for the interposition of the Seventh Fleet in the Formosan Straits, the American move constituted an intervention in China's internal affairs.   It obstructed the final outcome of the Chinese Civil War.   Although Britain was in no way directly involved in or committed to the defence of Formosa, the American decision to shield Chiang Kai-shek and perpetuate his rule over Formosa was received in London without any public disclaimers.[49]   Only a few left-wing Labou- rites expressed their dissent.   President Truman's statement that "the determination of the future status of Formosa must await the restoration of security in the Pacific, a peace settle- ment with Japan, or consideration by the United Nations,"[50] enjoyed Britain's tacit support.   London described American action as impartial neutralization of Formosa and sought to avoid giving the impression that the Western Powers were, in any way, committed to bolster Chiang Kai-shek. The British, at the same time, seemed to agree with the basic American policy of not allowing

> a territory of potentially considerable strategic importance, which is not yet legally a part of China and which American arms alone took from Japan, to pass under the control of Chinese Government in a period of dangerous armed conflict in the Far East.[51]

A communist attack on Formosa at that stage was viewed in official British and American circles as a factor disturbing peace and stability in the Pacific, making for the escalation of war and endangering the lives of British and American troops fighting in Korea.   At such a critical juncture, Britain could hardly afford to ignore American interests, feelings and opinions. Accordingly, London supported Washington's stand that Formosa was an international problem and that a peaceful settlement of the problem acceptable to all concerned was necessary.

During 1950-51 the British Government apparently thought of reconciling the American and Chinese interests by asking Peking to let UN objectives succeed in Korea and advising Washington to concede the Chinese viewpoint on Formosa. This was probably the import of Premier Attlee's 14 December 1950 statement, in which he observed :

> We seek a free and independent Korea....The Cairo Declaration, which was agreed on by all Korea's neighbours, expressed acceptance of two principles : non-aggression and no territorial ambitions.   It is for the Chinese Government to make it clear that they accept these principles, for their recent actions have thrown doubt upon this.   The question of Formosa, which was also dealt with in the Cairo Declaration, is one of the most difficult of all the problems facing us in the Far East.   There are mutual fears and suspicions to be got rid of before a solution can be found   It is right that everyone should try to understand the point of view both of the Chinese rulers and also of the United States of America.   Until China shows by her action that she is not obstructing the fulfilment of the Cairo Declaration in respect of Korea and respects the basic principle of the Cairo Declaration, it will be difficult to reach a satisfactory solution.[52]

The above-mentioned framework, Britain felt, could possibly provide a basis for "a genuine and satisfactory Far Eastern settlement." However, the first necessary step was "a settlement in Korea,"[53] *i.e.* Chinese acceptance of the UN objective of a unified Korea.

Since Korea is a peninsula of great strategic importance for China, Peking could not possibly accept the British idea of a trade-off between Korea and Formosa. Therefore, it was not possible for Britain to effect a settlement "by mutual consent" of the "great problems associated with Formosa" and involving "a great strategic conflict."[54]   Chinese intransigence in the Korean cease-fire negotiations led to a stiffening of the British attitude.   In his address before the US Congress on 17 January 1952, Sir Winston Churchill observed that free nations should neither facilitate nor encourage the bloody liquidation by the Chinese communists of these "free Chinese" on Formosa. He declared :

> We take our stand at your side....I am very glad, but whatever diplomatic divergences there may be from time to time about procedure, you do not allow the Chinese anti-Communists on Formosa to be invaded and massacred from the mainland.[55]

It was soon realized that a solution of the problem was not feasible on the basis of exchange of Formosa for Korea.   The Western Powers, therefore, floated other ideas like UN trusteeship, neutralization of Formosa or independent Taiwan—ideas which could hardly be palatable to Peking. Thus, the Washington correspondent of *The Times* observed on 9 April 1953 :

> There already seems to be a dawning recognition that a real solution of Far Eastern problems will entail eventually the admission that the Communists are the Chinese Government and, while Formosa can be set up as an independent state, it cannot any longer be encouraged to think of itself as having a future on the mainland.[56]

The failure of the Geneva Conference to reach an agreement on Korea proved beyond doubt that it was futile to hope for Communist acquiescence in the peaceful reunification of Korea on Western terms. In these circumstances, Churchill declared on 14 July 1954 :

> I certainly to do not see anything in the conduct of China which has yet happened which should lead the American Government to deliver Formosa to Communist China. Nor do I see any reason why at some subsequent date Formosa should not be...placed in the custody of the United Nations. I [do]...not want to harm our relations with the United States.[57]

While Britain did not assume any obligation for the defence of Taiwan, Foreign Secretary Eden supported the conclusion of the US-Chiang Mutual Defence Treaty of December 1954. He stated :

> Her Majesty's Government are satisfied that the Treaty is in fact purely defensive and that its object is to place relations between the United States Government and the Nationalist Chinese on such a basis as will result in a closer degree of consultation[58]....In their treaty with Chiang Kai-shek they have explicitly limited their own formal commitments to the defence of Formosa and the Pescadores.[59]

On 20 December 1954 Lord Reading, Minister of State for Foreign Affairs, declared that the British Government did not "regard it [Taiwan] as forming part of China,"[60] thereby setting the seal of official approval on a two-China solution of the Formosan problem.

In his message to Chou En-lai on 5 January 1955, Eden explained the British attitude towards the US-Chiang Security Pact in these words : Britain could not justifiably be accused of being guilty of bad faith; that nothing was to be settled by fighting; that in the opinion of Britain the American Nationalist Treaty would induce restraint; that, in any case, no one could expect Washington to give up its ally; and that one had to deal with the situation as it was. Anthony Nutting, in a statement in a television interview in New York, suggested that the United Nations would be fighting with the American forces in defence of Taiwan against Chinese attack and that British forces would therefore inevitably be involved. This statement, it was subsequently explained to the Chinese, only meant that an attack on

Taiwan would involve the danger of a wider conflagration; and that Britain had no obligation to defend Taiwan, only an obligation to act as a loyal member of the United Nations in accordance with a United Nations decision.[61]

The British stand as regards the Soviet proposal for convening a conference for settling the Far Eastern problems[62] further lent credence to the view that Britain supported the American idea of maintaining Chiang Kai-shek in power on Formosa. In its reply to the Soviet Government on 9 February 1955, London stated that a conference that excluded the parties most directly concerned (*i.e.* the Peking and Formosan regimes), could not be productive of results; that the position of the UN could not be overlooked; and that fighting must come to an end first.[63] It is significant to recall that in the Canadian proposal of 26 January 1951, Taiwan was not included as a participant in the proposed seven-nation conference (China, the Soviet Union, the USA, Britain, France, India and Egypt) to discuss both the Korean and Formosan questions.[64]

Britain did not think that maintaining Formosa as "a point of arms for a rival Chinese Government...situated within striking distance" and "being held there as a spear-head of a possible attack" against China[65] would serve any useful purpose. Likewise, the British had no faith in the "myth" that Chiang could ever hope to conquer the mainland. They were convinced of the "practical impossibility of such a venture."[66] Besides, it provided Peking with "a handy excuse for 'counter hostilities',"[67] which threatened peace in the Pacific and contributed to the heightening of tension in the area. Britain, at the same time, disapproved of Chinese attempts to "liberate" Formosa, or other disputed islands, by the use of force. Accordingly, London refused to regard the conflict between the Communists and the Nationalists as a civil war. In this context, the British Foreign Secretary observed :

Our objective is to secure general international approval of the contention that the status of these islands (Quemoy and Matsu) and of Formosa should not be settled by force. I know that there are some who say that because the conflict between the Chinese Communists and the Chinese Nationalists is of the nature of a civil war, we are not entitled to try to prevent these matters being resolved by force. I think that is a very dangerous argument, particularly when we remember that one participant in the civil war is closely allied to the Soviet Union and the other participant has a defence treaty with the United States of America. Those are facts, and they make the idea of settling this matter by force extremely dangerous. There are several countries in the world which are divided. There are other areas in the world whose status is not agreed, and I believe it should be our endeavour to prevent solutions of that kind of problem by force of arms. Of course, one way of preventing the use of force is to give in to the other side. That kind of appeasement can be very dangerous; that could lead to the overthrow of our friends and the withering away of independence in the area. The House should reflect upon the consequences, in the smaller countries of the South-East Asia and the Far East, of the United States giving in to the use of force over Formosa and the off-shore islands....One ultimate consequence might be the withdrawal of the United States from the great responsibilities she has undertaken in the Far East.[68]

Thus, Britain believed that any enhancement of Chinese military strength or the establishment of Communist bases on Formosa was a distrurbing factor for peace and stability in the Pacific and harmful to the vital interests of the Western Powers, particularly those of its ally, the USA[69] and its Commonwealth partner, Australia.[70] The occupation of Formosa by Peking also affected British national interests in Hong Kong, Malaya and the Indian Ocean area and endangered the mutually beneficial British trade with Taiwan.[71] London, therefore, deemed it necessary to oppose the forcible liquidation of Nationalist Formosa by Communist China for obvious strategic, political, economic and humanitarian reasons.

Chinese Stand

The presence of Formosa as the "free world's master strategic bastion" in the Pacific[72] enabled Washington to maintain its sway and influence over Japan, South Korea, the Philippines, etc.[73] But China considered it a potential threat to its security and a violation of its sovereignty. The liberation of Taiwan, Chou

En-lai contended, would mean not only safeguarding the sovereignty, unity and territorial integrity of China but also ensuring peace and security of Asia and the world.[74]   Thus, he sought to identify the national interests of China with the revolutionary cause of the world proletariat.

Since Peking considered the "liberation" of Taiwan to be an internal problem of China, it regarded the interposition of the Seventh Fleet between mainland China and Taiwan as interference in its domestic affairs.   In the beginning, the American move might have appeared as a temporary measure dictated by the exigencies of the Korean War,[75] but the conclusion of a Mutual Security Pact between the USA and the Republic of China[76] seemed to dash all hopes of an early withdrawal of the US Fleet.   The US-Chiang Pact was considered an open interference in China's internal affairs, a blatant infringement of its sovereignty and a provocation for war.[77]   Washington, it was stated, was "determined to remain in a position of permanent hostility" towards China.[78]

While the United States remained the prime target of Chinese attack and condemnation, Britain was also criticized by Peking for supporting such concepts as neutralization of Formosa, UN trusteeship, two Chinas, etc.   Commenting on the Truman-Attlee Communique of 8 December 1950 (which expressed belief in the consideration of the Formosan Question by the UN), the *People's Daily* remarked: "From this Communique one can make out that on the Formosa problem British imperialism is following US imperialism."[79]

Since China regarded US-Chiang military pact "a serious war provocation of the US aggressive bloc against the Chinese people and a great menace to peace in Far East and Asia,"[80] Peking considered British support of that pact as not only "tacit acceptance of American aggression and war"[81] but also open encouragement to American aggression against China. In his statement on 21 December 1954, Chou En-lai observed :

> During the Geneva Conference, through the efforts of both China and Britain, some improvement was made in the relations between the two countries. This is beneficial to world peace. However, recently, the British Government has been vigorously following the dangerous policy of the

United States aggressive bloc on certain major issues. Notably on the question of US aggression against the Chinese territory of Taiwan, the British Government even supported the so-called 'mutual security treaty' between the US Government and the traitorous Chiang Kai-shek clique and has encouraged the United States in its seizure of Taiwan. This contravenes the obligations underteken by the British Government in many solemn international agreements, and impairs the relations between China and Britain. The Chinese Government cannot but feel great regret at this attitude of the British Government.[82]

From the Chinese viewpoint, the presence of the American Seventh Fleet (and not Peking's attempts at the forcible "liberation" of Taiwan) was the fundamental cause of tension in East Asia. It also constituted a menace to peace and security in the Pacific.[83] Accordingly, Peking believed that the question of easing tension arising out of US action in the Taiwan area could be a matter of bilateral discussions between Washington and Peking or a subject of consideration at an international conference. The question of the "liberation" of Taiwan, on the other hand, was China's internal affair and could not, therefore, be a subject of discussion in any bilateral or multilateral forum.

On 4 February 1955, the Soviet Government proposed to Britain and India that the three countries jointly sponsor a conference between China, the USA, Britain, the Soviet Union, France, India, Burma, Indonesia, Pakistan and Ceylon, which could be held either at Shanghai or New Delhi in February 1955 to discuss the dangerous situation in the area of Taiwan and other coastal islands of China. While welcoming the proposal, the *People's Daily* reiterated that "the liberation of Taiwan" was entirely China's internal affair. It warned that should the UN or any international conference attempt to discuss China's domestic affairs, it would be deemed "intervention" in its internal affairs. Moreover, the *People's Daily* firmly opposed "pariticipation of the Chiang Kai-shek clique in an international conference to ease the Taiwan situation."[84]

In a statement issued on 12 February 1955, the British Foreign Office objected to the exclusion of the Chinese nationalist authorities from the proposed conference. It considered it "desirable that any meeting for the discussion of the situation in the area of the coastal islands and Formosa should be organised in a form acceptable to the United Nations."[85] Peking refused to accept London's stand. In this connection, the *People's Daily* observed :

> It is not difficult to see that the British Foreign Office in effect repeated Washington's nonsense. In point of fact, this behaviour of the British authorities is preventing a relaxation of the tension in the Taiwan area and encouraging U.S. aggression and intervention in China's internal affairs. Furthermore, it is impairing Sino-British relations. The Chinese people cannot help being indignant at such a policy which is also inconsistent with the British people's own interests.[86]

A formal offer to begin bilateral negotiations with the USA to ease tension in the Taiwan area was made by Chou En-lai at the Bandung Conference of Afro-Asian countries on 23 April 1955. However, this in no way signified that Peking was prepared to surrender its sovereign right of liberating Taiwan or make it a subject of Sino-American talks.[87] Chang Han-fu, the Chinese Vice-Foreign Minister, observed :

> China wants to eliminate tension in the Taiwan area through peaceful negotiation with the United States. But this allows no interpretation that China is prepared to give up its sovereignty over Taiwan. Whether China will liberate Taiwan by peaceful or other necessary means is an internal question for China with which the United States has no right to interfere.[88]

Sino-American talks began at ambassadorial level in Geneva on 1 August 1955 (the venue of talks was subsequently shifted to Warsaw). The negotiations dragged on for a number of years but no agreement was possible. The United States insisted that Peking renounce the use of force against the Republic of China and agree to a permanent cease-fire in the Taiwan Straits. Britain supported Washington's position in the matter.[89] China, on the other hand, expressed its willingness to settle outstanding disputes between China and the USA by peaceful means without any resort to the threat or use of force.

However, it refused to entertain the idea of a cease-fire or renunciation of the use of force against the remnant Chiang Kai-shek clique. Chou En-lai remarked :

> The so-called cease-fire between the People's Republic of China and the traitorous Chiang Kai-shek clique, which the United States Government and its followers are trying to engineer, is in actuality intervention in China's internal affairs and alienation of China's territory.[90]

From 1957 onwards, Members of Parliament belonging to both the Conservative and Labour Parties of Britain, journalists and others visited Formosa. An organization called the "Friends of Free China" became active in advertising the claims of the Formosan regime. Peking obviously disliked such things. Commenting on the visit of a British M.P. to Formosa in early 1957, the *People's Daily* observed that the activities of such people, "interested in creating two Chinas," could only "damage Sino-British relations and harm the Far Eastern situation." Chou En-lai expressed his indignation to a group of Labour M.P.s (who met him in 1957) about the recent development of relations between Britain and Formosa and the tendency to "treat Formosa as a government." In his report to the National People's Congress in February 1958, Chou En-lai stated that the "flirtation between the British Government and the Chiang Kai-shek clique" had, of late, notably increased and that Britain had become a "propaganda centre for the absurd contention that the status of Formosa was undetermined." China, he remarked, would never tolerate the British practice in following American attempts to create "two Chinas."[91]

The Formosan question was not only complicated in its legal and political aspects, but it also gave rise to a highly dangerous and explosive situation. How far the conclusion of the US-Chiang pact, designed to deter Mao Tse-tung "from reckless attempts" to "liberate" Formosa, had contributed or "will contribute to the peace and security of dangerous and sensitive zone"[92] is difficult to say. The Chinese continue to be as determined to "liberate" that island as the Americans seemed inclined "to keep it from falling into unfriendly hands."[93]

The stationing of a US Air Force unit, equipped with tactical missiles called Metador (in accordance with the 7 May 1957 agreement between Washington and Taipeh), was a clear indication of American resolve to defend Formosa even at the risk of a nuclear confrontation. While London seemed inclined to favour a "two China" solution of the difficult problem,[94] it, nonetheless, recognized its obvious limitations in the matter. "We cannot," Eden stated, "of course impose our views upon the parties most directly concerned, nor decide for them where their own true interests lie."[95]

The First Taiwan Straits Crisis, 1954-55

While the presence of a Nationalist administration in Formosa constantly reminded Peking of the existence of a rival regime on Taiwan, Taipeh's continued occupation of the offshore islands was considered a serious threat to the security of the Chinese mainland, the coastal areas in particular. These islands, situated just five miles off the Chinese coast, were used by Taipeh as a base for small-scale coastal raids, for naval blockading, and for gathering intelligence. Peking had so far refrained from launching direct military raids on Taiwan, thereby avoiding confrontation with the USA.[96] However, it had sought to assert its control over the offshore islands, and this had produced two Formosan Straits Crises— the first from December 1954 to February 1955 and the second in August-October 1958.

Britain acknowledged Peking's claim to the offshore islands, but it disapproved Chinese attempts to occupy them through resort to force. Foreign Secretary Eden declared :

> The Nationalist-held islands in close proximity to the coast of china are in a different category from Formosa and the Pescadores, since they undoubtedly form part of the territory of the People's Republic of China. Any attempt by the Government of the People's Republic of China, however, to assert its authority over these islands by force, would, in the circumstances at present peculiar to the case, give rise to situation endangering peace and security, which is properly a matter of international concern.[97]

During the Taiwan Straits Crises, British efforts were primarily directed to prevent the escalation of the conflict and to bring about the cessation of hostilities.[98] To that end, London had suggested that some of the disputed islands be evacuated and the Nationalist garrisons on the remaining islands be either withdrawn or reduced in strength. On 26 January 1955, while reviewing the recent events in the House of Commons, Eden observed :

> In this situation the first concern of Her Majesty's Government has been, and is, to stop the fighting. We have, therefore, continued to urge on all concerned the importance of doing this and of preventing a wider conflagration. Force is not the solution of these delicate and difficult problems. A settlement can only be arrived at by the peaceful process of patient negotiation. Her Majesty's Government are convinced that the object of the United States Adminstration has also been to reduce the risk of any extension of the fighting. Their treaty with General Chiang Kai-shek which defines their commitments was concluded with this object in view....We in this country respect President Eisenhower and know that he would sanction the use of United States forces only with the greatest reluctance and when, in his view, the circumstances constituted an immediate and serious threat to the security of Formosa and the Pescadores. This is not a new element in United States policy. On the other hand, Her Majesty's Government also understand that in the matter of the coastal islands the Chinese Government cannot be expected to act in such a way as might seem to prejudice what they regard as their rights. We are, however, convinced that the problem of the coastal islands is susceptible of a peaceful solution if only all concerned are prepared to work for it.[99]

In his statement on 8 March 1955, Anthony Eden stated :

> The United States Government have already given positive proofs of their desire to relax tension and reduce the risks of war....They have effectively restrained the Chinese Nationalists in recent weeks from initiating attacks against the Chinese mainland. They have persuaded the Nationalists to evacuate the Tachen and Nanchi islands....We would like to see them [Nationalists] withdraw their armed forces from the other coastal islands.[100]

Commenting on the problem of offshore islands, Prime Minister Churchill observed :

There is a great difference between the coastal islands of China and the island of Formosa. As there is no question of our being involved militarily or indeed of our being needed in the defence of the coastal islands, we should be careful of what advice we should offer our friends and allies upon it. The decision on whether, or when, these particular islands should be evacuated is not one the burden of which falls upon Her Majesty's Government, and we must recognise the natural pre-occupations of other Governments who are immediately affected by the threatened attack from Communist China. This is especially true at a time when the Chinese Communists keep stridently asserting that the islands are to be regarded as a steppingstone to the seizure of Formosa itself, with all that that must mean for the Chinese Nationalists under Generalissimo Chiang Kai-shek, who have been given shelter and protection there by the United States, and to whom the United States are bound by over 14 years comradeship in war, both against the Chinese Communists and the Japanese invaders of China.[101]

The statements quoted above amply prove that while counselling restraint and moderation upon its ally, the USA, the British Government had generally appreciated and sympathized with the American viewpoint. Like the Americans, the British did not wish that the offshore islands, which were defensible, should pass in the hands of Chinese communists, except as part of general settlement of the Formosan question. Thus, in his message to Chou En-lai on 28 February 1955, Eden enquired whether the Chinese Government would privately or publicly state that, while maintaining their claims, they did not intend to prosecute them by force. The message also contained a suggestion that if Peking could do that it might be possible to find a peaceful settlement of the question of the coastal islands. The British proposal to the Chinese, H. Trevelyan remarks, "was as much as to ask them to give up Taiwan for the coastal islands" and the Chinese could not be expected to agree to it. In his reply, Chou En-lai criticized the "dirty deal" by which the Americans wanted to trade their intervention in the islands against Chinese acceptance of their occupation of Taiwan.[102] However, since the Chinese found their ally, the Soviet Union, reluctant to become involved in a war with the United States on a issue which was not of the first importance for its security (it was a purely Chinese question and the result of the Chinese decision), Peking abandoned its plan, if any, of attacking Taiwan.

The Second Taiwan Straits Crisis, 1958

During the Second Taiwan Straits Crisis, London had no illusions about China's growing might and its aggressive intentions. Britain, therefore, supported Washington more firmly and more openly. The British Foreign Office declared :

> We have no obligation or commitment of any kind to take military action for the defence of Quemoy, Matsu or Formosa. Our only obligations are those in accordance with the Charter of the United Nations. As was stated in Washington yesterday, the United States Government have neither sought, nor, received, promises of British support in the event of war over the Chinese off-shore islands. With regard to the present situation, we regret the current indications that the Chinese Government wishes to settle the problem of the off-shore islands by force. We hope that further attempts will be made to solve the problem of the status of the off-shore islands by peaceful methods. The diplomatic discussions in Geneva since 1955, although they did not result in a solution, did seem to reduce the tension in the area. We regret that the Chinese Government should appear to be reverting to military methods. We strongly approve President Eisenhower's statement yesterday that he wishes these differences to be settled by way of negotiation. We hope that talks, whether in Warsaw or elsewhere, between representatives of the two Governments will begin speedily. We also welcome the President's statement of his hope that the United Nations could exert a peaceful influence on the situation if the bilateral talks do not fully succeed. It is important that the real issue should be appreciated. The immediate question is not the present or future status of the off-shore islands; it is whether a dispute of this nature should be settled by force; and upon that point we strongly support the American position.[103]

Unlike 1955, the British took no steps in 1958 to secure the withdrawal of Nationalist forces from the offshore islands. British ministers generally tended to support the American stand. Thus, on 15 September 1958, the British Prime

Minister rejected a suggestion by Gaitskell, the Leader of the Opposition, that the British Government publicly declare that it would not participate in a war fought for the defence of Quemoy and that, if necessary, he should fly to Washington to make these views known to the American Government. The change in the British attitude in 1958 was probably a "reflection of the general deterioration in the mood of British relations with China since the brief honeymoon period after Geneva." According to Donald Maclean, the reason for the British Government's refusal in 1958 to be drawn into public opposition to Washington and Chiang lay in a change not in British policy towards China but in Anglo-American relations. The special relationship with the USA was of much greater importance to Britain than its relatively small interests in China. Moreover, by that time, it has entered a new and, from London's point of view, favourable phase, bringing with it, among other things, a renewal of Anglo-American cooperation in the nuclear field and joint Anglo-American landings in Lebanon and Jordan. London, therefore, was quite keen to avoid giving offence in Washington. [104] Whatever be the justification for the change, the British public posture in the matter was not at all conducive to the improvement of Sino-British relations. The Chinese press remarked : "Lloyd and his like were openly conniving with and backing the United States policy of aggression and provocation against China."[105]

While Britain generally supported Washington, it was still opposed to the escalation of the conflict over the tiny islands in the far distant Pacific. Accordingly, London disapproved of Nationalist Chinese raids or similar provocative actions that invited Chinese Communist retaliation. Britain favoured a negotiated settlement which would remove the source of intermittent international tension and friction.[106] The Americans too were inclined to go along with Britain *provided* it could somehow prevent Formosa from falling into Communist hands. Secretary of State Dulles stated :

> The U.S.A. has no commitment and no purpose to defend the coastal positions as such. The basic purpose is to assure that Formosa and the Pescadores will not be forcibly taken over by the Chinese Communists.[107]

On 11 September 1958 President Eisenhower declared that the United States still believed "that diplomacy can and should find a way out." "There are measures," he stated, "that can be taken to assure that these offshore islands will not be a thorn in the side of peace."[108]

The coming into power of the Democratic Party in the United States in 1960 raised hopes about a settlement being reached on the question of the offshore islands.[109] While not in power, its leaders had made certain statements suggesting that they would have no objection to surrender these offshore islands to Peking if the latter responded by giving an undertaking that it would not seek to alter the present status of Formosa by force.[110] In the absence of such a commitment on the part of China, Democratic leaders desired that the countries of the world, including American allies, the uncommitted nations and the Soviet Union, should issue an open declaration condemning the use of force in the Taiwan Straits and agree to stand by the side of the USA in the defence of Formosa against any aggression.[111] However, after the Democratic Administration was installed in power, the crisis in the Taiwan Straits had subsided and, therefore, there was no occasion for Washington to express its wilingness to consider a deal as regards the offshore islands.[112]

The possibility of Quemoy and Matsu being considered, at some future date, as "virtually unrelated to the defence of Formosa and the Pescadores," and their abandonment could not be completely ruled out. It might be recalled that in the beginning of 1955 the Tachen Islands and Yushan and Pishan were written off and evacuated with the help of the USA in order "to avoid a bloody and wasteful battle."[113] The Western Powers, including Britain, were willing "to trade the reduction of the [Nationalist] garrisons on the offshore islands for a *de facto* recognition of the *status quo* in the Formosa Strait."[114] But no agreement had been reached on these lines because Peking had not, at any time, been inclined to pay the price. The situation in East Asia, particularly in the Taiwan Straits, therefore, had remained explosive—one of "a prolonged armed truce."[115]

Sino-US Rapprochement *and Change in British Attitude on Formosa*

During President Nixon's visit to China in February 1972, a final settlement of the Taiwan question could not be reached. However, the two countries most directly concerned with the problem took an important step in the direction of easing tension and facilitating an amicable solution of the intricate problem. In the Sino-US Joint Communique of 27 February 1972, Washington conceded that Taiwan was "a part of China" and that the Taiwan question should be settled "by the Chinese themselves." Nevertheless, Washington had reaffirmed "its interest" in a peaceful settlement of the problem. The security treaty with Taipeh had not been abrogated, but Nixon had agreed to progressively reduce US forces and military installations on Taiwan leading to their complete withdrawal in course of time.[116]

In 1970-71 the People's Republic of China was recognized by a number of countries. In establishing diplomatic relations with China, Canada and Italy took note of Peking's stand that Formosa was an inalienable part of China. In November 1971, the People's Republic of China replaced Taiwan as a member of the UN. These developments, particularly the expulsion of Taiwan from the world organization have considerably strengthened the Chinese case *vis-a-vis* Formosa and the offshore islands.

In these circumstances, the British attitude as regards the status of Formosa could not remain unchanged. Britain realized the incongruity of its low-level diplomatic relations with China at a time when Peking was coming out of its isolation in a big way and other West European countries, including West Germany, were moving ahead towards the establishment of full diplomatic relations with Peking. However, London was not inclined to hastily give up the bargaining counter which, unlike other West European States, it enjoyed as a signatory to the Cairo Declaration. It did not, therefore, wish to announce any change in its stand on the status of Formosa unless it received positive assurances from Peking about the establishment of full diplomatic relations at ambassadorial level and the future of Hong Kong. Accordingly, while replying to a question whether any change was contemplated in respect of maintaining a consulate in Taiwan, the British Foreign Secretary, Sir Alec Douglas-Home, simply observed (on 2 August 1971) that the British Consulate was not accredited to the Government of Taiwan. He refused to elaborate it or add anything further. However, this remark, as also his somewhat positive attitude on the question of Chinese representation (while expressing the view that the Important Question resolution might not be moved in the UN in 1971, he observed that there was only one seat for one country in the organisation),[117] was quite significant. It indicated that London meant business; that any change in the British attitude on Formosa and on the question of Chinese representation in the UN would depend on the progress in the Anglo-Chinese negotiations (resumed in the beginning of 1971) on the exchange of ambassadors between the two countries.

Towards the end of 1971, Britain, for the first time since 1961, voted against the US draft resolution which required two-third majority for a change in the Chinese representation in the UN.[118] In March 1972, an agreement was concluded to up-grade Sino-British relations to ambassador level. In the Joint Communique, that was issued on 13 March 1972, the British Government agreed to remove its official representation in Taiwan and to close its consulate in Taiwan. London also agreed to "acknowledge the position of the Chinese Government that Taiwan is a province of the People's Republic of China." The task of looking after British interests in Taiwan was entrusted to the Australian mission there. Explaining the Government's position in the matter in the House of Commons, Sir Alec Douglas-Home stated that at the time of the resumption of Sino-British discussions in early 1971, London had told Peking that if an agreement on an exchange of ambassadors was reached, Britain would be prepared to withdraw its consulate from Taiwan. He further pointed out that both the Government of the Peoples Republic of China and Taipeh maintained that Taiwan was a part of China. The Taiwan question, he observed, was "China's internal affair to be settled by the Chinese peoples themselves." British acknowledgement of the position of the Chinese Government that Taiwan was a province of the Peoples Republic of China and that the Taiwan question was an internal affair of China, he stated, was "in accordance with the views which the British Government took both at Cairo and at Potsdam," *viz.* that Taiwan should be restored to China. This view, Sir Alec added, had not changed.[119] In spite of the attempts on the part of the British Foreign Secretary to defend the position of the British Government as a return to the past, the fact remained that the stand he was taking in 1972 was in marked contrast to the British attitude in the 1950s and early 60s, when the British Government had publicly declared that the Taiwan question was an international problem to be decided in the world forum rather than an internal affair of China to be settled by the Chinese themselves.

CHAPTER FIVE

Southeast Asia

Unlike Korea, Britain had a direct interest in Southeast Asia—
"the rice-bowl of the orient"—because of its geographical
location, its enormous wealth in natural resources, especially in
strategic raw-materials,[1] and for reasons of safeguarding its
colonial possessions. Southeast Asia is the commercial and
strategic gateway between the Pacific and Indian Oceans as also
between Asia and Australia. Besides, all intercontinental airways in the Far East pass through this area. "The economic,
political and strategic importance" of Southeast Asia, the
British Commissioner General in Malaya, Malcolm MacDonald,
observed, had been "the ceaseless rivalry between democratic
and Communist forces for its possession" in the post-World
War II period.[2]

Britain was interested in the security of the area because it
wished to preserve an important market for British goods and
to safeguard its large investments in Malaya, Burma and Indonesia,[3] and the sea communications to Australia and New
Zealand. Foreign Secretary Bevin considered Southeast Asia
to be "the biggest area for capital development goods."[4] The
Indian Ocean was also vitally important for Britain. Two-
thirds of the area and four-fifths of the population of the
British Commonwealth lie in lands whose shores abut on the
Indian Ocean. Lord Killearn, therefore, called it "a Commonwealth waterway."[5] Britain endeavoured to maintain its control
over the Malacca Straits through which passed all shipping
between Europe and the Orient via the Indian Ocean. Besides,
Singapore had remained the centre and citadel of British power
in the Eastern seas and the place from where the British expected "to discharge commitments under the Manila Pact (SEATO)
and even, perhaps under CENTO."[6] It was not only the prin-

cipal naval and air base of Britain in the Far East, but it was also the world's most important warehouse and distributing point for rubber. This great commercial and trading centre handled nearly £700 million worth of trade every year and about 40,000 ships passed through it annually.[7]

British Stake in Malaya

Malaya is situated in the very heart of Southeast Asia. It was directly ruled by Britain till 31 August 1957 when it became a self-governing dominion within the Commonwealth. Of all the countries in the region, Malaya occupied a place of distinct importance both in terms of strategic location and production of natural rubber and tin.[8] In the post-war period, Britain faced an acute economic crisis and was left with no other choice except "a dollar pension and grim decline."[9] In these circumstances, Malaya, which was "the greatest dollar earner in the sterling area," proved to be of great help to Britain, particularly in balancing its overseas account with the dollar area. Moreover, Britain owned two million planted acres of rubber, 75 per cent of the tin mines and 95 per cent of big business in Malaya.[10] Earnings from these sources enabled London to pay for its imports. Thus, "the standard of living in Britain," the Correspondent of *The Times* remarked, was "directly related to prosperity in Malaya."[11]

Military Uprising

The aim of the territorist campaign, launched in the first half of 1948, was to sabotage "British imperialist production centres, transport and communications" and eliminate and punish "traitors, reactionary capitalists and contractors."[12] It threatened not only Malaya's solvency[13] but also Britain's position as the banker of the sterling area. The terrorist campaign was telling heavily on the Malayan economy, London's balance of payments position, the market potentialities for British goods in Malaya and overseas earnings of the United Kingdom.

In order to crush this challenge to its vital interests, Britain proclaimed a state of emergency in June 1948 and declared unlawful the Pan Malayan Federation of Trade Unions, the Malayan Communist Party (MCP), Malayan People's Anti-Japanese Army (MPAJA), Ex-Comrades Association, the New Democratic Youth League and Ikatan Pempela Tanah Ayers Malaya. The British Government endeavoured "in all possible ways to defeat and to destroy this menace in Malay" which sought "to reduce the economic life of that country to chaos by murder of the managements on the estates, both European and Chinese, and to impede Malayan recovery and create some other control over Malaya."[14]

Britain tried to suppress the civil disturbances in Malaya by adopting ruthless and repressive measures. It prescribed a death penalty for the possession of arms, causing an explosion likely to endanger life, and for collecting subscriptions or receiving supplies on behalf of the bandits. Air raids on the terrorists were frequent. Napalm bombs were used to burn jungles. Collective punishments were often imposed upon the entire group living in a village or urban areas that concealed information about rebels, "which some of them could hardly fail to possess."[15] They were punished because they had failed in their duty to cooperate with the authorities. Under emergency regulations, all men between the ages of 18 and 55 were made liable to compulsory part-time duties as home guards,[16] who enjoyed wide powers of search and arrest. By 15 October 1950, 10,949 persons, most of them Chinese, were under detention and by 10 March 1953, the British Colonial Government had deported nearly 24,036 Chinese and 1,893 other nationals—Indians, Ceylonese and Indonesians.[17] In order to effectively suppress the 7,000-odd terrorists, Britain deployed nearly 120,000 military and police personnel (in addition to a large number of home guards) and spent a large amount of money.[18] In spite of the denial by the Secretary of State for the Colonies,[19] the British Government had almost succeeded in creating a "police state" in Malaya.[20] Britain did not proclaim martial law because that would have added "nothing to the powers which already exist, but would in fact put fresh burdens upon the military which at the present time they are not required to shoulder, with the consequences that they are more free than they would be under martial law to carry out their military duties."[21]

Calcutta Conference of Asian Communist Parties, 1948

The military uprising in Malaya was accompanied by the outbreak of violent incidents in Burma and Indonesia as well. The British believed that this "whole sinister communist plan for revolution in Southeast Asia" was inspired by Moscow.[22] It was considered a part of the Kremlin's policy to institute the Berlin Blockade and instigate a great wave of strikes in Western Europe in the severe winter of 1947-48, thereby defeating the Marshall Plan, which was designed to restore the economic health of West Europe. Official British circles suspected that orders for an armed revolt in Malaya came from the Calcutta Conference of Asian Communist Parties held in February 1948. While referring to the decision of the Malayan Communists to take to open violence, the British Colonial Secretary observed : "Nor has it passed unnoticed that in February a 'Youth Conference' attended by Communists from Russia and Eastern Europe, and by delegates from Malaya was held in Calcutta."[23] He blamed Moscow (and not Peking) for "the vilification of Britain—the wilful lies in regard to the Malayan situation."[24]

It might be recalled that an article appearing in *Voprosy Istorii* (Moscow) described the Malayan Communist Party struggle as a "just and holy war against imperialism." The article referred to the "political achievements of Chinese People's Republic in the foreign sphere" (such as the recognition of the Democratic Republic of Vietnam) and asserted that the Chinese revolution exercised "a tremendous revolutionizing influence upon all peoples of the East, especially Malaya." The Chinese Communist victory, it added, intensified the crisis in the colonial system and aggravated "the general crisis of capitalism." The article expressed the view that Peking would not disappoint the hopes of the Singapore Committee (of the Malayan Communist Party) about gaining "ultimate victory in the national and revolutionary war."[25] By extending a helping hand in Malaya, Vasilyev wrote in *Pravda*,

China would not only be serving a revolutionary cause but
would be assisting its Chinese brethren who were being "subject-
ed to ridicule and repression on the part of the authorities for
many months."[26]

The British felt that, as an ambitious and expanding Great
Power, the Soviet Union had a two-fold objective in promoting
the Malayan insurgency : firstly, Moscow endeavoured to bring
about the economic and political collapse of Western Europe,
and secondly, it sought to instigate China into undertaking
an adventurous course of action in Southeast Asia, thereby
embroiling Peking in a confrontation with the Western Powers.
It was believed that Peking, at that stage, was not in a position
to assume an aggressive posture in the world and there were
no visible signs of Chinese expansionism.[27]

The Calcutta Conference was held at a time when the
Chinese people were still fighting "against foreign aggression...
[and] for complete national independence."[28] The Chinese
delegation to the Calcutta Conference stated that the realization
of Communist victory in China and the consolidation of the
people's gains required "the assistance and association of the
liberation campaign of the peoples of Southeast Asia,"
which would greatly encourage them in their fight.[29] Reliable
Communist sources in Hong Kong denied that there was any
connection between the Malayan Communist Party and the
Chinese Communist Party. The outbreak of violence in
Malaya was considered "purely an internal problem of the
Malayans and having absolutely nothing to do with the Chinese
Communist Party which never attempts to intervene in the
internal situation of any foreign country."[30]

Chinese Attitude

Confronted with the formidable task of socio-economic reconstruction and the problem of weeding out nearly 400,000 nationalist guerillas, the newly-established People's Republic of
China was hardly in a position to adopt an aggressive posture.
Food shortages, economic confusion and political instability at
home ruled out any Chinese involvement in a major war.
Moreover, considering China (and not Russia) to be "the great

reality" in Southeast Asia,[31] the British believed that there was no danger of an immediate armed aggression in the area.[32] Far from being a threat to the security of the region, China's weakness left it a helpless victim to Kremlin's machinations. "China to-day," G. F. Hudson remarked, "has the formal status of a Great Power, but has hardly any industrial or military strength of her own, and tends to become a battle-ground between Soviet and Western influence." Thus, it was assumed that for fear of losing Western economic aid, so necessary for its industrialization, China would not be inclined to take an adventurous course of action in Southeast Asia.[33]

Conscious of their problems and limitations, the Chinese leaders adopted a cautious and low-profile attitude which was evident from their attitude towards Hong Kong and Burma. Their attitude towards Malaya was also "relatively detached,"[34] which showed that Peking did not intend to interfere with British interests in Southeast Asia. The reason for this restraint might well have been, as Fitzerald points out, "not any lack of sympathy with the aims of the rebellion, but rather doubt as to its chance of success."[35] Speaking at a meeting of the Chinese People's Political Consultative Conference in September 1949, Liu Shao-chi stated : "If China doesn't go into socialism...China will become an imperialistic country." However, at the same time, he emphasized that this would occur only "after the completion of her industrialization." In 1949-50, he pointed out, an expansionist course of action "will never be allowed by the Chinese people nor by the peoples of the world." He, therefore, regarded "the socialist future of China" and the adoption of an aggressive policy as "matters of the very remote future."[36]

Compared to the speech of Louis Saillant,[37] General Secretary of the World Federation of Trade Unions (WFTU), Liu Shao-chi seemed to take a moderate line in his statement at the Conference of Asian and Australasian countries, which was held under the auspices of he WFTU in Peking in November 1949. Liu commended the path taken by the Chinese people to "the peoples of the various colonial and semi-colonial countries in their fight for national independence and People's Democracy" and described "the national liberation wars in Vietnam, Burma, Indonesia, Malaya and the Philippines" as entirely correct.[38] However, the Manifesto, that was issued at the end of the Conference, seemed to reflect the Soviet viewpoint that Britain should not be permitted "a way out of economic crisis which is already developing" and that Communist insurgents continue their fight to achieve that end. The struggle of the Malayan terrorists, the Manifesto added, was "not isolated" for they had the sympathy and support of "the workers throughout the world."[39] That the Chinese view was different from that of the Soviet Union on the issue of the liberation struggle in colonial areas and dependent countries was evident from a persual of the *People's Daily* editorial of 16 June 1950 and the editorial that appeared in the Cominform Journal on 27 January 1950. While accepting the Cominform approach that "armed struggle against imperialist aggression is essential for the liberation of many colonies and semi-colonies," the *People's Daily* asserted :

> But the time and place for conducting this kind of revolutionary armed struggle must be decided according to concrete conditions. It can by no means be conducted in any colony or semi-colony at any time without the necessary conditions and preparations.[40]

British Recognition of China and its Impact on Malaya

The victory of the Communists in China gave a fillip to the terrorists' morale. However, since Malaya neither had a common frontier nor adequate land communications with China, Peking could not render any direct material assistance to the Malayan terrorists. There was, in fact, no evidence that Malayan Communists were actually receiving any arms aid from China.[41] Therefore, there was no point in accusing Peking of hostile acts when there existed none. Baseless vilification of China would have only antagonized Peking, driven it closer to the Soviet Union and further complicated the British task of suppressing the communist insurgents. On the other hand, Britain stood to gain much by cultivating relations with China. In the first place, cordial relations with Peking would have reduced British anxiety about protecting Hong Kong and enabled

London to reinforce its garrisons in Malaya.[42] Secondly, Britain had realized the futility of depending solely on military means for the suppression of the Malayan insurrection. It was, therefore, believed that "some kind of political settlement with China" could bring the Malayan emergency to an end. "A directive from Moscow or Peking," Kenneth Younger stated, "could probably call them off tomorrow."[43] The only adverse effect of British recognition of China could possibly be the presence of Chinese consuls in Malaya, who might assist the rebels and thereby make the British task of bandit suppression more difficult.[44] However, the British Government was quite conscious of these "possible dangers in relation to Malaya,"[45] and was prepared to face them.

Thus, in according recognition to the Mao regime, London seems to have taken a calculated risk but the risk was not all that serious. By the end of 1949, both the number of weekly incidents caused by terrorist activity had "dropped steadily" (from an average of over 50 to 26) and the number of terrorists who surrendered had "considerably increased."[46] Moreover, British recognition of China tended to remove the fear from the minds of a considerable section of the Chinese people in the Federation of Malaya (which became less ready to cooperate with the Government and more disposed to insure themselves with the terrorists) that "if they openly sided with the Government in Malaya, their relatives or their property, or both, in China, would suffer at the hands of the Communist Government." Conciliation with China appeared to facilitate the British task of bandit suppression because it helped Britain in successfully organizing the Chinese community and bringing it "into a more satisfactory relationship with the State Government."[47]

In a broadcast over Radio Malaya on the day Britain announced its recognition of China, the British Commissioner General in Malaya criticized Moscow for interfering in the internal affairs of neighbouring countries, including China, and for fomenting trouble in Southeast Asia.[48] Addressing his remarks to the attention of Chinese leaders, he observed :

Recognition of the new Chinese Communist Government is accompanied by an assumption that they will regard their

Communism as an article for internal consumption by the Chinese, not for forced exports to neighbours. They must not interfere in the national affairs of people outside China. Some commentators in Peking are obviously extremely ignorant about affairs in Southeast Asia. Radio orators talk as if Communist terrorists in Malaya, who have spent the last 18 months murdering Malay, Chinese, and other citizens indiscriminately, are somehow a popular liberating army representing the Malayan peoples. We must see that such ignorant talk is not translated into equally misguided attempts to give practical assistance to local gangsters.[49]

Since Peking did not respond to the British recognition, Malaya did not have to face the possible dangers inherent in the presence of Chinese consuls in Malaya. However, Peking criticized British authorities for persecuting overseas Chinese.[50] After the Korean War, Peking also issued several official statements expressing concern about the oppression and expulsion of Chinese nationals in Malaya. But it studiously refrained from making any formal complaint or lodging protests with the British Government. Thus, on 30 September 1950, Ho Hsiang-ning, Chairman of the Chinese Overseas Affairs Commission, criticized British action in closing *Nan Chiao Daily* and *Hsien T'ai Daily*, describing it an "unreasonable" and "unfriendly" act. He called upon the "Malayan Overseas Chinese to unite together, and struggle continuously for obtaining their righteous rights."[51] In a statement issued on 29 December 1950, the spokesman of the Chinese Foreign Ministry demanded that Britain put an end to the persecution and deportation of Chinese nationals in Malaya. He also gave details of killings and tortures inflicted on both Malayans and Chinese by the British authorities.[52]

On 8 March 1951 the Chairman of a Peking-based "Relief Committee for Overseas Chinese Refugees from Malaya" sent a telegram to Premier Attlee informing him that the Committee had organized a team to proceed to Malaya to investigate the conditions of suffering Overseas Chinese. He demanded that necessary entry permits be issued to the members of the team. In this context, the British Secretary of State for the Colonies, James Griffiths, observed :

We have nothing to hide but equally we have no intention whatsoever of permitting such a mission now or at a later date to enter Malaya....The 11,000 Chinese held in detention camps in Malaya are in the main aliens who have been actively helping the terrorists. They would not be in detention camps now had the Chinese been willing to accept the obligations of a sovereign state to take back its own subjects when they are deported.[53]

London also tried to rid the Chinese schools of their "China consciousness" by dispensing with the necessity of depending "on textbooks imported from China."[54]

Change in Tactics of Communist Insurgents

Failure to get outside material aid, lack of firm support of the people, difficulty in setting up rural bases and obtaining a constant and adequate supply of food in the deep jungle[55] compelled Malayan terrorists to change their tactics. An early indication of change was evident in October 1951,[56] but the major shift from violent and destructive warfare to open political struggle occurred only when Communist countries moved *en masse* in the direction of peaceful co-existence with the West. Replying to a question whether British interests in Malaya "constitute an obstacle to Anglo-Chinese understanding," Chou En-lai observed in June 1954 : "Not at all; that was a matter for the British and the Malayan peoples....China did not regard Malaya as being within the Chinese sphere of influence." China, he asserted, was more interested in "closer Anglo-Chinese understanding" for the contributions that it would make to world peace, and in increasing the volume of trade between the two countries.[57] On 1 May 1955, Ng Heng, the representative of the "Malayan People's Liberation Army," offered to hold negotiations with the British Government. He said :

The sole aim of our struggle is, as it has always been, to achieve a peaceful, democratic, and independent Malaya. It is, as has always been, our aim to achieve this goal by peaceful means....We are willing...to send our representatives directly to Kuala Lumpur to discuss arrangements for negotiation....[58]

On 23 December 1955 the Malayan Communist Party (MCP) issued a statement calling upon Malayans, no matter to what nationality, social stratum or political party they belonged to, to come together in a common effort to win independence, democracy and peace. The statement included an eight-point programme to achieve these ends.[59] However, the statement did not signify that the "long-term goal of struggling for the achievement of people's democracy and socialism"[60] had been abandoned.

Peking believed that the eight-point programme of the MCP was "a true reflection of the urgent aspirations and common interests of the people of every nationality in Malaya," and "a reasonable approach for settling relations between Malaya and Britain." It formed a sound basis for negotiating "a cease-fire agreement on a fair and reasonable basis." Chin Chang's commentary in the *People's Daily* endorsed the MCP programme by stating that it took into account "the actual situation in Malaya today," and was "in short...Marxism in practice."[61] Peking looked forward to increased possibilities of trade and, therefore, welcomed the lifting of the "embargo" on the export of Malayan rubber to China in June 1956. Commenting on the visit of the first trade mission from Singapore and Malaya (which visited China in August 1956 and concluded trade deals amounting to £5 million), the Observer in the *People's Daily* optimistically remarked :

> The development of trade will have a positive function on improving mutual understanding and friendship. We hope that from now on trade and mutual visits between China and Singapore and between China and Malaya will be continuously strengthened and trade can be gradually normalised.[62]

Referring to the armed clashes, that were still continuing between the governments of Malaya and the Philippines, on the one hand, and the armed forces of the people on the other, Vice-Foreign Minister Chang Han-fu declared on 15 July 1957 :

> These are internal affairs of the two countries and have nothing to do with China. Not only has China not inter-

fered in the internal affairs of the countries, but it has always stretched out the hand of friendship to the Philippines and Malaya and is willing to co-exist peacefully with them on the basis of the five principles.[63]

Independence and After

By granting independence to Malaya, Britain sought to deprive the rebels of their political excuse for continuing the struggle (a revolt against colonialism) and forced the Chinese element in the population to accommodate itself to new conditions. Mao Tse-tung and Chou-En-lai sent congratulatory cables to Tuanku Abdul Rahaman, Head of the Federation, and Tengku Abdul Rahaman, Premier and Foreign Minister of Malaya respectively on the occasion of Malaya's independence.[64] However, relations between the two countries remained far from cordial. Towards the end of 1958, Peking suspended trade with Singapore and Malaya as a reprisal against the restrictions imposed by their governments on the import of cheap Chinese textiles and cement and the ban on certain Chinese publications. On 3 May 1959, the *People's Daily* Commentator listed the following among the unfriendly acts of the Malayan Government : discrimination and restrictions against trade with China; deportation of a large number of Chinese residents in Malaya; the closure of the Bank of China branch in Malaya; and the slanderous attacks on China contained in Malayan Government's White Paper of 28 March 1959 regarding subversive activities.[65]

On 31 July 1960 the state of emergency came to an end but normalization of relations between China and Malaysia took place only in May 1974 when the two governments recognized each other and diplomatic relations were established.[66]

British Interests in Other Countries of Southeast Asia

Unlike Malaya and Singapore, British interests in other countries of Southeast Asia were, for the most part, indirect. Among these states, the subordination of Thailand to the communists was considered a greater calamity than the fall of Indo-China because it was not only a source of food supply to Malaya and an important market for British goods,[67] but also because of its strategic position on Malaya's frontier. The British received valuable support from the Thai authorities in the suppression of the terrorist movement in their colony.[68] It was essential for the communists to subjugate Thailand before they could advance towards Malaya and the Indian Ocean. Britain, therefore, felt particulary concerned about the territorial integrity and independence of Thailand,[69] and, in the event of the total collapse of the French military position in Indo-China, was inclined to take joint Anglo-American military action to safeguard the frontiers of Thailand.[70] Again, in May 1962, when communist-led forces in Laos were approaching the Thai border and the Thai Government appealed for assistance, the British Government not only approved the despatch of US forces, but itself sent a squadron of Hunter jet fighters to Thailand. The British Prime Minister, when questioned in the House of Commons, emphasized that this force was intended not for intervention in Laos, but for the defence of Thailand, if its territory were attacked.[71] The British idea of turning Indo-China into a buffer zone, a neutral belt, or "a protective pad"[72] between China in the north and Malaya and its immediate neighbour, Thailand, in the south was likewise motivated by their desire to safeguard their vital interests in Malaysia and Singapore.

From the point of view of British foreign political strategy as a whole, Donald Maclean points out, former Indo-China, like China itself, is in a double sense a secondary front. It is not only far from the areas of primary concern to British foreign policy (Europe and the Middle East), but also, unlike Thailand and Indonesia, does not abut directly on the main surviving centre of British power in East Asia (Malaysia and Singapore) and, owing to years of first French and later American domination, has never been, and is not likely to become, of even commercial interest to London. Therefore, unlike the outcome of anti-communist struggle in Malaya, Britain did not feel much perturbed if the internal struggle in Vietnam and Laos went in favour of the communists. The British, Maclean observes, would have been glad if the French or the Americans had succeeded in bringing Ho Chi Minh and his men to heel, but did not regard it as a major tragedy when they failed to do so.[73] Britain and the West, William Haytor stated, were not engaged in a world-wide anti-communist crusade, but in protecting themselves and their own way of life in their own countries. He remarked : "We may think communism a detestable way of life for ourselves. But it is not for us to decide whether it is right or wrong for other countries, unless its adoption by other countries imperils us."[74]

However, Britain could not possibly remain unconcerned with the events taking place in Indo-China, which had a direct bearing on the British campaign against the communist guerillas in Malaya[75] and the French contribution to European defence.[76] London had not forgotten the Japanese invasion of Malaya through Indo-China and Thailand. It was, therefore, eager to keep the danger as far away from Malaya as possible. A communist victory in Indo-China was detrimental to British national interests. It tended to enhance the terrorists' morale in Malaya, and restricted "the free access of the western world to the trade and materials of Southeast Asia," which, in turn, adversely affected the balance-of-payments position of the sterling area.[77] In these circumstances, Britain deemed it necessary to check the advance of communism in Southeast Asia by actively cooperating initially with the French[78] and subsequently with the Americans.

War in Indo-China

The war in Indo-China began on 19 December 1946 and, for a number of years, the French were in a strong position. However, the communist victory in China "disagreeably transformed the situation" and rendered the political and military task of the French in Indo-China far more difficult. The Vietminh rebels could now "find refuge, equipment, money and training facilities across the Chinese border." With this assistance "they built up their strength from disorganized guerila bands to an army highly skilled in Indo-Chinese warfare, supported by numerous irregulars." Thereafter, the chances of French successes in the war became slender. "As

long as the Vietminh could find refuge in China," Eden
observed, "they could never be completely rounded up and
destroyed."[79]

The recognition of the Ho Chi Minh regime by Peking and
Moscow[80] was a matter of great anxiety to the Western Powers.
"The Russians," *The Times* correspondent remarked, "have
taken legal cover for a great deal more than they did in Greece,
and if their recognition means that the Chinese Government at
Peking can expect Soviet support for physical intervention in
Indo-China the outlook may be regarded as highly disquiet-
ing."[81] In the words of the British Minister of State, the
communist orientation of Ho Chi Minh, which was "fairly
clear from the very start,"[82] was now quite in the open.

The British were not fully satisfied with the appointment of
Bao Dai as the head of the newly-created Associated State of
Vietnam, within the French Union.[83] Nevertheless, they believed that "the interests of the Commonwealth [fundamentally of
Britain] would be best served by international support of the
Emperor Bao Dai."[84] This support was given by according
recognition to the Bao Dai regime by the UK, the USA and 25
other Western nations.[85] Washington, Eden stated, could now
render economic and military assistance to the French in Indo-
China "without bolstering colonialism."[86] In their communique
on 13 May 1950, the Foreign Ministers of the UK, the USA
and France took note of the serious situation developing in
Southeast Asia and "decided to coordinate their efforts to
prevent the smuggling of arms into the area and to take every
opportunity of exposing the aims and methods of Communist
imperialism."[87] American assistance to the French began in
May 1950. By May 1952, the USA was bearing nearly a third
of the total cost of the Indo-China war.[88] During the last
months of that war in 1954, Washington bore almost 80
per cent of the costs of French military operations in Indo-
China.[89]

China's Role in the Indo-China War

As soon as the People's Republic of China was established,
Voprosy Istorii emphasized the "extremely important signi-

ficance" of the communist victory in China to "the struggle of Vietnam for independence and democracy." The most difficult period of the Vietminh fight against "imperialist invaders," the Soviet paper added, "is coming to an end" for, in future, they "will have, in place of the hostile Kuomintang rear, the friendly, neighbourly Chinese People's Democratic Republic."[90] However, Peking was rather slow in rendering material aid to the Vietminh. In the first place, Chinese aid was given only after the Korean War broke out.[91] Moreover, as compared to the American assistance to the French in Indo-China, Chinese aid was very meagre. It was limited only to supplies, training and advice.[92] The primary motive behind Chinese aid seemed to have been the desire to safeguard their southern borders. Peking felt concerned about its southern borders because of its known weakness and confrontation with the Western Powers in the Korean War.[93] The absence of direct communication links with Indo-China[94] further limited Chinese capacity to render material aid to Ho Chi Minh in large quantities.

The *People's Daily* editorial of 19 August 1950 considered the international situation "obviously favourable to the Vietnam people's struggle for liberation." However, it merely offered its good "wishes to the Vietnam people for the early achievement of final victory."[95] The Vietminh struggle benefitted Peking in a number of ways. It weakened the Western Powers, distracted their attention and energy, discredited them in Asian eyes and ensured the safety of China's southern frontier by keeping hostile forces at a distance. For all these reasons, Peking felt happy at the "new situation in Vietnam," brought about by "the spectacular victories won by the Vietnam People's Army in its autumn and winter offensives" and began to pay increasing attention to the events in Southeast Asia. On 15 January 1953, the *People's Daily* observed :

These victories have expanded and consolidated the liberated areas in Northern Vietnam....To the South, the People's Army can join forces with the troops and guerillas in Central Vietnam and, at the same time, increase the threat to the Red River Delta. To the west, it can reach the liberated region of Pathet Lao, making it untenable for the French aggressors in that state....The Vietnam People's Army...besides its tested ability in guerilla and mobile warfare, is now capable to winning frontal attacks, as evidenced by the liberation of Nghialo, Mocchau and other enemy strongholds.   It has also proved its sustained combat power as it has kept up its offensive during the past three months, giving no respite to the enemy....Bigger victories are in store for the Vietnam People's while final defeat is not distant for the aggressors and interventionists.[96]

The Vietminh followed Peking's advice by invading Laos in April 1953.   Prior to that, hostilities had been confined to the fertile soggy delta in North Vietnam and the military situation could not be considered unfavourable to the French.[97] However, the penetration "in force for the first time into northern and north-central Laos" threatened the Laotian capital, Luang Prabang, and appeared to be the beginning of a concerted communist drive south towards Thailand.[98]   The Laos offensive was a matter of acute concern for the Western Powers because it sought to establish "in the northern and central areas of the region guerrilla bases, a Communist 'heartland' from which subversive activities in Burma and Siam can be directed, and local Communists [even in Malaya] armed and supplied."[99]   In 1953 and 1954, the Vietminh succeeded not only in occupying the province of Sam Neua in Laos and compelling French troops to evacuate Na-Sam and Lai-chau in north-western Vietnam, but also felt confident to carry the war into both Laos and Cambodia.[100]

Despite spectacular Vietminh successes, Chinese military intervention in the Indo-China War was considered highly unlikely for a number of reasons.   Firstly, Chinese participation in the Indo-China War would have been hazardous in view of the repeated warnings given by the Western Powers.[101] Secondly, Chinese military involvement in Indo-China so soon after the Korean War (and especially when its forces were still tied up in the north-eastern part of China and in Korea itself) seriously affected the economy of the country.   Thirdly, while it was quite certain that the Western Powers would fight to defend what they considered to be their "vital interests in Southeast Asia,"[102] Peking could not be cocksure about active Soviet involvement in the war, with the result that the main burden would have to be borne by China.   Any large-scale Soviet commitment or assistance to the communists in

Indo-China seemed out of question partly because, unlike Korea, Soviet interests in Indo-China were not that vital and partly because in 1954 the Kremlin was not only preoccupied with the pressing internal problems created by Stalin's death but also had to face a serious challenge posed by the formation of the European Defence Community and the growing strength of the NATO Powers.[103] In these circumstances, any Chinese involvement in a general conflict was fraught with the gravest dangers. Peking, therefore, desisted from intervening in the Indo-China conflict. Accordingly, China deemed it necessary to characterize as "totally false" the rumour about sending 300,000 Chinese troops to Vietnam, which, Peking stated, was intended to misguide world opinion and further enable the United States "to interfere and directly join in the Indo-China War."[104] In order to dissociate London from Washington, China made several friendly overtures towards Britain. For instance, it promised to expand trade, ease restrictions on the exit of British nationals in China, and despatch a Chinese *charge d'affaires* to London. Peking desired to isolate the United States and thereby prevent the internationalization of the Indo-China conflict which, in the peculiar circumstances of the case, would have, from the very start, developed into a war against China.

While direct Chinese intervention in Southeast Asia seemed unlikely, it was more or less certain that Peking would not allow hostile forces to come close to its southern borders and permit "a repetition of MacArthur's march to the Yalu."[105] The establishment of Western military bases along the borders of the Yunnan province would have threatened its security. Thus, in the event the Vietminh had to face a total defeat, Chinese military involvement in the Indo-China War could not altogether be ruled out. Accordingly, Britain endeavoured to give concrete assurances about the security of China's frontiers (including the establishment of buffer states in the areas adjacent to the borders) with a view to avert the possibility of Chinese intervention and to facilitate the task of a negotiated settlement. Before Britain committed itself, in any way, to the war in Indo-China, it considered it both necessary and desirable to explore all possibilities of a negotiated settlement. A military solution of the Indo-China problem entailed the serious risk of war with China and possibly with the Soviet Union as well because the two communist Powers were linked with a military alliance.

British Attitude

Like the Chinese, the British were also quite keen to avoid a general war. As early as May 1952, the British Government expressed its strong opposition to any course of action in Southeast Asia, which would be likely to result in a war with China.[106]   The British were acutely conscious of their limited military and economic resources, and their widespread commitments in Malaya, Kenya, Korea and West Germany. For Britain, Europe was "the decisive area" in the world, and the war in Indo-China, like the Korean War, appeared not only a "wasteful war," but also "the wrong war against the wrong man in the wrong place."[107]   Since the Indo-China conflict did not, in any way, directly threaten its home territories, Britain had no desire to become deeply involved in that war. Moreover, London seriously weighed the far reaching consequences of a global war. The British saw little justification for the Anglo-American intervention in Indo-China and the chances of success were also not bright. London believed that military intervention in Vietnam would probably lead eventually to action against the Chinese mainland. It was recalled that the Americans had failed to turn the tide of war in Indo-China in favour of the French by putting in "nine times more supplies of material than the Chinese" aid to Vietminh. Besides, the Americans were found reluctant to intervene by land forces, "the only effective way" in which aggression could be successfully met. Air and sea power were unlikely to be thoroughly effective substitutes for land forces. Therefore, there appeared no possibility of Western success in Indo-China against an enemy to whom the nuclear threat, though "grave...was not decisive."[108]

The Western Powers could hope to fight the massive land army of China only with the help of Asian manpower combined with American air and naval power. However, the Asiatic countries, particularly India, Burma and Indonesia, were not inclined to cooperate with the West in defence of what they regarded the colonial interests of the Western Powers. In this context, Younger observed :

> The case against international intervention in Indo-China war at the present time is overwhelming. To say that American intervention would call forth increased Chinese intervention, thereby enlarging the war, is only a part, though an important part, of the case. Equally important is the fact that the war in Indo-China differs from the war in Korea in that almost every Asian country has regarded it from the start as a war of liberation from French colonialism. Even the Nationalist Government of China shared this view after 1945, the anti-colonial cry is therefore no mere communist invention.[109]

Eden recognized the difficulty of finding a plausible excuse for Western intervention in the Indo-China war. He stated :

> There was never a national determination against Vietminh in Indo-China comparable to that in Malaya which enabled the jungle war to be won. There was no clear-cut breach of a treaty or international engagement which had to be respected in the world's interests, as there was later when the Suez Canal was seized in defiance of engagements recently renewed, the greatest international waterway passing under the control of one state. In these conditions a massive intervention in the conflict by France's allies could not have been justified, a limited one would have only made matters worse.

For the above-mentioned reasons, Britain was "strongly opposed to any course of action in Southeast Asia which would be likely to result in a war with China" and considered it necessary that "any provocative action must at all costs be avoided."[110]

Britain was not inclined to give any undertaking concerning British military action in Indo-China in advance of the results of the Geneva Conference. In the London Communique of 13 April 1954 Eden agreed with Dulles that attempts by the communist forces in Indo-China to overthrow the "lawful and friendly Government" of South Vietnam and their invasion of Laos and Cambodia "not only threaten those now directly involved, but also endanger the peace and security of the entire area of South East Asia and the Western Pacific, where our

two nations and other friendly and allied nations have vital
interests." However, in the paper prepared by the Foreign
Secretary, it was subsequently clarified that the London Communique did not commit Britain "to join in immediate
discussions on the possibility of Allied intervention in the
Indo-China war."[111]

One can speculate that the Soviet Union stood to gain in a
number of ways by the prolongation of the Indo-China conflict.
In the first place, it committed Western Powers' resources and
energies in a far distant peninsula. Secondly, it ensured
hostility between China and the Western nations. However,
there were reasons to believe that the escalation of the conflict
in Indo-China and the resultant general war would not have
been in Soviet national interests.[112] Ho Chi Minh would have
preferred to fight the war to the finish,[113] but there was little
he could do without the active support of China or the Soviet
Union. It was believed that the Chinese, conscious as they
were of the possible American reaction, would seriously think
of the dangers inherent in a world conflict.[114] Besides, they
could not ignore the racial problems, which were bound to
arise in the event of the whole of Indo-China being brought
under the Chinese communist control.[115] It was, thus,
assumed that Peking would try to restrain the Vietminh and
advise them not to drive the enemy to humiliation and
despair.[116] An indication of the Chinese desire to seek a
negotiated settlement was given by Peking both before and
during the Geneva Conference.

In its editorial of 3 April 1954, the *People's Daily* expressed
its belief that the Geneva Conference "will take a step forward
along the path of international consultation, toward the relaxation of international tension, a step that will lead to durable
peace in the Far East and the rest of the world." The Chinese
paper advised Britain to pursue an "independent foreign
policy" and not "to pull the chestnuts out of fire for the United
States," if it wanted to see the hopes of many of its people
regarding the easing of war tension and the opening of the
road for East-West trade fulfilled. The realization of these
hopes, it stated, would depend upon "the success of the Geneva
Conference." It added : "Clearly this is another testing time
for the ruling circles of these countries and their moves will be

closely watched by peace-loving people throughout the world."
If the UK followed the US policy of "united action" and
hostility toward China, the *People's Daily* warned, then it must
fully take into consideration the consequences of such an
action.[117]

The Geneva Conference

During the Geneva Conference, Chou En-lai agreed with Eden
that the possibility of a negotiated settlement in Indo-China
existed;[118] that the problems of Laos and Cambodia were
different from those of Vietnam, and that "the early and
simultaneous cessation of hostilities throughout Indo-China"
was "the most important and urgent step toward the restoration of peace in Indo-China." Chou En-lai's statement that
"the situations in the three states of Indo-China, namely, Viet
Nam, Khmer and Pathet Lao, are not entirely similar, so that
the measures for settlement will probably not be the same,"[119]
was in marked contrast to Soviet Foreign Minister Molotov's
assertion that "a war of national liberation is being waged, not
merely in Viet Nam, but also in Pathet Lao and Khmer."[120]
Chou En-lai even seemed inclined to abandon the claims of the
Pathet Lao and the Cambodian Communists for recognition in
the same manner as those of the Vietminh. In his statement
of 16 June 1954, he assured Eden that he would persuade
the Vietminh to withdraw from Laos and Cambodia (Chou
stopped short of saying that the Vietminh had invaded these
two states) and that China would recognize their governments
provided no American bases were set up on their territory.

Since Britain seemed hopeful that a negotiated settlement
was possible in the near future, Eden was determined not to
"endorse a bad policy for the sake of unity."[121] British policy
in Indo-China was based on a keen awareness of the dangers
inherent in the escalation of the conflict and a cool appraisal
of "what the prime Western interests in Southeast Asia are,
which of those interests cannot be given up, and how best they
can be upheld."[122] Needless to say, the primary British
interests in the area were the security of Malaya and the
overall stability in the region as a whole. In order to ensure

"an effective barrier as far north of that country [Malaya] as possible"[123] and to cultivate relations with Peking,[124] Britain deemed it necessary to reach a mutually agreed settlement of the Indo-China problem.   However, Britain was aware that any negotiated settlement "was bound to produce either a communist share in the government of most of Indo-China, or complete communist control of part of the country." The Western Powers could not hope to impose a "victor's terms... upon an undefeated enemy."   While both solutions were "disagreeable,"[125] Britain had to choose one. London preferred the second solution because it was felt that if it opted for the first (*i. e.* the establishment of coalition Governments), the communists might eventually come to dominate all the three Associated States of Indo-China. The precedent of Czechoslovakia, Eden said, could not be lost sight of. It would be better if "communism could be held at arm's length, clear of Cambodia and Laos, and halted as far north as possible in Vietnam." Thus, the partition of Vietnam appeared "preferable" since it was "the least damaging solution."[126] In the circumstances, it enabled Britain to terminate the eight-year old war in Indo-China and to cultivate good relations with Peking.   Accordingly, the partition of Vietnam was considered "not appeasement but realism."[127]

The Geneva Agreements of 1954 were not "completely satisfactory" from either the British or the Chinese viewpoint or even from that of the other parties concerned. Nevertheless, the Chinese felt satisfied with the arrangement which ensured that "the three Associated States must be independent, sovereign and neutral "[128] and free from foreign military bases.[129] Thus, China had North Vietnam as a friendly Communist State on its southern border and the possibility of making the whole of Vietnam Communist in the future could not be altogether ruled out. The British felt greatly relieved because the Geneva Agreements safeguarded their interests in Malaya; allowed "free life to some part of Vietnam;" gave "Laos and Cambodia the reality of independence;"[130] and facilitated their task of *rapprochement* with China. Anthony Eden described it "the best bargain" and took pride in the achievements of the Geneva Conference, which, he said, "stopped an eight year war and reduced international tension at a point of instant danger to world peace."[131] The Chinese also welcomed the Geneva Agreements. They paid tributes to the "energetic assistance" rendered by British delegation, which, as the *People's Daily* put it, "played a vital role in arriving at agreement."[132]

After Geneva

The Geneva Agreements put an end to the hostilities in Indo-China for the time being "on acceptable terms," but "the problems of Indo-China were by no means over."[133] The integration of the Pathet Lao in Laotian community and the unification of Vietnam presented serious difficulties and gave rise to new tensions and conflict in subsequent years.

Developments in Laos

The Armistice Agreements provided for the withdrawal of Vietminh troops from Laos but Pathet Lao troops were permitted to concentrate themselves in a regroupment area consisting of the two northeastern provinces of Phongsaly and Sam Neua. The contiguity of these provinces to China and North Vietnam and the mixed character of the population of the region made it difficult to check infiltration of men and material from across the border. Article 14 of the Agreement on the Cessation of Hostilities in Laos said : "Pending a political settlement, the fighting units of 'Pathet Lao,'...shall move into the Provinces of Phongsaly and Sam Neua....They shall be free to move between these two Provinces in a corridor along the frontier between Laos and Viet Nam...."[134] Elections, which were to form the basis of a political settlement in Laos, were held in December 1955. However, the Pathet Lao refused to participate in the elections. Therefore, elections could not be held in the two provinces which were under the control of Pathet Lao. Despite the decision of the International Supervisory Commission in Laos upholding the "Royal Laotian Government's right to administer the provinces of Sam Neua and Phongsaly," Pathet Lao forces continued to obstruct "the practical reunification of the country"[135] and occasionally launched attacks on the Royal Government troops in these provinces. [136] In these circumstances, Britain joined hands with the American and French Governments in presenting identical notes to the Royal Laotian Government on 16 April 1957. The Western Powers welcomed the firmness with which the Kingdom of Laos had resisted Pathet Lao manoeuvers of placing "extraneous conditions" upon their acceptance of the authority of the Royal Government and upon their integration into the national community. The three Western nations expressed their confidence that the Royal Government would continue in its determination that "the political future of the Kingdom of Laos shall not be dictated by dissident groups enjoying no constitutional status."[137]

The Laotian Agreements of November 1957 provided for a coalition government, the transfer of the administration of the two provinces of Sam Neua and Phongsaly to the Royal Laotian Government, and the incorporation of the Pathet Lao units into the Royal army, though Pathet Lao was allowed to maintain an independent organisation of its own. Accordingly, elections were held throughout Laos on 4 May 1958 and a coalition Government was formed. In February 1959, however, Washington supported the rightist Phoumi Nosavan clique's attempts to destroy the coalition Government and to start the civil war again. In the meantime, one Pathet Lao Battalion was integrated in the Royal Laotian Army on 18 May 1959. But the second Battalion, managed to escape. It moved towards the frontier with North Vietnam and grew in strength. A critical situation soon developed, which became the subject of discussion in the UN Security Council.[138]

While China considered Phoui Sananikone Government's action as regards disarming of the two battalions of the former Pathet Lao and other similar activities as "the gravest violations of the Geneva agreements,"[139] London did not think that Laotian Government actions in regard to the integration of two ex-Pathet Lao battalions, in any way, constituted a violation of the Geneva Agreement or the Agreements of November 1957. Britain also refused to support the Soviet suggestion that the International Commission for Laos be reconvened against the wishes of the Laotian Government.[140]

London held Pathet Lao and the North Vietnamese authorities, and not the Laotian Government, responsible for creating the critical "civil war" situation in Laos. Britain also refused to take any action on the Chinese suggestion in regard to the proposed trial of the leaders of the Neo Lao Hak Sat. It considered it to be a matter for the Laotian authorities in which it was improper for other Governments to intervene. The Laotian courts, the British reply to the Chinese note of 31 October 1959 stated, were fully competent to determine whether Neo Lao Hak Sat leaders had broken the law.[141]

In 1959 Britain found the Soviet proposal for a new Geneva Conference unacceptable and upheld the Royal Laotian Government's sovereign right no longer to submit to the supervision of the International Control Commission.[142] London also saw no reason why the United Nations should not deal with the problem or why it should abdicate its competence in favour of a new Geneva Conference. The British note to the Soviet Government dated 9 November 1959 stated that there would be no problem in Laos if the North Vietnamese authorities were to cease their encouragement and assistance to the Pathet Lao rebels and if the latter were to end the rebellion and act in accordance with Laotian law. Britain expressed the hope that all concerned, including the Soviet Government, would use their influence to see that the Geneva Settlement was observed and, in particular, the rebellion was brought to an end. This, the British note observed, would make a far more certain contribution to peace than the holding of a new Geneva Conference.[143]

Britain deplored the uprising of Captain Kong Lae's troops in August 1960. In a statement before the House of Lords on 19 December 1960, the British Foreign Secretary stated that steps should be taken to put a stop to the supply of assistance from outside the country to those who were in rebellion against the legal Government. However, like 1954, the British Government was opposed to direct military intervention on the part of the United States during the Laos crisis of 1960-61. It favoured a political settlement based on the Geneva Agreements —a settlement providing for communist participation in the Laotian Government. Thus, Alec Douglas-Home declared in the House of Lords that ever since the rebellion of Captain

Kong Lae's troops, British policy had been "to try and encourage the Laotians to form a Government of the national union."[144] The British Under Secretary of State criticized US policy in Laos by stating that the USA has done its best to destroy Souvanna Phouma, who represented the best hope of a noncommunist Laos. Washington, he added, was "backing a crooked right-wing gang." The impression of Washington always rushing about to prop up corrupt dictators in Asia, he warned, could not have happy consequences. A reassessment of the situation in Laos in White House, particularly after the installation of J.F. Kennedy as President, ultimately led to an agreement between the US President and the British Premier that while joint military intervention might be necessary in the last resort, a solution should be sought on the lines recommended by London, *i. e.* the formation of a neutral coalition government, including both communists and the extreme right and headed by Souvanna Phouma.[145] The way was thus opened for the conclusion of a ceasefire in Laos and for convening a 14-Nation International Conference on the Settlement of the Laotian Question at Geneva from 12 May 1961 to 23 July 1962.

After 15 months of hard and often frustrating negotiations, the participants in the Conference agreed to recognize, "respect and observe in every way the sovereignty, independence, neutrality, unity and territorial integrity of the Kingdom of Laos."[146] The neutralization of Laos was agreed upon because both Washington and Moscow recognized the futility of bringing Laos under their own exclusive sphere of influence. Pathet Lao was recognized and became a part of troika government in Laos. As a result of the neutralization of Laos, American Programme Evaluation Office (an euphemism for the American military command in Laos) was withdrawn. Neutralization of Laos ensured the decline of Soviet influence. Because of their geographical proximity, Peking and Hanoi continued to retain their influence in Laos. However, the woes of Laotian people were far from over. The attempt of a group of right-wing officers to over-throw Premier Souvanna Phouma, in the abort-*coup* of 19 April 1964, gave rise to a situation which was as menacing to international peace as the one which prevailed in 1960. It is stated that in the absence of active support from the

Western Powers, these officers wereforced to abandon their scheme.[147] In May 1965, Britain joined hands with its allies in the SEATO Council in condemning the presence of North Vietnamese forces in Laos and the use of Laotian territory as a channel for sending men and material to the Viet Cong.[148]

Unification of Vietnam

As regards the unification of Vietnam, the Geneva Agreements provided that elections should be held "under the supervision of an international commission" in July 1956. Consultations concerning these elections were to start from 20 July 1955 onwards. North Vietnam repeatedly urged the holding of such consultations and Peking consistently supported Hanoi in that regard.[149] However, consultations could not be held because the Ngo Dinh Diem Government in South Vietnam, backed by the United States, opposed them. It was believed that due to the disparity in the population of North (13 million) and the South (9 million) Vietnam, the communists would dominate both parts of Vietnam if elections were held. Since Britain's public stand seemed favourable to the holding of consultations for elections in Vietnam under the Geneva Agreements, the *People's Daily* welcomed the "expressed attitude" of the UK as "a step in the right direction."[150] In reality, Britain did not wish to see the *status quo* in Vietnam (the partition of the country along the 17th parallel) disturbed by the violation of the cease-fire agreements even if the elections provided for at Geneva were not held in July 1956. Therefore, London continued to recognize the Saigon regime as the only legal Government of Vietnam, and, accordingly, supported its admission into the United Nations. The reunification of Vietnam, British Foreign Secretary Selwyn Lloyd observed, should be achieved through "genuinely democratic procedures" which "must be agreed by the parties concerned."[151] In February 1962, it was openly stated on behalf of the British Government that conditions did not exist for "free and fair elections" and that the North Vietnamese people would certainly not be able to express their will freely.[152]

Formation of a Defence Organization in Southeast Asia

"The idea of a defence pact for Southeast Asia," Averell Harriman observed in 1954, "had been thought about for some two years" but it was the rapid deterioration of the French position in Indo-China that led to "its sudden revival, just on the eve of the Geneva Conference."[153]   In the summer of 1954, the United States vigorously pressed that idea in the hope that it would "strengthen the negotiating position of the free nations during the Indo-China phase of the Geneva Conference."[154] Britain, on the contrary, believed that while the formation of a defence organization in Southeast Asia "would be unlikely to help us militarily" it would harm "us politically by frightening off important potential allies."[155] The formation of a defence organization in Southeast Asia was more likely to prejudice the successful outcome of the negotiations at Geneva where the Western Powers "were committed to a discussion with the Soviet and Chinese Governments."[156] The British, therefore, wanted to fully explore all possibilities of a negotiated settlement with the Communist Powers[157] before they would commit themselves about the formation of a military alliance in Southeast Asia. Until the final outcome of the Geneva Conference was known, the British would not, at any stage, go beyond examination of the possibility of forming a mutual security system in Southeast Asia.[158]

Eden's Locarno Idea

Action on the formation of the SEATO was also delayed in the hope that the Geneva discussions on the cessation of hostilities in Indo-China might lead to a reciprocal guarantee of the settlement reached.   While an agreed settlement to stop the war in Indo-China was the "immediate task" of the British Government,[159] Eden's efforts at Geneva were not directed solely to the achievement of that aim. He endeavoured to establish "comprehending and friendly contacts with the members of the Conference,"[160] including China. One of the main objectives of the British Government was "to ensure that any acceptable settlement shall be backed by effective international guarantees."[161] Foreign Secretary Eden explained this idea on 23 June 1954 when he suggested that a reciprocal arrangement of the Locarno type might be possible in Southeast Asia. He observed :

> I hope that it will be possible to agree on some system of South-East Asian defence to guard against aggression....We could have a reciprocal arrangement in which both sides take part, such as Locarno. We could also have a defensive alliance such as N.A.T.O. is in Europe, and,...such as the existing Chinese-Soviet Treaty provides for the Far East... These two systems, I admit, are quite different, but they need be in no way inconsistent. My belief is that by refraining from any precipitate move towards the formation of a N. A. T. O. system in South-East Asia, we have helped to create the necessary conditions in which both systems can possibly be brought into being.[162]

In referring to "Locarno," Eden presumably had in mind not exactly a Locarno-type arrangement as such[163] as an agreement under which the whole or part of the Southeast Asian area would be neutralized and reciprocally guaranteed by the communist and non-communist Powers. Besides, he did not think that such an all-embracing arrangement (which included China) excluded a NATO-type collective security pact in Southeast Asia. The dual system of guarantees envisaged by him took into account the possibilities of communist aggression in Southeast Asia, the difficulties of stabilizing the vulnerable frontiers of the countries in the area, and the British desire to reach a *modus vivendi* with China. The purpose of a mutual security pact was to balance the existing Sino-Soviet alliance and to deter and warn a potential aggressor. It assumed that China was an expansionist Power. Eden's "Locarno" idea, on the other hand, was designed to secure peace in Southeast Asia on the basis of mutual trust. Its success depended on the degree of *rapprochement* with China, while the concept of a military bloc gave rise to tension and insecurity. It was, indeed, antithetical to the spirit of peace, which was so characteristic of Eden's proposal. However, the dual system of guarantees, contemplated by Eden, admirably served British interests in the region. It ensured American military support in safeguarding

British territorial possessions and economic interests in the area without alienating the sympathies of India or other Asian countries. At the same time, the idea of gaining China's goodwill was also not abandoned.

Eden was no doubt aware of the difficulties involved in realizing his scheme of reciprocal guarantees by China and the USSR, on the one hand, and the UK, the USA and France, on the other (and perhaps by India and a few other countries as well). He admitted that such an arrangement would not "resolve the problems of the world for all time" because the "ambitions of certain Powers" would not be satisfied. Nevertheless, Eden felt that the concerned States must be persuaded to agree to it "for reasons of coexistence," if for nothing else. He was also hopeful that, if agreed upon, the arrangement "might last." He emphasized the need to have an open mind "in these approaches," and keep an eye on the "differences between the Communist Great Powers" which, he stated, "exist...[though] they are not canvassed."[164] Since Eden's idea admirably suited British interests, he considered it worthwhile to pursue it with vigour and deemed it necessary to justify it even in his *Memoirs*. He observed : "The thought behind the Locarno Pact, that of a reciprocal defensive arrangement in which each member gives guarantees, was a good one and might well be applied to our problems in South-east Asia."[165]

The Americans and the Chinese were probably not enthusiastic about Eden's "Locarno" idea. The Americans objected to it because it did not help in countering the menace of communist subversion. Secondly, it was considered detrimental to the effective working of the mutual security pacts that Washington had so assiduously built over the years in various parts of the world.[166] Washington was also reluctant to guarantee a settlement that signified acceptance of communist domination over North Vietnam. Apparently, the Chinese did not wish their freedom of action to be restricted in a sector where they stood to gain and which afforded them an opportunity to divert the attention of American arms, that confronted Peking in the Korean and Formosan theatres. The Communist Powers, however, did not summarily reject Eden's proposal. They were willing to guarantee the Geneva Agreements *provided* action to implement that guarantee was taken only on the unanimous agreement of all the guarantors. This arrangement, Eden remarked, was "completely unacceptable to us" because it would have introduced "the principle of the veto"[167] and prevented the Western Powers from taking any military action even when the settlement was being violated. Evidently, the Western Powers, particularly the USA, would not want to foreclose the possibility of taking military action when necessary.

Britain Joins SEATO

Since it was not possible to obtain the kind of reciprocal guarantees that it had in mind, London agreed to join the SEATO. It was believed that a military pact would help the Western Powers in guarding against "new adventures...begun on miscalculation which could lead to war."[168] R.H. Turton, Joint Under-Secretary of State for Foreign Affairs, justified the setting up of SEATO in the following words :

> If there were no reciprocal international guarantee possible then it was absolutely vital that there should be the final declaration at the Geneva Conference and some collective safeguard; otherwise there would have been a very dangerous gap in this part of the world at that time.[169]

Britain was not completely satisfied with para 12 of the Final Declaration of the Geneva Conference (21 July 1954) in which "each member of the Geneva Conference," including China, undertook "to respect the sovereignty, the independence, the unity and the territorial integrity" of Cambodia, Laos and Vietnam and "to refrain from any interference in their internal affairs."[170] Britain did not think that the SEATO was "a conclusive answer" to the Soviet Union in that part of the world. Nevertheless, London considered it "valuable" in so far as it provided "the means of warning a potential aggressor that he will meet with the united resistance of the countries that feel themselves threatened, and an assurance that they can pursue their pressing problems of development in comparative security."[171]

British efforts to obtain a Locarno-type arrangement as well as their original plan of a NATO-type military alliance in Southeast Asia failed to materialize. Washington refused to commit its land forces for the defence of Southeast Asia. It preferred to rely primarily on its mobile naval and air power to "strike an aggressor wherever the occasion may demand."[172] As a result, the SEATO could neither have a standing army nor a unified command. Moreover, in the event of aggression, the parties to the Treaty were not bound by an automatic commitment to render military assistance. Each party agreed to meet the "common danger in accordance with its constitutional processes."[173] It was, indeed, a weak provision comparable to the one found in the ANZUS rather than in the NATO.

London had to be content with whatever it could get. However, it suggested certain changes in the American draft of the treaty and these were accepted. Since the words "communist aggression" in the Southeast Asian context referred only to Chinese expansionism, and, for that matter, hampered Sino-British *rapprochement*, Britain insisted that the word "communist" be deleted and "aggression" should remain undefined. While London agreed with the American idea of throwing "some mantle of protection" over Laos, Cambodia and Vietnam[174] (this was done by describing them as designated states for the purposes of Article IV of the Treaty), it succeeded in getting para 3 included in Article IV of the Treaty. Para 3 stated that no action "shall be taken" either against attack or subversion within the territory of these "designated" states "or on any territory so designated...except at the invitation or with the consent of the government concerned."[175] Under the provisions of the Treaty, the signatories committed themselves "to meet the common danger" only in case of an armed attack having taken place within the Treaty area. Under Article VIII of the Treaty, areas "north of 21 degree 30 minutes north latitude" were regarded outside the Treaty area. Thus, the British not only expressed their disagreement with Dulles that Chinese aggression anywhere would mean that Peking had decided on a general war in Asia[176] but also endeavoured to steer clear of Sino-American confrontation in the Formosan Straits.

Even after Britain joined the SEATO, it sought to explain

its membership to Peking by stating that it was not, in any way, deviating from its declared path of seeking a *modus vivendi* with China, but merely taking some necessary steps to safeguard its interests in the region. Speaking at the Bangkok Conference of SEATO Powers on 23 February 1955, Foreign Secretary Eden observed :

> In the sphere of defence our activities threaten no one. They form part of an effort to improve and strengthen our defense in a part of the world where it is clearly needed. The work done under this treaty can be an important contribution to these ends. We in Britain recognize, of course, that it is not the only contribution. There are many ways of strengthening peace; we wish them all well and support them wherever we can. We will always strive to extend the area of peaceful cooperation among the nations. But, at the same time, in the present state of the world, it is right and prudent that those with a common interest in the preservation of peace in a particular part of the world should work together in accordance with the Charter of the United Nations for their own common defense and welfare. To do so is a wise precaution and not a resounding menace.[177]

Chinese Reaction

The Chinese were not convinced of the British argument that SEATO was not directed against them. As early as 6 August 1954, the *People's Daily* commentator Wu warned that by participating in the organization of "a military bloc" in Southeast Asia, the UK was not only following "the U.S. policy of hostility to the Chinese people" but also "sacrificing its own national interests to the U.S." Wu referred to Anthony Eden's statement of 22 July 1954 (in that statement Eden had expressed the hope that the armistice in Indo-China "will lead to better relations elsewhere") and observed : "Active British support of the U.S. Southeast Asian aggressive bloc is contrary to its professed desire for peaceful coexistence and 'very unwise'...No good can come of following this U.S. policy."[178] Chou En-lai accused Britain of creating new obstacles to the improvement of Sino-British relations by becoming a member of SEATO. He criticized London for its failure "to make efforts to promote peaceful cooperation between China and Britain."[179] Peking had no misgivings about SEATO, which, it believed, was "directed against the People's Republic of China."[180] Commenting on the Bangkok Conference of SEATO Powers in February 1955, the *People's Daily* pointed out that the "intensified U.S. activities to undermine the Geneva Agreements seriously threatened not only peace in Indo-China but also China's security." It asserted that "the U.S. policy to sabotage the Geneva Agreements has the support of Britain and the approval of France" and warned these countries by stating that they "must bear full responsibility for the consequences of their efforts to sabotage the Geneva Agreements."[181] On 8 March 1955, the Observer's article in the *People's Daily* criticized the London Press Service for attempting "to create the impression that the inclusion of Laos, Cambodia and South Viet-Nam in the S.E.A.T.O. treaty was not violation of the Geneva Agreements." "The London Press Service," the article added, "is trying to whitewash British action in following the United States along the dangerous path of wrecking the Geneva Agreements."[182]

Vietnam Conflict in the 1960s

In view of the Russo-Chinese emphasis on peaceful coexistence in the mid-1950s, elections for the reunification of Vietnam were indefinitely postponed and the *status quo* in Vietnam was tacitly accepted by the Big Powers. Thus, in the message addressed to the two Governments of Vietnam on 8 May 1956, the Soviet Co-Chairman of the Geneva Conference agreed with his British counterpart that pending the holding of free general elections for the reunification of Vietnam, the two Co-Chairmen attached great importance to the maintenance of the cease-fire under the continued supervision of the International Commission for Vietnam.[183] However, in 1959 the Communist Party of North Vietnam resolved to liberate South Vietnam. The establishment of the National Liberation Front (NLF) in South Vietnam in December 1960 heralded the beginning of the liberation struggle. The British Government disagreed with the view that what was happening in South Vietnam was "the action of an oppressed rebel minority." London considered communist attempts to reunite the country by force "intolerable." What is taking place in South Vietnam now, Britain stated, was "a calculated Communist take-over bid...it is quite clearly directed and assisted from North Vietnam." Britain expressed its understanding of the American view that if Hanoi stopped its campaign to destroy the Republic of Vietnam the steps which the United States was taking to assist the South Vietnamese in their defence efforts would no longer be necessary.[184] The British Government also sent a small mission under a former Malayan civil servant, R.G.K. Thompson, to advise the Ngo Dinh Diem Government in Saigon on the civil and administrative aspects of the South Vietnamese efforts against the guerillas.[185] After the Tonkin Gulf incident (August 1964), Washington became deeply involved in the Vietnam conflict. Bombing of North Vietnam was commenced in February 1965. The Pentagon Papers, which were published in June 1971, revealed that the "secret war" phase culminating in the final US commitment in 1965 began six months before the Tonkin Gulf incident. The British Government expressed public support for the American action in the Tonkin Gulf by stating that it was an exercise of the essential right of self-defence and fully consistent with the UN Charter.[186]

The American decision to bomb North Vietnam was conveyed to Prime Minister Wilson as early as December 1964 during his visit to Washington. Apparently, the British Government felt reconciled to the US action and had no sympathy for the solution propounded by the Communist Powers, namely, that the United States unconditionally withdraw from the area. London expressed the view that the American action did not increase the danger of the situation in Vietnam and that it was a legitimate reaction to the help given by the Vietnamese in the North to the Vietnamese guerillas in the South. In his statement before the House of Commons on 1 April 1965, the Secretary of State for Foreign Affairs found fault not with Washington but with Hanoi for seeking to achieve its ends by direct action in preference to accepting a Conference from which a compromise could emerge. He expressed his understanding of the American position that the USA could not stop its bombing unless there was a

satisfactory assurance by North Vietnam that it was prepared
to cease attacks on the South and willing to consider a compromise, negotiated settlement.[187] The SEATO Council Communique of 5 May 1965 denounced in strong terms the aggression against South Vietnam "organised, directed, supplied and
supported by the Communist regime in North Vietnam." It
also affirmed its view that the defeat of the communist attack
on South Vietnam was essential to the security of Southeast
Asia as a whole and welcomed the American determination to
support the Saigon regime and, at the same time, to enter into
negotiations provided these were unconditional.[188] On 13
May 1965, the British Prime Minister supported the SEATO
point of view and expressed regret that the Communist Powers,
including China and the Soviet Union, showed no readiness
"to consider a negotiated settlement on anything but their
own unacceptable terms."[189] Hanoi, the British Secretary of
State stated, should openly declare that it was prepared to
negotiate, without first demanding the withdrawal of all
American forces. "If we ask for the cessation of United States
action against North Vietnam," he added, "we must in the
same breath and with the same emphasis ask for the stopping
of North Vietnamese infiltration against the South."[190]

In his telegram (dated 3 June 1965) to President Johnson,
Wilson expressed his sympathy with the former's efforts in the
direction of a negotiated settlement of the Vietnam problem.
Wilson, however, reiterated the earlier stand of dissociating
Britain from American bombing of oil storage depots near
Hanoi and Haiphong.[191] It was quite obvious that, unlike
1954, the USA was not at all amenable to British influence in
1964-65. It might be recalled that in January 1954 President
Eisenhower had approved a contingency plan to extend the
hostilities against China in order to save both the French from
defeat and the whole of Southeast Asia from communist
domination. But he disapproved of American intervention in
the conflict "except on a coalition basis with active British
Commonwealth participation." In 1954-55, Anthony Eden,
who was very perturbed at the prospect of the use of atomic
weapons and the conflict in Indo-China becoming "a bigger
affair than Korea,"[192] was able to prevail upon Washington to
restrain itself. In the 1960s, however, the British were in no

position to influence American decisions or to uphold a policy running directly contrary to that of their American partners.

Although the underlying objective of British policy had remained the same, namely to defuse the Indo-Chinese powder barrel, even if this meant recognizing the permanence of communist power in a large part of former Indo-China, there was a marked difference in the British attitude during 1960s as compared with 1954. In 1954 Britain's weight was thrown openly against American military intervention. But during the 1960s, both Conservative and Labour Governments, while still refusing to commit British forces to the defence of Vietnam or Laos and still expressing certain reservations about US policy towards Indo-China, gave it their moral support. Because of the sharpening conflict between the demands of the Anglo-American special relationship, prompting support for American escalation, and the demands of London's own order of priorities, prompting search for a political settlement, Maclean observes, the course of British diplomacy became increasingly tortuous and contradictory, so much so that at home it in the end aroused widespread opposition and contempt.[193]

British Proposals

The British Labour government combined mild protests against American bombing in Vietnam with certain proposals, which were unimpressive in form and ineffective in content. At a time when it was deeply entangled in the Indonesian-Malyasian confrontation in Borneo and stood in need of American help, Britain could ill afford to undercut American resolution in Vietnam. It appeared that despite initial reluctance on Washington's part, Premier Wilson and President Johnson eventually struck a bargain in December 1964, whereby American support for British policy in Malaysia was expressly balanced against British support for American policy in Vietnam.[194] The British proposals, therefore, were designed to help Washington to extricate itself out of a difficult situation and to silence opposition at home, particularly the vociferous members within the Labour Party. These proposals, it seemed, were

probably cleared with the US authorities beforehand and, therefore, treated by the latter as at worst innocuous, and at best
helpful, to their own policy. On 29 June 1966, Wilson and
his colleagues publicly regretted that US aircraft had attacked
"targets touching on the populated areas of Hanoi and
Haiphong" and dissociated themselves from that action. But,
at the same time, they reaffirmed their support for American
policy in Vietnam as a whole and considered that only Hanoi
and not Washington bore the onus of continuing the war.[195]

On Harold Wilson's initiative, the Commonwealth Prime
Ministers' Conference in June 1965 resolved that a mission,
composed of the leaders of some Commonwealth countries,
should "make contact with the Governments principally concerned with the problem of Vietnam in order to ascertain how
far there may be common ground about the circumstances in
which a conference might be held leading to the establishment
of a just and lasting peace in Vietnam."[196] The Commonwealth Mission, comprising Britain, Ghana, Nigeria and
Trinidad and Tobago and headed by Wilson, was expected to
visit Washington, Moscow, Peking, Hanoi and Saigon in its
quest for peace in Vietnam. Both Hanoi and Peking rejected
that proposal and, therefore, the idea of a peace mission was
soon given up. Chou En-lai denounced the proposed Commonwealth peace mission as a "hoax" designed to help the US to
"hang on in South Vietnam." The Chinese Premier observed :
"As Co-Chairman of the Geneva Conference, Britain has not
only failed to check United States acts of aggression in fulfilment of her duty, but has consistently supported them."[197] In
April-May 1965, it might be recalled, the Chinese and North
Vietnamese Governments had refused to see Gordon Walker.

At the Labour Conference held in Brighton on 6 October
1966, Foreign Secretary Brown made another set of
proposals and followed them up at the UN General Assembly.
He expected that at his meeting with his Soviet counterpart in
New York, he would be able to show some dramatic results.
There was, however, no chance whatsoever of any success in
the matter because the Russians demanded that the cessation
of American bombing of North Vietnam should be absolute
and unconditional. Commenting on Brown's proposals,
Izvestia asserted that their purpose was to force the victims of

American aggression to agree to talks under duress. Unlike June 1966, when Premier Wilson was courageous enough to oppose American bombing of Hanoi and Haiphong, London maintained (in December 1966) a discreet silence inspite of pressure from Members of Parliament and others.[198] Widespread dissatisfaction amongst the M.P.s in particular and the public in general, however, compelled Foreign Secretary Brown to take some initiative in the matter. On 31 December 1966, he sent out messages to the USA and to the Foreign Ministers of South and North Vietnam urging that a meeting of the members of the three countries take place at once to arrange the cessation of hostilities. Such a proposal stood no chance of success. Only the Government of South Vietnam came out with a positive response. President Johnson was "delighted" with the British proposal, but other American observers felt that it was nothing more than a gimmic, dictated by domestic Party considerations. Moscow dubbed it as a "manoeuvre." Hanoi Radio described Brown a messenger of the United States and dismissed his peace initiative as "an attempt to deceive world opinion." To Peking, the British appeared tied to the apron-strings of American policy and seemed incapable of taking any forthright stand on Vietnam—a stand that would be independent of Washington's position. China, therefore, found London of little use or no consequence.

Chinese Reaction

Foreign Minister Chen Yi conceded that Britain and America did not hold identical views on some concrete measures in the Vietnam war. Yet, he emphasized that there existed "no fundamental difference" between them when "it comes to the question of consolidating the world colonial system."[199] Peking regarded British role in Vietnam in the 1960s as subservient to the USA. Tung Fang-hsiang's article entitled "Britain's Shaky Labour Government" described the Wilson government as "the weakest, most unstable and most unpopular administration Britain has had since the end of World War II." He considered it "British monopoly capital's faithful watch-dog" and an active accomplice of US imperialism in Vietnam. The Labour government, Tung observed, supported US bombing and the use of poison gas in Vietnam; allowed the use of Hong Kong as a base of operations for US aggression; slavishly backed the US in escalating its war against Vietnam; and did everything in its power to popularize the Johnson Administration's "peace talks" hoax. Tung believed that the sharp decline in Britain's international position was the direct result of the Labour government's "reactionary home and foreign policies" and increasing dependence on the United States.[200] The *People's Daily* commentary of 18 February 1966 recalled Wilson's anti-China outcries of 1964 (when he accused China of engaging in subversion in Africa) and 1965 (when he criticized China's nuclear strength as posing a serious threat to neighbouring countries and considered Peking's role in the Indo-Pakistan conflict as fishing in troubled waters). It also referred to Wilson's 8 February 1966 statement in the House of Commons "applauding the resumption of U.S. bombing of North Vietnam...extolling the U.S. 'peace talks' swindle" and openly attacking China by insinuating that it was the "enemy of peace" and the "enemy of negotiations."[201]

Commenting on Wilson's talks in Moscow with Premier Kosygin in February 1966, the *People's Daily* Commentator laid bare the whole record of Anglo-Soviet collaboration in the service of US aggression and the "peace talks" swindle in Vietnam. In that connection, he referred to the February 1965 proposal about convening an international conference without preconditions on a so-called "peaceful solution" of the Vietnam question. He also referred to the April 1965 proposal in regard to the convening of an international meeting to discuss the Cambodian question, the aim of which was said to be to smuggle in Johnson's "unconditional discussions" on the Vietnam question. The so-called British Commonwealth "peace mission," the Chinese Commentator pointed out, was set up in June 1965 in order to sell Washington's "peace talks" formula. During his visit to Moscow, Foreign Secretary Michael Stewart urged the convening of a "conference of all the governments concerned" by Britain and the Soviet Union. Thus, the British Labour government was seen energetically serving "a faithful lackey of U.S. imperialism on the Vietnam question." By collaborating and taking united action with "such a notorious U.S. flunkey," the Commentator observed, "the Soviet leadership evidently also wants to give the Johnson Administration as much help as it can in promoting the 'peace talks' hoax." The duties of the Co-Chairmen of the Geneva Conference, the Chinese Commentator reminded, were to uphold the Geneva Agreements, which American imperialism had mutilated by its naked aggression against Vietnam. But instead of halting that aggression, the Co-Chairmen were seen as helping the Johnson Administration peddle its "peace talks" swindle. And instead of demanding the immediate withdrawal of American troops from South Vietnam, the Co-Chairmen "urge the Vietnamese people to stop their resistance." The Chinese Commentator remarked that this showed that the two Co-Chairmen were not at all interested in solving the Vietnam question on the basis of upholding the Geneva Agreements, but wanted the Vietnamese people to tolerate the occupation of South Vietnam by the United States and accept the division of the country. Acting in that manner, the Commentator added, the Co-Chairmen had long abandoned the proper stand they ought to take and had "degenerated into the assistants of the U.S. imperialists in their aggression against Vietnam."[202]

Wilson's hurried visit to the Soviet Union in July 1966 was also criticized in the Chinese press. A commentary, entitled "Peddling U.S. Peace Talks Fraud : Wilson's Unsavoury Role," described British and Soviet leaders as "running errands for the U.S. policy of aggression in Vietnam." The British Labour government, the Chinese commentary pointed out, had allowed its airforce to transport military supplies for the US aggressors in South Vietnam. Moreover, Britain sent a medical team to South Vietnam; placed Hong Kong at the disposal of Washington to be used as a base for the war of aggression against Vietnam; and virulently attacked China, "which firmly supports the Vietnamese people's struggle to resist U.S. aggression and save their country." Wilson, the Chinese commentary added, attacked Chou En-lai by name for his just stand on the Vietnam question and openly urged the British public to demonstrate in front of the Office of the Chinese *charge d'affaires* in London.[203]

Premier Kosygin's discussions with British leaders in February 1967 were, likewise, viewed with grave misgivings in the Chinese press. The British Labour Government was described as "a notorious broker for the U.S. 'peace talks' scheme" while Kosygin was criticized for his "open betrayal of the Vietnamese people." The Wilson-Kosygin talks, it was stated, were mainly aimed at stamping out the Vietnamese people's struggle against US aggression and for national salvation, and at stepping up the formation of a counter-revolutionary "holy alliance" against China. The direct tele-communications link between the Kremlin and Whitehall, it was further believed, would help them to carry on "their counter-revolutionary collusion."[204] Similarly, the British move to set up joint US-British military bases, including Diego Garcia, in the Indian Ocean was said to be motivated by the desire to encircle China and to fill the "dangerous gap" between the US 7th Fleet cruising in the South China Sea and the US 6th Fleet in the Mediterranean in order to suppress the national liberation struggles in Southeast Asia and areas around the Indian Ocean.[205] Wilson's discussions with President Johnson in Washington in February 1968 were also criticized in the Chinese press.[206]

Recent Developments, 1970-75

The extension of the war in Vietnam into Cambodia in the summer of 1970 was the subject of extensive debate in the British House of Commons. Members of the Opposition considered American action to be in violation of Cambodia's territorial integrity and, therefore, desired that it be condemned. The leaders of the British Government and M.P.s from the ruling party, on the other hand, endorsed the American move because they were convinced that the United States had no intention to either conquer North Vietnam or to escalate the conflict. Washington, they felt, was only interested in protecting the sovereignty of South Vietnam. The British Government seemed to accept the domino theory argument that if the communists succeeded in conquering Vietnam and the rest of Indo-China, they would also prevail in the whole of Southeast Asia. Cambodia, it was stated, outflanked Vietnam and, therefore, if the US withdrew its troops from there the fall of

South Vietnam to the communists could not be prevented. Furthermore, it was recognized that since it was only 20 minutes flying time from Vietnam to Singapore, developments in Vietnam and Cambodia had direct relevance to British interests in Malaysia and Singapore.

It was, thus, evident that the British Government was not prepared to find fault with American violations of the territorial integrity of Cambodia, which Prime Minister Harold Wilson stated, had already been "breached systematically and over a period of time" by the communists. He held both sides responsible for the extension of hostilities into Cambodia. Foreign Secretary Stewart openly denounced North Vietnamese and Viet Cong forces for using considerable parts of the territories of Laos and Cambodia in order to improve their military position in Vietnam, and thereby spreading the war into those states. He also found fault with the authorities in Hanoi for not adopting a constructive attitude during the Paris Peace Talks. The areas into which American forces had recently entered, Stewart remarked, could not be regarded in any real sense "neutral" areas since for a long time no Cambodian authority had either functioned or exercised effective control over those areas. They were, in fact, used by the communist forces for administration, command, control, supply and retraining purposes. Keeping these things in mind, he felt that there was no justification for condemning the US alone. Since the British Parliament had not condemned "earlier violations of Cambodian neutrality," Stewart did not think it was "sensible, logical, or, what matters most, constructive towards peace for us now to make a single pronouncement on the actions of the United States." The British Government saw no change in the American policy of Vietnamisation and of ending the war through negotiation at the Conference table. However, London could not but express concern about the resumption of bombing of North Vietnam and the extension of conflict into Cambodia. The British Premier was not sure as to "whether a decision taken with the declared end of achieving peace more quickly may not sometimes set in train both on the ground in the area concerned and more widely through world reaction, other events which are difficult to control." In short, a limited extension of the area of fighting might not remain limited either in area or in time. Prime Minister Wilson, therefore, emphasized the need of arriving at an agreed and negotiated settlement at the Conference table. He also advocated withdrawal of *all* foreign troops from the Cambodian and Vietnamese soil. He further recognized "the undeniable, very much wider fact which overlies all conflict in Asia" that the conflict of Southeast Asia, and every manifestation of that conflict, could not be decided on a world scale without the representation on a world scale, at the United Nations, of the Chinese Government and the Chinese people.[207]

After Sino-British relations visibly improved following the agreement on the exchange of ambassadors in March 1972, the British Government was careful not to speak of the Chinese role in Southeast Asia in critical terms. Thus, during the first ever visit of a British Minister from the Foreign Office to China, Anthony Royle did not deem it proper to discuss the embarrassing Vietnam question at all in the Great Hall of the People.[208] Obviously, the British did not wish to jeopardise their relations with China for the sake of Vietnam. The Chinese also became circumspect in criticizing Britain for its pro-US attitude in Vietnam.

The British Government felt "immensely relieved" when an agreement on ending the war and the restoration of peace in Vietnam was reached on 27 January 1973. The British Foreign Secretary congratulated the Governments concerned for their success in bringing about that agreement which, he said, "if observed in good faith, appears to offer the prospect of peace at last." Because of nearly three decades of war and near war, the history of Indo-China, the British Foreign Secretary stated, gave little scope for easy optimism. However, there was opportunity to achieve an enduring peace, and to extend the settlement into the neighbouring countries of Laos and the Khmer Republic (Cambodia). Britain, he added, had a definite role to play as Co-Chairman with the Soviet Union in securing the future peace of Laos and that Chou En-lai had been informed of this particular responsibility of Britain during his visit to Peking.[209]

The Paris Agreements on Vietnam of 27 January 1973 were subsequently endorsed and supported by an International Conference on Vietnam held in Paris from 26 February to 2 March

1973. Britain participated in it and signed the Act of the Conference. Speaking at the initialling ceremony on 1 March 1973, the Under Secretary of State for Foreign and Commonwealth Affairs, Anthony Royle, observed : "No document, no words, indeed, no conference, can ensure the maintenance of peace in Vietnam. This...must rest with the parties concerned on the ground. If they are determined that the Agreement will work, it will. If they are not so determined, it will not."[210]

In his statement before the House of Commons, Royle stated that Britain was not fully satisfied with the "reporting arrangements" instituted by the Act of the Conference; that the situation in Vietnam continued to be "very delicate"; and that a total end to all acts of hostility had yet to be achieved. However, he expressed the hope that Khmers would come together to settle their differences by peaceful rather than military means and that fighting in Laos would cease and that foreign troops would be withdrawn from Laos within 60 days. He explained that as far as he knew "the foreign forces in Cambodia today are North Vietnamese forces" and that Chinese forces were not involved.[211]

The Paris Agreements of 1973 proved to be a stop-gap arrangement. Ultimately, the problem of Indo-China was resolved in April-May 1975 when the Vietcong gained power in South Vietnam, the Khmer Rouge defeated the pro-US government in Cambodia and Laos succumbed to the controlling influence of the Pathet Lao. On 8 June 1975, the North Vietnamese National Assembly declared Hanoi to be the capital of United Vietnam, thereby confirming *de facto* reunification after more than 20 years.

CHAPTER SIX

Hong Kong

Writing about Hong Kong on the eve of communist victory in China, Lewis Gen observed :

> Of all the foreign settlements and concessions originally wrested from China, Hong Kong now remains the only foreign colony (barring the tiny Portugal one of Macao) yet to be returned. This is in the mind of every Chinese, the question being only how and when.[1]

The position today is not very different from what it was in October 1949 when the above-mentioned words were written. Peking has stated that Hong Kong will in due course return to China. It has frequently warned Britain to refrain from using Hong Kong for the purposes of subversive activities against China, and, at times, had used its political and economic leverage there to cause serious difficulties for the British colonial administration. But the Chinese leaders have not so far attempted to recover the colony either through resort to force or by negotiation. However, that does not, in any way, imply that Peking would continue to tolerate the existence of this colonial possession for all time to come.

Hong Kong is geographically, ethnically, culturally, and historically an integral part or "a segment of China."[2] The colony is in every way highly vulnerable—politically owing to the close ties of the population with the People's Republic, economically because of its dependence on the latter for food and water supplies, and militarily since it is indefensible against attack from that quarter. The British Government, therefore, desired a good working relationship between China and Britain and China and Hong Kong and took care to abstain from any provocative words or deeds.[3] Nevertheless, on certain issues (*e, g-,* regulations on the immigration of Chinese nationals in Hong Kong, the deportation of communist symathizers, and suppression of communist newspapers and educational under- takings) Peking has denounced the Hong Kong British authori- ties for what it had called unfriendly and hostile acts. To a certain extent, such an attitude on the part of China could perhaps justify the remarks that it offered "a clue...of ultimate intent to seize Hong Kong."[4] But hitherto the Chinese have kept their reservations and future plans to themselves and have found it expedient to maintain the *status quo.*

Britain had refused to consider any abdication of its autho- rity and responsibilities in Hong Kong partly because of its profitability. In 1965, for instance, earnings on direct British capital investment in the colony of 400 sq. miles, estimated at £7.4 million were comparable to those from the whole of Nigeria and more than those from Ghana. Britain's precarious position as regards Hong Kong was quite evident from the geographical location of the colony, the racial composition of its popoulation (98% of its total population of four million are Chinese), the inadequacy of its water supply, and its dependence upon the mainland both for water and food supply[5] and in matters of trade as well.[6] London, therefore, could not afford to antagonize Peking. Accordingly, an important objective of British diplomacy had been to prolong British tenure of Hong Kong for as long as possible.

Historical Perspective

Situated on the southeast coast of China, the British colony consists of the island of Hong Kong, Kowloon, and what is commonly known as the New Territories, which had been acquired at different dates and held under dissimilar treaty provisions. The island of Hong Kong spans an area of 29 square miles and is separated from the mainland by one of the finest natural harbours in the world. It came under British possession in January 1841. The Treaty of Nanking (29 August 1842), that brought the First Opium War of 1839-42 to an end, recognized its cession in full sovereignty to the British Crown.[7] The peninsula of Kowloon (area $3\frac{1}{4}$ sq. miles) is situated on the mainland and just across the island of Hong Kong. It was added, alongwith Stonecutters island ($\frac{1}{4}$ sq. miles), to the colony of Hong Kong by the Convention of Peking, 1860.[8] Under a subsequent Convention (signed at Peking on 9 June 1898), Britain acquired on 99-year lease $365\frac{1}{2}$ sq. miles of territory called the New Territories.   These Territories consisted of all the imme- diately adjacent mainland and numerous islands in the vicinity, such as Lantau, Lamma and Cheung Chou. The Convention of 1898 ceded the largest chunk of territory to Britain containing most of the colony's arable land, fishing centres, railways, water reservoirs, mining areas and manufacturing industries. It also defined the rights of the Chinese in and around Kowloon. The Convention provided :

> It is...agreed that within the city of Kowloon the Chinese officials now stationed there shall continue to exercise juris- diction except so far as may be inconsistent with the mili- tary requirements for the defence of Hong Kong. Within the remainder of the newly-leased territory Great Britain shall have sole jurisdiction. Chinese officials and people shall be allowed as heretofore to use the road from Kowloon to Hsinan. It is further agreed that the existing landing place near Kowloon city shall be reserved for the conve- nience of Chinese men-of-war, merchant and passenger vessels, which may come and go and lie there at their plea- sure; and for the convenience of movement of the officials and people within the city....The area leased to Great Britain...includes the waters of Mirs Bay and Deep Bay, but it is agreed that Chinese vessels of war, whether neutral or otherwise, shall retain the right to use those waters.[9]

Out of a population of over 3 million at the end of 1960, more than 99% were of Chinese origin. The geographical location of the colony and the Chinese component of its popu- lation make Hong Kong not only militarily indefensible[10] but also easily susceptible to political changes on the mainland. Thus, the anti-foreigner movement, which marked the Kuo- mintang's rise to power in 1922, was reflected in Hong Kong by considerable social unrest. A seamen's strike occurred in the same year, and in 1925-26 there was a serious general strike and boycott "plainly engineered from Canton."[11] The for- mer paralysed the harbour while the trade boycott of Hong

Kong, "with a mass withdrawal of the Chinese working population there, nearly ruined the colony and wrecked its trade."[12] These events showed beyond doubt that Hong Kong could not remain insulated from the widespread popular resentment on the mainland against the privileged status of the foreigners. However, it did not, in any way, signify that China had launched a movement for the recovery of the British colony. Such a question arose only during World War II, when the United States desired that Hong Kong be transferred to China[13] and the Western Powers agreed to surrender their special privileges in China by the Treaty of 1943. On the one hand, the renunciation of extra-territorial rights on the mainland made Britain anxious to retain Hong Kong as a "place of confidence, where business and similar transactions can be carried out."[14] On the other hand, it kindled hopes among the Chinese about taking possession of Hong Kong at the end of the war in the Pacific and thereby to do away with "the sole visible reminder of the old 'unequal treaty' system." The restoration of British rule in Hong Kong after the war appeared "by no means certain."[15] Chiang Kai-shek protested against British attempts to reestablish their authority in Hong Kong in 1945 by despatching Rear-Admiral Sir Cecil Harcourt with warships from the British Pacific Fleet to accept the surrender of Japanese troops in Hong Kong and proclaim British control over the island. In the circumstances, Harcourt accepted the surrender of the Japanese in Hong Kong on behalf of both British and Chinese Governments.[16]

The British authorities suspected that movement of Chinese troops to Kowloon to board ships for service in Manchuria was part of a Chinese attempt to take over the colony. The transfer of power from the military to civilian authorities (which was scheduled to have taken place on 1 April 1946), was postponed till 1 May 1946.[17] The agitation in China for the return of the colony continued throughout the remaining period of Nationalists' rule and, therefore, Britain's relations with Chiang Kai-shek remained tense. In January 1946 there were student demonstrations in Nanking and Shanghai. The Kuomintang also endeavoured to assert its control over the trade union movement, the teachers organization, and the newspapers of the colony.[18]

Kowloon City Incident of 1948

In January 1948 the forcible eviction of about 2,000 Chinese squatters from Kowloon City as "precautionary measures against epidemic diseases and fire"[19] was the cause of acute friction between the British and the Nationalist Government of China. It gave rise to an anti-British movement in China and produced riots not only in Hong Kong but also in Canton, where the office of the British Consulate and the premises of some British firms were burnt down. The Chinese Government emphatically reiterated its jurisdictional rights in the City of Kowloon on the basis of the provisions of the 1898 Convention,[20] which were interpreted differently by the British and the Chinese. The British Government insisted that Chinese jurisdiction of the city came to an end with the withdrawal of the "Chinese officials now stationed there," who were compelled to leave the city in 1899 by force of arms and under protest. The Chinese Government, on the other hand, contended that the term "Chinese officials" included not only persons then holding office in the city but all their successors as well. It held that the provision about the Chinese officials continuing to exercise jurisdiction in Kowloon "except so far as may be inconsistent with the military requirements for the defence of Hong Kong" was only a limitation on the exercise of the duties of the said Chinese officials and not a condition on the continuation of Chinese jurisdiction there. The Chinese reply note of 5 February 1948 to the British further added :

> China yielded to the force of circumstances by agreeing only to meet the military requirements of the Powers concerned without renouncing her jurisdiction in the respective reserved areas. That the failure of Great Britain to observe even this reservation in respect of Kowloon, which stands now as the last vestige of an outmoded system, would have the most unfortunate repercussions in China may well be imagined.[21]

Since the Hong Kong British authorities could not possibly afford to displease China, they tried to repair the damage done by the "Kowloon City Incident." As a "gesture of cooperation and friendliness," they "responded to an urgent appeal in November for assistance from Shanghai by the immediate despatch on loan of 10,000 tons of rice to relieve a critical food shortage which had arisen" there. They also warned "dissident Chinese political groups out of sympathy with the Chinese Government" that they should not abuse the privilege of asylum and the freedom of press and of speech they enjoyed by attacking "in immoderate terms the established Government of China." On 18 October 1948 the China-Hong Kong Customs Agreement for the prevention of smuggling was finalized. It permitted the Chinese Maritime Customs to maintain collecting stations in Hong Kong and Kowloon and to patrol specified areas in Deep Bay and Mirs Bay. These and similar other concessions, the British Colonial Office Report for the year 1948 stated, represented "a considerable derogation of sovereignty on the part of Hong Kong" and were "a real and concrete gesture of goodwill towards China in her post-war difficulties."[22]

Trade with Nationalist China

In coming to terms with Chiang in 1948, even at some "sacrifice," Britain took into consideration the vital role that Hong Kong could play in promoting trade relations with China. It also recognized the fact that "Hong Kong's economic future is so closely linked with economic developments in China, and particularly in south and west China, that in most respects the two must be considered together." However, American predominance in Chinese markets in the immediate post-war years, the chaotic political conditions in China and the stringent import controls and restrictions[23] (these led to the "grave reduction in Hong Kong's trade" with China, the stockpiling of commodities, the fall in prices and recession in trade[24]) were matters of serious concern to Britain. The silver lining in the dark clouds was increased trade with North China,[25] which was then in communist hands. This seemed to augur happy tidings for the future. However, the Nationalist blockade of Chinese ports, which was proclaimed in June 1949, threatened to undermine the prospects of expanded trade with North China. Nevertheless, the Colonial Office Report on Hong

Kong for the year 1949 was optimistic. It was in marked contrast to the gloomy 1948 report which forecasted that "no improvement in the China trade can be expected in the near future."[26] It stated :

> Before the normal pattern of trade was disrupted by the outbreak of the Sino-Japanese war in 1937, over 40% of the Colony's total trade was conducted with China, and it is true to say that in the long run, the trade of the Colony must continue to be linked with that of China, whatever temporary shifts in pattern have been brought about by the unsettled conditions prevailing in that country during the past few years....The Colony's trade for 1949 showed a great increase over 1948, which had itself been considered a boom year....Trade has risen steadily throughout the year. At the time when Shanghai was occupied by the communists, much cargo originally consigned to that port was off-loaded in Hong Kong, leading to acute shortage of godown space. This situation was aggravated by the subsequent Nationalist blockade, but later on much of the cargo in question was shipped to Tientsin, and goods are once again on the move. One of the most interesting features of the year's trade has been the rapidly mounting volume of trade with North China, which indicates that a brighter future may be in store for the Colony in its trade relations with China, which have been so adversely affected by the past four years of civil war in that country....The steady decrease in trade with China, which has been the most disturbing feature of the post-war period was arrested in 1949. Imports from China increased by 38% over the previous year, whilst exports to China more than doubled. The change of government in China had resulted in change in the nature of the Colony's exports to that country, raw materials and industrial merchandise having taken the place of consumer goods and general cargo. It is to be hoped that the return of more settled conditions to China will cause a gradual swing back towards the Colony's traditional trade pattern.[27]

Communist Take-over in China and After

With the establishment of the People's Republic of China, prospects of trade with China considerably improved.[28] Peking did not question British treaty rights in Hong Kong[29] and embarked on an ambitious programme of industrialization of the country. Moreover, it appeared keen to cultivate mutually beneficial economic relations with all countries of the world, the capitalist nations included. Hong Kong could not afford to indulge in quarrels with Communist China any more than with the Kuomintang. Since an armed attack upon the colony seemed "very improbable,"[30] it was imprudent on the part of British authorities in Hong Kong to unnecessarily pick up quarrels with the Peking regime. However, since a time of change is a time of potential danger, Britain deemed it necessary to despatch "substantial reinforcements,"[31] as a precautionary measure against military adventures and in order to strengthen the law and order situation in the colony; adopted certain other security measures;[32] and took steps to curb the activities of Chinese personages and groups,[33] and to restrict the large inflow of Chinese immigrants into Hong Kong.[34] Although the British military reinforcements were "sufficient to put the colony on a war footing,"[35] they were, in no way, adequate for the defence of Hong Kong against an actively hostile China. "The real defence of Hong Kong," Conservative Party spokesman R. A. Butler declared, "depends not so much upon the brigades which the Minister of Defence is so rightly mustering, but upon the mobilisation of all our strategic and diplomatic resources."[36] "A trade agreement with the Chinese People's Government," another British M. P. remarked, "would be immensely more valuable than trying to pretend that, in the event of a world war, we could possibly hold the Island of Hong Kong against the Chinese, when we could not hold it against the Japanese."[37]

Trade with Communist China

Even before the establishment of the People's Republic of China, trade dealings with communist-controlled North and Central China had provided sufficient ground to hope that "when it comes to trade, the Chinese will not be unduly influenced by political considerations."[38] There was no indication in 1949 that direct trade, that had become firmly established between the Wars, would supplant the Hong Kong entrepot trade.[39] The British authorities, therefore, were determined not to miss any "opportunity to widen the traditional entrepot function between China and the West."[40] British recognition of the Peking regime was expected to facilitate expansion of trade. Shortly after Britain recognized China, Chinese businessmen in Hong Kong antcipated that the Canton-Kowloon through railway service would reopen soon. The prices of the metal products and industrial chemicals rose appreciably in expectation of increased shipments to China.[41] In his despatch from Hong Kong on 25 September 1950, *The Times* Correspondent wrote :

> A new feature of trade between Hong Kong and the mainland is the hunger of the new regime for goods necessary for carrying out industrial plans. Communist State traders here have told merchants that they are anxious that ships sailing to China should have full holds....The Chinese Communists now possess an unprecedented surplus of foreign exchange which they are intent on using to buy the imports they need for industrialization. Pressure to buy from stocks in Hong Kong is accentuated by the difficulty in buying direct from abroad....Hong Kong's total exports during the first eight months of this year were worth $2,000 m. compared with $1,300 m. in the same period of 1949.[42]

Hong Kong's trade reached its post-war peak in 1950, the first year of communist rule in China. A comparison with 1948 figures revealed that the colony's exports increased more than five-fold, while its imports from China nearly doubled.[43] Because of the unprecedented expansion of trade with China during 1949-51, the volume of Hong Kong's foreign trade also considerably increased and the colony's merchants inordinately fleeced the inexperienced communist representatives.[44] However, the embargo resolution of the UN General Assembly (18 May 1951) and action taken by the Hong Kong British authorities in pursuance to that resolution seriously affected trade relations.[45] Exports to China declined sharply,[46] with the result that the total value of Hong Kong's trade was drastically reduced. Sir H. Shawcross, President of the Board of Trade, emphatically asserted that Britain could not agree to impose a total embargo on trade with China because that would entail enormous difficulties for its colonies, particularly

Hong Kong.   He remarked :

> We cannot, of course, disregard the geographical situation of Hong Kong....It is the exports from the Colonial Territories to China which have presented by far the greatest problem....In relation to any attempt to restrict trade with China the position of Hong Kong is manifestly more difficult than that of any other territory in the world....Entrepot trade...is the life blood of Hong Kong, and without it it could not possibly maintain its economy or support its population of 2,500,000 people. In particular it depends on China for considerable part of its food supply, particularly fresh foods which could not easily be obtained from elsewhere; and the water supply although not...coming actually from Chinese territory comes from the mainland and is extremely vulnerable in its situation. Moreover, 95 per cent of the population are Chinese, many of them recent refugees and almost all maintaining close personal ties with China. It must be clearly realised by those who criticise Hong Kong policy in regard to trade with China that any serious food shortage, or any considerable unemployment in Hong Kong would provide opportunities for economic and political difficulties of a most serious kind. A military victory against Communism at the front door is of no good if Communism is infiltrating through the back door owing to economic, social and political difficulties. In spite of the obviously high degree to which Hong Kong's economy depends on trade with China the Hong Kong Government have imposed a total prohibition on the export to China of over 200 items of industrial equipment....All this in addition to the obvious things like arms, aircraft and munitions.[47]

The Korean War and Embargo

Hong Kong's industries had developed and expanded at an unprecedented pace since 1945. But in the wake of the Korean War, they were confronted with the worst crisis in their short history in early December 1950. In view of active Chinese intervention in the Korean War, the United States Government deemed it necessary to impose a virtually complete embargo (which was strictly enforced) on all shipments of goods to China.[48] This severely affected the colony's entrepot trade.[49] It also facilitated closer trade links between China and the Socialist countries of East Europe, including the Soviet Union.[50]

Speaking at the annual General Meeting of the Chartered
Bank of India, Australia and China on 2 April 1952, Vincent
Alpe Grantham, Chairman of the Bank, observed :

> One major development, unforseen at first, has been the
> extent to which China has been turning to Russia for more
> and more of her requirements, and although the trade bet-
> ween Hong Kong and the China mainland remains
> considerable, it is no longer so confidently accepted that
> China could not do without Hong Kong's assistance in
> trading with the outside world. This is a development of
> some importance which only adds to the uncertainty sur-
> rounding Hong Kong's continued existence as a world port
> and manufacturing centre.[51]

Hong Kong's share in the total Chinese imports fell drastically
from 66.9% in 1950 to 11.1% in 1953.[52] When asked "How
do Hong Kong traders feel about the embargo?" the Governor
of Hong Kong, Sir Alexander Grantham, replied :

> They feel much as a man feels when you give him a knife
> and tell him that it is in the interest of the community at
> large that he should cut his throat....A trade embargo which
> is a form of blockade, does not harm an agricultural country
> like China nearly as much as it would an industrial country
> like Britain. Traders here would like to see the embargo
> lifted.[53]

Political changes in China, the Three-Anti and Five-Anti
movements in particular, were equally harmful to Hong
Kong's economy.[54] The liquidation of British business interests
in China further affected the possibilities of trade through Hong
Kong.[55] Hong Kong's exports to China, which declined from
£72 million in the first half of 1951 to £28.25 million in the
second half of that year, continued to fall, with the result that
in the first six months of 1952 they stood at the low figure of
£10.4 million.[56]

A slight improvement in the situation was noticeable in the
second half of 1952 and the first half of 1953, when Hong Kong
exports to China increased to £22.10 million and £22.75
million respectively.[57] However, any substantial increase in
Hong Kong's exports to China depended, to a great extent, on the
relaxation of political tensions in the Far East. In his budget

speech on 4 March 1955, the Governor of Hong Kong referred to the courage shown by Hong Kong businessmen in overcoming the difficulties and observed : "The solution lies elsewhere....What we and the rest of the world want is real peace and a general easing of tension, especially in the Far East, of which there seems scant prospect at present."[58] After the Korean Armistice was signed, the British Secretary of State for Colonies observed :

> The embargo has imposed a severe strain upon Hong Kong's economy and despite the success of manufacturers and merchants in finding new business must continue to do so as long as the traditional Chinese market is largely denied to Hong Kong. Our international obligations preclude any relaxation in Hong Kong controls at the present time. I am, however, deeply conscious of the hardships suffered in Hong Kong and I shall do my best to ensure that the benefits of any relaxation which may attend a political settlement in the Far East are enjoyed by Hong Kong in equal measure and at the same time as they are available to other friendly countries.[59]

Britain was quite conscious of the difficulties faced by Hong Kong traders because of "their very loyal observance" of the embargo.[60] However, there was little London could do in regard to revision of embargo since the US Government was firmly opposed to any relaxation of trade controls with Communist countries, especially China.[61] Prospects of Hong Kong-China trade, therefore, remained dismal. Exports to China continued to decline. In 1955, they stood at "almost exactly one-half of 1954, one-third of 1953, and one-eighth of 1950."[62] The *Far Eastern Economic Review* remarked :

> The United Nations action restricting trade with China only tended to speed up Peking's trade policies which were aimed at direct trade and gradual exclusion of middlemen and entrepots (like Hong Kong). Even if exports of selected strategic materials could be shipped to China, Hong Kong would not much benefit from such a partial lifting of the 'embargo'. Prospects of Hong Kong-China trade remain dismal and practical businessmen cannot optimistically view these commercial relations....Imports from and exports to China via Hong Kong, are bound to slowly decline because of

1. increasing barter and direct (bilateral) trade, 2. low export earnings by China which depress its purchases, and 3. Peking's selectivity in purchases, often of industrial equipment which can be supplied by European industry with no middlemen being required.[63]

Utility of Hong Kong for China

The relative importance of Hong Kong in China's external trade considerably declined. However, the usefulness of Hong Kong for Peking had not altogether disappeared. In this connection, Yuan Li-wu states :

> The diminishing importance of Hong Kong in Communist China's foreign trade does not really reduce Hong Kong's economic usefulness to Communist China seriously. Consequently, one might be justified in deducing from this the conclusion, which is probably comforting to many diverse interests, that the existence of Hong Kong as a British colony would continue to be unaffected in the immediate future. First, trade with Hong Kong has since 1952 yielded an export surplus in favour of Communist China. Since Hong Kong has a free foreign exchange market, this exports surplus can be used to help pay for Chinese imports from all other countries in all currency areas. Second, a preponderant part of Communist China's exports to Hong Kong consists of foodstuffs and other commodities for consumption in Hong Kong by the local population. This source of foreign exchange supply, which cannot be replaced by any other visible source, would disappear if Hong Kong became a part of Communist China.[64]

Hong Kong remained useful for China for a number of reasons. In the first place, it enabled Peking to earn valuable foreign exchange. It provided financial facilities which no longer existed on the mainland, and a growing market for Chinese exports. Thus, in 1967 it was estimated that Peking's receipts from the British colony were running at no less than £250 million a year. The main part of this came from China's enormous trade surplus with Hong Kong, arising chiefly from the sale of foodstuffs amounting to nearly £170 million. Large sums in foreign exchange also accrued from remittances, which the Overseas Chinese sent to their families in China through Hong Kong, and from the profits of China's own business interests in the colony. Secondly, it helped the Chinese Government to keep in touch with Overseas Chinese and Southeast Asia in general since there were no restrictions on entry from the mainland. It, thus, enabled Peking to spread its political and economic influence in Afro-Asian countries, particularly Southeast Asia.[65] Thirdly, in view of the prevailing Sino-Soviet rift and the withdrawal of Russian technicians from China, it had become increasingly difficult for China to procure capital goods it needed from the Soviet Union. Moreover, it was not in Peking's interest to remain exclusively dependent on Moscow. It was, therefore, assumed that China would seek to diversify its trade and endeavour to expand its economic relations with the Western World. The value of Hong Kong would then be greatly enhanced.

Hong Kong did not represent a security threat to China. If it was a Nationalist base for spying on the mainland, it was also a Communist base for spying on Taiwan. The British colony helped nearly two million people of the neighbouring Kwangtung province to earn their livelihood by supplying Hong Kong with fresh food and other daily necessities. Moreover, the existence of the British colony as a "hostage for Britain's good behaviour"[66] enabled Peking to exert pressure on London so as to keep British foreign policy on an even keel (particularly in so far as its support to the USA was concerned) and to play off London against Washington. By taking any hostile action against Hong Kong, on the other hand, China would not only have driven the UK and the USA closer together but would also have lost an important diplomatic leverage to encourage conciliatory tendencies in British policy and to exploit policy differences, if any, between London and Washington, thereby contributing to the isolation of the United States from its Western allies in Far Eastern matters. The recent Chinese policy of cultivating the European Powers in the EEC and in the NATO as a countervailing force to the two super Powers, particularly the Soviet Union, has further induced Peking not to risk alienating Britain's sympathies by engaging in hostile confrontation over Hong Kong.

Above all, the primary concern of Chinese policy was the

recovery of Taiwan.   As long as that goal remained unfulfilled,
Hong Kong, it was believed, was comparatively safe in British
hands.   For all these reasons, China had refrained from taking
any military action against Hong Kong, which could possibly
have resulted in confrontation with the United States.

Chinese Attitude

The Chinese attitude towards Hong Kong was neither one of
friendship nor that of hostility.   The Colonial Report of 1953
described it as "cold, aloof and ambiguous."[67]   The Colonial
Reports referred to a number of minor frontier incidents,[68] a
few cases of shooting of naval ships or aircraft, and protest
notes against the persecution of Chinese residents in Hong
Kong.   Peking had also accused Britain of permitting its colony
to be used as a base for hostile activities.   The Chinese
protests, accusations and frontier incidents, multiplied after the
Korean War.   Soon after the establishment of Chinese garrisons on the islands to the south and southwest of the colony
in the summer of 1950, British ships passing in the vicinity of
these islands, the British authorities contended, were "fired on
without warning."[69]   However, in a statement issued on 24
August 1950, General Yeh Chien-ying, Governor of Kwangtung asserted that the British warship intruding into Chinese
waters on 17 August 1950 had been properly and "immediately
warned."   He considered violation of Chinese territory, territorial waters and airspace to be "provocative acts," which were
stated to be "inseparable from the foreign policy of
imperialism."   The Hong Kong authorities, he added, must
shoulder full responsibility for all the consequences of these
"obviously planned encroachments of our country's
sovereignty."[70]

In the beginning of September 1950, Peking Radio and the
official communist newspaper in Canton accused the Hong
Kong Government of persecuting Chinese residents.[71]   When
the issue of crossing the 38th parallel by UN troops in Korea
was discussed, Chou En-lai utilised the grievances of the Overseas Chinese in British colonies to pressurize London.   On 30
September 1950, he observed : "Britain's extremely unjustifi-

able and unfriendly attitude towards Chinese residents in Hong Kong and other places cannot fail to draw the serious attention of the Central People's Government."[72] In a statement issued on 5 April 1951, Yeh Chien-ying, Governor of Kwangtung, condemned "as unlawful and outrageous the action of the Hong Kong British authorities in openly shielding the US-Chiang bandits who seized the [five] Chinese fishing vessels."[73]

On 25 January 1952 the Chinese Ministry of Foreign Affairs protested against the arrest and deportation of eight cinema workers and others in Hong Kong. The protest note accused British authorities of sending "small groups of bandits led by Hsiao Tien-lai and other Chiang Kai-shek remnants to sneak across the Chinese border to rob the people, plant explosives and distribute reactionary leaflets." This series of persecutions and provocations, it added, were not "local incidents but...a new development in the hostile policy of the United Kingdom towards the People's Republic of China."[74] Serious riots broke out on 1 March 1952 in Kowloon following the Government's refusal to allow the Canton Communist "comfort mission" to enter the colony to "succour" about 25,000 refugee fire victims.[75] Peking refused to consider the British demand for compensation when a Royal Naval launch was fired on in the Pearl River Estuary on 9 September 1953 "without provocation by a Chinese naval craft."[76] China, however, agreed to pay £367,000 as compensation for the loss of the British Cathay Pacific Airways Skymaster airliner, which was shot down by Chinese fighters off Hainan island on 23 July 1954.[77]

Peking criticized British authorities for the aircrash of the Indian plane, "Kashmir Princess," that carried a Chinese delegation and Chinese and foreign correspondents to the Afro-Asian Conference at Bandung. The plane had taken off from Hong Kong on 11 April 1955 and exploded near Sarawak, North Borneo, the same day. The Chinese Ministry of Foreign Affairs observed :

The British Government and the British authorities in Hong Kong bear a serious responsibility for this unfortunate incident. We demand that the British Government...conduct a thorough investigation into this incident and arrest and punish according to law the secret agents taking part in this sinister plot so as to place the responsibility where it belongs.[78]

Peking addressed three protest notes to Britain in regard to the landing in Hong Kong on 31 January 1956 of an unarmed Chinese Nationalist fighter aircraft, which, it was stated, had violated the airspace of Fukien and Kwangtung provinces and which was allowed to depart for Formosa on 12 March 1956.[79]

Kowloon Riots, 1956

The most serious outbreak of violence in the post-war history of the colony occurred in Kowloon on 10 October 1956 on the "Double Tenth" anniversary of the founding of the Republic by Sun Yat-sen.[80]   Chou En-lai summoned O'Neill, the British *charge d'affaires*, and expressed indignation and concern over the casualties suffered by Chinese inhabitants in Kowloon and the "grave" damage done to their property as a result of "cold-blooded murders and looting by Kuomintang agents." He protested against what he described as the failure of the British authorities to adopt effective measures to stop the violence and disturbances "organised and fomented by Kuomintang agents." He demanded that the Hong Kong authorities severely punish the miscreants and take effective steps to protect Chinese inhabitants and the organs and enterprises of the Chinese Government in Hong Kong.   The Chinese Government, he stated, reserved the right to raise demands in the future.[81] This, in effect, implied that if the hostile activities of Kuomintang agents were not curbed by the Hong Kong authorities, China would take whatever steps it deemed necessary to maintain the law and order situation in the colony.   On 19 October 1956, Chang Han-fu, Vice-Foreign Minister, received the British *charge d'affaires*.   He castigated British statements disclaiming responsibility for the riots and lodged a stern protest.[82]   On 24 October 1956, the *People's Daily* warned :

> The Chinese people will not stand quietly by and disregard the safety of the Chinese who live in Hong Kong and Kowloon.   We are not prepared to tolerate the use of Hong

Kong and Kowloon as a base for acts of sabotage against China....We demand Hong Kong authorities to immediately change such attitude which we cannot bear, thoroughly to take measures regarding this riotous affairs, strictly punish criminal head of Kuomintang agents and indeed to take care of the life and security of the Chinese residents.[83]

The Chinese Ministry of Foreign Affairs statement of 22 January 1957 criticised the Report, issued by the British authorities in Hong Kong on 1 January 1957, on the "Riots in Kowloon and Tsuen Wan," for whitewashing the crimes of Kuomintang agents and for its failure "to provide responsible assurances for the future security of the life and property of the Chinese inhabitants." The Ministry took strong exception to the mention made in the Report of the Chiang Kai-shek group in Taiwan as the "National Government in Formosa," and suspected that it reflected "the British Government's design of creating 'two Chinas'."[84] On 9 April 1958, the Chinese Government protested against the British decision to allow the military aircraft of the Chiang Kai-shek clique to land in Hong Kong and "to be flown back to Taiwan." Peking warned :

Such action of the British Government and the British authorities in Hong Kong extremely unfriendly and harbouring hostility towards the Chinese Government and people will certainly adversely affect Sino-British relations, and that the British Government will be held responsible for all the consequences.[85]

Other Chinese protest notes to Britain were related to the Hong Kong Government's order prohibiting Chinese residents in Hong Kong from hanging up the Chinese national flag and singing the Chinese national anthem;[86] the forcible closure of *Chung Hua* Middle School; "British police brutality against Chinese correspondents;" and the deportation of Parker Tu, Principal of the *Peichiao* Middle School. "If Britain continues to indulge in provocations," a *Peking Review* editorial warned, "it must be prepared to face the consequences."[87] Numerous protests were lodged by the Chinese Ministry of Foreign Affairs against the infringement of Chinese airspace by British aircraft. The protest note of 27 August 1958 recalled earlier protest notes of 24 May, 18 June and 5 August 1958 and observed :

> Occurring at a time when the United States and its lackey,
> the Chiang Kai-shek clique, are creating tension in the
> Taiwan Straits, these activities of military reconnaissance
> and harassment take on an extremely serious character....
> The Chinese Government holds that the British Government
> should apologize to the Chinese Government for the intru-
> sions into Chinese territorial air by British aircraft, punish
> the personnel who have engaged in these provocations, and
> guarantee against similar incidents in the future....If these
> activities are not stopped, the British Government and the
> British authorities in Hong Kong must be held responsible
> for all the consequences.[88]

On 4 September 1958 the People's Republic of China
extended its territorial air and water limits to 12 miles. Since it
placed Hong Kong within the territorial limits of China, the
British *charged' affaires* in Peking was instructed to inform the
Chinese Government that Her Majesty's Government could not
recognize the Chinese claim as valid under international law.[89]
In January 1963 the British decision to demolish old houses in
the Kowloon city called forth a strong protest from China.
New China News Agency considered it "a gross violation of
Chinese sovereignty" and "intolerable." The official protest
note of Chinese Government was, however, not so violent as
the *New China News Agency* account of it. Moreover, when
N. Khrushchov rebuked Peking for tolerating colonial regimes
(in Hong Kong and Macao) right at its droorstep, the *People's
Daily* replied by saying that in dealing with "various imperialist
countries," China took differing circumstances into account and
made distinctions in its policy accordingly. "When conditions
are ripe," the Chinese paper remarked, the questions of Hong
Kong, Kowloon and Macao, "should be settled peacefully
through negotiations and pending a settlement, the *status quo*
should be maintained."

Cultural Revolution

During the "Cultural Revolution" phase in China (1965-68),
Hong Kong was also the scene of disturbances (May-September

1967) in which 51 people lost their lives, over 800 sustained injuries and more than 5,000 were arrested. In the face of persistent demonstrations and riots, the Portuguese in Macao capitulated to the Chinese Communist and Red Guard demands on 30 January 1967. In these circumstances, Yang Kuang advocated shaking "the foundation of the reactionary British rule in Hong Kong" too. Yang was the chief of a newly-formed front organization of communists and fellow-travellers called the "Committee of Hong Kong-Kowloon Chinese Compatriots of All Circles for the Struggle Against Persecution by the British Authorities in Hong Kong." During the communist-inspired demonstrations, strikes, riots, etc., a Hong Kong police inspector was kidnapped by Chinese nationals across the border.

A number of border incidents occurred. While Hong Kong authorities considered them a serious affair, they did not regard them as an attempt at armed invasion of the colony. There were also occasional exchanges of fire, which led to the closure of the border bridge of Man Kam To and the stringing of barbed wire along the border. On 20 October 1967 the Chinese Foreign Ministry lodged a serious protest with the British Government about the matter and demanded that London instruct the British authorities in Hong Kong to immediately remove the obstacles and barbed wire, restore normal traffic and order on the border and guarantee against the recurrence of similar incidents. After negotiations, a settlement was reached on 25 November 1967 when normal traffic at the busy Man Kam To Bridge was restored.[90]

Peking provided help to the rioters by contributing H.K. $20 million to a strike fund. The amount was remitted (first instalment of $10 million on 13 June 1967 and the remaining amount on 30 July 1967) by the All-China Federation of Trade Unions in care of the Hong Kong and Kowloon Federation of Trade Unions to the Committee of the Hong Kong-Kowloon Compatriots of All Circles for Struggle Against Persecution by British imperialism and against British violence.[91] Moreover, in order to boost the morale of the striking workers, Peking repeatedly protested against British "atrocities" in Hong Kong and massive rallies were held in Canton in support of the Hong Kong compatriots. Food shipments to Hong Kong, which constituted nearly 30% of the colony's imports from

China, were stopped for four days (from 29 June to 2 July 1967). This produced a serious food shortage and led to a rapid rise in food prices. As regards water supply, while Peking refused to sell additional water to the drought-affected colony, the existing agreed water supply from the Chinese-built Shumchun reservoir on the Chinese side was continued without any interruption.

At times, Peking took some retaliatory measures against the British. For instance, on 22 May 1967 China decided to annul the 1954 arrangement by which the British *charge d' affaires* Office was allowed to post personnel in Shanghai in charge of the affairs of British nationals there. Accordingly, Peking demanded that P M. Hewitt leave Shanghai within 48 hours.[92] On 21 July 1967 the freedom of movement of Reuter's Peking correspondent (Grey) was restricted in retaliation for Hong Kong authorities' persecution of the correspondents of the Hong Kong Branch of *Hsinhua News Agency* and "other patriotic newsmen."[93] On 30 August 1967, it was announced that no personnel of the Office of the British *charge d' affaires* in China could leave Chinese territory without the permission of the Chinese Foreign Ministry. The exit visas that had been issued to them earlier were also cancelled.[94]

The British *charge d' affaires*, D.C. Hopson, was summoned several times (on 15 and 22 May, on 29 June, on 9 and 22 July, on 20 and 30 August, on 9 October and on 6 December 1967) and was handed over the most urgent and most vehement protest statements. The statement of 15 May 1967 contained five "solemn and just demands" of the Chinese Government. The British Government was asked to instruct the British authorities in Hong Kong as follows :

1. immediately accept all the just demands put forward by Chinese workers and residents in Hong Kong;

2. immediately stop all fascist measures;

3. immediately set free all the arrested persons (including workers, journalists and cameramen);

4. punish the culprits responsible for the sanguinary atrocities, offer apologies to the victims and compensate for their losses; and

5.   guarantee against the occurrence of similar incidents.[95]

On 29 June 1967 a protest note against intrusion of Chinese airspace by British military planes was delivered to the British diplomat in Peking.[96]   The Chinese note of 9 July 1967 demanded public apologies for the 8 July armed provocation in Sha Tau Kok (along the border); immediate punishment of the culprits; compensation for all losses; and release of arrested persons.[97]   The Chinese note of 20 August 1967 demanded cancellation, within 48 hours, of the ban on the three Hong Kong newspapers, *Hong Kong Evening News*, the *Tin Fung Daily News*, and the *Afternoon News*, and the release of the "19 patriotic Chinese journalists and 34 staff members" of these papers.[98] The note of 9 October 1967 accused Hong Kong British authorities of sabotaging "our patriotic fellow countrymen's National Day Celebrations."[99]

The disturbances in Hong Kong subsided by October 1967. However, they did a great deal of harm to Hong Kong's economy.   The Crown colony's exports fell by 31%, its total imports by 18% and total trade by 18%. Peking also did not remain unaffected by the undeclared boycott of its products by numerous Hong Kong citizens. It suffered a 17 to 18 percent loss in its 1967 trade earnings from Hong Kong, which stood at about the same level from 1956 onwards but grew rapidly during the period 1962 to 1966.

In 1968 Peking extended its moral support to the struggle of "patriotic fellow countrymen in Hong Kong and Kowloon" against British outrages. On 18 February 1968, the three Hong Kong patriotic Chinese papers—the *Hong Kong Evening News*, the *Afternoon News* and the *Tin Fung Daily News* resumed their publications after six months suspension. This was greeted by the All-China Journalists Association (A.C.J.A.) as another victory for patriotic compatriots and journalists in Hong Kong in their struggle against British imperialist outrages.   The A.C.J.A.'s message assured them of the Chinese people and journalists' firm support in their anti-British brutality struggle.[100]   On 15 March 1968, Hopson, the British *charge d' affaires*, was summoned by a responsible member of the West European Affairs Department of the Chinese Foreign Ministry.   A serious protest was lodged with the British Government against the British authorities' attempt to "deport" two patriotic Chinese film workers (Fu Chi and Shih Hui). This was considered an act of persecution making for renewal of "tension in Hong Kong and on the border." The British diplomat was told that the Chinese patriotic compatriots in Hong Kong had "the sacred right to live and work there, a right which they cannot be deprived of by anyone." The Chinese official demanded immediate acquittal of the two film workers and restoration of their personal freedom, safety, etc., failing which the British were warned that they would be held responsible for all the consequences arising therefrom.[101]

On 27 May 1968, another protest note was handed over to Hopson by Lo Kuei-po, Vice-Minister of Foreign Affairs, against the entry of the US nuclear-powered aircraft carrier *Enterprise* into Hong Kong. The note criticized Britain for abetting US imperialism and allowing Washington to use Hong Kong as a base of operations for its war of aggression against Vietnam. The turning of Hong Kong into a base of operations for US nuclear-powered warships, the Chinese note asserted, not only exposed the British Government as an accomplice of the US in its aggression against Vietnam, but also constituted "an ever more serious menace to China's security," a direct grave threat to the lives of Chinese inhabitants in Hong Kong," and "a serious provocation against the people of China, Vietnam and all Southeast Asia." The note demanded that the American aircraft carrier be ordered to leave Hong Kong immediately.[102] In July-August 1968, the British cancelled the registration of the *Chung Wah* Middle School (it was closed on 28 November 1967). Peking considered the closure of the school as an unwarranted and reactionary attack on and a fascist outrage against the patriotic educational institutions in Hong Kong, a grave step making for tension in Hong Kong, a new provocation, and an infringement of their sacred right to disseminate and study Mao Tse-tung's Thought.[103] The Chinese Foreign Ministry expressed serious concern about it and later lodged a serious protest with the British Mission in Peking.[104]

Thus, Peking had, over the years, built a record of complaints against British rule in Hong Kong and had claimed the crown colony as Chinese territory. However, it had refrained from taking any serious step to reunite Hong Kong with China.

It had continued to tolerate the imperialist stronghold right on its doorstep despite Khrushchov's taunts in the matter. Although the situation in 1967 seemed ripe for "liberating" Hong Kong, Peking desisted from seriously contemplating such a course of action primarily because the British colony served as a major outlet for Chinese exports and China's trade surplus with the crown colony was an important source of foreign exchange earnings, nearly US $600 million per year in convertible currency. It was more than 50% of Peking's total foreign exchange earnings by 1967.

Chinese Representation in Hong Kong

Peking exercises considerable influence over the labour movement, the press and the educational institutions in Hong Kong. It also regards the majority of the inhabitants of the colony as Chinese nationals and had repeatedly asserted its right to protect their life, property, freedom, etc. There is hardly any matter within the competence of the Hong Kong Government which does not, in some degree, affect the welfare of these Chinese nationals. In these circumstances, the presence of Chinese consuls in Hong Kong could have opened the way "for almost unlimited interference by the Chinese Government in the domestic affairs of the colony."[105]

The revival of Chou En-lai's proposal of 1955 about the establishment of Chinese diplomatic representation in Hong Kong, therefore, is regarded by the British as "a calculated projection of politics into the apolitical colonial atmosphere of Hong Kong," almost a disturbance (or a step in that direction) of the *status quo*. The Chinese proposal, therefore, is unlikely to find favour in London any more now than it was 20 years ago or even 105 years ago. Alexander Grantham, then Governor of Hong Kong, commenting on Chou En-lai's proposal, reportedly remarked : "I would resign first. There's no room for two governors in Hong Kong."[106] While the British *charge d' affaires* was said to have welcomed Chou En-lai's proposal for its favourable impact on Sino-British relations, Grantham rejected it because he felt that a Chinese representative in the British Colony (with its 99% Chinese population) would have had such ill-defined duties, status and authority that interference in Hong Kong's internal affairs would have been inevitable.[107]   For all the above-mentioned reasons, Britain had been averse to accept the Chinese proposal to set up in Hong Kong "an office of a Commissioner of Foreign Affairs of the People's Republic of China with diplomatic and other staff."[108]

The Future of Hong Kong

On several occasions, Peking had brought to bear considerable political pressure on the colony. However, it had so far refrained from making a major issue of Hong Kong's status, partly because the continued existence of the colony served many a useful purpose and partly because China did not wish to provoke a head-on clash with the British while Taiwan remained under American protection. After the Chinese conquest of Formosa, the British position in Hong Kong would become even more untenable.

Even if Peking did not intend to take Hong Kong by force and the colony did not succumb to communist control as a result of internal decay and depression,[109] the retrocession of the crown colony might yet possibly take place in 1997, when the lease of the New Territories expires.[110]   Some people think that after the surrender of New Territories, "the interests of the people in Hong Kong" would be "best served" by transforming the colony into "a self-governing area, backed by some sort of United Nations or other international support."[111]   However, Peking is unlikely to agree to such proposals. After China became a member of the United Nations it refused to describe Hong Kong as a colony, and thereby place it under UN tutelage or supervision. The Chinese population in Hong Kong is described by Peking as compatriots, and not *hua chiao*, *i.e.*, Overseas Chinese living in foreign lands.

In this connection, it is also pertinent to recall what the *People's Daily* wrote about Macao. Commenting on the large-scale "celebrations" by the Portuguese authorities on the occasion of the 400th anniversary of their seizure of Macao, the Chinese paper observed :

This news has evoked the utmost indignation of the Chinese people. Macao is Chinese territory. The Chinese people have never forgotten Macao, nor have they forgotten that they have the right to demand the recovery of this territory from the hands of Portugal....The fact that Macao has not yet been returned to China does not mean that the Chinese people can tolerate long continuation of occupation of Macao.[112]

The above remarks apply with equal force to Hong Kong. The problem of the return of Hong Kong, it is stated, "will be solved when the time is ripe." In the meantime, the *status quo* has to be maintained because it serves Chinese interests fairly well. Therefore, it was not surprising that during British Foreign Secretary Sir Alec Douglas-Home's visit to China in 1972, an understanding was said to have been reached on the continued existence of the crown colony. It was agreed that any uncertainty about the future status of Hong Kong should not be allowed to disrupt the fast developing Sino-British friendship. Moreover, it was believed that Peking had given an assurance that it would not press for the restoration of the 400 square mile territory for an indefinite period. Britain, on its part, had agreed to ensure that Hong Kong would, in no way, be used by outsiders for purposes hostile to China. It was also agreed that all round cooperation between Hong Kong and China—in trade, communications, transportation and power, etc.—would be established and developed further.[113]

A glimpse of the benign, though anomalous, attitude of Peking towards Hong Kong's political future was available during Queen Elizabeth II's visit to the crown colony in May 1975. She was the first reigning British monarch to set her foot on Hong Kong soil. In a casual reference to the colony's political congruence (and this was her sole reference to China), she observed : "You live in harmony with the Chinese People's Government : you benefit from the confluence of the two great cultural streams of East and West." The British colony, which is claimed as Chinese territory, could indefinitely prolong its lease of life by maintaining harmonious relations with Peking and by proving economically useful to both Britain and China.

CHAPTER SEVEN

Chinese Representation in the UN

Even before the People's Republic of China was admitted to the United Nations in November 1971, the question of Chinese representation in the UN had appeared to be a minor problem as compared to the "great strategic conflict"[1] in regard to Formosa. In fact, this question would have been resolved much earlier had it not been considered to be closely interlinked with the problem of Formosa. The Western Powers insisted on keeping Peking outside the UN for 21 years and had been reluctant to expel Taiwan from the world organization primarily because they believed that it would enable them to push through their plan to create "two Chinas" or an independent Taiwan and thereby keep this strategic island in friendly hands. China has, at the same time, sought to become a member of the UN[2] not only because it would have enhanced its prestige and reduced its diplomatic dependence on the Kremlin but also because its admission in the UN and the expulsion of Taiwan would have greatly strengthened its case *vis-a-vis* Formosa. Peking's presence at UN headquarters would also have facilitated the establishment of Chinese contacts with a large number of countries.

Britain has changed its stand on the question of Chinese representation in the UN quite often, depending on the exigencies of the situation and consideration of its national interests. Since London seemed reconciled to the conquest of Formosa by the Chinese Communists in the beginning of 1950, it was inclined to support Peking's case in the UN and even "help to shepherd China into the United Nations rather than to oppose her entry and cause unnecessary frustration."[3] After the Korean War, however, Britain modified its attitude. It took into account the manifest Chinese hostility towards the West as evidenced by the non-establishment of diplomatic relations with the UK and active intervention in Korea; the US commitment to defend Formosa from unfriendly hands; and the emergence of Communist China as a possible threat to Hong Kong. However, in the early 1970s Britain was convinced of the severity of the Sino-Soviet confrontation and the desire of China to terminate its isolation and seek wider contacts in the world. Thus, in the wake of President Nixon's visit to China, the British Government again changed its attitude on the question of Chinese representation in the UN.

British Abstention in the Security Council

As early as 15 November 1949, Chou En-lai addressed a telegram to Carlos P. Romulo, President of the UN General Assembly, in which he challenged the legal status of the Kuomintang (Formosan) delegation and questioned its right to represent China in the UN.[4]   The question of Chinese representation was not raised in the Security Council until January 1950, although at the 458th meeting of the Council on 29 December 1949 the Soviet delegate, Malik, considered "it necessary to state that it will not regard Mr. T. F. Tsiang, the Kuomintang representative on the Security Council, as representing China, nor as being empowered to represent the Chinese people in the Security Council."[5]   On 8 January 1950, *i.e.* two days after British recognition of China, Chou En-lai sent another telegram to the UN declaring the presence of the Kuomintang delegate in the Security Council illegal and demanding his expulsion.[6] On 10 January, the Soviet delegate raised the question of Chinese representation in the Security Council before it proceeded to adopt its agenda.   "Upon instructions" from his Government, he stated :

> Should the Security Council fail to take appropriate measures for the exclusion from its membership of the representative of the Kuomintang group, the delegation of the U.S.S.R. will not participate in the work of the Security Council as long as the representative of the Kuomintang is not excluded from that body.

Malik also submitted a draft resolution which declared the representation of the Kuomintang group as "illegal" and demanded its exclusion from the Council.

The President of the Council, who happened to be the representative of Nationalist China, ruled that the Soviet proposal would be printed and distributed to the members and a special meeting called for its consideration. Malik, however, insisted that the Security Council take a decision on the matter then and there. He stated : "Should the English and French texts of that proposal not be ready, I suggest that the meeting be suspended for a few minutes until the text is available and that my proposal be then put to vote."[7] The delegations of the USA, the UK, and Nationalist China took objection to the Soviet attitude, which, they believed, was in violation of the rules of procedure and amounted to dictating terms to the Council. Sir Alexander Cadogan, the British representative, considered the Soviet proposal as having been "raised prematurely." He remarked :

> At this moment not many Governments have recognized the new Government of China, and, therefore, it might be premature and precipitate on the part of this organ of the United Nations to take, or attempt to take, a definite decision in the near future.[8]

From this statement and the British vote in favour of the President's ruling that the Soviet proposal be considered at a subsequent meeting of the Council, Moscow came to the conclusion that Britain was unlikely to support the Soviet stand "in the near future." Accordingly, at the subsequent meeting of the Council, held on 12 January 1950, Malik accused Britain, alongwith the USA and France, of having been "actuated by the desire to bolster the sorry remnants of the Kuomintang clique." He criticized the Anglo-American bloc, headed by the United States, for preventing the adoption of the Soviet proposal.[9] Referring to Britain in particular, Malik observed :

> The somewhat peculiar situation results that, while some countries sign notes through their Foreign Ministers recognizing the Central People's Government of the People's

Republic of China, they vote, through their representatives in the Security Council, in support of the representative of the Kuomintang group with which they have broken off diplomatic relations, and speak in favour of his remaining in the Security Council [10]

He denounced British attitude in the matter as "double-dealing... hypocritical...Janus-faced."[11] On 13 January 1950, the Soviet proposal was put to the vote and defeated. Britain abstained. Thereafter, Malik declared that the Soviet Union would "not recognize as legal any decision of the Security Council adopted with the participation of the representative of the Kuomintang group." The Soviet Government, he stated, would not be guided by any such decisions.[12] He also staged a walk-out from the Council chamber. Britain later accused Moscow of using the question of Chinese representation in the UN for making "more enemies for the Western Nations."[13]

From 13 January 1950 to 1 August 1950 (when the Soviet delegate resumed his seat in the Security Council), the Soviet Union continued to stage walk-outs from other UN bodies. Throughout this period Britain abstained on the question of Chinese representation partly because of the resolute American stand in the matter and party because of its own reluctance to submit to Soviet pressure and give up a bargaining counter which, it thought, could profitably be used in the Anglo-Chinese discussions on the establishment of diplomatic relations. However, British public opinion was getting disillusioned since the Government's attitude proved unproductive, its objectives in China remained unfulfilled, and the work of the UN had been brought to a standstill.[14]

The Korean War

Though Britain continued to abstain even after the Korean War broke out, the grounds of its abstention had somewhat changed. Hitherto, Britain had disliked yielding to Soviet pressure, but now the factor of appeasing and encouraging aggression entered into the picture. At a time when the Western Powers were engaged in meeting "a direct challenge to the world authority,"[15] to accede to Prime Minister Nehru's appeal to settle the Korean problem by admitting Chinese Communists to the UN[16] seemed tantamount to a "decision... dictated by an unlawful aggression."[17] Thus, on 1 August 1950 Britain, alongwith the USA, voted in support of the majority Security Council resolution, by which the ruling of the Soviet representative (as President of the Security Council) to the effect that the Kuomintang member was not the lawful representative of China was overruled. However, on 3 August 1950 Britain voted with India, the USSR, Yugoslavia and Norway in favour of the Soviet proposal to place the question of Chinese representation on the agenda of the Security Council. It appeared that while Britain was opposed to the immediate admission of Peking and the simultaneous expulsion of the Kuomintang delegate from the Council, it was not averse to the question of Chinese representation being discussed in the Council.

The British stand perceptibly changed in September 1950 when the North Korean armies were forced to retreat by UN forces. Peking had by that time begun to denounce American troops in Korea of "provocative and atrocious acts of invading the air of China...encroaching upon China's sovereignty, killing Chinese people, and attempting to extend the war and violate peace."[18] China also accused the British authorities in Hong Kong of encroaching upon China's territorial waters and air-space, of spying and of shelling rounds of ammunitions on Chinese troops. "The above-mentioned matters occurring again and again," Yeh Chien-ying, Chairman of the Kwangtung People's Government, observed on 24 August 1950, were "obviously planned encroachment on our country's sovereignty." Such "provocative actions and the imperialist foreign policy," he added, "are inseparable."[19] In his telegram dated 17 September 1950 to Trygve Lie, Secretary-General of the UN, Chou En-lai warned :

> Should the United Nations General Assembly accept the illegal 'delegation' of the Chinese Kuomintang reactionary remnant clique...the Central People's Government of the People's Republic of China would consider this a most unfriendly action toward the Chinese people on the

part of the United Nations.[20]

The United Kingdom did not intend to be "bogged down in China with a China war," since it suited Russia's strategy of "keeping Europe clear for themselves."[21] It, therefore, viewed with grave concern the above-mentioned Chinese statements. Besides, it was believed that the Chinese anxiety in regard to the Anglo-American policy of carrying out expansion in Manchuria was not entirely unfounded. Peking's propaganda in this particular instance, Bevin admitted, was "reinforced by memories of the Japanese occupation," and hence, it "was having marked effect all over China." London, therefore, deemed it necessary to check, counter and "correct" all propaganda of that nature. Accordingly, Britain sought to assure Peking that the Western Powers had no intention whatsoever of attacking Manchuria.[22] Peking could not be convinced of the *bonafides* of the Western Powers by mere words alone. Therefore, one way by which Britain thought of demonstrating to China that the Western Powers were not hostile to it was by way of supporting Peking's case for admission in the UN. Britain, thus, decided to vote in favour of the Indian resolution in the General Assembly in September 1950.[23] However, in spite of the British vote in favour of the Indian resolution, it was evident to all concerned that their real sympathies were with the Canadian resolution,[24] which sought to postpone any action on the question of Chinese representation till the conflict in Korea was brought to a successful conclusion. The clear import of Foreign Secretary Bevin's speech in the General Assembly on 25 September 1950 was that after Korea was united under UN auspices, Britain and other Western Powers would sympathetically consider China's case for admission in the UN.[25] In other words, he hinted that London was quite willing to grant Peking's demand in regard to admission in the UN *provided* it refrained from combat in Korea.

The British attitude in the Security Council was in no way different from its stand in the General Assembly. In the beginning of September 1950, the Soviet representative submitted a draft resolution (S/1759) "to invite the representative of the People's Republic of China to the meeting of the Security Council" in connection with the complaint about bombing by

UN air forces of Chinese territory.   At the Council meeting on 11 September 1950 while the USSR and France considered Article 32 of the Charter as applicable in the case, the representatives of China, Cuba, Ecuador and the USA maintained that that Article was inapplicable. In supporting the Soviet draft resolution, the Indian representative observed that rule 39 of the rules of procedure could be applied to the case, even if some members of the Council regarded Article 32 inapplicable. The British delegate stated that Article 32 could not be invoked so long as the Council was of the opinion that Peking should not represent China in the Council.   He further stated that rule 39 did not oblige the Council to invite the representative of the People's Republic of China.   He did not believe that much would be gained by hearing a representative of China in the Council when Peking's detailed evidence could better be presented to a commission on the spot.   Washington had suggested the establishment of such a commission and Britain considered that proposal as "entirely fair and, indeed, very generous." Nevertheless, the British delegate expressed the view that in equity—as opposed to law—Peking, if it so wished, had a right to submit its views before the Council.

On 28 September 1953, Britain voted in favour of inviting China during the discussion on Peking's complaint regarding an armed invasion of the island of Taiwan (Formosa) under rule 39 of the rules of procedure, the invitation being effective only after 1 December 1950. The consideration of the question had to be deferred till then. At the 519th meeting of the Security Council on 8 November 1950, the British delegate himself moved an amendment (S/1890) to the effect that Peking be invited, in accordance with rule 39 of the rules of procedure, to present its case on the special report of the UN Command on Chinese intervention in Korea. Although Peking's attitude did not, in his view, justify the extension of a general invitation to it, he thought that the Chinese People's Republic, having been arraigned by the UN Command, ought to be allowed to make a statement on its behalf.

One can argue that had Peking been admitted into the UN in September 1950, it would not have intervened in the Korean War. However, it was doubtful if China, even after it became a member of the UN, would have allowed the entire Korean peninsula to pass under the influence of the Western Powers. Perhaps, if the question of Chinese representation had not been closely connected with the problem of Formosa, or if the fighting in Korea had no relationship with the control of Formosa the British attitude on the question of Chinese representation might have been different. However, in the circumstances of the case in which Peking's admission in the UN was closely interlinked with the question of Formosa,[26] Britain could hardly expect its ally, the USA, to adopt a course of action that meant taking double risks in regard to both Korea and Formosa. Such a step entailed many disadvantages. It signified unilateral concession to Peking on the question of representation in the UN. It weakened the case for the defence of Formosa against Communist Chinese attack. Finally, it affected the morale of UN troops then fighting in Korea and jeopardized the successful outcome of the attempt at resisting aggression.

If Peking had given firm indication that it would not challenge the authority of the UN in Korea, then London might have openly supported the Chinese demands as regards its representation in the UN and its claim to Formosa. That was probably what Premier Attlee had in mind when he spoke of strict adherence to the Cairo Declaration of 1943 *by all the Powers.*[27] Sino-US *rapprochement* was possible only by a process of give and take. It was precisely for these reasons that London was unwilling to support the Soviet proposal that the Kuomintang delegate be expelled and that Peking be admitted into the UN immediately.[28] The Chinese were quite critical of the equivocal attitude of Britain and other countries that had announced their willingness to establish diplomatic relations with China but refused to support the Russian proposal. The spokesman of the Chinese Foreign Ministry observed: "The Chinese people continuously and closely watch these countries' attitude in the United Nations for the inconsistency in words and deeds." The UN resolution, he stated, deferred the issue for the time being so as to allow the US "aggressors" to control the whole of Korea. He therefore, considered it one more step in "the plot of encroachment on China and extension of war."[29]

Chinese Intervention in Korea and British Reaction

After the Chinese intervention in the Korean War, it became increasingly difficult for Britain to bring about a *rapprochement* between China and the USA. British support in favour of Peking's admission into the UN was considered appeasement and was the subject of much "misunderstanding" in the USA.[30] After the Chinese participation in the Korean War, London could no longer take the stand that it neither saw nor heard any accusations against the Government of China "of instigating, or having any lot or part in, the North Korean aggression."[31] However, it was agreed at Washington that every effort must be made to prevent the conflict in Korea from spreading and becoming a conflict with China from which might flow a world war.[32] Thus, British support for Peking's entry into the UN, which continued till 1 February 1951, was part of British "tactics"[33] to hold out the prospect of China's ultimate admission in the UN but seeing to it that the UN did not immediately take a decision in the matter. Britain also wished to maintain its trade relations with China, which continued to flourish until May 1951 when the UN-sponsored embargo was imposed. Britain seemed to take the view that while the Soviet Union would like to prolong the war in Korea, "China really wants to stop this fighting."[34] However, Britain could not ignore the fact that any unilateral concession in favour of China would be tantamount to appeasement and was likely to whet Peking's appetite for further aggression. On the other hand, it was realized that by closing all doors in regard to China's admission and by treating it as an outcast, the Western Powers would be unnecessarily antagonizing and provoking Peking.

For nearly a year, *i.e.* from September 1950 to 1 February 1951 (when the UN General Assembly declared China an aggressor in Korea), Britain supported Peking's admission in the various organs of the UN.[35] However, after China "launched offensive after offensive against the United Nations forces,"[36] thereby frustrating all hopes of an early cease-fire in Korea, Britain supported the US resolution in the UN General Assembly declaring China an aggressor. London also began to vote against Peking's entry in the UN and in favour of US proposals to postpone consideration of the question of Chinese representation.   Foreign Secretary H. Morrison conceded "in principle" that the delegates of the People's Government of the People's Republic of China should represent China in the UN.   Nevertheless, he observed on 27 June 1951 :

> In view, however, of that Government's persistence in behaviour which is inconsistent with the purpose and principles of the Charter, it now appears to His Majesty's Government that consideration of this question should be postponed *for the time being*.[37]

This view was subsequently reaffirmed on a number of occasions with the result that "for the time being" turned out to be ten years, despite repeated efforts behind the scenes to get Washington to see reason.[38]   The coming into power of the Conservative Party did not alter this stand of the British Government.[39]

In the first half of 1951, the UN forces (mostly American) suffered heavy losses at the hands of the so-called "Chinese People's Volunteers."   President Truman declared a national emergency in the country and China was condemned for aggression by the UN.   In April 1951 Peking was unseated from the Universal Postal Union—the only organ of the UN where its representatives had been seated in May 1950 on a Swiss motion. On 18 May 1951 the General Assembly imposed an embargo on trade with China.   In these circumstances the question of Chinese representation was relegated to the background.[40] Conscious of the strong American opposition in the matter, the British delegate to the UN even declared on 11 November 1951 that "even if the armistice negotiations being conducted in Korea were successful in the near future," it would be quite "inopportune for the vexed question of the representation of China to be debated in the General Assembly."[41]   There was no perceptible change in the British attitude during 1952 except that London refrained from making any statement that it would not reconsider its attitude towards Chinese representation in the UN even after the armistice had been signed.[42]   The British reticence in the matter, which was in marked contrast to their November 1951 statement, was probably due to their desire to see an early end of the Korean hostilities.   London did not, in any way, wish to jeopardize the truce negotiations that were going on intermittently at Panmunjon. However, since these negotiations were unduly prolonged, Western Powers deemed it necessary to pressurize China so as to compel it to sign the Korean armistice at an early date. Soon after the visit of a British delegation to the United States, the British Government announced measures to tighten shipping controls on China. As regards the question of China's admission in the UN, Anthony Eden declared on 17 March 1953 :

> Whatever the past history may have been I am not prepared, so long as I am Foreign Secretary of this country, to advocate to the United Nations the recognition of a Government who are in full aggression against the United Nations and are shooting down our troops.[43]

As compared to his earlier statement of January 1953,[44] the above-mentioned remark of Eden was stiffer in tone, if not in content.

The prospects of an early armistice in Korea improved after Chou En-lai's statement of 30 March 1953, *i.e.* after Stalin's death.[45] Britain, therefore, once again began to speak in a milder tone so as not to jeopardize the chances of an early conclusion of a Korean truce, which was essential for promoting British trade with China. Speaking in the House of Commons on 12 May 1953, Selwyn Lloyd, Minister of State for Foreign Affairs, observed :

> While that conflict is still in progress it seems quite out of the question to support the Central People's Government's claim or to promise to support it in a contingency which has not yet arisen. When peace has been established in Korea, a different situation will arise, and that is one of the matters which will have to be discussed. I can assure the House that Her Majesty's Government will have a clear viewpoint on that matter at that time.[46]

On 21 July 1953, the Chancellor of the Exchequer, R. A. Butler, stated :

> Our policies on such subjects as Chinese representation and the strategic embargo will have to the reconsidered in con-

cert with the other members of the United Nations at the appropriate time after an armistice, depending on how events develop in the Far East.[47]

The cautious, noncommittal and vague words mentioned above indicated that while Britain did not wish to prejudice the conclusion of an armistice in Korea, it was not prepared, in any way, to commit itself as regards Peking's admission to the UN. In fact, in promising to reconsider the issue, London did not depart from its basic policy of not granting unilateral concessions to China. The communique issued by the Foreign Ministers of the USA, the UK and France on 14 July 1953 stated that "in existing circumstances and pending further consultation, the common policies of the three Powers towards Communist China should be maintained."[48] After the Korean Armistice was signed, the Chancellor of the Exchequer elaborated the three-Power statement in the following words : "While any immediate change of policy would be impracticable until the situation in clearer, this question could be further examined in the light of experience gained after the armistice." Keeping in view the strong feelings of the Opposition in the matter, he softened his tone and stated that the Government "have not adopted any rigid attitude on this question, and the position in this matter, which is of such interest to the House of Commons, is open, as it should be." While endorsing the statements of 27 June 1951 and 18 June 1952, he made the following "accretion or addition" : "We hope and trust that the day for settling this and other problems will have been brought nearer by the armistice."[49]

British Policy After the Korean Armistice

Selwyn Lloyd, Minister of State, made a clear and detailed statement on the question of Chinese representation in the UN on 30 July 1953. The signing of the armistice, he stated, "has certainly brought us one stage further forward." However, the government did not hold the view that "automatically on the signing of the armistice there should be the recognition and admission of Communist China to the United Nations."

According to him, the British attitude on the question of Chinese representation in the UN, depended on the following four factors :

(a) the observation of the armistice agreement—"an exceedingly complicated" matter which afforded "ample opportunity for friction between the parties to it";

(b) progress at the political conference on "the very thorny problem of Korea." By this Lloyd obviously meant the political settlement of Korea which would bring about the peaceful unification of the country. In other words, Britain was now asking Peking to accept a solution of Korea which it refused to accept two years back. What the Western Powers could not achieve by force, they now desired to accomplish by diplomacy and peaceful methods;

(c) the development of British relations with the People's Government of China and the way in which their mission was treated there, *i.e.* the establishment of full diplomatic relations; and

(d) the question of the treatment of British traders in China, which could not be described as "good treatment."

"These are all matters," Lloyd asserted, "which must be considered and which must enter into our judgement."[50]

In view of the above-mentioned pre-conditions, it seemed highly unlikely that London would support Peking's case for admission in the UN. However, since the major obstacle in the way of China's admission to the world organization (the continued aggression in Korea and attack upon UN forces there) had been removed, it was felt that Peking's case would be vigorously advocated in the forthcoming eighth session of the General Assembly beginning in September 1953. The Soviet delegate pressed the issue at the Assembly meeting on 13 September 1953, *i.e.* even before it had elected its office bearers. John Foster Dulles, US Secretary of State, deemed it necessary to personally move the resolution for postponing the consideration of the question for the rest of the eighth session. The British delegate, Sir Gladwyn Jebb, expressed the hope that "the day for settling the question of Chinese representation will have been brought nearer by the signature of the armistice." However, he supported the US resolution by stating that it was "entirely appropriate." "We must wait and see," he remarked "if our great hopes" regarding "a satisfactory political settlement" of the Korean problem "are going to be fulfilled."[51] The US resolution was adopted but votes cast in favour of Peking increased to 10 as compared with 6 in 1952.

Hopes about Britain modifying its stand on the question of Chinese representation in the UN failed to materialize partly because the American attitude in regard to both Formosa and Peking's entry in the UN had considerably hardened[52] and partly because the UK considered China, even after the Korean truce, "still technically at war with the United Nations."[53] Moreover, London was acutely aware of the very serious situation in Indo-China in which China was stated to have "played so great a part." In these circumstances "to try to force the entry of Communist China into the United Nations," Churchill remarked, would not only "complicate altogether the very grave affairs we have to deal with in so many other questions," but would also "be regarded as a most harsh and uncalled for act of unfriendliness by the mighty people of the United States, to whom we all owe much...."[54]

Indo-China Conflict

In the first half of 1954, therefore, the question of Chinese representation came to be linked with the situation in Indo-China. Cessation of hostilities in Indo-China was considered the most urgent and pressing problem. However, the two main parties in Britain held divergent views on the ways and means to achieve that end. While the Labour Opposition in Parliament believed that Peking's admission in the UN would create favourable conditions for a successful outcome of the Geneva talks on Indo-China,[55] the ruling Conservative Party felt that any attempt or "agitation" at that time in favour of Peking would rouse American feelings and Washington would conclude that the Chinese had succeeded in "shooting their way into" the UN. Thus, it would have complicated and made "more difficult" Eden's task at Geneva—a declicate task of bringing together both the USA and China to a settlement on the problem of Indo-China. Since the British Government had no desire to jeopardize the "prospect of success" at Geneva,

Premier Churchill acknowledged that it was inconceivable "in principle" that China should forever be excluded from the UN. In practice, however, he felt that "it might be better" if the question of China's entry in the UN (which was to be discussed in the UN in September 1954) was "postponed until a later date."[56] Mrs. Castle interpreted Churchill's statement to mean that even if China showed goodwill in the negotiations over Indo-China, Britain would not support its admission in the forthcoming session of the General Assembly. This interpretation was considered "a complete misrepresentation" of the Premier's words by Douglas Dodds Parker, Joint Under-Secretary of State for Foreign Affairs.[57] However, Selwyn Lloyd, Minister of State, gave no assurance to Mrs. Castle (M. P.) that the Government would support China's case for admission in the UN in case peace was restored in Indo-China. Even if efforts at Geneva were crowned with success, Lloyd remarked, arrangements for a ceasefire and a settlement in Indo-China would be "extremely complicated and very difficult indeed to carry out, and their successful carrying out must depend upon good faith" which must be shown by "deeds and not just by words." "Surely it is complete folly," he said, "to suggest that at this moment we should seek to force this through against the view of our American allies." Lest these words might offend China and thereby prejudice the Geneva talks, then in a crucial stage, he, at the same time, stated that "far from it being a disadvantage to the free world to have the Peking Government take the China seat in the United Nations, it may well be an advantage." He did not think that "we have" in any way suffered from Russian participation in the UN debates.[58]

That Britain would not support Peking's case at the ensuing session of the General Assembly was also evident from Foreign Secretary Eden's remark soon after the signing of the armistice in Indo-China and the initialling of the Geveva Agreements.[59] However, the truce in Indo-China and the signing of the Joint Statements, embodying the much-advertised Five Principles of Peaceful Co-existence between Chou En-lai and the Premiers of India and Burma, created a favourable situation for the discussion of the question of Chinese representation in the UN. Several members of the UN, which formerly voted to put off consideration of the issue, began to favour taking it up after the Geneva Agreements of July 1954. Denmark, Iceland and Norway, for instance, had supported the US motion to postpone consideration of the Chinese question in 1953, while Sweden had opposed it. But in their Joint Statement of 31 August 1954, all four Nordic countries reached unanimity of views that it was desirable that the Peking Government should represent China in the United Nations within the near future.[60] However, as compared to 1953, Peking secured less votes in its favour in 1954.[61] This was partly because of Chou En-lai's violent speech of 11 August 1954 about the liberation of Taiwan ("liquidating the traitorous Chiang Kai-shek group") and the heavy artillery bombardment commenced by Peking on 3 September 1954 (just 18 days before the General Assembly voting on the issue) against the islands of Quemoy and little Quemoy.[62]

Before casting his vote in favour of the US proposal to postpone the consideration of the question of Chinese representation in the General Assembly on 21 September 1954, the British delegate (Sir Pierson Dixon) referred to these "incidents and statements," which, he said, "have disquieted us all." He observed :

Her Majesty's Government does not consider that it would be wise or timely to debate the question of Chinese representation at the present. Differing views upon it are strongly held. In a matter of this sort it is unwise to force to a vote an issue on which this Assembly is so deeply and so evenly divided. Our overriding purpose must be to hold this organisation together and so make it possible gradually for it to gather strength. In our view debates on this violently controversial matter would do more harm than good and would place an intolerable strain upon the United Nations.[63]

In his speech before the National People's Congress on 23 September 1954, Chou En-lai criticized Britain for participating in the US-sponsored military alliance in Southeast Asia and also for following the American policy of preventing China from acquiring its rightful position in the United Nations.[64]

Peking's Bid for Admission in the UN, 1955

In 1955 Peking made a determined bid to become a member of the United Nations. At first, it adopted pressure tactics and, when that failed, it assumed a peaceful posture on the international plane. When the Formosan Straits Crisis was at its height, the Security Council decided (on 31 January 1955) to include on its agenda both the New Zealand item (concerning the question of hostilities in the area of certain islands off the coast of Mainland China between the People's Republic of China and Nationalist China)[65] and the Soviet item (complaint regarding United States aggression against the People's Republic of China in the area of Taiwan and other islands of China).[66] The Council invited Peking to participate in the discussion of the first item which was to be considered first. In his reply cable to the UN Secretary General on 3 February 1955, Premier Chou En-lai categorically refused to send a representative to take part in the discussion of New Zealand's proposal. That proposal, Chou stated, obviously meant intervention in "China's internal affairs" and, as such, constituted a "direct violation of the fundamental principles of the United Nations Charter." He expressed his readiness to send the Chinese representative to take part in the deliberations of the Security Council

> only for the purpose of discussing the resolution of the Soviet Union and only when the representative of the Chiang Kai-shek clique has been driven out from the Security Council and the representative of the People's Republic of China is to attend in the name of China.[67]

After this attempt to pressurize the UN failed, Peking sought to convince the world of its peaceful intentions in the international field. It refuted the Western Powers' allegation that the Chinese attitude was neither peaceful nor consistent with the purposes and principles of the UN Charter. Thus, in his speech before the Helsinki Peace Congress on 23 June 1955, Kuo Mo-jo asserted : "As a Charter member of the United Nations China and her people have consistently supported the purposes and principles of the United Nations Charter."[68] The *People's Daily* cited numerous examples of Chinese efforts to ease international tension and strengthen mutual trust and cooperation among nations. Among these efforts were : termination of the war in Korea, that was "made possible through the initiative" of China; the "great contributions" made to the peaceful solution of the Indo-China question at the Geneva Conference; participation in the Asian-African Conference at Bandung; the upholding of the Five Principles of Peaceful Co-existence; and the establishment of peaceful, friendly relations with its neighbours.[69] The Sino-American Ambassadorial Talks on the problem of Formosa commenced on 1 August 1955 and 11 US airmen and four fighter pilots were also released by China (their release was reported by the UN Secretary-General just 11 days before the General Assembly vote on 20 September 1955). Thus, Peking asserted : "Ever since its founding, the great People's Republic of China has been steadfastly pursuing the policy of preserving peace and friendship among nations."[70]

In these circumstances, Krishna Menon of India was in a better position to make a strong case in favour of Peking at the tenth session of the General Assembly. He stated :

> Nothing was more striking at Bandung than not only the willingness but the enthusiasm, the insistence of the Chinese Government to express its allegiance to the Principles of the Charter of the United Nations and also to claim its position as a founding Member.

If Peking did not accept the legality of UN resolutions passed in its absence, he added, it was because it had been "wrongly excluded" from the UN. Hanifah of Indonesia said : "The Bandung Conference has...shown that the Government of Peking is quite capable of contributing its share to the easing of international tensions, for peaceful relations in the world of today." Unable to refer to any aggressive action on the part of China, the British delegate simply stated : "The time has not yet come when it would be in the interest of the United Nations to discuss this question. That is why we shall support the United States motion."[71] Addressing the General Assembly on 30 September 1955, the British Foreign Secretary, H. Macmillan, admitted that there was a marked improvement not only in the European but in the Asian theatre as well. "Both in Korea and Indo-China," he said, "fighting has stopped. Even in the problems surrounding China and the narrow seas, there has been a marked relaxation of tension." Referring to the question of Chinese representation in the UN, he remarked :

> We do not believe that the time has yet come to take up this problem. Nevertheless it must be settled before fully peaceful relations can be established in the Far East. But, as so often in human affairs, it is not only the question of what ought to be done but the question of when it ought to be done.[72]

The adoption of the US proposal, that postponed the consideration of the question of Chinese representation in the UN, was criticized by Peking. The denial of "inviolable and inalienable" rights of the Chinese people in the UN was considered "extremely unjust and unreasonable." Such an action, the *People's Daily* editorial stated, "breaches the Charter of the United Nations," lowers the prestige and standing of the UN and "grossly violates the interests of world peace and security." The Chinese paper observed :

> Without the participation of the People's Republic of China, it is utterly impossible to settle major international issues. It is inconceivable that world-wide agreement can be reached on general disarmament and the prohibition of the use of atomic weapons in exclusion of the People's Republic of China.

The *People's Daily* criticized Britain by referring to it as "certain Western countries...which have always talked about wanting to establish normal or even friendly relations with China," but had followed the United States year after year in agreeing to postpone "consideration of the lawful position of the Chinese People's Republic in the United Nations on the pretext of avoiding controversy and 'holding together' the United Nations." Such tactics, the Chinese paper stated, were only a "cover for an unfriendly attitude towards the Chinese People's Republic," which would never succeed. Since "so many countries which love peace and are concerned about the United Nations have expressed great dissatisfaction" at the exclusion of "a quarter of the human race," the continuation of this state of affairs "instead of holding the United Nations together...will, clearly, only impair its unity."[73]

Chinese efforts in 1955 to gain admission into the UN had not been entirely in vain. Peking received 12 votes in its favour, as compared to 7 in 1954. It was realised that sole reliance on the support of the Socialist bloc and few Asian nations was not enough. After Secretary of State Dulles threatened to use veto in the Security Council, Peking could hope to get entry into the UN only through the General Assembly. The universal membership of the UN, especially the admission of the newly-independent Afro-Asian countries and of those States (including communist nations) which had recognized the Peking Government but had not yet been admitted into the world organization, was, therefore, helpful to Peking. China endeavoured to gain recognition from as many countries as possible. At the same time, it championed the cause of newly-independent Afro-Asian countries and supported their case for admission into the UN. By so doing, Peking was indeed, facilitating its own admission into the world body. Accordingly, the *People's Daily* fully endorsed the 25-nation draft resolution on admission of a number of countries to the UN. That resolution, it stated, reflected "the common desire of an overwhelming majority of nations" and deserved "serious consideration of all UN members." The Chinese paper observed :

> If adopted the 25-nation draft resolution will undoubtedly greatly increase the universal character of U.N. membership and improve the present inadequate representation of Asian and African nations in the U.N. This will help the U.N. play its role of safeguarding the cause of peace.[74]

Of the 16 nations admitted to the UN on 14 December 1955, six were Afro-Asian states and four communist countries. Votes in favour of Peking at the General Assembly session in 1956 therefore, increased to 24, *i.e.* double of what they were in 1955.[75]

British Reservations Continue, 1956-60

In private discussions with Washington, London seems to have pleaded the case for Peking's admission into the UN.[76] However, its public posture remained unchanged in 1956 and thereafter. Year after year the British delegates to the UN repeated the same arguments about untimeliness and deep divisions and "opposing views...so strongly held" that any discussion of the question, far from contributing to "a solution"[77] of the problem, would only increase tension and prove harmful to the world organization. Thus, in 1956, Crosthwaite, the British delegate, considered the time inopportune "to attempt to settle that question." He stated : "A discussion of it would merely exacerbate feelings and would not be in the United Nations interests."[78] A year later, Sir Pierson Dixon observed : "Time was not yet ripe."[79] In 1958 again, he "could not help but feel that the reasons underlying its previous attitude were still valid."[80] In 1959 Dixon reiterated the same view.[81] He admitted that the General Assembly "does of course, discuss each year a considerable number of controversial questions," but "this question" of Chinese representation, he pointed out, "appears to us to be on a different level since it affects the very structure of our organization and since the feelings which it evokes are particularly strong."[82]

A fitting reply to British objections was given by Krishna Menon of India. He repudiated the British contention about untimeliness in the following words :

> When has one heard of an imperial country ever thinking that progress was timely ? There is always the phrase 'Always too late and too little' applied to those who are in the exercise of authority without the consent of peoples. Therefore, the question of timeliness is one on which we must agree to differ.

Referring to the charge of deep division on the issue, Menon observed : "The best way to deal with division is to discuss it." He saw no reason "why it should not be argued."[83] He also quoted the following remark of the representative of Finland : "My delegation fails to see how the successful activity of the United Nations could be furthered by not considering this matter here."[84] The Indian request to include the question of Chinese representation on the agenda of the General Assembly, the representative of Iraq stated, "is both appropriate and necessary." The rejection of that request, he observed, would not be "in the interests of our organization and would certainly not help to ease international tension."[85]

It was, thus, becoming increasingly difficult for the United States to secure General Assembly endorsement of the recommendation of the General Committee about postponing the consideration of the issue and preventing it from being included on the agenda of the Assembly. The problem of disarmament further added to the urgency of admitting China in the deliberations of the world organization. Claude Corea of Ceylon asked : "Can anyone envisage the banning of atomic tests or the banning of atomic weapons unless the People's Republic of China is a party to the ban ?"[86] Krishna Menon observed :

> It is impossible to think of any scheme of disarmament, let alone atomic weapons, when a country reputed to have a standing army of 5 million people and probably another 5 or 10 million in reserve is outside the ambit of the discussions. I would say that it does not seem sound and reasonable, to put it very mildly.[87]

He then quoted Lester Pearson (Canada), former President of the General Assembly, who earlier remarked :

> How long are we going to be able to support the United States position, because it is a United States position, that this question cannot even be talked about at the United Nations....How could Peking be asked to accept and carry out any such obligations, take part in control and inspection, which we rightly claim to be essential, and yet be considered as unrecognizable. It does, to say the least, present a dilemma.[88]

Apparently Peking was quite aware of the "dilemma" of the Western nations. It also took into account the fact that the aggressive foreign policy that it pursued from 1958 onwards—in 1958 in the Taiwan Straits, in 1959 in Tibet and in 1960 in Laos—did not in any way decrease the number of votes cast in its favour. Therefore, Peking began to assert that the restoration of its seat in the UN was "primarily not an urgent need of

China, but of the United Nations as a world organization."[89]
By denying China its "lawful seat" in the UN, the *People's Daily* asserted, "it is not the international status of China, but the prestige of the United Nations which has been more and more impaired." Commenting on the General Assembly's vote on the question of Chinese representation at its 15th session, the *People's Daily* quoted Comrade Shehu of Albania who had said that "to vote against the restoration of the rights of the Chinese Republic at the United Nations is to vote against peace, against disarmament." A significant addition among Peking's supporters in the UN in 1960 was Cuba—"the first Latin American country to have won independence and rid itself of the control of the United States." Peking's case was likely to be supported by more nations if they overthrew imperialist domination and enslavement. Accordingly, it was in Chinese interest to support the "national democratic movements in Asia, Africa and Latin America" and to cultivate relations with those countries. Peking also relied on making "more and more people...realise that no major current international issues can be settled without China's participation."[90] Peking, thus, adopted an intransigent and aggressive attitude and wanted to remain free from any moral pressure or influence of world public opinion that the membership of the UN might have entailed.

Towards a "Two-China" Solution, 1961-70

The Western Powers felt concerned about the aggressive international posture of China and the prospect of it becoming a nuclear-weapon Power. They realized the urgency of solving the problem of arms control by bringing Peking in the world organization. They also could not remain indifferent to the "serious risk"[91] of being outvoted in the 1961 session of the General Assembly on the question of placing the problem of Chinese representation on the agenda. Motivated by these considerations, rather than any anxiety to gain the goodwill of the uncommitted countries, Britain began to have second thoughts about following America in the matter. London also felt encouraged by President Kennedy's success in the USA. Thus, Foreign Secretary Sir Alec Douglas-Home observed on 8 February 1961 :

> One must admit that a country which has lately smothered Tibet, is infringing India's frontiers and rejecting all attempts at conciliation, and which has publicly proclaimed its belief in the necessity of war, has few of the credentials of a peace-loving nation in the United Nations. All that is true. Nevertheless, we have always felt, and we feel now, that the facts of international life require that Communist China should be seated in the United Nations....We can make no progress with disarmament unless China is there. I do not know whether we can make very much progress if she is, but that remains to be seen. But the United Kingdom's position is plain and consistent. We recognize Communist China and we have our representative there. We have supported the moratorium in the debates on whether or not Communist China should be seated in the United Nations, because the choice, until now, has been between the admission of Communist China and the break-up of the United Nations. So long as that was the choice there was only one answer. It is for the United States to say, in their own time, what their attitude will be, but, of course, we are in close touch and our approach to this problem is well-known to them.[92]

The Democratic leaders of the USA also realized the necessity of making a reappraisal of Washington's China policy. As early as 11 November 1960, Chester Bowles spoke of the solution of the problem of China's entry in the UN "through some kind of a 'two China' policy'."[93] Adlai Stevenson, the new US Resident Representative at the UN, in his press conference on 27 January 1961, stated that while the US sought to "achieve peaceful relations and restore harmony with Communist China," it would not be at the cost of the US determination "to stand by our treaty commitments with our allies," including the Republic of China. He regarded Communist China's threat to take Taiwan by force if necessary "inconsistent with the renunciation of force which is an obligation of all members of the United Nations."[94] In other words, the United States demanded that as a price for its admission in the UN, Peking should issue a public statement renouncing the use of force as regards Taiwan and express its willingness to co-exist in the UN with the Nationalist regime of China. Secretary of State Dean Rusk made that abundantly clear when he observed :

> We recognize and support the membership of the Government of the Republic of China and will continue to do so. The authorities in Peiping have indicated that they are not interested in relationships unless Formosa is abandoned. It may be that the question comes up as to whether they have any interest in membership in the United Nations under these circumstances.[95]

The question of Chinese representation in the UN was, for the first time, debated in the General Assembly at its 16th Session in 1961. Before the discussion on the subject began, Peking criticized the US policy of "two Chinas" and observed that while it was interested in becoming a member of the world organization, the representative of the "Kuomintang clique" must be expelled first.[96] The United States seemed willing to consider the case of Peking's admission in the UN, but was not at all prepared to acquiesce "in Communist China's design to conquer Taiwan." Peking's demand for the expulsion of Nationalist China from the UN was considered "absurd and unthinkable" because it would have given the organization's seal of approval to the "conquest and overthrow" of the Nationalist regime in Formosa. Since Peking appeared in no mood to compromise on this score, Adlai Stevenson found it "impossible to speak seriously...of 'bringing communist China into the United Nations'." He lamented : "No basis exists on which such a step could be taken."[97] The US, therefore, submitted a resolution, along with four other countries, which declared that any proposal to change the representation of China was "an important question," requiring a two-thirds majority under Article 18 of the Charter. This five-Power resolution was adopted by 61 votes to 34 with 7 abstentions. Britain voted in favour of this resolution and explained its vote in the following words :

> No one who has followed the course of this problem through the last decade, in this Assembly as well as elsewhere, can deny that it is an important question....It is, therefore,

reasonable that it should be dealt with in accordance with the procedure for reaching decisions on important questions in the General Assembly. Her Majesty's Government in the United Kingdom wishes to make it clear that its objective in supporting this draft resolution is not—I repeat, is not—to find some new means of pushing this important problem aside. It is not the policy of Her Majesty's Government to deny a seat in the United Nations to the People's Republic of China. On the contrary, as my Secretary of State, Lord Home, said in the British Parliament last February, we believe that the facts of international life require the presence of the People's Republic of China in the United Nations. Her Majesty's Government in the United Kingdom believes that the aim of the United Nations must be to reach a solution to the question of Chinese representation acceptable to wide majority of Member States and as fair to all the interested parties as circumstances permit.[98]

The British delegate also voted in favour of the Soviet draft resolution and the three-Power amendment, the practical effect of which would have been the seating of Communist China in the UN and the removal of the Formosan delegate from the world body.[99] However, both the Soviet resolution and the three-Power amendment thereto were defeated. Godber explained the British vote by stating that the UK voted for them because "the sense" of both these proposals was that "the People's Republic of of China should be seated in the United Nations as representing the State of China." That, however, did not mean, Godber added, that Britain supported Peking's claim to represent Formosa in the United Nations. Since sovereignty over the island of Formosa, in the view of Her Majesty's Government, was undetermined, the question as to "who should represent Formosa in the United Nations," was also undetermined. That was a matter that had yet to be decided and on which Her Majesty's Government was free to take any position it liked. Moreover, the General Assembly, Godber remarked, could only bind itself and its subsidiary organs but not the "other principal organs of the United Nations" (*i.e.* the Security Council) to whom it could only make recommendations.[100] It appeared that Britain was not prepared to support Peking's case for permanent membership in the Security Council unless it accepted a "two China" solution by accommodating Taipeh in the UN.[101]

From 1961 to 1970, Britain continued to vote in favour of the resolution sponsored by Albania and others demanding the admission of Peking and expelling Taiwan from the UN as also in support of the US draft resolution declaring the question of Chinese representation in the UN to be "an important question" requiring a two-thirds majority. Thus, speaking in the debate on the question of Chinese representation in 1969, the British representative, Lord Caradon, remarked that the two resolutions before the UN General Assembly were "all too familiar." The British Government, he stated, had "regularly and consistently voted in favour of them both" and that "we shall certainly do so again." He conceded that the admission of China in the UN was important "for the Chinese people...for this world Assembly" and that every effort should be made to bring about the entry of the Peking regime into the international community. But, at the same time, he did not abandon the position that a two-thirds majority was required in the matter.[102]   This attitude was no doubt inconsistent with the British recognition of the Peking regime and, in effect, it delayed, if not prevented, China's admission in the world organization. The British were quite aware of the contradiction in their approach but they were not inclined to give up their bargaining counter and to displease Washington.

Replying to a written question in the House of Commons on 29 May 1970, the British Joint Under-Secretary of State for Foreign Affairs observed that his Government had always believed that the representation of the Chinese Government and the Chinese people at the United Nations was a prerequisite to the solution of major world problems.[103] But this did not produce any change in the British voting in the UN on the question of Chinese representation even though a majority of member states had, for the first time, voted in favour of the Albanian resolution.

Speaking in the General Debate in the UN General Assembly in 1970, the British Foreign Secretary, Sir Alec Douglas-Home, expressed concern about not all the major Powers being represented in the United Nations. He made a specific mention of China in that regard and stated : "This has made it undoubtedly more difficult for us to tackle effectively in this forum some of the most pressing and dangerous problems that trouble the world." He appealed to Peking to give up the rigidity of its political doctrine and think of the influence it would gain from joining the UN and of the advantages accruing from expanding trade, from prosperity and from interdependence.[104] Inspite of such a patronizing attitude and moral overtones, Britain continued its dual policy of supporting both the US and the Albanian draft resolutions in 1970. The Albanian draft, it is worth recalling, was approved by 51 votes to 49, with 25 abstentions. Thus, a simple majority of UN members for the first time pronounced itself in favour of Peking's admission and Taiwan's expulsion from the world organization.

Peking's Admission in the UN, 1971

The year 1971 witnessed a marked improvement in Sino-British relations and a significant change in the international situation. The hostility between Washington and Peking was giving place to Sino-US *rapprochement* in the wake of Nixon's visit to China and Peking appeared keen to stage a come-back on the international diplomatic scene. A number of West European countries were moving fast in establishing diplomatic relations at ambassadorial level with China. In this situation, Britain realized the incongruity of its low-level diplomatic relations with the Peking regime. Chou En-lai's apology (alongwith an undertaking to reimburse the cost) for the sacking of the British Mission in Peking in August 1967 and the release of British nationals detained in China gave sufficient indication of the Chinese desire to improve relations with Britain. Anglo-Chinese negotiations on the exchange of ambassadors were resumed in early 1971. In these circumstances, London once again modified its attitude on the question of Chinese representation in the United Nations.

Even before the question of Chinese representation was debated in the UN General Assembly in 1971, a change was noticeable in the British attitude in the matter. Speaking in the House of Commons on 2 August 1971, Sir Alec Douglas-Home referred to "a recent improvement" in Sino-British relations and to the discussions that were continuing about the exchange of ambassadors. He very much doubted that an Important Question Resolution would be moved in the fall of 1971. While keeping an open mind on "what form resolutions may take at the United Nations," Sir Alec proceeded to define the basic guidelines of British policy on the subject in the following words : "We have consistently voted for the Albanian resolution to seat Communist China, and I should add that there is only one seat for one country in the organization." Replying to a query as to whether any change in the position of maintaining a consulate in Taiwan was contemplated, Sir Alec observed that the Consulate was "not accredited to the Government of Taiwan." He declined to further elaborate that statement. He remarked : "At the moment I would rather not add to what I said just now."[105]

When the question of Chinese representation in the UN came before the General Committee of the UN in September 1971, the British delegate expressed his doubts as to the compatibility with the Charter of any proposal providing for dual representation. Thereafter, speaking in the debate on the subject, Sir Colin Crowe (UK) referred to President Nixon's initiative to forge a new relationship between the USA and China and to the virtual consensus in favour of seating Peking's representatives in the UN. Chinese participation in the deliberations of the world organization, he stated, was "a matter both of justice and of urgency." As a nuclear-weapon Power, China should participate "in our discussions on disarmament." Moreover, the UN could not hope to live up to its potential either as a world organization or as a centre for harmonizing the actions of nations unless and until the representatives of the People's Republic of China were able to come "into our midst," for which, Sir Colin Crowe remarked, "the time has surely come."

Explaining the British attitude on the question, Colin Crowe observed :

The Government of the People's Republic of China is the sole legal Government of China and is, therefore, entitled to occupy the place which the Charter accords to that State. There is no question here of the expulsion of a Member State, it is, rather, a question of who should represent an existing Member State. In the light of that my delegation will vote against any substantive draft resolution or amendment which provides for dual representation.

Britain, he further stated, would vote against the draft resolution contained in document A/L. 633, the amendments contained in document A/L. 637, as also against any procedural proposals which would have the effect of further delaying the entry of the Peking regime in the United Nations.[106] The views expressed by Colin Crowe in 1971 were in marked contrast to those previously held by Britain on the subject and contributed, in no small measure, towards the establishment of full diplomatic relations at ambassadorial level between Britain and China in March 1972.

Thus, for the first time in 1971, Britain voted against the US draft resolution requiring two-thirds majority for Peking's admission in the UN. The US draft was rejected by 59 votes to 55, with 15 abstentions and the Albanian draft resolution secured more than two-thirds majority—75 votes in favour, 35 against with 17 abstentions. Even if the US draft had been approved that year, it would not have prevented Chinese entry into the UN in 1971. Communist China joined the world organization in November 1971 itself, Taiwan was expelled and Peking simultaneously became a permanent member of the Security Council.

After the General Assembly adopted the resolution admitting the People's Republic of China and expelling Taiwan, Minister of State Godber explained the British attitude in the matter in the House of Commons on 4 November 1971. "What was at issue on this occasion," he said, "was quite simply who should represent China at the United Nations." Both the Government in Peking, and the authorities in Taiwan, claimed to be the rightful representatives of the people of China. There had been a lot of sympathy for the proposition that both Mainland China and Taiwan should be represented in the UN. The "two Chinas" solution, Godber observed, was superficially attractive, but it did not take into account the fact that neither Peking nor Taiwan was willing to accept that there could be a two Chinas solution, since they both claimed to represent the whole of China. In these circumstances, Godber remarked, Britain took the view that the exclusion of 14 million inhabitants of Taiwan was a lesser evil than the continued exclusion of the representatives of 750 million people in China. He considered that to be "the best solution." Accordingly, Britain decided not to support the procedural "Important Question" resolution, which was designed to delay Peking's entry.[107] Since mainland China represented "one of the great realities of power in the world,"[108] it was believed that admission of China would help impart some new sense of realism to discussions in the United Nations. Godber welcomed the arrival of Chinese representatives and expressed his willingness to listen to their views with interest. Britain, he stated, would assess their words and actions at the United Nations realistically, on the basis of how they affected Britain's interests and Britain's position in the world. Godber also expressed the hope that Peking's entry in the UN would lead to closer bilateral contacts between China and other nations, including Britain.[109]

CHAPTER EIGHT

Trade

Sino-British trade could make little headway in the immediate post-war period (1945-49) because of the Chinese Civil War and the failure of the corrupt Kuomintang government to curb inflation, conserve foreign exchange, have a balanced budget or to promote exports. Therefore, it was believed by the British Trade Mission, that visited China in 1946, that once conditions of peace and economic stability were established within China, the way would be "open for an incalculable development of trade between our two countries."[1] The prospects of such conditions being restored under communist rule in China seemed bright. The People's Republic of China also embarked on an ambitious programme of industrial development,[2] which could be succesfully carried out only with "an extensive exchange of goods and services with countries overseas."[3] Moreover, as compared to the Nationalist Government of Chiang Kai-shek, the trade and banking regulations of the Mao regime were much "more liberally framed"[4] and apparently Peking did not discriminate between the British merchants and their Chinese counterparts.[5]

However, in the beginning, British firms in Shanghai faced certain difficulties as a result of drastic steps taken by the People's Republic to check inflation and balance the budget; its policy of extending the sphere of state activity in the economic field and the non-establishment of diplomatic relations between the UK and China. But the bombing and blockade of Chinese ports by Chiang Kai-shek (effective since 26 June 1949) was much more damaging.[6] On 24 May 1950, Foreign Secretary Bevin observed :

The British interests in China have been hurt more by that (nationalist blockade) than by what the Communists have done. The Commmnists have taxed them, charged them and done all sorts of things, but I think that in all probability their difficulties could have been got over if the blockade had not been put in operation.[7]

As soon as Peking became aware that lack of experience and revolutionary zeal were causing harm to the national economy, it did not hesitate to modify its policies. British recognition of China and the "liberation" of Hainan and Chousan islands further improved prospects of more fruitful trade between the two countries.[8]

Effect of Korean War

The improvement of conditions in the summer of 1950 enabled British firms to transact sizable business for nearly a year. However, Sino-British trade suffered a severe setback in the wake of the Korean War. The imposition of an embargo by the UN in May 1951 proved injurious to Chinese economic recovery and compelled Peking to take the course of autarchy and economic integration with the Soviet bloc.[9] Peking diverted its energies from economic reconstruction to defence production, instituted stringent economic controls and accelerated the process of socialization of industry and commerce. Pressures on the business community increased considerably after the imposition of embargo, particularly during the Five-Anti Movement.[10] There was a marked expansion of the State or public sector in industrial production and in domestic as well as foreign trade. Whereas the output of industrial goods from state-owned enterprises in 1949 was only 43.8% of the total output, by 1952 it rose to 67.3%. The Government controlled over 90% of all loans and deposits through the People's Bank.[11] By the end of 1952 private enterprises accounted for only 36% of the total wholesale trade, 58% of retail trade and 39% of factory production, as compared to 76%, 84% and 52% respectively in 1950.[12] Of the total foreign trade, private merchants accounted for 31.65% in 1950 but they handled 8.21% in 1952, 7.88% in 1953 and as little as 1.83% in 1954. Since then, their share virtually disappeared.[13] Thus, on 23 September 1954 Chou En-lai claimed that "state-operated commerce" dominated domestic trade and had "in its charge the whole of the foreign trade."[14]

Problems of British Enterprises in China

The attempts by Peking authorities to bring foreign, as well as internal, trade under state control and to regulate the supply of raw materials to industries, the sale of their goods and their profits[15] adversely affected British industrial and trading concerns in China. The imposition of large fines during the Five-Anti Campaign led to "great shortage of money, and to the inevitable slowing down or stopping of industries, and therefore, to potential unemployment."[16] The restriction of the volume and area of business of private international trading companies (by 1953 they accounted for only 8% of total foreign trade) affected their capacity to pay the wages to workers and taxes to the Government. In these circumstances, British firms naturally contemplated a reduction in the number of employees to a size commensurate with the reduced volume of trade, but they were not allowed to do so. G.E. Mitchell, Secretary and Vice-Chairman of the China Association,[17] stated :

> By regulations, labour cannot be dismissed, and no industrialist may retrench without the agreement of the appropriate union, nor may a business close down without the permission of the authorities, so the situation has been that the big British factories have been compelled to continue to maintain on their pay rolls their full labour forces, and to pay them their full wages, despite the fact that they were at times doing practically no work and making practically no sales. In one instance, which Mr. Eden quoted in the House of Commons, one British factory had had 20,000 men on its pay roll for more than two years with no work for them to do.[18]

Although Chinese merchants did not get any preferential treatment, they were still better off in two ways : firstly, they were allowed to "revalue their assets in terms of the new exchange value"[19]; and secondly, they had no European staff problem.

The problem of recalling back the European employees of British firms arose out of the need to carry out retrenchment and the extremely strict attitude adopted by the People's Government in granting exit permits.[20] Before granting an exit permit to any European employee of British firms, a thorough examination of all his affairs was undertaken to ensure that he did not leave behind any unpaid debts or other obligations. Closely connected with the surplus Chinese and European staff problem was the doctrine of personal responsibility, *i.e.* the practice of holding senior staff personally responsible for any claims against the company.[21]

Previously, British firms bore their losses in the hope that conditions would improve,[22] but now their difficulties were all due to the deliberate policy pursued by the Chinese Government. Lord Reading, Minister of State in the Foreign Office, stated :

> It is the deliberate policy of the Chinese Government to render it impossible for most British and foreign firms to remain in China and to force them to surrender their assets. The reduction in assets is mainly due to the Chinese authorities forcing British firms into debt by restrictions, regulations and taxes et cetera, so that they have been unable to carry on, and in order to be able to liquidate and leave China they have had to surrender all their assets to the Chinese authorities. Only a comparatively small part of the reduction in assets is due to direct expropriation and confiscation by the Chinese.[23]

Giving information about Chinese requisitions of British property to the House of Commons on 15 October 1952, Foreign Secretary Eden observed :

> The present Chinese Government requisitioned certain property, equipment and buildings, belonging to two British firms, at Hankow, Chungking, and other ports in late 1950 and early 1951. In April 1951, they requisitioned all the property of the Shell Company in China, with the exception of some office accomodation. In August 1952, they requisitioned two British dockyards at Shanghai. Among other property taken over by the Chinese authorities is land belonging to the Shanghai and Tientsin Race Course Companies and some privately-owned houses and building land.[24]

The Chinese requisition of the property of Shanghai Dock-yard Ltd. and of M/s. Mollars Ship Buildings and Engineering Works on 16 August 1952 was in retaliation to the British decision to transfer 40 aircraft impounded at Hong Kong to American Airlines. In October 1952 the Supreme Court of Hong Kong decided that the remaining 31 aircraft should also be transferred to the American company.[25] China protested against this judgement and retaliated (on 21 November 1952) by requisitioning the property of four more British companies including the Shanghai Water Works Company.[26] Except for a sum of £13,710, which Peking agreed to remit in May 1956 to the management of the Company in respect of the pensioners, China refused to accept any other claim in that regard.[27] On 24 February 1953, Tsao Jo-ming, Director of the Foreign National Affairs Office of the Canton Military Control Committee, issued orders requisitioning wharves and go-downs and all the property (excepting the business premises) of the British firm Messrs. Butterfield and Swire.[28] In nearly all these cases, the British Government made representations to the Chinese Government and reserved full rights of the owners. All these requisitions, however, represented only a small portion of the assets surrendered by British firms in China.

The Chinese Government deliberately pursued a policy of requisitioning foreign enterprises only on a very limited scale. Peking intended to deprive them of even the technical "title to their properties" and of any "hope of making a claim if it should ever be possible to do so later on."[29] Peking was quite aware that the British merchants could not continue to sustain heavy losses for a long time. Thus, the only course left open to British firms was to seek permission to close their businesses. When they found that the winding up of their businesses was also not an easy job,[30] they sought the help of their Government.

Representations and Protests

The British Government could not be expected to remain indifferent to the interests of its nationals in China. In its protest note of 1 September 1951, the British Foreign Office complained of "arbitrary arrests and detention for indefinite periods" of British nationals. It also protested against the Chinese practice of holding "individuals personally responsible for the transactions and liabilities" of the firms which employed them and of refusing to allow them to leave China. After denouncing such actions as contrary to "generally accepted principles," the note expressed grave concern at the Chinese policy towards foreign nationals. It requested that steps be taken in the near future to rectify the situation. On the specific difficulties of British firms in China, the protest note stated :

> Although British business and other interests have been encouraged to remain in China by their understanding that the Central People's Government wish to maintain commercial relations with other nations, they have been subjected to constant uncertainties and hindrances which have caused grave disappointment and anxiety. For example, employers of labour are not even able to go into voluntary liquidation when, as a result of lack of materials or other circumstances beyond their control, they are no longer in a position to maintain their output. They are in fact prevented from reducing their pay roll, with the result that they are often forced to incur heavy losses. They may then he held personally responsible for liabilities so incurred, as already explained.[31]

On 12 April 1952 Her Majesty's *charge d' affaires* in Peking delivered another formal note which enumerated the difficulties experienced by British firms as follows :

(i) the making of each individual manager personally responsible for the policy and acts of his company, in some cases for acts before he became manager;

(ii) the increasing restrictions on the entry and exit of foreign staff;

(iii) the cancellation by the Chinese Government's trading organisations of former contracts, even though raw materials have been paid for and processed;

(iv) taxation and legal judgements which both appear to be discriminatory against foreigners;

(v) uncertainty caused to British subjects by the fear of arrest and detention incommunicado and without charges being preferred; and

(vi) pressure by the labour unions and reluctance by the local authorities to give any protection to firms who are being accused by the unions of malpractice.

"If this situation continues," the note warned, "it can only result, sooner or later, in the elimination of British business interests in China to the detriment of friendly relations between China and the United Kingdom."

On 19 May 1952, the British Government addressed yet another note to Peking at the request of the China Association. The note stated :

Nearly all, if not all, of the British companies in China, have come to the conclusion that this change in conditions necessitates a corresponding change in the nature of their organisations and in the scope of their activities. Many feel they can no longer operate satisfactorily in China and can serve no useful purpose in the future. Consequently they feel that the proper course is for them to arrange for the transfer as going concerns, custody or closure, of their businesses. The needs of individual companies will vary with their particular circumstances, and applications appropriate thereto will be made by them in due course.

In paragraph 3 of the Note, London referred to the belief of "a number of important British companies...that they can still perform a useful service in the interests of Sino-British trade." Britain also sought "the good offices of the Central People's Government" in regard to the following matters :

(a) approval of the termination of the services of redundant staff;

(b) the issue of exit permits for non-Chinese staff;

(c) the setting up of machinery to deal with custody or transfer as going concerns of any businesses to which this treatment is appropriate;

(d) taking of the necessary steps to deal with the suggestion in paragraph 3 above.

In view of the prolonged period during which many companies

had been operating under economically adverse circumstances, Her Majesty's Government requested that early and favourable consideration be given to the representations made in the note.[32]

In a statement before the House of Commons on 20 May 1952, Anthony Eden explained that the decision to wind up their business had been taken by British enterprises "reluctantly" and that in endorsing that decision "Her Majesty's Government for their part fully realise the gravity of this step." But since "British firms in China have for reasons beyond their control been facing...increasing difficulties" and "operating at a loss for a considerable period...it is difficult to see how the firms could have made any other decision."[33]

In reply to the British note of 19 May 1952, Chang Han-fu, Vice-Minister for Foreign Affairs, stated that the "serious but unnecessary difficulties" of British firms had been due to "their bad management" and to the "depressed state of trade between the two countries." The latter, he asserted, was brought about by the "discriminatory trade policy against China" pursued by the British government. He observed :

> The predicament of the British firms in China is the bitter fruit of the policy of trade control and embargo of the British Government. This alone suffices to prove that by following the United States in carrying out the trade control and embargo, the British Government not only contravenes but also jeopardises the interests of the British people.
> Due protection shall be afforded to the British companies and manufacturing firms in the territories of the People's Republic of China by the authorities of the People's governments of all levels, provided that they abide by the laws of the Chinese Government. In case they wish to wind up their business voluntarily, no matter what form of wind up they may take, they may apply to the People's government at their respective localities, and the competent authorities will deal with each case according to its own merits and the regulations. In the course of winding up, any question that may arise relating to the termination of services of employees and workers, the applications for exit permits, and the disposal of the enterprises, may be expeditiously and reasonably settled on the merits of each case and in accordance with the regulations.[34]

Subsequent events seemed to prove that "the Chinese were not disposed to let their victims go without wringing the uttermost farthing out of them."[35] British firms duly submitted their applications for winding up their businesses, but the Chinese authorities did not adopt a sympathetic attitude. Accordingly, another British note was delivered to Peking on 8 January 1953. It reminded the Chinese Government of its assurance and complained that most British firms "have been unable to make any appreciable progress"[36] in regard to the winding up of their business. Meanwhile, their employees were presenting them with "unreasonable and exhorbitant demands for settlements."[37] *The Sunday Times* report of 18 January 1953 that there had been a change for the better in the attitude of Chinese officials towards British firms in China was discounted by Lord Reading, Parliamentary Under-Secretary of State for Foreign Affairs. He stated that only a small proportion of British firms had applied for permission to wind up their activities in China. The Chinese authorities not only delayed granting such permission but also continued to detain many members of senior staff of British firms. Lord Reading mentioned 11 specific cases of businessmen whose departure was being delayed.[38] On 30 July 1953, Selwyn Lloyd, Minister of State, observed : "Our traders really have not had a fair deal."[39] On 22 February 1954, Foreign Secretary Eden characterized the treatment of British interests, including business and trade, as "most unsatisfactory." He remarked : "I regard this position as in every way unjust and unsatisfactory as far as British interests are concerned. If the Chinese Government want to improve relations with us, the best thing they can do is to treat our interests in China with ordinary courtesy and justice."[40]

As a result of the fruitful negotiations between Chou En-lai and Eden at Geneva, the Chinese adopted, a somewhat liberal attitude in issuing entry and exist permits.[41] However, their fundamental attitude towards British firms and other foreign firms remained unchanged.[42] British firms, therefore, continued to surrender their assets in China to Chinese authorities. It was disclosed on 26 July 1955 that Jardine Matheson and Company, which had extensive interests in 14 major Chinese cities, brought to an end its 120 years connection with China

when it surrendered its Shanghai establishment, the last to be
so liquidated, to Chinese authorities.[43] On 27 January 1958,
a British M.P. asked : "What steps have been taken to date
to obtain compensation for British property seized on the
Chinese mainland since 1949; and what is proposed to be done
in the future." Ian Harvey, Joint Under-Secretary of State
for Foreign Affairs, replied :

> Representations have been made to the Chinese authorities
> in those cases in which the owners requested such action.
> When, as I am sorry to say have been the general rule, the
> reply received has been unsatisfactory, the full rights of the
> owners, where they so desire, have been reserved against the
> time when it may be possible to discuss the matter further
> with the Chinese authorities.[44]

In spite of the fact that British firms and nationals were
being treated very badly by the Peking authorities, the British
Government could hardly take any retaliatory measures against
China. The developed country (Britain), H. Trevelyan points
out, had invested heavily in the underdeveloped country (China)
but the latter had no investments in the former. The seizure of
the Chinese Embassy in London, he stated, would have invited
immediate seizure of the rest of the British compound in Peking
and the consular property which they still had round China.
If the Hong Kong Government took measures against the Bank
of China in Hong Kong, the British diplomat remarks, Britain
would have invited hostile Chinese reaction against Hong Kong,
which daily received a large supply of fresh vegetables, fruit,
meat and poultry from Communist China, whose trade unions
were riddled with Communist agents, but which was at
that time less troubled by subversive action than in the days of
Nationalist power. As regards refusal to trade with China,
H. Trevelyan observes, it was by no means certain that British
firms would be willing to forgo their lucrative trade and see it
fall into the hands of their European competitors or the few
British firms which were in the hands of the fellow-travellers
and could therefore hope to receive favours from the Communists. One British firm, he says, was even negotiating a
profitable long-term contract for the sale of Chinese produce

at a time when its own business in China was being held to ransom and its manager harassed and denied the right to leave. Trevelyan does not blame that firm because if the firm refused the new contract, it would neither help the manager in his difficulties nor improve the chance of getting the Chinese to agree to the old branch being closed without the firm having to pay to give it up.[45]

Trade with China

The elimination of British merchant houses in China was "an extremely important and serious step" in British relations with China.[46] It snapped an important link in British trade with China. However, it did not imply the total cessation of trade between the two countries.[47] The British were fully convinced of the desirability of continuing trade with China. In a note delivered to the Chinese Government on 18 April 1952, the British Government stated :

> Her Majesty's Government have received unofficial reports of statements recently made in Moscow indicating that the Central People's Government (C. P. G.) is prepared to increase substantially China's trade with the United Kingdom.[48] Her Majesty's Government have noted this decision with interest and hope to receive from the C.P.G. an early intimation of the nature of its proposals and of the channels through which it intends to pursue the suggestions outlined in Moscow. In this connexion Her Majesty's Government point out that there are numerous established British merchants in Shanghai and Hong Kong who are well qualified to negotiate any such arrangements with the C.P.G. or its representatives.[49]

In the British note of 19 May 1952, Peking was informed of the decision of British firms to close down their businesses. However, London did not forget to mention that in order to carry on trade between China and Britain, British companies "contemplate setting up a new form of organisation...better suited to current conditions." This body, it was stated, could, "in fact, act as a permanent Trade Mission."[50] Chang Han-fu, in his reply, welcomed the British suggestion and recognized the need of continuing trade relations between the two countries. He stated :

> Recently, at the International Economic Conference, convened in April of this year in Moscow, the Chinese and British delegations reached an agreement for trade exchange to the amount of 10 million pounds on either side in 1952. On the basis of this agreement, the Chinese and British representatives for trade negotiations signed on June 9, in Berlin, a proforma contract to the amount of 6,500,000 pounds for the first instalment of goods.[51] All these facts amply prove that the Chinese government and people are willing to develop between China and Britain a normal trade relationship on an equal and mutually beneficial basis....The Central People's Government considers that the active promotion of the trade relations between China and Britain on a basis of equality and mutual benefit is conducive to the recovery and development of industrial and agricultural production in both countries, as well as to the improvement of the living conditions of the peoples of both countries. Therefore, any British company and manufacturing firm, or any such in the territory of China, as well as any organisation jointly formed by the British companies and manufacturing firms, provided that they do not harbour monopoly designs and are willing to trade with China on a basis of equality and mutual benefit, may all approach at any time the private and state trade organisations of China, establish contacts with them and conduct specific business negotiations with them.[52]

It was, thus, evident that both the British Government and traders were "exceedingly reluctant" to give up their commerce with China. On the contrary, they were quite keen to "build it up."[53] China too considered it beneficial to continue trade relations with Britain. Trade between the two countries continued to flourish until the middle of 1951,[54] when, under heavy pressure from Washington, London was obliged to give a draconian interpretation to the UN General Assembly resolution of May 1951 calling for an embargo on the shipment of strategic materials to China.[55] However, it was still believed in British commercial circles that the communist countries of Europe, including the Soviet Union, would not be able to supply the required goods and machinery to China either in the desired quantity or at reasonable prices. Accordingly,

China would remain interested in the East-West trade.[56]

Sino-British trade reached an "abnormally low" level in the first quarter of 1952,[57] and this was a cause of serious concern to both China and Britain. That China was quite keen to resume trade relations with the West, particularly Britain, was evident from the establishment on 4 May 1952 of a China Committee for the Promotion of International Trade to implement the resolutions passed at the Moscow International Economic Conference; the renewal of trade with Hong Kong towards the end of 1952; the establishment of an office for trade purposes in Berlin; trade negotiations with the representatives of British industrial and commercial circles in Moscow[58] and Peking;[59] and official Chinese statements.[60] Britain, on its part, was no less eager to continue its trade with China and, if possible, to expand it. Harold Davies, M.P. and a member of the British delegation to the Moscow Economic Conference, revealed that the British delegation was "the first to get down to business talks with the Chinese." Britain, he remarked, could no longer sit back and wait for trade to come to its doors. "We must go out and seek our markets," he said.[61] Britain was particularly interested in the export of textile goods, which constituted 35% of its total exports under the Moscow Agreement of 1952. Hopkinson, Secretary for Overseas Trade, observed :

In view of conditions in Lancashire and Yorkshire the export of British textiles is of paramount importance and we must neglect no opportunity of fostering this trade. In these circumstances, sensational reports of offers emanating from the Moscow Economic Conference have, naturally, aroused the greatest interest.[62]

As compared to 1952, there was marked improvement in Sino-British trade in the beginning of 1953.[63] However, it still remained far below West European countries' trade with China.[64] Because of the world-wide business recession, declining British exports, falling invisible earnings and keen competition from other nations, Britain became anxious "to increase its share of export markets, above all in the non-sterling world." The *Economic Survey for 1953*, presented by the Chancellor of the Exchequer to the Parliament (March 1953), concluded : "The most important task facing British industry today is to expand exports."[65] In these circumstances, British manufacturers and businessmen began to lay stress on expansion of Sino-British trade.[66] They felt encouraged by the Korean Armistice (July 1953) and recalled the words of P. Thorneycroft, President of the Board of Trade, who had said that "any improvement in the international situation with regard to peace will be a very helpful thing so far as the promotion of trade is concerned."[67] However, it was difficult for Britain to contemplate trade relations with China in strategic goods because Washington was firmly opposed to it.[68] Nevertheless, London considered itself morally free to continue and expand trade with China in non-strategic goods.

Towards the end of 1953, therefore, the China Association, the London Chamber of Commerce and the Federation of British Industries, held consultations to explore what could be done within the permitted limits of trade between the two countries. "With this end in view, and with the approval of H.M. Government," the three organisations addressed (on 29 March 1954) a letter to Yeh Chi-chuang, Minister of Foreign Trade in Peking.[69] In his reply, Lei Yen-min, Chinese Vice Minister for Foreign Trade, expressed his willingness to discuss the proposals contained in the letter. Accordingly, Peter Tennant of the Federation of British Industries held two series of meetings with Chinese officials in Geneva on 6-7 and 26-28 May 1954. Subsequently, the three British organizations, alongwith the Association of British Chambers of Commerce and the National Union of Manufacturers, formed the Sino-British Trade Committee (SBTC). "With the approval of H.M. Government,"[70] the SBTC arranged the visit of a Chinese trade delegation to Britain in June-July 1954. The SBTC held discussions with the visiting Chinese delegation with a view "to open up opportunities of business between the Chinese State trading organisations and British industrial and commercial firms, and to seek an expansion of trade" between United Kingdom and Hong Kong on the one hand and China on the other. The statement, issued at the end of the talks, reported "satisfactory progress towards reaching an understanding on the matters discussed."[71] In pursuance of the Chinese invitation and in order to follow up the series of useful discussions, a British trade mission, sponsored by the SBTC, visited China in November-December 1954 and signed contracts worth £3 million.[72]

Thus, during 1954 trade delegations of the two countries exchanged visits. There also appeared signs of a "new Chinese attitude to Western trade." The Chinese seemed willing to adopt "easier and more normal trading terms," to utilise the facilities offered by British banks in China,[73] and to accord a somewhat better treatment to British firms in regard to the grant of exit visas to some British residents. With the establishment of diplomatic relations at *charge d' affaires* level, the handicap which British businessmen had hitherto suffered on account of the absence of a Chinese Government representative "in any British territory with authority to issue visas" for travel in China was also removed.[74] British merchants hoped that commercial attaches would soon be added to the diplomatic missions of the two countries and that Peking would agree to open "a branch office of the China National Import and Export Corporation in London."[75]

Two British trade delegations visited China in 1955. The first, sponsored by the British Council for the Promotion of International Trade, a Communist front organization, visited China in February and signed 130 contracts totalling about £4 million sterling.[76] The second delegation, sponsored by the SBTC, visited Peking in March-April 1955. It renewed old acquaintances and received many enquiries, but it could sign contracts worth only £1 million.[77] Its discussions were not "entirely confined to trade talks." The exchange of technicians was discussed and "agreed in principle," though it was to be put into effect only "when trade expands further." In a statement issued prior to its departure from Peking, the delegation stated that there was a great scope for expansion of trade provided the barriers which prevent the full exploitation of the trade potential of the two countries were removed and trade relations normalized.[78] Tsao Chung-shu, acting Manager of the China National Import and Export Corporation, observed :

We are engaged in expanding industry and agriculture on a scale which necessitates very large imports and has made it possible for us to export much more than ever before. We are interested not so much in consumer and luxury goods as in industrial and building supplies for a giant, long-term programme creating the foundation of real nation-wide prosperity. While this requires certain changes in the thinking of some who traded with China in the past, it offers a basis for healthier and more extensive business connections than have hitherto existed.[79]

Thus, it was realized on both sides that trade between the two countries had not "developed to the degree that it might and could have done."[80] The main difficulty was in regard to embargo. Unless China was assured of an uninterrupted supply of capital goods from the West, it was unlikely to divert its exports from other markets (particularly the USSR and other communist countries) from where it obtained the machinery and other capital goods it needed.[81] Tsao Chung-shu referred to the anomalous situation of maintaining the embargo even after the Korean Armistice and the cease-fire in Indo-China. He observed :

There are broad prospects for Sino-British trade if normal conditions can be established, and it should not be difficult to arrive at a trade figure of £100 million per annum. To create such a favourable situation the embargo has to be removed first. British firms should insist on changing the Embargo policy and we shall fully cooperate with our Western friends to achieve this.[82]

The Embargo and its Relaxation

Although the export of certain goods to China from Britain was subject to licensing even before the embargo was imposed by the UN General Assembly on 18 May 1951,[83] a formal export licence control on all goods was introduced only from 25 June 1951 onwards, when the Assembly resolution came into effect. The critical Korean situation necessitated that economic sanctions "designed to deny contributions to the military strength of the forces opposing the United Nations in Korea" be applied forthwith as part of "additional measures...to meet the aggression in Korea" and "to support and supplement the military action of the United Nations in Korea." The Assembly resolution recommended that every State should impose "an embargo on the shipment...of arms, ammunition and implements of war, atomic energy materials, petroleum, transportation materials of strategic value and items useful in the production of arms, ammunition and implements of war" against China and North Korea. However, it left it to the discretion of each state to "determine which commodities exported from its territory fall within the embargo." The states were required to cooperate with each other in the application of the embargo and to prevent by all means within their jurisdiction "the circumvention of controls on shipments applied by other States pursuant to the present resolution."[84]

The British delegate to the UN was not convinced of the wisdom of imposing an embargo unless, he said, "we are certain and demonstrably certain of...the impossibility of a peaceful settlement" of the Korean problem. He added : "My Government quite frankly has the gravest doubts whether any punitive measures can be discovered which are not dangerous, double-edged or merely useless nor any which will materially assist our brave troops now fighting in Korea."[85] Britain reluctantly agreed to support the embargo resolution since all UN approaches of peaceful settlement had failed to evoke "a favourable response from the Chinese Communists."[86] The selective embargo imposed by the UN was, indeed, a compromise between what the USA and the UK had desired. London sought to strike a balance between jeopardising its "friendship and the understanding" with Washington and jeopardising "the possibility of confining this conflict and localising it to Korea itself." The escalation of conflict threatened "the military and the political security" of British Colonial Territories in the Far East.[87] While announcing the decision of the British Government to implement the UN resolution from 25 June 1951 onwards, Sir H. Shawcross, President of the Board of Trade, observed :

It is not our intention to impose a total embargo on trade with China, and export licences for goods which are not considered to be of military or strategic importance to China will be granted freely, subject to availabilities and the prior claims on our resources. On the other hand, licences will not be granted for export to China of goods which *in present circumstances* could be of strategic and military importance.[88]

Evidently, the British Government considered the imposition of an embargo a necessary evil and a temporary measure designed to meet the specific situation of the Korean War. In his discussions in Washington in March 1953, the British Foreign Secretary endeavoured to overcome American objections[89] in regard to the relaxation of the embargo. However, since the Korean truce was still eluding them, Britain had to agree to tighten shipping controls on China.[90] Thus, platform and fork-lift trucks were added to the embargo list.[91] In spite of all the steps it took, London never denied "the potential importance of the Chinese market to British trade and commerce." Lord Mancroft, Minister without Portfolio, complained that "many other countries do not carry out their part of the bargain with the same scrupulous accuracy as we do." However, he could not give any "specific answer" or assurance in regard to the problem of embargo so long as war in Korea continued.[92]

Chou En-lai's statement of 30 March 1953 seemed to pave the way for the signing of the Korean Armistice. Therefore, the spokesman of the British Government held out the prospect of modifying the embargo. On 28 April 1953, Nutting, the Joint Under-Secretary of State for Foreign Affairs, stated :

> Sould an armistice prove possible in Korea, the situation under which the United Nations Resolution [of 18 May 1951] arose would be altered and therefore the policy of all the nations concerned would naturally and immediately come under review.[93]

The President of the Board of Trade, P. Thorneycroft, also hinted at the relaxation of embargo. On 18 June 1953, he remarked : "Any improvement in the international situation with regard to peace will be a very helpful thing so far as the promotion of trade is concerned."[94]

Because of American objections, the embargo could not be modified even after the conclusion of Korean Armistice. In a statement issued on 22 October 1953, Thorneycroft recognized that "an extension in East-West trade would...undoubtedly be in our economic interests." However, he expressed his inability to do anything *substantial* in the matter save "in consultation and agreement with the other countries who are associated with us in this matter" of embargo. Nevertheless, he observed that the British Government did not consider "security controls...inflexible" and that "we shall introduce such modification as may be justified by changing circumstances."[95]

In spite of Lord Mancroft's assertion that trade restrictions on China were imposed only for the duration of the Korean War and that they "cannot possibly be extended to any general overall peace plan stretching far and away beyond Korea,"[96] the United Kingdom came to link the question of embargo with the situation in Indo-China. Minister of State Selwyn Lloyd characterized the truce in Korea as a "step in the right direction." "The next step to take," he added, "is to stop the fighting in Indo-China."[97] The outcome of the Geneva Conference, the Joint Under-Secretary of State for Foreign Affairs stated, "may yet open the way for a reconsideration of the strategic embargo on trade with China."[98] After the cessation of hostilities in Indo-China, London tried to justify its continued adherence to the embargo on grounds of "security" and non-fulfilment of the UN objectives in Korea.[99] These lame excuses failed to satisfy British businessmen, who viewed with growing concern the critical position of Hong Kong, Malaya's difficulties in selling its rubber, and the growing dependence of China on the Soviet bloc for the supply of capital goods. Lord Chorley countered the Government argument that any consideration of the relaxation of the embargo "must depend on the more favourable development of events in the Far East,"[100] by the following remark : "Undoubtedly this drying up of trade is a great hindrance to the growth of a peaceful relationship between our two countries. Undoubtedly a much larger volume of trade would foster peace."[101]

The continuance of strict controls on the China trade seemed all the more galling to British businessmen after trade restrictions on the Soviet bloc were relaxed.[102] The anomaly of according differential treatment to the Soviet bloc was evident to all concerned. China succeeded in procuring all the goods denied to it by Britain and other Western countries indirectly through the good offices of other communist countries, thereby frustrating UN controls. Moreover, stricter trade controls on China made Peking "ever more dependent on Russia for supplies and shipping,"[103] perhaps to a greater extent than "even Peking would have desired."[104] But since the question of embargo on exports to China was "an international issue of considerable...explosive possibilities," the British Government considered it "wise to handle it with caution."[105] It seemed as if London was convinced of the desirability of relaxing controls, but deemed it necessary not to take any action in the matter unilaterally.[106] In the second half of 1955, signs of a "marked relaxation of tension" were visible not only in Europe but in the Far East as well.[107] British businessmen, therefore, were quite vocal in their criticism of the Government's policy. They pleaded that the Chinese embargo list be made similar to the Russian list. They also pointed out that both Hong Kong and Malaya would continue to suffer as a result of the embargo "if no substantial relaxation comes soon" and that "the trade lost may never be regained."[108]

The question of restrictions on trade with China, which was unpopular with all sections of public opinion in Britain, came to a head in 1956-57. British firms had suffered as sellers, buyers, shippers, insurers and bankers. They suffered both in direct British-Chinese trade and in trade between China and Hong Kong, Malaya, Singapore, Ceylon and Indonesia, a great deal of which was in their hands. Politically, the restrictions cut across the general line of British policy towards China. They were also unacceptable to the Government of Ceylon and caused acute complications in Malaya, both countries being major exporters of rubber to China.[109] Therefore, during his visit to Washington in February 1956, Anthony Eden pressed the issue of reducing the forbidden export in the China List with President Eisenhower and his advisers. He laid particular stress on the undesirable political effects of the existing restrictions in Malaya and Ceylon. Malaya, he argued, could sell rubber to Russia and the latter could resell it to China, but direct sale from Malaya to China was forbidden. This, he said, was damaging to Malaya's interests and inexplicable to its leaders and its peoples, who were rapidly approaching independence. Ceylon, he observed, had already acted in defiance of the

United Nations resolution and made substantial shipments of rubber to China. He, therefore, felt that a start must be made at once in revising the list of forbidden items. In spite of his efforts, Eden failed to convince the American leaders. Finally, it was agreed that the controls "should continue and should be reviewed now and periodically as to their scope in the light of changing conditions, so that they may best serve the interests of the free world."[110]

After British attempts to secure relaxation of restrictions on trade with China failed, London decided to take a decision on its own in the matter. Thus, the export of 60 tractors to China was allowed.[111] The Chinese Foreign Ministry's favourable reply of 13 April 1956 as regards the problem of the registration of trade marks[112] further encouraged London to announce (on 14 May 1956) its intention to make extensive use of the exceptions procedure so as to permit the export of forbidden goods to China in "suitable" cases.[113] In pursuance of this policy, London decided on 4 June 1956 to lift the ban on the export of natural rubber from Malaya and Singapore to Peking. In the absence of any general relaxation of China trade controls, the exceptions procedure afforded Britain "some lattitude"[114] in the matter. London used that method to the maximum with a view to permit "reasonable exports in appropriate cases" to China of goods which were not on the Soviet lists.[115] However, the exceptions procedure was slow and cumbersome. It represented "a hole-in-the-corner" method and a very "elaborate process." It also entailed many hardships to British firms because no precise lists were available "giving information of what is exceptionable."[116] Therefore, it neither satisfied British businessmen nor the Chinese.[117] The British Government was aware of the difficulties but was unable to do anything further in the matter. The procedure, it was stated, could not be simplified "consistently with obligations accepted by all countries" in the Paris Consultative Group that administered trade controls on communist countries.[118] In these circumstances, London felt reconciled to the "unfortunate effects" of the China embargo being subject to consultation and agreement by the Paris Group.[119] The British Government placed the matter "very forcibly" before its allies in the China Committee more than once.[120]

Unfortunately, the discussions in the China Committee were unduly prolonged.[121]

In the meantime, pressures for revision of trade controls continued to mount. In 1956 there was 20% increase in China's trade with the West while its trade with the Soviet bloc declined from $3.807 billion in 1955 to $3.469 billion in 1956.[122] It seemed that Moscow was unable to meet all the requirements of China in regard to capital goods and Peking had to buy certain goods from the capitalist countries even at a higher price.[123] It might be recalled that China's ambitious Second Five-Year Plan contemplated doubling of its capital investment during the next five years, from 42.7 million yuan in the First Plan to 85.5 million in the Second.[124] Apparently, Britain was much impressed by China's expanding foreign trade[125] and its increased capacity to pay for imports from the West because of large sterling balances accumulated during 1952-56 when Peking could buy little from the sterling area due to the embargo.[126] Britain also took into account its failure to increase its exports to China "as rapidly as the other major West European countries"[127] and the loss of trade in the Middle East as a result of the Suez War.

In these circumstances, British business circles expressed their dissatisfaction with the exceptions procedure. The Government's inability to modify trade restrictions, it was stated, was "slowly strangling the goose that could lay a golden egg for British industry and business."[128] In a letter to the President of the Board of Trade, the SBTC strongly pleaded for applying the same controls to exports to China as it applied to exports to the Soviet bloc,[129] *i.e.* substantially reduce them. The Federation of British Industries and other trade associations made separate representations and D. Eccles, President of the Board of Trade, assured them that the Government would give "full weight to their views."[130] On 1 April 1957, Foreign Secretary Selwyn Lloyd gave advance notice of the British Government's intention to proceed unilaterally if no decision was arrived at in the Paris Consultative Group.[131]

At Britain's instance, the question of China trade controls was urgently studied in the China Committee of the Paris Group in the month of May 1957. However, no agreement could be reached. London, therefore, decided to proceed unilaterally.

It informed its associates that, in future, it would "adopt the same lists for China and the Soviet bloc"[132] and expected them to follow suit. Lloyd announced this decision in the House of Commons on 30 May 1957. He observed :

> This decision will mean no change as regards items which are embargoed for both the Soviet bloc and China. But certain items now embargoed for China will either be transferred to the quantitative control list, or to the watch list, or completely freed. The necessary detailed arrangements will need to be discussed in the China Committee.[133]

The British move cleared the principal obstacle on the British side to the development of Sino-British trade. The Board of Trade talked of doubling British exports to China from £10 million to £20 million.[134] However, the relaxation of trade restrictions did not instantly result in any significant increase in Sino-British trade. This was partly due to the general slackening in China's foreign trade[135] and partly because many of the goods so freed were already being exported to China under the extended use of exceptions procedure. Nevertheless, the British decision marked a beginning in the direction of further relaxation of embargo[136] and created favourable atmosphere for starting afresh trade discussions between China and Britain.

On 3 June 1957, the SBTC addressed a telegram to Peking asking whether a British trade mission might visit China. The Committee also renewed its invitation to the Chinese authorities to send an exploratory technical mission to Britain. It was believed that a technical mission, which would survey British industry and make favourable reports to state trading organizations of China, would do much more "to enhance the long-term prospects of the United Kingdom exporters" than an actual trade mission.[137] The Chinese Economic and Technical Mission of 20 experts headed by Chi Chao-ting, Vice-Chariman of China Committee for the Promotion of International Trade, made a six-week extensive tour of industrial centres in Britain. It visited nearly 200 firms, spending as much as five days with firms whose activities were of particular interest to them.[138] In an interview just before his departure on 6 December 1957, Chi Chao-ting stated that the Chinese experts were greatly impressed by what they had seen of British industry and commerce. The knowledge acquired by the Mission, he added, would enable it to make recommendations to the appropriate authorities in China and pave the way for increased Sino-British trade in the future, in goods as well as in 'know-how'.[139]

Frederick Erroll, Parliamentary Secretary to the Board of Trade, was the first British Minister to visit China in two decades. He made an exploratory study of China's industrial requirements and suggested that British consulting engineers might be sent to China to assist with projects. The Chinese responded by asking for a full list of the available experts.[140] On his return from China, Erroll told the House of Commons on 3 December 1957 :

> The Government are in earnest about the development of trade with China....I think that we may expect to see a steady but not a sudden or spectacular increase in our exports to China...China is a country with about one quarter of world's population. At present, only about one-third of 1 per cent of our export trade goes to China. There is surely scope for an increase, and I believe that with good-will on the part of both countries we should see this trade growing steadily during the coming years.[141]

With "a substantial relaxation of the embargo list" by the Coordinating Committee at Paris (COCOM) in August 1958, "Her Majesty's Government's objective of confining the list to items of real strategic significance," was "in great measure achieved."[142] The relaxation of trade restrictions, the severance of Sino-Japanese trade relations,[143] and the Chinese anxiety to utilize the accumulated sterling balances[144] facilitated a great upsurge in Sino-British trade, especially in British exports to China, in 1958.[145] By 1958 it also became fairly easy for British businessmen to get visas and consequently some of them regularly visited the biennial trade fair at Canton.[146]

Chinese Reaction to British Policy on Trade Controls

The UN resolution of 18 May 1951, Peking believed, was passed "under the control and duress of the United States Government.". It was considered by China as a "continuation of the illegal and shameful resolution falsely accusing China as aggressor" and "an important step in U.S. Government's intention of extending aggressive war." The spokesman of the Chinese Foreign Ministry, therefore, warned Britain in the following words :

> We should point out that before this illegal U.S. proposal was passed, the British Government had already adopted a series of unfriendly acts regarding trade, thereby revealing its determination to be the enemy of the Chinese people. All those countries following U.S. in imposing embargo against China and Korea must shoulder all the consequences of this hostile action against our country.[147]

Peking desired that London should dissociate itself from Washington in regard to the imposition of artificial trade barriers. Chou En-lai, therefore, welcomed the British announcement about the extended use of the exceptions procedure and lifting the ban on the export of rubber. He observed :

> The countries which are forced to implement the policy of embargo are finding that their own markets have been greatly reduced and their domestic economic difficulties aggravated. Recently, these countries have been trying to break through the embargo restrictions. This is understandable and is also to be welcomed. But, in order to effectuate the breakdown of the embargo and the development of trade, it is necessary...to abolish all kinds of artificial international trade barriers.[148]

The British decision of 30 May 1957 was widely acclaimed in China. The *People's Daily* Observer welcomed it for its "beneficial effects on the improvement of East-West friendly cooperation and economic intercourse." While depicting it as far from being a radical one, he yet regarded it as opening "a big hole in U.S. 'embargo'."[149] Chi Chao-ting described British move "a bold action," a wise decision, "a worthy initiative, serving the interests of the world peoples," and "a step forward" towards easing of international tensions. He added :

> Nonetheless it is only a first step. For the peaceful, prosperous life of all nations, there must be peaceful, prosperous

international trade. This can only be built on the mutual benefit and equality of the parties free from any discrimination.[150]

The Minister of Foreign Trade, Yeh Chi-chuang, considered the British decision of 30 May 1957 "a positive step" making for normal trade between China and the West. However, he regretted : "These countries have not entirely abandoned their discriminative trade policy. They retain more than 200 major items on their embargo lists. This is still a big obstacle to developing normal trade with them."[151]

After the COCOM decision of August 1958 on a substantial relaxation of the embargo list, China went on a buying spree in West Europe and soon exhausted all its sterling reserves. The *Hsinhua News Agency* correspondent remarked :

> Although this (COCOM) resolution is rather late and not thorough but this has proved that the US-advocated embargo policy is useless. At last it has to be withdrawn. It also reflects the British and other Western countries' urgent need for new markets to save their decayed industry, to reduce the pressure of economic crisis.[152]

Peking regretted that even after the relaxation of embargo, many goods continued on the forbidden list and that "some new items" had been added to that list.[153] Yeh Chi-chuang complained that certain Western countries adopted "various kinds of discriminative measures to limit our export to their countries." This, he stated, "will lead China to reduce her imports from those countries, with the result that their foreign markets will be curtailed and it will be difficult for them to sell their goods."[154]

Problem of Supplying Strategic Goods to China

As compared to 1958, the Sino-British trade declined in 1959. This was due to a number of factors : firstly, the Soviet attempts to prevent excessive reliance of China on West Europe;[155] secondly, the resumption of trade relations between China and Japan;[156] thirdly, the drying up of China's sterling reserves;[157] and lastly, the imposition of import restrictions by the British Board of Trade in November 1959.[158] However, under pressure from trading interests, who criticized the policy of licensing and quotas on imports from China, and in order "to meet the possibilities of increased trade with China,"[159] the British Government subsequently decided to modify the quota limitation imposed in November 1959.[160]

However, in the absence of mutual trust and friendly political relations, London could not be expected to altogether scrap or further revise the embargo list which was confined "solely to items of strategic significance."[161] In 1950, it was universally recognized that, "in China, the chief objectives of the economic development programmes have been the improvement of the people's livelihood and the bringing about of a balanced, equitable and democratic economy."[162] However, in view of Peking's aggressive international posture in the late 1950s and the whole of 1960s, and its attempts to become a militarily strong nation, London became reluctant to supply industrial raw-materials and equipment and strategic goods, in which China was mainly interested. On 9 May 1957, the Secretary, of State for Commonwealth Relations, Alec Douglas-Home, stated :

> We are aware of this problem of the necessity, if we can, to increase our export trade, we will do anything reasonable to that end; but, of course, it would be extremely foolish, for the sake of a little temporary increased income, to sell certain materials to countries who might use them against us in case of war. We must be careful and sensible, and strike a proper balance.[163]

Sober-minded British businessmen were also aware of the problem of strengthening China's war machine. For instance, in his address before the Royal Central Asian Society on 30 September 1953, H. J. Collar had observed:

> As merchants, and in so far as we are anxious to fill the stomachs of our own workers here, we are anxious for Chinese trade, but we must consider carefully where we are going. Do we want to meet all China's needs for her programme of industrialization ? What are we going to build if we do ? A Frankenstein monster, another enormous

adjunct to Soviet power in the Far East ? Or is there a
chance we may be able to build a powerful but friendly
nation ? It is an extremely important question and one we
must try to answer. One cannot, however, give an answer
one feels happy about.[164]

Sino-Soviet Rift and China's Trade Relations with the West

The growing Sino-Soviet rift in the 1960s created favourable conditions for the expansion of China's trade
relations with the Western nations, including Britain. Soviet
deliveries of industrial equipment to China dropped from $600
million in 1959 to about $27 million in 1962. Peking switched
a major part of its foreign purchases from the Soviet Union to
the Western countries. Accordingly, China's trade with
communist countries dropped from US $2985 million in 1959
to US $785 million in 1969 while its trade with non-communist
countries recorded an increase from US $1310 million in 1959
to US $3070 million in 1969. In 1955, as much as 75% of
China's trade was with the Soviet bloc and 25% with other
nations. By 1964, only 30% of that trade was with the Soviet
bloc, the remaining 70% was with the rest of the world. This
was, indeed, a remarkable swing, and an encouragement not to
be overlooked in Western commercial circles.[165]

In January 1965, Lin Hai-yun, Vice Minister of Foreign
Trade, observed that Peking's trade relations with Western
countries had grown in the last few years "under the influence
of our foreign trade policy of equality and mutual benefit."
Since the second half of 1963, he said, trade talks were held
with manufacturers and firms in various Western countries,
including France, Sweden, Holland, the United Kingdom,
Italy and West Germany. Chinese purchases of "a number of
complete industrial plants from them" aroused interest and
attention in industrial and commercial circles in many Western
countries. Lin criticized the "bankrupt US policy of obstruct-
ing and sabotaging" such trade. During the first half of 1964,
he asserted, more than 140 groups of representatives of foreign
firms, industrialists and businessmen and economic and trade
delegations from France, Switzerland, Sweden, Denmark,

Norway, Holland, the UK, Italy, Canada, Belgium, Australia and West Germany visited China.[166]

In these circumstances, Britain did not wish to lag behind. The rising trend in British exports following the relaxation of restrictions was sharply, though temporarily, reversed in 1961 and 1962 partly because of the difficult internal economic situation in China and partly because of the severe competition that British companies had to face from rival firms in Western Europe and Japan. However, in the spring of 1963, the Chinese Vice-Minister of Foreign Trade came to Britain. The Chinese delegation visited the works of a number of leading British firms, including ICI, Vickers-Armstrong, Courtaulds and Rootes and evinced keen interest in the purchase of aircraft, trucks, tractors, tin plates, steel plates aud fertilizers. In September 1963, a 16-member delegation of the "48 Group" arrived in Peking and Mrs. John Robinson, Vice-Chairman of the British Council for the Promotion of International Trade, also paid a seven-week visit to China.

Douglas Jay, the President of the Board of Trade, visited Peking in November 1964. He opened a British Industrial and Machinery Exhibition, which was the largest to be held in China by any Western country since 1949.[167] The area occupied by the exhibition amounted to 130,000 sq. ft.; 230 firms exhibited their products and 350 British executives participated therein. The exhibition was sponsored by the Sino-British Trade Council which was not a trading organization, but a Promotional Group comprising the Association of British Chambers of Commerce, the London Chamber of Commerce, the Federation of British Industries and the China Association—the most comprehensive group of Chambers and Associations in the whole country, covering every aspect of industry and commerce. The exhibits consisted almost entirely of engineering products and nearly all the products on view were sold at the end of the show. Douglas Jay considered the British exhibition a great success and "an outstanding landmark in the development of Sino-British trade relations." He observed :

In the medium and long terms the China market offers a large potential outlet for British goods, particularly those used in the heavy industrial and engineering fields. Although it would be over-optimistic for us to expect any dramatic increase in our sales to this market immediately, I am sure that the exhibition has done much to stimulate further the steady improvement which is now taking place.[168]

The British firms, John Keswick stated, "gained a new insight into the China market, a new appreciation of the advances made in China and of what Chinese requirements are and are likely to be."[169] Towards the end of 1964, China ordered 500 Land Rovers from Britain at an estimated cost of $840,000 and placed its first shipbuilding order with Britain for two 15,000 ton cargo vessels. Britain also sold several Viscount planes to China. The use of British aircraft for the internal airlines of China, it was believed, would entail, in terms of spare parts, servicing etc., a very close relationship between the two countries.[170] The British trade with China in 1964 showed a marked improvement over 1963—£42.3 million as against £31.7 million.

In 1965 the Chinese Trade Minister visited Britain and signed a contract for £220,000 worth of machine tools with Churchill & Co. Another contract worth £360,000 was signed for equipment used in the production of moulding carbon track potentiometers, which were required for communications, automation and television. Even though the British Embassy in Peking was burnt in September 1967, the British held an exhibition in Tientsin in less than a month of that incident and British trade with China during the first nine months of 1967 reached the record figure of £33 million as compared to £21 million in 1966.

While trade between Britain and China continued during the Cultural Revolution, the relations between the two countries were far from good. A number of British citizens were detained. In a statement made on behalf of the British Government on the floor of the House of Commons on 17 November 1969, it was stated that even after the six British subjects were released "not long ago," nine British subjects still remained under detention in China (on 20 July 1970, seven British subjects were stated to be under detention in China). The Chinese attitude towards some of the British detainees was described as "deplorable." London expressed "grave concern" in the matter and made repeated representations to the Chinese Government.[171] The continued detention of British subjects in China was considered a "serious obstacle" to the improvement of Sino-British relations.[172] However, as relations between the two countries improved, the British citizens were slowly and gradually released and this, in turn, contributed, to a certain extent, to the further improvement of their relations.

Recent Developments and Outlook for the Future

The establishment of full diplomatic relations at ambassadorial level in March 1972, the improvement in relations and the initiation of contacts at the highest levels (this was signified by British Foreign Secretary Sir Alec Douglas-Home's visit to Peking in October-November 1972 and the visits of Chiao Kuan-hua, Deputy Foreign Minister, and Chi Peng-fei, Foreign Minister, to Britain in November 1972 and June 1973 respectively) facilitated development of trade relations between the two countries. In view of the Sino-Soviet confrontation and intense hostility between the two largest communist Powers and the growing Sino-US *detente,* there appears little ground for suspicion like the one alluded to by Collar about creating a "Frankenstein monster, another enormous adjunct to Soviet power in the Far East"—a Chinese dragon emitting fire from its nostrils and in alliance with a diabolical Russian bear.

The agreement on the exchange of ambassadors in March 1972 inaugurated a fruitful period of widespread cooperation in both the political and economic fields between Britain and China. A few days after the agreement was signed, it was announced that a British Industrial Technology Exhibition would be held in Peking in March 1973. A Great Britain China Committee was also established to promote contacts of all kinds between the two countries. In March 1972 itself a number of Chinese delegations, including those from the Chinese Oceanography Society, the Technical Study Group of Synthethic Fibres of China, the Chinese Mechanical Engineering Society and the Chinese Aeronautical Society, visited Britain. These visits were considered "successful" and contributed to the further development of trade and cooperation between China and Britain.[173]   China represented potentially the biggest single market in the world.   Therefore, the British Premier expressed his desire to see "as rapid an expansion of trade as possible."   Three Chinese trade missions, he said, were visiting Britain and four British trade missions were either visiting China or were about to go there.   The exchange of these trade missions, he stated, would greatly encourage trade between the two countries.[174]

Anthony Royle, the British Under Secretary of State for Foreign Affairs, visited China in the summer of 1972.   He was the first Minister from the British Foreign Office to visit the People's Republic of China.   He had long discussions with the Chinese Foreign Minister and the Chinese Vice-Ministers of Foreign Affairs and Foreign Trade, which lasted for more than 14 hours.   In the course of these discussions, an agreement was reached that a framework "now exists for the gradual but steady development of exchanges in industrial, scientific and technological experience, trade and sport."   Royle confidently remarked that Sino-British relations were "now better than they have been at any time for very many years."   He also looked forward to their continued improvement.[175]

In May 1972, a BOAC delegation visited Peking and the British Government proposed that inter-governmental negotiations on air services should begin as soon as practicable.[176] Substantive discussions on the conclusion of an air services agreement began a year later. During British Foreign Secretary's visit from 29 October to 2 November 1972, it was confirmed that the Chinese Government would send upto 200 students to Britain within the next year to study English.   During 1972, Peking decided to buy three Anglo-French supersonic Concorde airliners (two from Aerospatiale and one from the British Aircraft Corporation), and twenty British Trident aircraft.   China also showed keen interest in buying VC 10.   Commenting on the reasons behind Chinese support for British entry into the European Common Market, the British Minister of State (Amery) stated that in their "search for peace and *detente* the Chinese Government naturally welcomed any development that would strengthen the cohesion of the Western European countries and their ability to contribute to economic prosperity and to peace."[177]

The British Minister of Trade, Peter Walker, visited China in March 1973, when a British exhibition was held in Peking. More than 350 British firms displayed a wide range of goods particularly those reflecting modern British technology. The exhibition, Peter Walker observed, "was the largest that has ever been staged by a foreign country in Peking" and it proved "a major success." Chou En-lai paid a two-hour personal visit to the British Exhibition. By July 1973, negotiations had been opened for over 50 contracts. These were in addition to those signed during the Exhibition itself.

Commenting on his visit to China and the series of discussions which he had with the Chinese Ministers, including Chou En-lai, Peter Walker expressed his confidence that trade and cultural relations between Britain and China would greatly increase. It was also agreed that a programme for an exchange of trade missions between the two countries over the next two years be drawn up. Peter Walker outlined the positive steps which the British Overseas Trade Board had taken to encourage trade with China. He confidently remarked : "We can now look for a period of sustained growth in our trading relationships with China." He saw great scope for the export of mining engineering equipment, offshore oil drilling and other sophisticated equipment and laid stress on the advantage of trying to seek a constant relationship. He acknowledged that no problem of strategic nature was involved in the supply of aerospace equipment and other such equipment to China. In this connection, he drew attention to the fact that at the moment the Americans were also trying to negotiate the sale of many aircraft to Peking. He, therefore, did not think that the restrictions on trade with China, because of strategic limitations, would stand in the way and inhibit the expansion of Sino-British trade in the future.[178]

In the first six months of 1973, British exports to China increased to £36.3 million as compared to £12.2 million in the previous year. British exports also covered a much wider range spread of goods. Encouraged by the large-scale expansion of trade relationship and the highly successful industrial exhibition of March 1973, the British Government held yet another exhibition of the latest machine tools and scientific instruments in Shanghai in March-April 1975. Over 60 British companies participated in that exhibition : about 300 representatives were sent to Shanghai. The direction of China's foreign trade had remained heavily weighed in favour of the non-communist countries—as much as 83% of the total Chinese trade had been with the non-communist world. In view of the removal of trade restrictions, the existence of high-level contacts and exchange of visits, the continuing Sino-Soviet rift, and the growing Chinese interest in developing trade links with West European countries, Britain can look forward to a considerable expansion of the mutually beneficial trade links with China in the future.

CHAPTER NINE

Conclusion

The foreign policy of a country is determined mainly by considerations of its geographical position, international conditions, economic and military capabilities and national habits and traditions. In order to facilitate its economic recovery and rectify the imbalance of power on the European continent, Britain entered into an alliance with the United States after World War II. On the other hand, China, for reasons discussed in Chapter Two, adopted a "lean to one side" policy towards the Soviet Union. The alignments of the two countries with their senior partners and the polarization of the world into two rival blocs created difficulties in the way of their coming closer together and hampered their pursuit of an independent foreign policy. However, both Britain and Communist China looked forward to playing a major role in world politics in the post-1945 period.

Britain accepted American economic aid under the Marshall Plan and sought to ensure the defence of West Europe under Washington's protective umbrella. However, London disliked the idea of either remaining on "a dollar pension"[1] for long or becoming a subservient ally of the United States. Since its standard of life depended almost entirely on its exports, Britain could not possibly ignore a market of 600 million people and contemplate severing relations with countries most suitable to its trade. Being an underdeveloped country, China constituted a natural market for British industrial goods. The industrialized economies of the UK and the USA, on the other hand, were not complementary but rather competitive. In fact, in the second half of the 1940s, the United States had emerged as Britain's most formidable competitor in China. However, as G.F. Hudson rightly points out, Britain could hardly afford the luxury of two separate policies in Europe and Asia; to combine with America in order to resist Soviet expansion in Europe and to combine with the Soviet bloc in order to thwart American policy in the Far East. British manoeuvers to exert pressure by forging diplomatic combinations with communist states against America, he added, could only have served communist purposes.[2]

For obvious reasons, the Anglo-American alliance was considered by Britain to be of much greater importance than the relatively small interests in China. Accordingly, when Sino-American relations were strained, London was often compelled to follow or support policies which created strains in Sino-British relations. However, its economic interests, Hong King's precarious position and the need to prevent China from becoming too much dependent on the Soviet Union led Britain to persist in its quest of cultivating normal, diplomatic relations with China and to restrain Washington in its hostility towards Peking so as to avoid an all-out war with China.

By establishing cordial relations with the People's Republic of China, Britain hoped to derive certain "immediate and tangible" advantages, such as the expansion of trade, protection of its investments in China and the preservation of its hold over Hong Kong. However, these advantages appeared "insignificant when weighed in the balance of enduring interests of this country [Britain] and of the peace of world."[3] The normalization of Sino-British relations, thus, had a deeper purpose, the creation of a "better equilibrium in the world"[4] —a world in which the British Commonwealth and China could act as major centres of power capable of pursuing policies independent of both Moscow and Washington.

The polarization of the world into two rival blocs, one led by the USA and the other by the USSR, was an unwelcome development which restricted the British as well as the Chinese freedom of action in foreign affairs and impeded the expansion of trade to the maximum extent possible. In 1949-50, therefore, Britain refused to "accept the concept of a world divided into East and West."[5] Even when circumstances drove London to take sides in the East-West conflict, it strove to minimize the rigours of rigidity within the blocs. It endeavoured to

keep China outside the pale of the Cold War even though it
was "all too easy to regard the Chinese problem, even in its
early stages, as merely one more aspect of the world-wide
struggle between the Soviet Union and the United States."[6]
British policy was based on the belief that it was in the best
interests of China that it should not be driven into irrevocable
hostility to the non-communist nations and into a position
where it could not avoid becoming a mere pawn in Soviet
policy. It was recognised that the Chinese Government was
a communist Government and so started with an ideological
bias against the democratic world. But there had been signs
that it was also a profoundly practical Government and that,
other things being equal, practical considerations might at
least mitigate the rigours of ideology in foreign affairs. This
being so, the immediate aim of British foreign policy was to
do nothing which would make it appear to the Chinese
Government that it had no real alternative to unquestioning
collaboration with the Soviet Union however much the policies
of that country might conflict with the real interests of China [7]
Peking seemed to be following a similar policy towards
Britain.

It was quite evident that a deterioration in Sino-Soviet
relations would oblige Peking to seek extensive Western
economic and military support. A Sino-Soviet rift would not
only have reduced Soviet pressures in Western Europe and the
Middle East—areas more vital to Britain—but would also have
compelled both China and the Soviet Union to look more and
more to West European countries and the USA for accomodation, support and closer relations, as recent events have substantially proved. London, therefore, endeavoured to establish
political, economic and cultural contacts with new China with
a view to safeguard its interests in China and Hong Kong, to
promote trade, to acquire an independent say in world affairs,
to draw China away from the Soviet orbit and, if possible, to
"win over China into the society of free nations."[8] A Sino-
Soviet confrontation, the British felt, was a far more effective
check on Soviet ambitions than spending more on NATO
defences.

The recognition of the People's Republic was the first step
in the direction of befriending China. Mao, as already stated,

adopted a "lean to one side" policy towards the Soviet Union. However, the Peking leadership was well aware of the difficult problems it faced at home, *e.g.* the consolidation of the gains of their victory, restoration of economic stability and industrialization of the country. Consequently, Peking was prepared to establish diplomatic relations with Britain in the beginning of 1950. However, London's hesitation in casting its vote in favour of China's admission in the United Nations and to transfer the 71 aircraft stationed in Hong Kong to Peking created difficulties. In adopting such an attitude, Britain might have been motivated by the desire to act, as far as possible, in concert with the USA and also, perhaps, from its own inclination not to relinquish its bargaining counters. But this stand was in conflict with the main aim of British policy towards China, *viz.* the search for a *modus vivendi* in Sino-British relations. Accordingly, London gave verbal assurances promising British support for Chinese admission in the UN and took steps to permit aircraft spare parts to be flown to Peking. In these circumstances, fruitful trade on a fairly extensive scale was continued, friendly visits between the two countries became more frequent and Anglo-Chinese discussions on the establishment of diplomatic relations began in right earnest in Peking in March 1950.

However, before negotiations on the exchange of ambassadors could come to a satisfactory conclusion, war broke out in Korea. The Korean War created an embarrassing situation for Britain. It exposed Britain's dual policy, *viz* of maintaining a special relationship with America and, at the same time, seeking accomodation with China. Though Britain joined hands with Washington in countering aggression but, at the same time, it endeavoured to restrain Washington so as to avoid a full-scale war with China, because that would have cut off trade and imperilled Hong Kong. Britain supported the US-sponsored resolution in the United Nations condemning China as an aggressor in Korea and acquiesced in imposing a selective embargo on the shipment of goods to Peking. The British attitude towards the question of Chinese representation in the UN was also far from favourable to Peking.

The Western Powers' policies compelled China to forge closer political, economic and cultural relations with the Soviet bloc countries. The embargo produced a major shift in the direction of China's foreign trade. In the wake of the Korean War, Peking also resorted to such expedients as the seizure of foreign investments and increasing restrictions on private enterprises—expedients which were detrimental to British commercial interests. British firms were gradually squeezed out of China and Hong Kong's position as a great entrepot trade centre was undermined.

In the beginning of 1950, the British were fully reconciled to, and would have even welcomed, Taiwan's seizure by the communists. However, in the wake of the Korean War, they gradually veered round to the American view that Formosa must not be allowed to fall into communist hands and that it should better be placed under the trusteeship of the United Nations. The present author does not intend to discuss here such hypothetical questions as : (i) had China been admitted to the UN in the beginning of 1950, the Korean War would never have broken out;[9] (ii) had the Korean War not broken out, Peking might have liberated Formosa without international complications;[10] and (iii) if China had not intervened in the Korean War, it would have been admitted into the United Nations.[11] However, one thing is certain : in the wake of the Korean War, both China and Britain came to hold divergent views on certain issues and adopted measures which could hardly be to the liking of the other party. Nevertheless, both nations realized that they must refrain from taking any action that might lead them into direct conflict with one another. Peking, on its part, desisted from attacking either Hong Kong or Taiwan, while London exerted itself to limit the war in Korea, in Indo-China and the Formosan Straits and to avoid an all-out war against China.

Even after the Chinese intervention in the Korean War, Bevin talked of preventing China "from lining up permanently with Soviet Russia"[12] and the British delegate to the UN warned against the danger of "consciously cutting China off from the free world and from the generous and civilising influences that flow from it."[13] The Conservative Government continued the Labourite policy of seeking a *modus vivendi* with China and cultivating trade relations with it. Eden declared :

It is our policy—I declare it again on behalf of Her Majesty's Government from this Box—to work for peaceful relations with China. Just as we did not hesitate to take our part in the decision of our predecessors to resist Chinese aggression in Korea, so we should be the first to welcome a reversal of Chinese policy. It must surely be in China's own interest to keep open the lines of contact with the Western world. We should be ready to help her to do so, but this of course assumes that the policy of Chinese aggression against a neighbour is for all time abandoned.[14]

During 1954-55 there was a distinct change in China's diplomatic posture both in relation to its neighbours and towards the "imperialists."[15] At the Geneva Conference in 1954, China and Britain developed close contacts and it was agreed that diplomatic relations should be established at the *charge d'affaires* level. Many of the troubles of the British community in China were also resolved. Exit permits were granted, negotiations for the closure of British firms began to move forward, a British deserter from Hong Kong was handed over and all British prisoners were released except Ford and one man convicted of murder. Eleven British sailors, who were arrested for their illegal entry into Chinese territorial waters in June 1954, were released and the two countries agreed to exchange trade delegations. A month after the Geneva Conference ended, a civil airliner of the Cathay Pacific Air Line was shot down by Chinese fighters off Hainan islands. Several passengers, including some Americans, were drowned. Contrary to one's expectations, the Chinese Government promptly acknowledged that a mistake had been made, tendered a full apology and paid a cheque for £367,000 in compensation.[16]

Both Britain and China contributed their share in bringing about the cessation of hostilities in Indo-China. Peking stood in need of a breathing spell to recuperate and reconstruct its economy, while London, owing to its stable economic position in 1953-4,[17] felt confident enough to assert itself so as to remind Washington that the Americans should not "think the time past when they need consider the feelings or difficulties of their allies."[18] While sufficient progress was made towards improving Sino-British relations, Geneva did not "in fact prove to be as fateful a turning point in the Far East as was the Washington Conference in 1922-3, and the solution of Anglo-Chinese conflict in 1926-7."[19] The Korean question remained unresolved and no settlement could be reached about £ 250 million worth of British property and investments "lying idle, requisitioned, leased or confiscated"[20] in Chinese hands. Peking's demands in regard to admission in the UN and possession of Formosa remained unfulfilled. Eden's project of a Locarno-type arrangement in Southeast Asia failed to materialize and an overall and lasting solution of important Far Eastern problems could not be reached. Thus, what was achieved at Geneva was an *ad hoc* settlement of more or less a local problem rather than a general settlement of all outstanding questions with China.

Nevertheless, Geneva ushered in a period of fruitful contacts between China and Britain, particularly in the sphere of trade. Obviously, communist China and capitalist Britain had to learn to live together with each other and strive to maintain trade relations.[21] Since the embargo stood in the way of expansion of Sino-British trade, Britain played a leading part in bringing about its relaxation. Britain also welcomed the widening Sino-Soviet rift[22] and the effect it was having in slowing down the quantum of trade between China and the communist countries of East Europe.[23]

In these circumstances, Peking was anxious to maintain and increase its volume of trade with West European countries. Thus China purchased six Viscount aeroplanes from Britain towards the end of 1961,[24] sent a high-powered trade delegation under the Vice-Minister of Foreign Trade on a visit to the United Kingdom during 1963 and looked forward to an expansion of trade relations with Britain and other West European countries. Access to "free world" markets enabled China "to attain the best commodity terms of trade between the two world markets."[25] It was evident that in seeking to rely less on the Soviet bloc Peking would not like to depend solely on the Western Powers either. While China was conscious about Britain's inability to supply war material to it in open defiance of American views,[26] Peking stood to lose nothing by taking advantage of the contradictions among the Western Powers. Consequently, there was, at times, a marked decline in Chinese propaganda against Britain and a growing recognition, on the part of Peking, of "Britain's role as a 'go-between' in East-West relations." The Chinese magazine, *World Culture*, admitted that "Britain has occasionally struck a different note from the U.S. on certain problems of East-West relations." It accused the Kennedy administration in the United States of striking "a heavy blow at Britain's international position" and observed: "The sharpening of U.S.-British contradictions... will inevitably hasten the disintegration of the imperialist camp."[27]

There is no immediate possibility of a general Far Eastern settlement being reached or the stalemate in Korea being broken. The armed truce in the Taiwan Straits is likely to continue for some more time. Nevertheless, the ice had melted and rigid postures had given way to flexibility in the wake of President Nixon's visit to China in February 1972. Peking's admission in the United Nations had been effected and there are indications of closer economic and political contacts between China and West Europe. In these circumstances, London extended its whole-hearted support to China's admission in the UN and modified its attitude on the Taiwan question. Consequently, diplomatic relations between China and Britain were established at ambassadorial level in March 1972. In view of the beginning of the North-South Korea dialogue, the situation on the Korean peninsula seemed to have somewhat eased though the North Korean ambition to reunify Korea (in the wake of the communist victories in South Vietnam, Cambodia and Laos) might create tension in the future. Britain at no time had any illusions about the credibility of the SEATO for the protection of its interests in the Far East. SEATO, Christopher Mayhew observed in 1966, "has been almost a total failure. It was the child—a sickly child—of Mr. Foster Dulles' passion for anti-communist pacts.... It was far too white and far too Western....The organisation has never yet acted collectively on any military question. It is safe to forecast that it never will."[28] Britain did not insist on the inclusion of Hong Kong in the defensive perimeter of SEATO partly because London wished to steer clear of any commitment in regard to Taiwan and desired to maintain, as far as possible, an inoffensive and unprovocative attitude towards China in order to improve Sino-British relations. Britain, therefore, would not mind the dissolution of SEATO.

Britain is acutely conscious of the fact that Hong Kong is in every way highly vulnerable. One British writer had gone to the extent of saying that if Peking wanted to annex Hong Kong, it was not necessary for it to move its troops across the 17-mile border. All it has to do is to withdraw frontier army guards, raise the sliprails and simply let thousands of unarmed civilians flood the crown colony. Therefore, this "borrowed place living on borrowed time" would continue to be under British control only as long as Peking tolerates it. President Nixon's visit to China in February 1972, Peking's peaceful posture and its quest for international acceptance had given "a fresh lease of borrowed time" to the crown colony.[29] Britain's membership of the EEC and the considerable expansion of China's trade relations with West European countries had further increased Hong Kong's utility to Peking as an important economic, trading, communications and intelligence link for China with the Western world.

Since 1967 Hong Kong has not emerged as a point of friction between Britain and China and has apparently ceased to be a problem hampering the development of fruitful relations between the two countries. Royle was the first British Minister from the Foreign Office to visit China soon after the announcement about the exchange of ambassadors. He returned to Britain with "the greatest confidence in the future of Hong Kong" as a result of his discussions in Peking. Apparently, Peking had assured him that it had no wish to alter the *status quo* in the near future.

The preservation of the *status quo* in Hong Kong is in the mutual interests of both Britain and China. A working arrangement between the two countries, therefore, seems to have been reached during the British Foreign Secretary's visit to Peking in 1972. A more enduring solution of the problem is possible through mutual consultations at the apropriate juncture, say about the time the lease of the New Territories expires. The terms of a settlement would depend on the then prevailing circumstances. In the meantime, both China and Britain will endeavour to reap benefits from the existence of Hong Kong as a crown colony. Peking is not likely to disturb the *status quo*, while the British would take special care that nothing is done that might be deemed prejudicial to Chinese national interests.

Britain and China might hold divergent views on certain international issues, but no serious problem now seems to exist which can possibly disturb the fast developing economic and political relations between the two countries. Peking's criticism of British colonial policy towards Northern Island and of the proposed Anglo-Rhodesian settlement (negotiated in 1971), though displeasing, did not seem to have had any adverse impact on their relations. The continued British membership of SEATO hardly bothers Peking. No longer there seems to exist any ground for the Chinese complaint about the British attitude towards Taiwan or the question of Chinese representation in the UN. With Peking trying to restrain North Korea, the unresolved Korean question is not likely to be a source of friction either. Full diplomatic relations have been established and there are bright prospects for developing mutually beneficial trade relations.

Britain's failure to evolve a coherent policy towards Peking in the 1950s and the 1960s was due to its weak economic and political position in the world and excessive dependence on the USA for its economic well-being and security. London's desire to patch up with China and, at the same time, placate Washington led to a certain contradiction in its policy so long as Washington and Peking remained hostile to each other. This contradiction (or rather duplicity) in British policy was manifest in its attitude on the question of Chinese representation in the UN, the Taiwan problem, the Korean War, the embargo issue and the Vietnam conflict. On all these problems, London was in a dilemma of finding a *via media* between the viewpoints of two antagonistic Powers—the USA and China. Had Peking been completely free from Soviet influence, especially during the initial period of the establishment of the People's Republic, or had Britain been able to resist American pressures, a deterioration in Sino-British relations might, perhaps, have been avoided. But the international situation being what it was, Britain and China adopted attitudes and postures that created complications in their relations. Britain's separate recognition of China, Kenneth Younger remarks, was announced in 1950 in the belief that many others would follow suit. It had little effect either upon Chinese action or upon events in East Asia because

British power alone was no longer sufficient for the purpose.[30] It was not possible for Britain to maintain a foreign policy in excess of its strength or its resources.

Loss of nearly £250 million worth of British investments in China and a delay of nearly 23 years in the establishment of full diplomatic relations had led some people to think that immediate gains from British recognition of the Peking regime had been quite negligible; that London should have accorded only *de facto* recognition and that too after extracting certain guarantees or assurances. It is stated that British recognition entailed certain risks, like those inherent in the presence of Chinese communist consuls in Malaya and Peking's exploitation of Anglo-American differences by playing off London against Washington. Such assertions seem to be based on misconceptions, which are borne out of ignorance of the reality of the situation. A *de facto* recognition of Peking would have been meaningless. Delay in according recognition in the hope of extracting concessions or guarantees from Peking would have served no useful purpose. The British recognition of China was an acceptance of reality, a convenience to protect and promote their national interests. It was neither a favour nor a gift. The British commercial and strategic interests dictated the realistic course of according *de jure* recognition to a government which was, in fact, exercising *de facto* authority over mainland China.

There is, likewise, no justification in the viewpoint, often put forward by some British commentators, that the substantive British decision to recognize China was the outcome of Indian influence. If British writers had sought to make out Indian influence over British policy in this regard as a factor in according recognition, it seems to be motivated primarily by their desire to moderate the sting of American criticism of British policy towards China rather than to risk American goodwill for the fanciful advantage of gaining transitory Indian goodwill. The British recognition did not save the liquidation of British assets in China (ranging between £200 to £250 million). Nevertheless, it contributed towards developing trade relations and preserving the status of Hong Kong. It also facilitated the establishment of much-needed contacts between Eden and Chou En-lai at the Geneva Conference on Indo-China in 1954, and thus helped in bringing about a mutually acceptable settlement of the Indo-China problem.

Furthermore, the accusation that the British recognition of China produced strains in Anglo-American relations does not seem to be quite correct because as late as June 1950 Washington was in no way committed to prevent the seizure of Taiwan by the Peking regime. In fact, the United States had full sympathy with the British desire to prevent the Peking leadership from pursuing an extremist policy at home and moving closer to the Kremlin. The USA itself would have followed Britain in recognizing Communist China had the Korean War not complicated matters for Washington. If Bevin's hopes of achieving a Sino-Western *detente* did not materialize in 1950 it was partly because both Britain and China were not then in a position to pursue a line of action completely independent of or altogether free from the influence of and pressure from their predominant partners—the USA and the Soviet Union. In spite of the constraints imposed by the division of the world into two rival blocs, London endeavoured to adopt an independent posture which was evident from its dissociation from Washington's decision to throw a protective shield over Taiwan (in the wake of the Korean War) and its efforts to restrain Washington from escalating the War. However, the fact remained that on certain vital issues, such as the branding of Peking as an aggressor in Korea, the imposition of an embargo, blocking China's admission in the UN, the problem of Formosa, etc. London was obliged to toe the American line.

In the 1960s, Britain supported India in the Sino-Indian conflict of 1962 and, together with America, embarked on joint measures to reinforce India's defences against China. London also felt concerned about Chinese activities in Africa, particularly Chou En-lai's remark during 1963-64 that Africa was ripe for revolution. But British efforts to reach a *modus vivendi* with Peking continued, though there were, at the same time, the beginning of Anglo-American military contingency planning in the Far East directed against China somewhat comparable to those in Europe directed against the Soviet Union. However, Britain did not believe that Communist China was expansionist in the sense of conventional military aggression. The dichotomy between Peking's words and deeds was noted and Peking was considered capable of "only subversion, provocation and above all propaganda and bluff." Furthermore, owing to continuing internal disorders during the "Cultural Revolution" period, it was believed that China would, for some time, be too isolated, weak and divided to be dangerously aggressive.[31]

The Chinese news media was critical of Anglo-American military cooperation East of the Suez and their policy of "containment of China." Peking denounced their plan to set up military bases in the Indian Ocean, Diego Garcia in particular, for providing the so-called nuclear protective umbrella against China. It sought to expose the hollowness of Britain's special relationship with the United States by pointing out to the latter's attempts to place West Germany on an equal footing in NATO through multilateral nuclear force plan and the weakness of the Commonwealth by drawing attention to various internal contradictions within the ranks of its membership.[32]

With the widening Sino-Soviet rift and confrontation between the two communist giants and Sino-US *rapprochement*, contradictions in British policy (the duality of approach inherent in its desire to follow America and cultivate relations with China in conditions of Sino-US estrangement) had almost disappeared. All the road blocks that had hitherto hampered the growth of friendly relations between Britain and China (*e.g.* Peking's admission in the UN, the embargo on trade and the British attitude on the Taiwan question) had been cleared and relations at ambassadorial level had been established. The joint Anglo-American base in Diego Garcia no longer bothers Peking. In fact, it is regarded a legitimate response to the expansion of Soviet naval forces in the Indian Ocean. (Incidentally, Peking has also dropped its opposition to the US military presence in East Asia, which is now considered as a useful countervailing force to the Soviet expansionist designs in Asia). Thus, the "period of pregnancy"[33] in Sino-British relations, which took an unusually long time of 22 years, has now come to an end. The two countries are no longer inhibited by the over-shadowing or dominating influence of either the USA or the USSR. In fact, Peking now faces Moscow squarely on its borders as well as in international forums and Britain has deemed it necessary to join the EEC, thereby shedding the stigma of being a camp follower of the United States. It has now become part and parcel of a grouping, "European Europe," which is expected to be independent of both the super Powers. The Chinese believe that this new grouping would play a useful role in opposing the hegemony of "US imperialism" and Soviet "social-imperialism." The British entry in the EEC was an important reason for China's adoption of a positive attitude towards Britain. It might be recalled that Peking's reappraisal of the EEC occurred only during 1970-71 when it considered Western Europe a conglomeration of States capable of throwing "many obstacles in the way of the two super Powers." Peking desired that members of the EEC should assert themselves politically against the hegemony of the super Powers. Peking believes that the major danger facing the people of the world is the scramble of the two super Powers for world hegemony, with Europe as the strategic focus of their rivalry. The Chinese leaders contend that they do not fear an imminent attack from the Soviet Union, even though one million Soviet troops are concentrated on the Sino-Soviet border. The main threat, according to Peking, is Soviet expansionism in Europe. China therefore, would like to see a self-reliant Western Europe based on a self-defence community independent of the United States and able to stand up to Soviet pressure.

Chinese opposition to the super Power hegemony, particularly that of the Soviet Union, had been an important factor in Peking's policy of wooing West European states. China has stressed that West Europe must follow up its economic and political integration with military coordination as well. Accordingly, China has not only approved NATO's existence and the role it can play in countering the Soviet threat but it has also supported moves to strengthen West European armed forces. Peking has warned West European states against being duped by the Soviet policy of *detente* and weakening of the NATO alliance by the withdrawal of American troops from Europe or unilateral cuts in defence expenditure. For that matter, Peking has been critical of the Conference on Security and Cooperation in Europe and the talks being held in Vienna on the mutual reduction of armed forces in Europe.

The improvement in Sino-French relations, following French recognition of China in 1964, received a setback after France moved closer to the Soviet Union in the late 1960s. It was only after President Pompidou's visit to China in September 1973 that relations between the two countries showed signs of improvement once again. Teng Hsiao-ping returned that visit in May 1975 (it was his first visit abroad after he became the senior-most Vice-Premier), an important result of which was the agreement to hold regular consultations at the Foreign Ministers' level. In 1974 a number of West European dignitaries, including the Prime Minister of Denmark, the Foreign Minister of Holland and the opposition leaders of Britain and West Germany, visited China. By the middle of 1975 the Dutch Foreign Minister, the Belgian Prime Minister, West German Opposition leader Franz-Josef Strauss and EEC Commissioner for External Affairs, Christopher Soames, had also visited China.

Edward Heath was Prime Minister in 1972 when he was invited to Peking but was the Conservative leader of the Opposition by the time he arrived in Peking in May 1974. He was nevertheless given a welcome befitting a Head of State primarily because of his contribution to the strengthening of Sino-Brirish relations, and more important, to the strengthening of West Europe. He was also granted an audience with Mao Tse-tung, a rare honour indeed. At a banquet given in honour of Heath on 25 May 1974, Teng Hsiao-ping recalled that it was under the Prime Ministership of the Conservative leader that agreement had been reached on the exchange of ambassadors. The British Government also acknowledged that Taiwan was a province of China under his leadership. Teng praised Heath for consistently standing for unity of the West European countries and the strengthening of their own independence and sovereignty. He had firmly led Britain, Teng added, "in returning to Europe...an important event in the interest of the West European people's struggle against hegemonism."[34]

Heath stated that Britain should remain "an active and energetic member of the European Community." It is in the interests of the world as a whole, he observed, that "Europe should increasingly unite and speak with a common voice." After asserting that the affairs of the world could not be left to the decisions of the two super Powers, Heath went on to remark : "It is right that you in China and we in Europe and many other countries across the world should have our say—and that when we speak the super Powers should listen."[35]

Commenting on the unusual welcome accorded to Edward Heath in China, Radio Moscow (27 May 1974) observed : "Peking's interest in London's foreign policy developed especially after the Tory government expressed its intention to use Britain's entry into the Common Market to strengthen NATO and set up so-called European nuclear forces." The Chinese, it added, did not conceal their delight that British Conservative leaders acted as pioneers of what the Soviet broadcast called behind-the-scenes intrigues by the North Atlantic bloc against European *detente*.[36]

Owing to its present anti-Soviet bias, Peking desires to see a strong and united Western Europe as a deterrent to the alleged Soviet ambitions and to counter the hegemony of the two super Powers. In pursuance of its policy of caution near at home (as was evident from Mao's restraining influence on the militant zeal of the North Korean President) and belligerence by proxy far away, China seems quite keen to egg on West Europe to be more uncompromising in its confrontation with the Soviet Union, a message which it had tried to impress upon all visitors from West European capitals. This serves Chinese interests because it obliges Moscow to maintain a large force on its Western frontier rather than on its long border with China. Accordingly, China was more favourably disposed towards some of the opposition leaders of West European countries, including Heath, than government leaders who seemed to be sympathetic to the idea of cooperation and *detente* in Europe. Thus, Labour Prime Minister Harold Wilson's Moscow visit in February 1975 was apparently disliked in Peking. A Chinese commentary drew attention to Soviet espionage activities which, it stated, were the "very opposite to friendly ties and *detente*." For similar reasons, Herr Brandt's *Ostpolitik* was considered dangerous flirtation with the Soviet bloc, while opposition politicians Helmut Kohl and Franz Josef Strauss were warmly greeted in Peking.

Peking welcomed Britain's vote in favour of remaining in the EEC (at a referendum held in June 1975) since it ensured continued membership of Britain into the main stream of political and economic life of West Europe. China established official relations with the EEC in May 1975 when it decided to nominate an envoy to the EEC in Brussels. It might be recalled that the EEC is China's second largest trading partner after Japan. Recent contracts concluded by West European firms with China involved a sale of 30 British Trident aircraft, with deliveries extending to 1976, a $264 million steel making complex for Wuhan, to be constructed by a West German consortium and operational by 1977, and $1 billion worth of orders from French firms for transport equipment and petro-chemical plants. Thus, China looks to West Europe as a supplier of sohphisticated technology and equipment which it is unable to get either from the Soviet Union or the United States.

Since a "United Western Europe" could better serve China's purpose of countering super Power hegemony and of acting as a buffer against the Soviet Union, Peking wishes to see West Europe as strong as possible in the economic, political and military fields. For that matter, China has also welcomed the development of co-operation between the Second and Third World countries, particularly the oil-rich Arab nations and the west European consumer countries. According to the "three worlds" concept, propounded by Teng Hsiao-ping (in his address before the UN General Assembly in April 1974), all the countries of the Second (the industrialized developed nations of West Europe and Japan) and Third World (the developing countries of Asia, Africa and Latin America) are imbued, in varying degrees, with the desire of shaking off super Power (First World) enslavement or control and safeguarding their national independence and the integrity of their sovereignty.[37] Thus, Peking supports and encourages World, Second World countries and identifies itself with the Third which is regarded as the most vital force for change in international affairs. The Chinese leaders also intend to form a broad united front of Second and Third World countries under their leadership and against the two super Powers. The charges of colonialist plunder and exploitation are now increasingly confined to only the two super Powers. West European countries are exempted from that charge and their agreements with the Third World countries are described in Peking as agreements concluded in the spirit of mutual benefit and equality. Thus, the Lome Convention between the EEC and 46 African, Carribean and Pacific developing states was hailed by the *New China News Agency* as a "big event in the development of relations between the Second and Third World countries" which should aid the world-wide struggle "against the super Powers and their hegemonistic practices." The recent improvement of French relations with Algeria was also looked upon with satisfaction in Peking. In short, the EEC, of which UK is now a part, and China can hope to play independent roles in the world keeping their own national interests in view. The constraints inherent in Sino-Soviet monolithic solidarity and Anglo-American special relationship, against which both London and Peking had worked in the 50s and the early 60s, no longer exist. Therefore, China and Britain can now look forward to a steady growth in their trade relations, free from political inhibitions and restrictions, and the development of fruitful political contacts at the highest level.

Abbreviations Used in Notes

AFP	*American Foreign Policy, 1950-55 : Basic Documents*, US Department of State (Washington, 1957).
BTJ	UK, *Board of Trade Journal* (London).
CD	*China Digest* (Hong Kong).
Cmd/.Cmnd.	UK, *Command Papers.*
CMR	*China Monthly Review* (Shanghai).
CPS	*Chinese Press Survey* (Shanghai).
CT	*China Today* (Embassy of People's Republic of China, New Delhi).
CWR	*China Weekly Review* (Shanghai).
DSB	*Department of State Bulletin* (Washington).
EW	*Eastern World* (London).
FEER	*Far Eastern Economic Review* (Hong Kong).
H.C. Deb.	UK, Parliamentary Debates, *House of Commons.*
H.L. Deb.	UK, Parliamentary Debates, *House of Lords.*
JMJP	*Jen-min Jih-pao (People's Daily)* (Peking).
JRCAS	*Journal of the Royal Central Asian Society* (London).
NB	*News Bulletin* (Embassy of People's Republic of China, New Delhi).
NCNA	*New China (Hsinhua) News Agency.*
NYT	*New York Times* (New York).
PC	*People's China* (Peking).
PR	*Peking Review* (Peking).
SCMP	*Survey of China Mainland Press* (US Consulate-General, Hong Kong).
SPT	*Soviet Press Translations* (Washington).
TMER	*Three Monthly Economic Review of China, Hong Kong, North Korea* (Economist Intelligence Unit, London).
UN Doc.	United Nations Document.
WWCC	*Chung-hua Jen-min Kung-he-kuo, tui Wai Kuan-hsi Wen-chien Chi* (Shih-chieh Chih-shih Ch'u-pan hsie, Peking).

Notes

Chapter One : Historical Background

1 N. Gangulee, compiled, *The Teaching of Sun Yat-sen* (London, 1945) 128.
2 Despatch from Lord Palmerston to the Minister of the Emperor of China. See Sir Frederick Whyte *China and Foreign Powers* (London, 1928) 45-6.
3 Godrey E.P. Hertslet, *Treaties etc. Between Great Britain and China*, I (London, 1908) 10.
4 Sir John T. Pratt, *The Expansion of Europe into the Far East* (London, 1947) 176.
5 See A. J. Sargent, *Anglo-Chinese Commerce and Diplomacy* (London, 1907) 295, Footnote.
6 Despatch from Clarendon to Dr. Bowring, Her Majesty's Plenipotentiary and Chief Superintendent of British Trade in China, 13 February 1854. H. B. Morse, *The International Relations of the Chinese Empire* (London, 1910) 672.
7 Hertslet, n. 3, 22.
8 Sargent, n. 5, 141-2.
9 *Ibid.*, 243.
10 John T. Pratt, *War and Politics in China* (London, 1943) 167.
11 *Ibid.*, 102 and 108-9.
12 *Ibid.*, 167.
13 Exchange of Notes between Claude M. MacDonald and the Tsungli Yamen, 9 February 1898. Quoted in Pratt, n. 10, 113.
14 *Ibid.*, 119.
15 Sargent, n. 5, 297.
16 Whyte, n. 2, 37.
17 *Ibid.*, 38.
18 Pratt, n. 10, 180.
19 Group V of the Twenty-One Demands were postponed and ultimately relinquished at Washington in 1922.
20 "The legal basis for our collective action in the Far East was established by the Washington Conference of 1921-22, particularly in the Nine-Power Treaty concerning China. This was a codification of the Open Door doctrine in expanded form." John King Fairbank, *The United States and China* (Harvard, 1948) 324.
21 Pratt, n. 10, 9.

22 Fairbank, n. 20, 320-1.

23 *Ibid.*, 320.

24 The revolution of 1911 started in the South and there was, for a period, a complete cleavage between the North and the South. However, all customs and other revenues from the South were sent to Peking. This greatly tipped the balance in favour of the Peking regime, and therefore, naturally caused a great deal of resentment among the nationalist revolutionaries.

25 Pratt, n. 4, 136-7.

26 The British disregard, or hostility, towards the communist doctrine and policy and Lenin's theory of imperialism and strategy for a communist world revolution was another important factor which embittered relations between the UK and the Soviet Union.

27 Ronald Farquharson, "China—Past, Present and Future," *JRCAS* (April 1952) 105-6. Britain's decision not to defend that concession was taken in order to save 90 per cent of its interests situated outside the concession.

28 Without Russian support and backing of Chinese communists, who had gained a footing among the workers and started organising them, the Kuomintang might not have hoped to challenge British power. In this way, Sun Yat-sen came to formulate his "Three Great Policies" of alliance with the USSR in foreign affairs; a united front with the Chinese Communists in internal affairs; and cooperation with the Chinese workers and peasants. Chiang Kai-shek publicly declared in 1923 that "China's revolution must be led by the Third International." Chiang Kai-shek, *China's Destiny and Chinese Economic Theory*, notes and commentary by Philip Jaffe (New York, 1947) 100 and 108-9 footnotes. Soviet help "ran into many millions sterling." Pratt, n. 10, 260.

29 "Much of the success that attended Soviet policy in the early 1920's was due to the moral fervour with which it was pursued." Pratt, n. 4, 183.

30 The complete neglect and disdain with which the UK treated China as a nation is apparent from the deal it made with Russia in 1899 regarding the mutual recognition of each other's sphere of interest in the development of railroads in China.

31 Pratt, n. 4, 168. He cites two glaring instances in this regard : (a) a mixed court in Shanghai, which was formerly entirely under Chinese control, but now came to be controlled by foreigners; and (b) the new arrangements made for the collection and custody of the customs revenues.

32 Ho Kan-chih, *A History of the Modern Chinese Revolution* (Peking, 1959) 27-8. The official communist historian asserts: "This was the first anti-imperialist strike of the working class in the history of China. The working class was the most powerful contingent in the ranks of the May 4 Movement."

33 Benjamin Schwartz, *Chinese Communism and the Rise of Mao* (Harvard, 1952) 25. Li Ta-chao and Chien Tu-hsiu were not only

"spiritual fathers of Marxism-Leninism in China and the first founders of the Chinese Communist Party," but also the leaders of the May 4th Movement. They were mainly responsible for the founding of the Society for the Study of Marxism at the Peking University in the spring of 1918. Mao also belonged to this student group. *Ibid.*, 26.

34 *Ibid.*, 215.
35 The surrender of foreign post offices and wireless stations on Chinese soil were agreed at Washington.
36 Jane Degras, ed., *The Communist International* : 1919-43, *Documents Vol. I* (1919-22) (London, 1956) 292.
37 *Ibid.*, 425.
38 Conrad Brandt, Benjamin Schwartz and John K. Fairbank, *A Documentary History of Chinese Communism* (London, 1952) 62-3.
39 Ho Kan-chih, n. 32, 90.
40 *Ibid.*, 92. After the May 30 Movement gained momentum, the membership of the Communist Party jumped from about 900 to about 20,000.
41 Fairbank, n. 20, 326.
42 Pratt, n. 4, 171.
43 As early as 1902, Article 11 of the Commercial Treaty between the UK and China provided that the former is "prepared to relinquish her extra-territorial rights when she is satisfied that the state of the Chinese laws, the arrangement for their administration, and other considerations warrant her in so doing." Hertslet, n. 3, 182. Twenty years later, the Washington Conference went no further than to appoint a commission of inquiry. The commission, in its report signed on 16 September 1926 by representatives of the 13 Powers, recommended that, when certain conditions have been satisfied, the Powers concerned shall relinquish extra-territorial privileges. *Cmd.* 2774.
44 Whyte, n. 2, 52-5. In the Nine-Power Treaty on the Chinese Customs tariff, the Powers assembled at Washington agreed to an immediate increase of a surtax of $2\frac{1}{2}$ per cent above the effective 5 per cent. But the Tariff Conference, which was to give effect to this increase, did not meet for three years though it was called upon to meet three months after ratification.
45 *Ibid.*, 59 and 62-3.
46 Yin Ching Chen, ed., *Treaties and Agreements Between the Republic of China and Other Powers*: 1929-1954 (Washington, 1957) 65-6. The remission of the Boxer funds was thus "calculated both to increase British prestige in China and to increase British exports to China in a period of declining world market." Irving S. Friedman, *British Relations with China*: 1931-39 (New York, 1940) 16.
47 See Whyte, n. 2, 59.
48 See G. E. Hubbard, *British Far Eastern Policy* (New York, 1943) 51 and Fairbank, n. 20, 196.
49 In December 1929 and again in December 1930, the Nationalist

Government set a date for the return of China's jurisdictional rights. In May 1931 the "Regulations for Controlling Foreign Nationals in China" was published. They were to become effective as of 1 January 1932 but were subsequently postponed as a result of the Japanese invasion of Manchuria. Chiang Kai-shek attributed the failure of these attempts partly to the breaking out of civil war and partly to the "policy of watchful waiting adopted by all the foreign powers." Chiang Kai-shek, n. 28, 132-3. As late as 2 November 1940, Sun Fo observed : "After even thirty years, our nationalist movement has not yet reached its goal....Today, all the unequal treaties, with the Treaty of Nanking at the head of them, are just as binding as ever. We are still far from being a free and independent country." Sun Fo, *China Looks Forward* (London, 1945) 39.

50 Evan Luard, *Britain and China* (London, 1962) 52.

51 Royal Institute of International Affairs, *Survey of International Affairs* 1939-46 : *The Far East* 1942-46 (London, 1955) 23.

52 *Ibid.*, 115.

53 *H. L. Deb.*, 126 (1943) 431. While the US loan or credit of £100 million was free from any restrictions, £40 million of the £50 million British aid to China was tied to purchases within Britain. *Ibid.*, 672.

54 *Ibid.*, 690-1.

55 G. E. Mitchell, "China and Britain : Their Commercial and Industrial Relations," *JRCAS* (Jul-Oct 1952) 248.

56 Hubbard, n. 48, 76.

57 Yin Ching Chen, n. 46, 142-4.

58 *H. C. Deb.*, 437 (1947) 1960-1.

59 UK Board of Trade, *Report of the United Kingdom Trade Mission to China* (London, 1948) 35.

60 *Ibid.*, 52.

61 *Ibid.*, 47. These goods were also subject to an additional luxury tax of 50 per cent of the import duty.

62 The British draft of the Treaty was presented in June 1946. In January 1947 the Chinese Government sent its counter-draft. *H. L. Deb.*, 145 (1947) 158.

63 As the US-Chiang Treaty of 4 November 1946 was regarded as conferring immense benefits on the Americans in matters of carrying on commercial, manufacturing, processing and scientific activities and in exploiting the mineral resources of China, British M.P.s consistently urged their Government not to lag behind the USA in this matter. Lord Cranborne on 23 January 1947 referred to the US-Chiang Treaty as giving the USA "very considerable commerical advantages," and complained "why are our negotiations lagging behind ?" *H. L. Deb.*, 145 (1947) 150. Anthony Eden made a similar plea in the House of Commons on 15 May 1947. *H. C. Deb.*, 437 (1947) 1753-4.

64 *H. L. Deb.*, 126 (1943) 684-5.

65 The Minister of Economic Affairs, Dr. Wong Wen-hao, anticipated the import of US $10 billion worth of capital goods soon
after the War. David Nelson Rowe, *China Among the Powers*
(New York, 1945) 92.

66 Statement by Lord Chancellor, Viscount Jowitt, 23 January 1947.
H. L. Deb., 145 (1947) 157.

67 *The Times*, 4 Feb 1948.

68 UK Board of Trade, n. 59, 13.

69 *The Times.* 6 Jan 1948.

70 The figures of imports and exports in 1946, issued by the Chinese
Maritime Customs and converted into sterling at the average offi-
cial rate for each months showed :
Foreign Trade, 1946 (Millions of £ Sterling)
Imports 156.3
Exports 37.9
UK Board of Trade, n. 59, 20.

71 On 9 April 1948 the Special Correspondent of the London *Times*
in Southern China, wrote : "The first thing the visitor must do is
to brush up his arithmetic. Lunch, on my first day in Shameen,
cost $225,000.... Most shopkeepers refused to accept denominations
lower than $500." *The Times*, 9 Apr 1948.

72 *H. L. Deb.*, 145 (1947) 149.

73 *H. C. Deb.*, 433 (1947) 2305. Here Bevin makes a reference to
Stalinist policies of the period.

74 *The Times*, 12 Feb 1948.

75 Statement by Mayhew, Under-Secretary of State for Foreign
Affairs in the House of Commons, 27 February 1947. *H. C. Deb.*,
433 (1947) 2399-2402.

76 *The Times*, 6 Jan 1948.

77 *Ibid.*, 12 Feb 1948.

78 The declaration of the Foreign Ministers of the USA, the UK and
the USSR in Moscow on 27 December 1945 falls into four parts :
"The three foreign Secretaries exchanged views with regard to the
situation in China. They were in agreement as to the need for
a unified and democratic China under the National Government
for broad participation by democratic elements in all branches of
the National Government, for a cessation of civil strife. They
reaffirmed their adherence to the policy of non-interference in the
internal affairs of China." Yin Ching Chen, n. 46, 241. On 11
March 1948 President Truman said : "We did not want any communists in the Government of China or anywhere else if we could
help it." US Department of State, *United States Relations with
China* (Washington, 1949) 273.

79 "Apart from the gift or loan of a few small warships to the
Chinese navy and some provision for the training of Chinese sailors
in England, the British Government had done nothing that could
be construed as assistance to Generalissimo Chiang Kai-shek....
The British Government could therefore view with relative

equanimity the prospect of a predominantly communist administration in China." F. C. Jones in Royal Institute of International Affairs, *Survey of International Affairs :* 1947-48 (London, 1952) 311.

80 F. C. Jones, *Manchria Since* 1931 (London, 1949) 240-1.

81 The prolonging of the Civil War, Lord Lindsay of Birker stated in the House of Lords on 11 June 1947, "is encouraging the Communists to believe that their only hope is in Russia." *H. L. Deb.*, 148 (1947) 526-7. As early as 23 January 1947, Lord Chancellor, Viscount Jowitt, observed : "While rigidly adhering to our decision not to interfere in Chinese affairs, which are matters for the Chinese, we earnestly hope that there may soon be a happy issue out of these afflictions, and that we will do everything which lies in our power to assist *anyone* bringing that about." *H. L. Deb.*, 145 (1947) 159.

82 *The Times*, 12 Feb 1948.

83 According to official information contained in the "China White Paper," the USA provided "more than 2 billion dollars in the form of grants and credits" to China since VJ Day. In addition surplus property valued at over $1 billion was sold to China for $232 millions. US Department of State, n. 78, 405.

84 "Between 1927 and 1945 the Chinese Communists received no direct help from Soviet Russia or the Comintern, not for lack of sympathy, but because to have encouraged separatist movements would have weakened and distracted China and have reduced her value as a bulwark against Japan." Pratt, n. 4, 187. After 1945 it was no doubt in Russian interests to encourage communists and foster separatist tendencies in China but apart from the complicity of the USSR in allowing the Chinese Communists to take hold of Japanese arms and areas in Manchuria and thus indirectly helping them, we have "no evidence that Soviet military advisers are assisting the communist armies in the field. No Soviet aircraft have made their appearance in the Civil War. Reports that Soviet instructors are training troops in Manchuria may possibly be true..." *Times* correspondent in Peking. *The Times*, 12 Feb 1948. On 1 July 1949, Mao Tse-tung denied that he had received any material help from Russia. He said : "We are indebted to Marx, Engels, Lenin and Stalin for giving us a weapon. The weapon is not a machine gun, but Marxism-Leninism." Mao Tse-tung, *On People's Democratic Dictatorship* (Peking 1953) 2.

85 Grover Clark, *Economic Rivalries in China* (New Haven, 1932) 105.

86 UK Board of Trade, n. 59, 162.

87 *Ibid.*, 28, 53 and 42-3.

88 *Ibid.*, 97 and 145.

89 *Ibid.*, 23-9.

90 *The Times*, 17 Feb 1948. See also *Ibid.*, 6 Feb 1948.

91 *The Times*, 4 Feb 1948.

92 A.S.B. Olver, *Outline of British Policy in East and Southeast Asia 1945-May* 1950 (London, 1950) 20.
93 Statement of the Foreign Secretary, Bevin, in the House of Commons, 16 November 1949. *H. C. Deb.*, 469 (1949) 2015.
94 *Ibid.*, 2015. From November 1949 onwards two Royal Navy frigates were kept off the mouth of the Yangtze to assist British merchant ships. Luard, n. 50, 133.
95 "The Russians did not lift a finger to help Mao rid himself of a disastrous nuisance when it would have been easy to lend only a few planes to dispose of it." Robert Gullain in Otto B. Van Der Sprenkel, ed., *New China : Three Views* (London, 1950) 115.
96 Statement in the House of Commons, 24 May 1950. *H. C. Deb.*, 475 (1950) 2086.
97 *The Economist*, 7 Jan 1950, 10.

Chapter Two : British Recognition and Peking's Reaction

1 Kenneth Younger, "A British View of the Far East," *Pacific Affairs* (Jun 1954) 101-2.
2 See Kenneth Younger, "An Analysis of British and U. S. Policies in the Far East," *EW* (Mar 1953) 10.
3 *SPT* (15 Oct 1950) 566-7.
4 V. Maslennikov in *Voprosy Ekonomiki* (Moscow) (No. 9, 1950) as translated in *SPT* (15 Mar 1951) 138.
5 Shanghai contained 80 per cent of the country's entire light industry and 25 per cent of the heavy industry. E. Vysokov in *Pravda*, 24 Sep 1951. *SPT* (1 Nov 1951) 590. Of the one million workers engaged in Shanghai's industry, more than 60 per cent were employed in private enterprises.
6 L. Baranov in *Pravda*, 5 Jan 1950. *SPT* (1 May 1950) 268-9.
7 Chinese Communist Party's May Day slogans, 1 May 1948. *CD* (18 May 1948) 10.
8 *SPT*, n. 3, 566-7.
9 Mao Tse-tung, *On Coalition Government* (Peking, 1955) 49.
10 Mao Tse-tung quoted by *Pravda*, 23 Sep 1950. *SPT*, n. 3, 566-7.
11 Edgar Faure, *The Serpent and the Tortoise* (London, 1958) Preface.
12 *Rude Pravo* (Prague), 22 Jan 1953, quoted by Paul E. Zinner, "Soviet Policies in Eastern Europe" in Philip E. Mosley, ed., *Russia Since Stalin : Old Trends and New Problems* (Philadelphia, 1956) 158.
13 Quoted by Pospelov, Editor of *Pravda* in a speech on 21 January 1949. Royal Institute of International Affairs, *Documents on International Affairs* : 1949-50 (London, 1953) 126-7.
14 *Ibid.*, 126.

15 Sir Roger Makins, "The World Since the War : The Third Phase," *Foreign Affairs* (Oct 1954) 6.
16 C. M. Woodhouse, *British Foreign Policy Since the World War* (London, 1961) 22.
17 *H. C. Deb.*, 482 (1950-1) 1456.
18 *NYT*, 19 May 1951.
19 *SPT*, n. 4, 131.
20 *The World Today* (Dec 1952) 497.
21 Younger, n. 1, 100.
22 Younger n. 2, 10.
23 See statement by British Foreign Secretary, Bevin, 24 May 1950. *H. C. Deb*, 475 (1950) 2083.
24 *NYT*, 19 May 1951.
25 C. P. Fitzerald, *Revolution in China* (London, 1952) 215.
26 *Ibid.*, 217.
27 "Not one of these reasons for so grave a step as the rebuff to friendly intercourse was adequate," Fitzerald asserts. *Ibid.*, 216.
28 *Ibid.*, 218-9.
29 Michael Lindsay, *China and the Cold War* (New York, 1955) 19.
30 *Ibid.*, 20-1 and 10.
31 Article in *Hsueh-hsi* (Peking), 24 Oct 1949 as translated in *CPS* (11 Nov 1949) 42.
32 Mao Tse-tung, quoted in *CD* (22 Mar 1949) 21.
33 Harrison Forman, *Blunder in Asia* (New York, 1950) 160.
34 Speech by Nan Han-chen, Director of the People's Bank of China, 8 October 1951. Quoted in Sunder Lal, *China Today* (Allahabad, 1952) 183.
35 US Department of State, *United States Relations with China* (Washington, 1949) IV.
36 See Report by Ma Shun-ku, Director of the Labour Bureau of the Shanghai People's Government, 16 October 1950. *CMR* (Dec 1950) Supplement 10-1.
37 *CWR* (22 Jul 1950) 141.
38 *CMR* (Dec 1950) 119.
39 Mao Tse-tung, *On People's Democratic Dictatorship* (Peking, 1952) 30.
40 Article by Vladimer Poptomov, Bulgarian Foreign Minister in *For A Lasting Peace, For A People's Democracy*, 6 Jan 1950. Broadcast by Moscow Radio on 7 January 1950. See *White Book* issued by the Yugoslav Foreign Ministry (Belgrade, 1951) 270.
41 Francis C. Jones, "Recent Developments in Manchuria," *JRCAS* (Apr 1957) 121.
42 In 1943 Manchuria produced 49 per cent of the entire country's coal output, about 87 per cent of its pig iron, 93 per cent of its steel products and 78 per cent of its electric power. *CWR* (17 Jun 1950) 53-4.
43 Alignment with the Soviet Union, Chang Min-yang observed in *World Culture* on 21 October 1949, was necessary to safeguard "the

fruits of our victory" and to ensure against "our enemies from within and without who may want to stage a comeback." *CPS* (Nov 1949) 10.

44 *Ibid.*, (11 Jan 1950) 33.
45 *Ibid.*, 32-3.
46 See Article by Chang Min-yang in *World Culture*, 5 Aug 1949 as reproduced in *CWR* (27 Aug 1949) 238.
47 Mao Tse-tung, *On People's Democratic Dictatorship* (Peking, 1950) 33-4.
48 *CD* (29 Jun 1948) 13.
49 *Ibid.*, (5 Apr 1949) 2.
50 Mao Tse-tung, n. 47, 34,
51 *CWR* (10 Dec 1949) 31.
52 *CPS* (11 Jan 1950) 33.
53 In communicating the British Government's decision to recognize China, Foreign Secretary Bevin not only repeated the words "the basis of equality, mutual benefit," etc. but also informed the Chinese Government about the severance of British relations with the Kuomintang. *The Times*, 7 Jan 1950.
54 Communist authorities had placed placards on 6 January 1950, on the gates of the British and American Consulate Generals' and French and Netherlands Embassy Offices announcing the requisition of the buildings. The British Consulate General conveyed the British Government's note of recognition during the day and the placard was removed during the night. O. Edmund Clubb, "Chinese Communist Strategy in Foreign Relations," *Annals of the Academy of Political and Social Sciences* (Philadelphia) (Sep 1951) 164. While the barracks belonging to the other governments were requisitioned, the British barracks, covering by far the largest area of land, were for the time being spared. They were seized on 11 April 1950.
55 Statement by the Spokesman of the Chinese Foreign Ministry, 22 May 1950. *PC* (1 Jun 1950) 26.
56 *WWCC* : 1949-50, 19.
57 *Ibid.*, 17.
58 *CPS* (21 Jan 1950) 62-4.
59 *Ibid.*, 62-4.
60 Stalin, quoted by Chen Po-ta in his article written on the occasion of Stalin's 70th birthday, December 1949. *CWR* (21 Jan 1950) 124.
61 Of the total value of China's foreign trade in 1949, the share of the USSR was 7.76 per cent, of the UK 6.98 per cent, of Hong Kong 28.29 per cent and of the USA 24.46 per cent. Li Ching-yun, "New China's Foreign Trade," *PC* (1 Apr 1951) 5.
62 Fitzerald, n. 25, 214, 219 and 212.
63 *H. C. Deb.*, 475 (1950) 2085.
64 UN Doc. S/PV 459 (10 Jan 1950) 3.
65 *SPT* (15 Mar 1950) 167.

66 Statement by the Spokeman of the Chinese Foreign Ministry, 22 May 1950. *PC* (1 Jun 1950) 26.
67 See editorial in *People's China. Ibid.*, 2.
68 *H. C. Deb*,, 475 (1950) 2083.
69 *NYT*, 6 Apr 1950. Britain was busy encouraging other governments, including those of the Commonwealth countries, to recognize Peking and canvassing support for seating China in the UN. On 21 March 1950, a British Foreign Office Spokesman said that Cuba, Ecuador and Egypt had not yet replied to British attempts to end the deadlock in the UN Security Council over the admission of Chinese People's Government. Press reports that the approaches had failed were untrue, he added. *CWR* (1 Apr 1950) 83. See also statement by the Minister of State in the Foreign Office, Younger, 24 May 1950. *H. C. Deb.*, 475 (1950) 2188.
70 Statement by the Minister of State for Colonial Affairs, John Dugdale, 31 March 1950. *Ibid.*, 473 (1950) 744.
71 *Ibid.*, 743-4.
72 The British Government abstained on votes relating to the admission of Communist China into the UN till September 1950. Thereafter, they voted in favour of seating Peking in the UN on six occasions till February 1951 when China was condemned for aggression in Korea. Thereafter, upto December 1961 London voted against the seating of Communist China in the UN.
73 *PC* (1 Jun 1950) 26.
74 Statement by Liu Shao-chi, 1 May 1950. *CWR* (15 May 1950) 195-8. These measures included various tax relief measures, such as reduction in the deliveries in kind to the state and abolition of some 500 items of tax. See E. Kovalyov, "The Agrarian Policy of Chinese Communist Party," *SPT* (1 Apr 1951) 167, and also report by Chen Yun, Chairman of the Committee of Financial and Economic Affairs, 14-23 June 1950. *CWR* (1 Jul 1950) 88-90.
75 See editorial in *Ta Kung Pao*, 27 Feb 1950. *CPS* (Mar 1950) 129.
76 See article by Chen Nan Li, Associate Director of the Economic Research Department of the Bank of China. *CWR* (24 Jun 1950) 60.
77 *JMJP* quoted by Allen S. Whiting, *China Crosses the Yalu* (New York, 1960) 179. See also article by Chang Min-yang in *World Culture*, 14 Apr 1950, as translated in *CWR* (20 May 1950) 207.
78 See Statement by Foreign Secretary Bevin, 14 December 1950. *H. C. Deb.*, 482 (1950-1) 1458. See also Chapter Seven.
79 *JMJP* as translated in *PR* (6 Oct 1961) 21.
80 Chou En-lai's report on the Work of the Government, 23 September 1954. *PC* (16 Oct 1954) 23.
81 Tsiao Kuan-hua, "The Chinese People's Republic : A Bulwark of Peace," *International Affairs* (Moscow) (Jun 1955) 30-1.

Chapter Three : The Korean Question

1 Statement by the Spokesman of Chinese Foreign Ministry, 11 November 1950. *PC* (1 Dec 1950) Supplement 3. "China and Korea," General Yang Yung stated on the 10th anniversary of China's entry into the Korean War, "are separated by only a river. They are as dependent on each other as the lips and the teeth....The security of China is closely connected with the survival of Korea." *JMJP*, 24 Oct 1960.

2 Quoted in *Contemporary Japan* (Oct-Dec 1950) 351-2.

3 A.C. Wedemeyer, *Report on Korea* (Washington, 1951) 14, 24-5 and 8. American policy-makers and strategists, including Dean Acheson, later recommended evacuating American forces from South Korea because their presence seemed to serve no purpose.

4 The US Government realized the difficulty of defending Korea from a "base of supplies...5,000 miles away." Report by the US President to the Congress, 19 July 1950. *AFP*, 2556.

5 On 26 June 1950, Premier Attlee announced British decision to support the US action in Korea by immediately placing their naval forces in Japanese waters at the disposal of the US authorities to operate on behalf of the Security Council in support of South Korea. "Orders to this effect," he said, "have already been sent to the naval Commander-in-Chief on the spot." *H.C. Deb.*, 476 (1950) 2323.

6 Message from the US Secretary of State to the Prime Minister of India, 18 July 1950. *AFP*, 2551,

7 Statement by President Truman, 19 July 1950. *Ibid.*, 2557.

8 Although Korea was not a member of the UN, it "was a State created by the United Nations, guaranteed by the United Nations, and with a United Nations Commission there." Speech by Foreign Secretary Ernest Bevin, 5 October 1950. *Report of the 49th Annual Conference of the Labour Party*, 1950, 148.

9 Address by President Truman, 1 September 1950. *AFP*, 2567. See also statement by Premier Attlee, 12 September 1950. *H.C. Deb.*, 478 (1950) 953-5.

10 With Sakhalin in the north and Korea to the south, John Foster Dulles stated on 1 July 1950, "Japan would be between the upper and lower jaws of the Russian Bear." *DSB* (10 Jul 1950) 50. See also G. F. Hudson, "Korea and Asia," *International Affairs* (London) (Jan 1951) 21.

11 "The prospects of peace and stability in the Far East have been much set back by the fighting in Korea." Statement by Foreign Secretary H. Morrison, 25 July 1951. *H.C. Deb.*, 491 (1950-51) 476. Hong Kong could not have remained safe in these circumstances. In his letter to President Truman on 6 July 1950, Premier Attlee expressed his acute concern about the "problems which are likely to face us as the situation in Korea develops." He added : "We cannot

ignore the possibility of Chinese attack on Hong Kong." Francis Williams, *A Prime Minister Remembers* (London, 1961) 230-1.

12 Address by the US Assistant Secretary of State for Far Eastern Affairs, Dean Rusk, 18 May 1951 *AFP*, 2473.

13 John T. Pratt, *The Expansion of Europe into the Far East* (London, 1947) 114. The reasons which impelled Japan to forestall "Russia before the railway link with Vladivostok was completed," also led the West to resist North Korean attack before Moscow came to control the whole of Korea.

14 Address by Foreign Secretary Bevin at the Labour Conference, 5 October 1950. *Report of the 49th Annual Conference of the Labour Party*, 1950, 150.

15 Since Japan was the industrial rival of Britain, an independent and friendly China fitted well in Britain's strategy to effect balance of power in East Asia.

16 "It was the Soviet Union that trained and equipped the North Koreans for aggression," President Truman stated on 11 April 1951. *AFP*, 2611. While referring to China as "a great pacific nation," in his speech before the Annual Labour Conference on 5 October 1950, Foreign Secretary Bevin spoke of "Russia and her accomplices" being "in possession of all Korea in the event of aggression in Korea coming out successful." He called it "a deliberate organisation for aggression: because the tanks the North Koreans used were not made in Korea, they were sent there." The North Koreans, he added, "have been pushed into this. They have been the victims of machination." *Report of the 49th Annual Conference of the Labour Party*, 1950, 148.

17 Speaking of the Chinese intervention in Korea, the Assistant Secretary of State for Far Eastern Affairs, Dean Rusk, in a speech on 18 May 1951, observed : "China has been driven by foreign masters into an adventure of foreign aggression which cuts across the most fundamental national interests of the Chinese people." *AFP*, 2474.

18 *H.C. Deb.*, 478 (1950) 951.

19 Statement in the House of Lords, 14 December 1950. *H.L. Deb.*, 169 (1950) 1059. As late as 22 July 1955, Minister of State, Selwyn Lloyd, remarked : "We have not yet got parity with the Soviet Union." *H.C. Deb.*, 518 (1952-53) 401.

20 See Francis Williams, n. 11, 175.

21 Statement by Premier Attlee, 28 June 1950. *H.C. Deb.*, 476 (1950) 2292.

22 From the very outset of the Korean War, Churchill stated on 30 January 1952, he was "disquieted by seeing...the attention and resources of the United States being diverted from the main danger in Europe to this far distant peninsula in the China areas....When the main dangers are so much nearer home, we do not want to see ourselves tied down or entangled in a war in Korea—still less in a war in China." That would indeed, as General Bradley so forcibly said, "be the wrong war, in the wrong place, at the wrong time."

H.C. Deb., 495 (1951-2) 199.
23 *H.C. Deb.*, 496 (1951-2) 1018.
24 *H.C. Deb.*, 481 (1950) 1335-6.
25 Premier Attlee's reply to a letter of Fenner Brockway, back bench Labour member, seeking assurance from the Government that British support in Korea would not be extended to action unauthorised by the United Nations against China. For text of Attlee's reply, see *The Times*, 16 Aug 1950.
26 See *AFP*, 2541-2. See also Trumbull Higgins, *Korea and the Fall of MacArthur* (New York, 1960) 84.
27 See *H.C. Deb.*, 477 (1950) 954-5. In his reply to Fenner Brockway, Attlee bluntly stated that Britain's undertaking to give military assistance in Korea did not extend to Formosa. *The Times*, 16 Aug 1950.
28 *Cmd.* 8078, 11, 25-6 and 28.
29 *Ibid,*, 12. Speaking in the UN General Assembly on 25 September 1950, Foreign Secretary Bevin declared : "In our view there must no longer be South Koreans and North Koreans, but just Koreans." *UN Doc.* A/PV 283 (25 Sep 1950) 88.
30 *Cmd.* 8078, 12.
31 See *The Economist* (26 Aug 1950) 399.
32 This was done only after the Chinese intervention in Korea was reported to the United Nations by General MacArthur in his Special Report on 5 November 1950. See *Cmd.* 8366, 17-8.
33 See statement by the British delegate in the General Assembly *UN Doc.* A/PV 292 (6 Oct 1950). See also *Contemporary Japan* (Oct-Dec 1950) 616.
34 *Cmd.* 8366, 7-8.
35 "All that the North Korean authorities have to do now," Gladwyn Jebb, the British delegate in the UN, said on 30 September 1950, "is to sue for peace. Now that their cause.. seems to be quite hopeless...bombing of military targets in North Korea cannot be abandoned, since no commander can be expected to allow the enemy to reinforce his front line troops if he can possibly prevent it." UN Doc. S/PV 508 (30 Sep 1950) 7.
36 Speaking in the First Committee of the UN, British Minister of State Younger pleaded for not missing the opportunity then afforded of putting an end to the "present tragic and unnatural division" of Korea. UN Doc. A/C. 1/PV 347 (30 Sep 1950) 11.
37 See *The Economist* (26 Aug 1950) 399-400.
38 *Ibid.* (7 Oct 1950) 570. "The 38th parallel," Foreign Secretary Bevin stated on 14 December 1950, "was artificial." He added : "I also visualised that if we perpetuated the 38th parallel we should be in the difficulty, for a long time to come, of having two armies lined up, one on each side of it." He, thus, offered "no apology" for the 8-Power resolution which indirectly sanctioned the crossing of the 38th parallel. *H.C. Deb.*, 482 (1950-1) 1459.
39 Statement by Bevin. See *Report of the 49th Annual Conference of the*

Labour Party, 1950, 148.
40 See address by Bevin at the Labour Conference, 5 October 1950. *Ibid.*, 150.
41 UN Doc. S/PV 506 (29 Sep 1950) 5.
42 *The Economist* (7 Oct 1950) 569.
43 The UN troops, Younger stated, would remain in Korea so long as the task of unifying Korea was not finished. UN Doc. A/PV 292 (6 Oct 1950) 197-8.
44 Statement by Bevin, 14 December 1950. *H.C. Deb.*, 482 (1950-1) 1459.
45 See Evan Luard, *Britain and China* (London, 1962) 53-4.
46 *H.C. Deb.*, 482 (1950-1) 1460. "The relationships between the soldiers of the United States and ours there is not consultation of the sort where one makes representations and then walks out. It is a question of always attempting to agree... We are not in the position in which we were in the war." Statement by Bevin, 14 December 1950. *Ibid.*, 1460-1.
47 Statement by Bevin, quoted in Luard, n. 45, 91.
48 "Not until 13 August 1950, did the first Chinese ambassador present his credentials in Pyongyang, only to depart within a few months, leaving a *charge d'affaires* to represent Peking until 1955." Allen S. Whiting, *China Crosses the Yalu* (New York, 1960) 44.
49 *Ibid.*, 34 and 44-5.
50 "There is no clear evidence of Chinese participation in the planning and preparation of the Korean war....In Korea the initial responsibility clearly lay with Moscow." *Ibid.*, 51. Here it may be added that the possibility of North Koreans initiating an attack in the hope that the Kremlin would eventually be forced to support them cannot be ruled out. Whether any previous agreement between the Chinese and Soviet governments existed regarding an attack on South Korea is difficult to say.
51 Luard, n. 45, 93,
52 *PC* (1 Sep 1950) 4.
53 *WWCC* : 1949-50, 19.
54 See Chou En-lal's protest note to the US Government on 27 August 1950 and his two messages to the UN dated 27 August 1950 and 30 August 1950. *PC* (16 Sep 1950) 26-7.
55 *WWCC* : 1949-50, 148. This transfer of ethnic Korean troops, MacArthur observed, represented "substantial if not decisive military assistance" to the North Korean regime. Whiting, n. 48, 93.
56 *PC* (1 Oct 1950) 26-7.
57 *Ibid.*, (16 Oct 1950) 7.
58 Whiting, n. 48, 88.
59 W. W. Rostow, *The Prospects for Communist China* (New York, 1954) 69.
60 Statement at the Geneva Conference, 11 May 1954. *Cmd.* 9186, 42.
61 Statement at the Geneva Conference, 28 April 1954. *Ibid.*, 17,
62 In a motion submitted by a group of 29 Labour members in the

House of Commons, the Government was asked "to instruct its representatives on the United Nations Interim Committee to seek immediate agreement on the line beyond which the United Nations forces will not advance, with a view to bringing the fighting to an end as quickly as possible." *Daily Herald*, 18 Nov 1950. Quoted in Elaine Windrich, *British Labour's Foreign Policy* (London, 1952) 221.

63 Communique by the Commander-in-Chief' United Nations Command, 6 November 1950. *AFP*, 2583.

64 Statement by the US Secretary of State, Dean Acheson, 16 November 1950. *Cmd.* 8366, 20.

65 *Ibid.*, 20-2. On 8 November 1950 the UN Secretary-General communicated to Peking the Security Council decision inviting a Chinese representative "to be present during discussion by the Council of the Special Report of the United Nations Command in Korea." *Ibid.*, 18.

66 Kenneth Younger, "An Analysis of British and U.S. Policies in the Far East," *EW* (Mar 1953) 10.

67 *H.C. Deb.*, 483 (1950-1) 38.

68 See J.P. Jain, *A Documentary Study of the Warsaw Pact* (Bombay, 1973) Introduction.

69 See Statement by Lord Chancellor Viscount Jowitt, 1 March 1951. *H.L. Deb.*, 170 (1951) 798.

70 *Cmd.* 8366, 57.

71 Statement by Foreign Secretary, H. Morrison, 11 April 1951. *H.C. Deb.*, 483 (1950-1) 1023.

72 See John W. Spanier, *The Truman MacArthur Controversy and the Korean War* (Harvard, 1959) 140-1.

73 *Cmd.* 8366, 57.

74 The preeminent power position enjoyed by the USA in the post-war years was not as yet translated into forces in being. Address by Charles E. Bohlen, Special Assistant to the Secretary of State, 23 May 1961. *DSB* (19 Jun 1961) 967-8. The West badly needed time to strengthen the defence of Western Europe, which was, at that stage, "not strong enough to man a proper defence line." Statement by the British Defence Minister Shinwell, 14 February 1951. *H.C. Deb.*, 484 (1950-1) 409. Britain, therefore, considered it "unwise to contemplate at the present time any extension of the war." Statement by Lord Chancellor, Viscount Jowitt, 2 May 1951. *H.L. Deb.*, 171 (1951) 682.

75 Younger, n, 66, 11. See also Spanier, n. 72, 176.

76 Statement by Premier Attlee, 12 February 1951. *H.C. Deb.*, 484 (1950-1) 60.

77 See *The Economist* (11 Aug 1950) 724.

78 *PC* (16 Dec 1950) Supplement 16.

79 *New York Herald Tribune*, 6 Dec 1950. Quoted in Spanier, n. 72, 147.

80 At his press conference on 30 November 1950, Truman remarked that the use of the atomic bomb was under "active consideration"

and that "the choice of weapons was a matter for the military commander in the field." *NYT*, 1 Dec 1950.

81 Francis Williams, n. 11, 234-6.

82 In an urgent letter addressed to the Prime Minister, many Labour members, including Ian Mikardo, Tom Driberg and Alice Bacon of the National Executive Committee of the Party, urged the government to "dissociate Britain from the use of the atom bomb, emphasise that this country cannot be committed to any action outside the decisions of the United Nations and warn that any unilateral action would be followed by the withdrawal of British forces from Korea." *Daily Herald*, 1 December 1950. Quoted in Windrich, n. 62, 224.

83 Attlee had full support of the French Government and Commonwealth countries in the matter. See Francis Williams, n. 11, 235 and 240. See also *External Affairs* (Dec 1950) 436.

84 See Council on Foreign Relations, *The United States in World Affairs* : 1950 (New York, 1951) 427 and *Cmd.* 8110.

85 *Cmd.* 8366, 25.

86 UN Doc. A/C. 1/PV 410 (8 Dec 1950) 406.

87 *Cmd.* 8366, 27.

88 This resolution was introduced in the First Committee of the General Assembly on 12 December 1950. It envisaged the convocation of a Conference on the Far East "for the peaceful settlement of existing issues." *Ibid.*, 24-8.

89 *PC* (1 Jan 1951) 4-5 and 29.

90 *Cmd.* 8366, 29.

91 This was proposed in the statement of the US representative before the UN General Assembly on 6 December 1950 and the United Nations agreed to discuss it. See *AFP*, 2593-4.

92 UN Doc., A/C. 1/PV 421 (8 Jan 1951) 472.

93 Washington saw little chance of success in making an approach to Peking. Nevertheless, it endorsed the Five Principles out of deference to the belief of "many members that the Chinese Communists might still be prevailed upon to cease their defiance of the United Nations" and their pleadings that "the United Nations should leave no stone unturned in its effort to find a peaceful solution" and that "opposition or abstention by the United States would destroy any possibility of success which the proposal might have." Statement by the US Secretary of State, 17 January 1951. US Department of State, *United States Policy in Korean Conflict*, July 1950-February 1951 (Washington 1951) 34.

94 *PC* (1 Feb 1951) 30.

95 UN Doc. A/C. 1/PV 426 (18 Jan 1951) 507.

96 Statement on 23 January 1951. *H.C. Deb.*, 483 (1950-1) 40.

97 On 19 January 1951 the House of Representatives passed a resolution demanding that Communist China be immediately branded as aggressor in Korea. The next day the US delegate in the UN introduced a resolution to that effect in the First Committee. The

Senate passed a similar resolution on 23 January 1951. *AFP*, 2602.
98 Gladwyn Jebb in the First Committee UN Doc., n. 95, 507.
99 *H.C. Deb.*, 483 (1950-1) 40.
100 Statement by the Minister of State Younger, 12 February 1951. *Ibid.*, 484 (1950-1) 153.
101 Attlee added : "For our part, we have not lost hope that China may yet be ready to play her traditional part in the world affairs and live on friendly terms with other members of the world community." *Ibid.*, 483 (1950-1) 41-2.
102 *Ibid.*, 40. A similar explanation was given in China's reply to the Indian ambassador on 22 January 1951. For text of reply, see *PC* (1 Feb 1951) 29.
103 *AFP*, 2605.
104 Explaining these new features on 25 January 1951, Gladwyn Jebb stated : "In the first place, and most importantly, it is clear that the Peking Government does not entirely reject the principles of a cease-fire before negotiations....At least they talk of a cease-fire for a limited time period to be agreed upon as a first step, thus enabling more general negotiations to proceed...Secondly, it was made at least reasonably clear that the withdrawal of foreign troops from Korea was meant to include the so-called Chinese 'volunteers.' Thirdly, it is now made clear that the principles on which the internal affairs of Korea are to be settled by the Korean people are to be a matter for discussion at an eventual conference, whereas previously it had appeared that Peking's intention was to leave this question entirely to the Koreans....While I do not for a moment wish to read too much hope into these 'clarifications,' I do think that some of the criticism to which they have been exposed do them rather less than justice." *Cmd.* 8159, 8.
105 *Ibid.*, 9-14.
106 Britain considered the US resolution declaring China an aggressor as both untimely and unhelpful to negotiations. The resolution, London felt, subordinated negotiations "to an immediate study of further measures which might broadly be called sanctions," and which, as Gladwyn Jebb put it, were likely to be "dangerous, double-edged, or merely useless." Britain exerted all its influence to alter the resolution so as to keep the door open for negotiations. It voted in favour of the amended resolution because otherwise there was every possibility of the original resolution "more harmful to negotiations," being passed by a very large majority. Statement by Minister of State Younger, 12 February 1951. *H.C. Deb.*, 484 (1950-1) 155. Although Britain voted in favour of the US resolution, it declined to co-sponsor it.
107 British objections to the original resolution had been to the statements contained in paragraphs 2 and 8, one of which was "inaccurate and the other of which was unwise." Statement by Lord Chancellor Viscount Jowitt, 1 March 1951. *H.L. Deb.*, 170 (1950) 795. Paragraph 2 was amended to read that the Chinese Government "had not

accepted United Nations proposals" instead of the phrase "had rejected all United Nations proposals." In the case of paragraph 8 an important addition was made. "The effect of this addition was to defer consideration by the Assembly of further measures in the event of the Good Offices Committee reporting progress. Thus the essential principle is maintained that the United Nations will continue its efforts to arrange for a peaceful settlement and that there can be no question of the United Nations proceeding to further measures until it has become apparent that those efforts have failed." Statement by Premier Attlee, 1 February 1951. *Cmd.* 8159, 17. "The important thing about this amended resolution, Lord Henderson, Parliamentary Under-Secretary of State, remarked, "is that 'additional measures' will not become a live issue until the Good Offices Committee has reported failure in its efforts. Even then the application of 'additional measures' will not be automatic." *H.L. Deb.*, 170 (1951) 650.

108 *Cmd.* 8159, 16.
109 *PC* (16 Feb 1951) Supplement 2-3.
110 Statement by Attlee, 1 February 1951. *Cmd.* 8159, 17.
111 Statement on 28 February 1951. *H.L, Deb.*, 170 (1951) 650.
112 Statement on 12 February 1951. *Cmd.* 8366, 42. London did not think that naming China an aggressor had closed the door of negotiations.
113 Statement on 5 February 1952. *H.C. Deb.*, 495 (1951-2) 834.
114 Statement by Lord Henderson, 28 February 1951. *H.L. Deb.*, 170 (1951) 650. Drawing attention to the large-scale massacre of the Chinese in Korea, Premier Churchill said that Chinese Communist Government not only have their troops "being slaughtered at the rate of about 40 to 1 by the United Nations forces," but they also "had a terrible mass of wounded and invalids flung back upon them far beyond their resources to handle." Statement on 30 January 1952. *H.C. Deb.*, 495 (1951-2) 202. See also Statement by Henderson, 28 February 1951. *H.L. Deb.*, 170 (1951) 650.
115 See *Cmd.* 8366, 61-2. Ser also Chapter Eight.
116 Harold Davies, "Westminister and the East," *EW* (Jul 1951) 6.
117 UN Doc. A/C. 1/PV 505 (29 Jan 1951) 6.
118 Statement by Chou En-lai, 14 December 1952. *PC* (1 Jan 1953) Supplement 2-6. See also statement by Selwyn Lloyd, 30 October 1952. *Cmd.* 8793, 21.
119 See *Cmd.* 8716, 4-5. The UN, thus, receded from the principle of "voluntary repatriation" to that of "no forced repatriation."
120 For text of resolution, see *Ibid.*, 18.
121 See Foreign Office comment of 31 January 1953. *Cmd.* 8793, 13.
122 Revised Mission of the United States Seventh Fleet in the Formosa Area. Message by the President to the Congress. *AFP*, 2475. See also Robert J. Donovan, *Eisenhower : The Inside Story* (New York, 1956) 30.
123 The British did not consider it a step in the right direction and

"at once made known their concern at this decision which, they feared, would have unfortunate political repercussions without compensating military advantages." Statement by Foreign Secretary Eden, 3 February 1953. *H.C. Deb.*, 510 (1952-3) 1674.

124 See Chapter Eight.
125 Special Report of the Unified Command on the Armistice in Korea, 7 August 1953. *Cmd.*, 8938, 3 and 8.
126 *PC* (16 Apr 1953) 5-7.
127 Statement by Bedell Smith, 5 June 1954. *Cmd.* 9186, 71. "There is fundamental disagreement, not only about the method of translating these principles into reality but even about the meanings of the principles themselves. Even the same words have different meanings according to which of us uses them." Speech by McIntosh, Acting Head of New Zealand Delegation, 11 June 1954. *Ibid.*, 85.
128 Chou En-lai criticized those who sought to utilise that principle for effecting Korean unification. The protagonists of this view, he stated, "overlook the fact that opposition to the principle of mutual agreement between the two sides is nothing but an attempt to impose forcibly the will of one side on the other—an attempt which has long since been proved abortive even when supported by foreign armed forces." Statement at Geneva Conference, 22 May 1954. *Ibid.*, 57.
129 Speech by Nam Il, Minister for Foreign Affairs of the Democratic People's Republic of Korea, at the Geneva Conference, 22 May 1954. *Ibid.*, 52-3.
130 Statement by Foreign Secretary Eden, 11 June 1954. *Ibid.*, 88.
131 Speech by McIntosh, 11 June 1954. *Ibid.*, 85.
132 Speech by Bedell Smith, 5 June 1954 "The United Nations," he added, "has the competence, the experience, the authority, the impartiality and the facilities to perform this task." *Ibid.*, 71.
133 Speech by Soviet Foreign Minister, Molotov, 11 May 1954. *Ibid.*, 40.
134 Speech by Chou En-lai, 5 June 1954. *Ibid.*, 73.
135 Statement by Molotov, 11 May 1954. *Ibid.*, 39.
136 Statement by Chou En-lai, 22 May 1954. *Ibid.*, 57.
137 Statement on 11 June 1954. *Ibid.*, 88.
138 *Ibid.*, 57 and 73.
139 Statement by Bedell Smith, 5 June 1954. *Ibid.*, 69.
140 *Ibid.*, 88.
141 Report of the UN Members which participated in the Korean War to the UN Secretary-General on the Results of the Geneva Conference, 11 November 1954. *AFP*, 2698.
142 *Cmd.* 9186, 48 and 88. Eden made it plain that the West was not ready to accept Communist Nations, such as Poland and Czechoslovakia, as neutral nations.
143 Statement by C.A. Ronning, Acting Head of the Canadian Delegation, 11 June 1954. *Ibid.*, 83.
144 Statement by Chou En-lai, 5 June 1954. *Ibid.*, 74.

145 The Communist proposal of a simultaneous withdrawal of the forces of the two sides, certain Member States of the UN that participated in the UN action in Korea stated in their Report to the UN Secretary-General on the Results of the Geneva Conference, "amounted to a demand that the aggressor forces in Korea should be placed on a plane of equality with the United Nations forces which are in Korea in accordance with United Nations resolutions to repel aggression." *AFP*, 2699.

146 Anthony Eden, *The Full Circle* (London, 1960) 28.

147 See UN General Assembly Resolutions A/Res 2466 dated 20 Dec 1968, A/Res 2516 dated 25 Nov 1969 and A/Res 2668 dated 7 Dec 1970.

148 UN Doc. A/C. 1/PV 1670, 48-51.

149 UN Doc. A/C. 1/PV 1637, 42-8.

150 UN Doc. A/C. 1/PV 1687, 25-31.

151 UN Doc. A/PV 2035 (22 Sep 1972) 47-51.

152 UN Doc. A/PV 2181 (28 Nov 1973) 6.

153 UN Doc. A/C. 1/PV 1966 (21 Nov 1973) 31-40.

154 UN Doc. A/9973.

155 UN Doc. A/C. 1/PV 2031 and 2039.

156 UN Doc. A/C. 1/PV 2036 (5 Dec 1974) 69-75.

157 The South Korean press has started advocating deployment of an international peace-keeping force in the demilitarized zone along the entire truce line. Since a force composed of small non-aligned countries might not be able to withstand the thrust of military action from the North, it is desired that such a force should be drawn from the four Powers whose conflicting interests converged on the Korean peninsula.

158 UN Doc. S/11737.

159 The North Korean President threatened the United States with a more disastrous course than Indo-China if it did not withdraw its troops from South Korea. *Times of India*, 31 May 1975.

160 The influential North Korean paper, *Rodong Sinmun*, in a commentary in April 1975, referred to the "decisive step in Indo-China" and observed : "It is the irresistible trend that the traitors like Rhee, Chiang Kai-shek, Diem, Thanom, Lon Nol and now Theiu are punished by the people and Pak Jung Hi traitorous clique cannot extricate themselves from it." While in Peking, Kim warned : "If the enemy ignites war recklessly, DPRK will resolutely answer it with war and completely destroy the aggressors. In this war DPRK will only lose the military demarcation line and will gain the country's reunification."

161 North-South dialogue received a set-back in the middle of 1975 when the meetings of the North-South Coordinating Committee and that of Red Cross working-level officials were suspended.

Chapter Four : Formosa and the Offshore Islands

1 "Ilha Formosa," the beautiful island, was the name given to it by the Portuguese when they reached the island in 1590. To the Chinese and the Japanese it is known as Taiwan, which is derived from two Chinese characters—the first meaning a "plateau" and the second "bay."

2 The forefathers of the Taiwanese or native Formosans came to the island from China towards the end of the Ming dynasty.

3 See Article on "Formosa," by Eugene H. Dooman, Hugh Borton, Cabot and Coville, officials in the State Department. *DSB* (3 Jun 1942) 1019.

4 See statement by Dean Acheson, former Secretary of State, 6 September 1958. *NYT*, 7 Sep 1958.

5 See statement by President Truman, 5 January 1950. *DSB* (16 Jan 1950) 79.

6 See President Eisenhower's message to the Congress, 24 January 1955. Council on Foreign Relations, *Documents on American Foreign Relations: 1955* (New York, 1956) 294.

7 See article by Frank H.H. King, "British Trade with Nationalist China," *FEER* (17 Jun 1954) 747.

8 *H.C. Deb.*, 530 (1953-4) 494.

9 *DSB*, Vol. 9 (1943) 393.

10 *DSB*, Vol. 13 (1945) 137.

11 *DSB* (27 Aug 1951) 349. The Soviet Union, though invited to the Conference, refused to sign the document. Communist China and Nationalist China were both excluded from participation in the San Francisco Peace Conference, as no agreement could be reached between the UK and the USA—the two countries responsible for framing the San Francisco treaty documents.

12 *China Handbook : 1952-53* (Taipei, 1952) 154.

13 Article V of the Treaty of Mutual Defence between the United States and the Republic of China says : "Each Party recognizes that an armed attack in the West Pacific Area directed against the territories of either of the Parties would be dangerous to its own peace and safety and declares that it would act to meet the common danger in accordance with its constitutional processes." *DSB*, Vol. 31 (1954) 899. Commenting on it in the Senate Committee on Foreign Relations, Secretary of State Dulles observed that reference in the Treaty to "the territories of either of the Parties" was language carefully chosen to avoid denoting anything one way or another as to sovereignty over Taiwan. *AFP*, 963.

14 *H.C. Deb.*, 595 (19 Nov 1958) 1140.

15 Quincy Wright, "The Status of Communist China," *Journal of International Affairs*, Vol. 11 (No. 2, 1957) 181. See also Quincy Wright, "Non-Recognition of China and International Tensions," *Current History*, Vol. 34 (1958) 153.

16 Statement by Premier Churchill, 1 February 1955. *H.C. Deb.*, 548 (1954-5) 602.

17 *Ibid.*, 478 (26 Jul 1950) 60 Written Answers. The British Under-Secretary of State for Foreign Affairs, Mayhew, said: "Any change in the legal status of Formosa can only be formally effected in a treaty of peace with Japan." *Ibid.*, 469 (14 Nov 1969) 1679.

18 *Ibid.*, 536 (1954-5) 159. Written Answers.

19 *Ibid.*, 540 (1955-6) 1870-1.

20 To the British, the Chiang Kai-shek regime in Formosa was, perhaps, a provincial authority at best and a bandit or rebel group at worst. The Foreign Office, in a certificate issued in connection with legal proceedings in the English courts, stated that "Her Majesty's Government did not recognise that any government was located in Formosa in July and August 1953." Nevertheless, Her Majesty's Government had maintained a consul at Tamsui till 13 March 1972 and had presented through him to the National authorities a number of claims arising out of damage done to British vessels by Nationalist forces based in Formosa. See J.P. Jain, "The Legal Status of Formosa : A Study of British, Chinese and Indian Views," *American Journal of International Law* (Jan 1963) 28, footnote.

21 Georg Schwarzenberger, "Title to Territory: Response to a Challenge," *Ibid.* (Apr 1957) 315.

22 For a further discussion on the problem of the legal status of Formosa, particularly the idea of a condominium over Formosa being exercised by the co-signatories of the San Francisco Treaty, see J.P. Jain, n. 20, 29-30.

23 *AFP*, 2468.

24 *AFP*, 2477.

25 *H.C. Deb.*, 478 (15 Sep 1950) 174. Written Answers.

26 *Cmd.* 8110, 4.

27 *H.C. Deb.*, 487 (1950-1) 2311-2. In proposing the settlement of the question of Formosa by the United Nations, the Western Powers probably thought of making use of Article 107 of the Charter, which says: "Nothing in the present Charter shall invalidate or preclude action, in relation to any state which during the Second World War has been an enemy of any signatory to the present Charter, taken or authorized as a result of that war by the Governments having responsibility for such action."

28 *Ibid.*, 496 (1951-2) 1027

29 *Ibid.*, 530 (1953-4) 496. For a comparison between the views of Britain and the USA on the subject, see J.P. Jain, n. 20, 31-2.

30 The Cairo and Potsdam Declarations, Chou En-lai observed in his cable to the UN Secretary-General on 24 August 1950, were "both binding international agreements which the United States Government has pledged itself to respect and observe." Foreign Languages Press, *Important Documents Concerning the Question of Taiwan* (Peking, 1955) 22.

31 *Ibid.*, 34.

32 *NB* (9 Feb 1955) 8. Mei Ju-ao also refutes arguments advanced by the United States and "their accomplices, among whom are the British politicians and propagandists in particular," to justify the U.S. "aggression" under the "legal cloak" of "such nonsense" as the "neutralisation" of Taiwan, placing it under the UN "trusteeship", making Taiwan an "independent State" or recognizing two "Chinas". *Ibid.*

33 Address before the Foreign Policy Association, New York, 16 February 1955. *Free China Review* (No.3, 1955) 61.

34 *H.C. Deb.*, 536 (1954-5) 206. Written Answers.

35 As early as 28 November 1950, *i.e.* before the signing of the San Francisco Peace Treaty, the Communist Chinese representative, Wu Hsiu-chuan, observed: "The status of Taiwan was determined long ago. The question of the status of Taiwan simply does not exist....To argue that because the Peace Treaty with Japan is yet to be concluded the status of Taiwan remains undetermined and must await consideration by the United Nations—to argue thus is to make a mockery of history, of realities, of human intelligence, of international agreements. To argue thus is to make a mockery of the United Nations Charter." *Important Documents Concerning the Question of Taiwan*, n. 30, 41-2.

36 See statement by Chou En-lai, 28 June 1956. *PC* (16 Jul 1956) Supplement 12-3.

37 See statement by Chou En-lai, 24 January 1955. *PC* (No. 4, 1955) Supplement.

38 The Chinese complaint regarding "armed invasion of Taiwan by the United States" was submitted by Chou En-lai in his cable to the United Nations on 24 August 1950. See *Important Documents Concerning the Question of Taiwan*, n. 30, 21-2. In a letter addressed to the President of the General Assembly (U.N. Doc. A/1375) dated 20 September 1950, the Secretary General of the Soviet delegation requested, "as a matter of importance and urgency," the inclusion of the item "United States aggression against China" in the agenda of the General Assembly. During the debate, Gladwyn Jebb, the British delegate, observed that it was not clear what document A/1375 referred to. He seemed to differ from, or at least to cast doubt about, the Soviet representative's view that China included Formosa, "an assumption," Spender of Australia said, "which prejudged the issue." See UN Doc. General Committee, 69th Meeting, 21 September 1950, 5-6. On 30 November 1950, the Security Council rejected by a 9-1-1 vote the Soviet resolution which would have condemned the United States.

39 Premier Chou En-lai characterized the decision of the General Assembly to include the "Question of Formosa" on its agenda as "an unjustified decision in violation of the United Nations Charter and international law...in violation of the sovereignty and independence of China." *Important Documents Concerning the Question of Taiwan*, n. 30, 25.

40 In its editorial on 29 January 1955, the *People's Daily* declared that neither the United Nations nor any other state has "any right to intervene in the liberation of Taiwan which is by its nature within the domestic jurisdiction of China." *JMJP*, 29 Jan 1955.

41 *Important Documents Concerning the Question of Taiwan*, n. 30, 41. See also statement by Wu Hsiu-chuan before the Security Council, 28 November 1950. UN Doc. S/PV 527, 10.

42 Statement by Chiang Kai-shek, 8 February 1955. *Free China Review* (No. 3, 1955) 52-3. For detailed discussion of the Nationalist Chinese attitude on the subject, see J.P. Jain, n. 20, 37-8.

43 Statement by the British Foreign Secretary, 19 November 1958. *H.C. Deb.*, 595 (1958-9) 1141.

44 Statement by the Joint Parliamentary Under Secretary of State, Lord Lansdowne, 11 December 1958. *H.L. Deb.*, 213 (1958-9) 216.

45 Statement by Foreign Minister Chen Yi. Quoted in Gerald Clark, *Impatient Giant: Red China Today* (London, 1960) 46.

46 Statement by the British Foreign Secretary, 19 November 1958. *H.C. Deb.*, 595 (1958-9) 1141.

47 See *The Economist* (13 May 1950) 1050.

48 See H. Trevelyan, *Worlds Apart : China 1953-55 Soviet Union 1962-65* (London, 1971) 148.

49 "The American Seventh Fleet has...been carrying out a thoroughly respectable police operation off Formosa; admittedly, it is intervention in the Chinese civil war, but its purpose is to localise the battle now raging in Korea." *Ibid.*, (29 Jul 1950) 203-4.

50 Royal Institute of International Affairs, *Documents on International Affairs*: 1949-50 (London, 1953) 632.

51 *The Economist* (8 Jul 1950) 67. See also *Ibid.*, (12 Aug 1950) 298.

52 *H.C. Deb.*, 482 (1950-1) 1354-5.

53 Statement by H. Morrison, Secretary of State for Foreign Affairs, 11 May 1951. *Ibid.*, 487 (1950-1) 2302.

54 *Ibid.*, 482 (14 Dec 1950) 1462.

55 *DSB* (28 Jan 1952) 118.

56 Quoted by Lord Elibank. *H.L. Deb.*, 181 (1952-3) 1189.

57 *H.C. Deb.*, 530 (1953-4) 494.

58 *Ibid.*, 535 (8 Dec 1954) 939.

59 *Ibid.*, 538 (8 Mar 1955) 160.

60 *H.L. Deb.*, 190 (1954-5) 511.

61 See H. Trevelyan, n. 48, 133-7.

62 On 4 February 1955 the Soviet Minister for Foreign Affairs proposed· to the British Ambassador in Moscow that a conference be held in Shanghai or New Delhi to consider the position in the Formosa Straits area.

63 *Commonwealth Survey*, Vol. I (1955) 175.

64 The British Government considered the Canadian proposal "a positive programme" and commended it for acceptance to China. However, before the proposed Conference could discuss "the related problems of Formosa and the assumption by the Peking representa-

tive of China's seat in the United Nations," it had to make arrangements for a cease-fire in Korea and to discuss "the withdrawal of all non-Korean troops from Korea and the unification of the country." See statement by the Parliamentary Under-Secretary of State for Foreign Affairs, Lord Henderson, 28 February 1951. *H.L. Deb.*, 170 (1951) 650- 4.

65 See statement by C.R. Attlee, 5 February 1952. *H.C. Deb.*, 495 (1951 -2) 838.

66 Chester Bowles, "The 'China Problem' Reconsidered," *Foreign Affairs* (Apr 1960) 481. As early as April 1953 Minister of State Selwyn Lloyd observed: "Her Majesty's Government have repeatedly pointed out that...few adventures could be less fruitful or successful than the launching of these Nationalist troops on the mainland of China." *H.C. Deb.*, 513 (1952-3) 1192.

67 Chester Bowles, n. 66, 480-1. According to Britain, no useful purpose would be served by the Nationalist air and sea raids against the mainland which could not produce any decisive results. Their chief effect would only be to intensify Chinese Communist hostility to their authors and drive the Chinese people, especially those suffering directly from the raids, into the arms of the Communists. The British Government, therefore, "made known their concern" at the decision of the Eisenhower Administration to free Chiang from the obligation not to invade the mainland in February 1953. See statement by Foreign Secretary Eden, 3 February 1953. *H.C. Deb.*, 510 (1952-3) 1674-5.

68 *Ibid.*, 594 (1958-9) 327-8.

69 The US Ambassador to Australia, Sebald, emphasized the importance of Formosa in the following words: "Not only does Taiwan (Formosa) in friendly hands constitute an important bastion of the free world and a deterrent to Chinese Communist expansion, but the Republic of China offers the only alternative for the loyalty of millions of overseas Chinese as well as countless millions of non-Communist Chinese on the mainland....A change in the status of Free China would, I believe, have a chain reaction effect which would seriously weaken the free world. The United States has a mutual defence treaty with the Republic of China. This is an important element in the complex of bilateral and multilateral pacts which have contributed to the stabilization of the Far East." Address on 26 July 1957. *DSB* (2 Sep 1957) 390.

70 "For the defense of Australia, Canberra desires that Formosa be kept out of Peking's grasp. It also wants Britain to cling to Singapore, a naval base whence Japan threatened Australia during World War II." Lionel Gelber, *America in Britain's Place* (New York, 1961) 172.

71 Even after the Chinese Government agreed to set up a diplomatic mission at *charge d'affaires* level in London, Britain continued to maintain a consular post in Formosa and an official of the Board of Trade paid a visit to the island to discuss commercial matters.

Evan Luard, *Britain and China* (London, 1962) 212.

72 *The Times*, 7 Feb 1953.

73 See Gerald Clark, n. 45, 40.

74 Cable to the UN Secretary-General, 10 October 1954. Embassy of the People's Republic of China in India, *China Will Liberate Taiwan* (New Delhi, 1955) 25-6.

75 In his statement on 31 August 1950 President Truman declared that the United States' Seventh Fleet was guarding Formosa until the end of the war in Korea. *NYT*, 1 Sep 1950

76 When asked whether the purpose of the Treaty was more diplomatic than military, Secretary of State Dulles replied: "It has a diplomatic purpose...which is very considerable. From a purely military standpoint, it changes the situation in this respect, perhaps, that the authority of the President to use there the armed services of the United States, which originally derive from the Korean War, may be tending to become obsolete from the lapse and passage of time, and the conclusion of the armistice in Korea." News Conference on 1 December 1954. *DSB* (13 Dec 1954) 897.

77 Declaration of the First Plenary Session of the Second National Committee of the Chinese People's Political Consultative Conference, 25 December 1954. *China Will Liberate Taiwan*, n. 74, 41.

78 See *JMJP* Editorial, 16 July 1954. The Paper seriously warned the United States of the "protracted grave consequences arising out of such a situation." *NB* (28 Jul 1954) 6-8.

79 Editorial on 13 December 1950. *Hsin-hua Yueh-pao* (The New China Monthly) (Jan 1951) 569-71.

80 Statement by Chou En-lai, 21 December 1954. *China Will Liberate Taiwan*, n. 74, 35. Commenting on the statement of the Spokesman of the British Foreign Office dated 1 December 1954, which stated that the British Government had for a long time been "generally informed" of the negotiations on this treaty and was "in contact all the time with the US Government about the general situation in the Far East," the *People's Daily* of 5 December 1954 remarked : "This shows that it was concluded not only with British concurrence but that the British Government also had a finger in the pie." *Ibid.*, 69.

81 *JMJP* Editorial, 5 Dec 1954. *Ibid.*, 70.

82 *Ibid.*, 36-7.

83 See statement by Chou En-lai, 24 January 1955. *PC* (16 Feb 1955) Supplement.

84 *JMJP* Editorial, 16 Feb 1955. *NB* (2 Mar 1955) 6-7.

85 Royal Institute of International Affairs, *Documents on International Affairs* : 1955 (London, 1958) 454.

86 *NB* (2 Mar 1955) 7.

87 See statement on Sino-American talks by the Spokesman of the Chinese Foreign Ministry, 18 January 1956. *PC* (1 Feb 1956) Supplement.

88 *CT*, 25 Jul 1957.

89 As early as 8 March 1955 Foreign Secretary Eden stated: "Her Majesty's Government trust that they (the Central People's Government)...while maintaining intact in all respects their position in regard to Formosa and the Pescadores...will not prosecute their claims by forceful means....Any indication that, in prosecuting claims, force will not be used would, I believe, reduce the tension at once and perhaps enable us to make headway." *H.C. Deb.*, 538 (1954-5) 160 and 163.

90 *PC* (16 Feb 1955) Supplement.

91 Luard, n. 71, 212-3.

92 Report of the Senate Committee on Foreign Relations, 8 February 1955. *AFP*, 964-5.

93 *Ibid.*, 965.

94 The international recognition of the Peking regime as the Government of China and of the Nationalists in Taiwan as the Government of Formosa, Evan Luard believed, was "the simplest, and indeed self-evident, solution of the problem." Luard, n. 71, 245.

95 *H.C. Deb.*, 538 (1954-5) 160.

96 Speaking of the second crisis in the China seas in 1958, Tang Tsou remarked : "Nationalist ships were effectively running the Communist blockade; Chiang Kai-shek's planes maintained air superiority over the Strait, and the presence of eight-inch hotwitzers on Quemoy presented Mao with the danger of nuclear war." Tang Tsou, "Mao's Limited War in the Taiwan Strait," *Orbis* (Oct 1959) 346.

97 *H.C. Deb.*, 536 (4 Feb 1955) 159. Written Answers. On 26 January 1955 Eden remarked: "Formosa had never in this century been a part of China and the status of Formosa...was dealt with by the Treaty of San Francisco...The off-shore islands have always been regarded and are now regarded by us as part of China. We have always been careful to draw that distinction." *Ibid.*, 160.

98 Through its ambassador in Moscow, Britain tried to enlist the support of the Soviet Union "to achieve at least a *de facto* cease-fire" in the Formosan Straits. William T. Stone, "Problem of Formosa," *Editorial Research Reports* (Washington) (16 Feb 1955) 122. At the same time, London also endeavoured to restrain Washington. While refusing to accept the claim of Chinese Communists "in its entirety,' *The Economist* warned the United States that "in standing up to Communist pressure on this particular question (of offshore islands) the United States runs an unpleasant risk of impairing the full support of its main allies." *The Economist* (5 Feb 1955) 431.

99 *H.C. Deb.*, 536 (1954-5) 158-9. Speaking in the Security Council debate on 31 January 1955 the British delegate Sir Pierson Dixon observed : "The only immediate purpose of British policy in this affair is to bring hostilities to an end and prevent the danger of a wider conflagration. Our objective is simple and constructive, as our motives are disinterested. Our design is to stop the fighting, to ease tension, and to promote peace. In our minds it is not necessary, or indeed expedient, to go into the past. There is no question of

allocating here blame to either side for the past. If the fighting can
be stopped, there is no doubt in the minds of Her Majesty's
Government that this would increase the possibility thereafter of
peaceful rather than violent adjustments of the problems involved."
UN Doc. S/PV 690, 6-7.

100 *H.C. Deb.*, 538 (1954-5) 160. On 13 and 26 February 1955, the
People's Liberation Army landed on the Tachens, the Yushan, Pishan
and Nanchi Islands. *PC* (1 May 1955) Supplement 3.

101 *H.C. Deb.*, 537 (23 Feb 1955) 158-9. Written Answers.

102 See H. Trevelyan, n. 48, 144-5.

103 Statement of 13 September 1958. See Central Office of Information,
Formosa and the Off-shore Islands, R. 4149 (London, Jan 1959) 21.

104 Donald Maclean, *British Foreign Policy Since Suez* 1956-1968 (London,
1970) 297.

105 Luard, n. 71, 172-3.

106 "Our policy," Foreign Secretary Macmillian stated on 27 April
1955, "has always been to try to get a cease-fire and to see the problems of Formosa and of the offshore islands settled by negotiation.
We have been in continuous communication with the parties concerned in order to obtain these objectives." *H.C. Deb.*, 540 (1954-5)
911-2.

107 Statement on 16 February 1955. See *Hindustan Times*, 18 Feb 1955.
On 5 April 1955 Dulles stated: "We all realize it is a highly dangerous situation, and we want to eliminate to the maximum degree
possible the dangerous elements." *AFP*, 2494.

108 Council on Foreign Relations, *The United States in World Affairs*:
1958 (New York, 1959) 322.

109 See *The Times*, 30 Nov 1960.

110 "If the People's Government of China will officially, publicly and
unequivocally renounce the use of force in settling the Formosa
question...the United States will urge the Chinese nationalists to
give up their present position on Quemoy and Matsu, as we previously
urged them to leave the Tachens." Chester Bowles, Letter to the
Editor, 29 March 1955. *NYT*, 4 Apr 1955.

111 "Fortified by such an international declaration denouncing the use
of force, with the assurance of such collective support for the defense
of Formosa, and with the addition thereby of moral solidarity to
military strength, I should think that Quemoy and Matsu would
have little further importance to the Nationalists, let alone to us.
And that they could then be relinquished before we stumble any
further down the dismal road to war that nobody wants." Radio
talk by Adlai E. Stevenson, 11 April 1955. *Foreign Policy Bulletin*
(15 May 1955) 133.

112 In his statement of 27 June 1962 President Kennedy reiterated President Eisenhower's view that the United States would not remain
inactive in the face of any aggressive action against the offshore
islands which might threaten Formosa. *NYT*, 28 Jun 1962.

113 See statement by Secretary of State Dulles before the Foreign Policy

Association, 16 February 1955. *Foreign Policy Bulletin* (15 May 1955) 132. Although Dulles emphatically declared that "Formosa and the Pescadores are not on the bargain counter for international trading," he never said anything like that about the offshore islands. See News Conference of 1 December 1954. *DSB* (13 Dec 1954) 896.

114 Tang Tsou, n. 96, 348.

115 *Ibid.*, 350. Some even expressed doubt whether the surrender of Formosa would change the "prolonged armed truce" into any permanent settlement with Communist China so long as the Peking regime persists in their present belligerent mood.

116 *Statesman*, 28 Feb 1972. According to reliable reports, by the middle of 1975 the US military strength in Taiwan was reduced from 4,000 men to 2,800 men and the last squadron of 18 F-4 Phantom jet bombers (which have nuclear capability) was also withdrawn. While President Ford is likely to visit Peking in the fall of 1975, he may not take a decision on shifting diplomatic recognition from Taiwan to Peking in view of the forthcoming 1976 Presidential elections and the influential Republican lobby in favour of Taipeh. See *Times of India*, 9 Jun 1975.

117 *H.C. Deb.*, 822 (2 Aug 1971) 1068-9.

118 See Chapter Seven.

119 *H.C. Deb.*, 833 (13 Mar 1972) 31-5.

Chapter Five : Southeast Asia

1 "Southeast Asia is the world's largest exporter of natural rubber, copra, quinine, kapok, rice, teak, pepper, tapioca flour, and tin ....Currently the area produces rice for its own needs and a surplus of almost 4 million tons for export; its rubber plantations provide the world with about 90 per cent of its crude rubber ; its mines provide about 60 percent of the world's tin; and it produces some 84 percent of the world's copra and coconut oil." US Department of State, *Background : Southeast Asia, Area of Challenge Change and Progress* (Washington, 1959) 5. It also has the largest oil reserves in the Far East Pacific region.

2 Regional Information Office, *Malaya : The Road to Independence* (Singapore, 1957) 7.

3 These investments were estimated at $860 million before the Second World War. Lenox A. Mills and Associates, *The New World of Southeast Asia* (Minnesota, 1949) 5.

4 *H. C. Deb.*, 475 (1950) 2093.

5 *H. L. Deb.*, 181 (1953) 1166.

6 Lionel Gelber, *America in Britain*'s *Place* (New York, 1961) 158.

7 UK High Commission in India, *British Information Services*, 14

Apr 1959.

8 Malaya provides over 40% of all the natural rubber produced in the world and nearly a third of the world's total output of tin. Economist Intelligence Unit, *An Economic Geography of the Commonwealth* (London, 1957) 206-8.

9 *The Times*, 10 Mar 1948.

10 "The Chinese in Malaya," Editorial in *EW* (Mar 1954) 7. "British vested interests produce some 60 per cent of the rubber in Malaya, and 60 per cent of the tin. The gold dollars earned by these two industries alone amount each year to more than three times the dollars earned by all exports from Britain." Alliance Platform for the Federal Elections, *Menuju Kearah Kemerdekaan* (*The Road to Independence*) (Kaula Lumpur, 1955) 24. The British continued to dominate the economies of Malaysia and Singapore even after their independence. According to official statistics, the earnings from British companies there were £22.4 million in 1964, most of which came from rubber and tin industries in the hands of British firms. See Donald Maclean, *British Foreign Policy Since Suez* 1956-1968 (London, 1970) 243.

11 *The Times*, 9 Jun 1950.

12 Joint Statement by the Pan Malayan Federation of Trade Unions and Malayan Communist Party. *CMR* (Sep 1950) 16-7. Particular stress was, therefore, laid on slashing of rubber tress thereby curtailing the main source of revenue of the British people and the Malayan Government.

13 "Considerable anxiety is felt in the Malayan Federation over the financing of the emergency, the cost of which is rising steadily....The Federation is at present spending 45.1 per cent of its annual revenue on defence and internal security, including squatter resettlement. This is approximately four times what any other colony in the Empire spends on defence." *The Times*, 9 Jun, 1950. "In the past six years," the Alliance Platform for the Federal Elections observed, "the Federation has contributed nearly $1200 million of her own resources to the cost of fighting the Emergency with the result that she faces financial stringency. *Menuju Kearah Kemerdekaan* n. 10, 24.

14 Statement by the Secretary of State for the Colonies, Creech Jones, 8 July 1948. *H. C. Deb.*, 453 (1948) 603-5.

15 Royal Institute of International Affairs, *Survey of International Affairs* : 1952 (London 1955) 438. Under emergency regulation 17 D, which was revoked on 25 November 1953, a reign of terror was let loose on villages by the British authorities. Villages were cleared at short notice and destroyed by a mixed contingent of troops and social workers. Collective fines were also imposed. These were sometimes as high as "a minimum of $15 per head for all males over the age of 18." *Ibid.*, *Survey of International Affairs* : 1951 (London, 1954) 466.

16 Men, called upon for compulsory duty, had to show good cause

to the district officer before they could be released. A penalty of three months imprisonment was provided for guards failing to report or to do duty, and three months imprisonment or a fine of 1,000 Malayan dollars for obstruction of a guard, refusal to answer his questions, or to produce documents." *The Times*, 15 Sep 1950. The decision to form a Home Guard force was announced in April 1950. *The Hindu*, 3 Sep 1950.

17 Command Paper No. 24 of 1953 of the Federation of Malaya. Deportation was preferable to holding persons in custody in detention camps for an indefinite period because the latter was a costly business entailing an expenditure of $3,941,778 each year. However, the work of repatriation was obstructed after the Chinese Communists gained control of the southern parts of mainland China and shipping services were dislocated. Britain still repatriated 140 persons to Hainan but in September 1950 Peking refused to receive Chinese nationals repatriated from Malaya to Hainan and consequently the repatriation programme virtually came to a standstill.

18 In 1949, the Emergency cost $112 millions; in 1950, $136 millions; in 1951, $240 millions and in 1952, $265 millions. *Malay Mail*, 25 Nov 1953. As late as September 1957, Ismail, Malayan delegate to the UN, spoke of Malaya "still spending at the rate of about $100,000 a day in fighting the Communists in the Malayan jungles. UN Doc. A/PV 686 (24 Sep 1957). According to Lord Mancroft, it cost about 1 million Straits dollars (500,000 US dollars) for each guerilla eliminated. *The Hindu*, 27 Sep 1950.

19 *H. C. Deb.*, 453 (1948) 603-5.

20 The Singapore correspondent of *The Times* wrote : "Communist propagandists say that Malaya is police state, and so in a way it is. The emergency regulations have increased the power of the executive at the cost of the individual. The effective Government is a military oligarchy, with a command apparatus demanding absolute obedience, which is also a system of police surveillance. The power of the security forces is almost absolute....Curfews are imposed at will, food rations reduced, villages evacuated, and individuals detained indefinitely." *The Times*, 2 Oct 1953.

21. Statement by the Minister of State Younger, 24 May 1950. *H. C. Deb.*, 475 (1950) 2189.

22 *The Times*, 22 Sep 1948.

23 *Cmd.* 7709, 61.

24 *H. C. Deb.*, 453 (1948) 603-5.

25 G. Bondaryevsky, "The Post-war Struggle of the Malaya Peoples for National Liberation," *Voprosy Istorii* (No. 4, 1950) as translated in *SPT* (15 Sep 1950) 503.

26 *Pravda*, 6 Oct 1950, as translated in *Ibid.*, 650.

27 "Any territories which the Chinese may have annexed or on which they may have designs are at the instigation of Russian rather than Chinese policy." Ronald Farquharson, "China—Past, Present And Future," *JRCAS* (Apr 1952) 116. While refuting Soviet accusations

that the wars in Korea, Vietnam and Malaya were "colonial enterprises designed to suppress nationalist movements and permit the continued exploitation of the subject populace," the British delegate to the UN Political Committee observed : "It was to be hoped that they did not mean that the Soviet Union had persuaded Communist China to undertake aggressive adventures in Southeast Asia." UN Doc. A/C.1/PV 503 (28 Jan 1952) 267.

28 The Observer in *CD* (24 Feb 1948) 10.

29 *Ibid.* (9 Mar 1948) 13.

30 *Ibid.* (29 Jan 1948) 17.

31 Kenneth Younger, "A British View of the Far East," *Pacific Affairs* (Jun 1954) 102.

32 Military observers in Singapore, Tilman Durdin stated, "forsee no possibility of an opening blitz attack against Malaya....Neither China nor the Soviet Union has the naval power based at present far enough south to provide consistent aerial support." *NYT*, 4 Jan 1951.

33 G. F. Hudson, "China Since 1927" in W. E. Soothill, *A History of China* (New York, 1951) 124.

34 G. F. Hudson, "British Relations with China," *Current History* (Dec 1957) 331.

35 C. P. Fitzerald, "Peace or War with China," *Pacific Affairs* (Dec 1951) 342.

36 *CWR* (1 Oct 1949) 64.

37 See *Ibid.* (26 Nov 1949) 205-6.

38 Speech by Liu Shao-chi, 16 November 1949. See People's Publishing House, *Working Class in the Struggle for National Liberation* (Bombay, 1949) 30.

39 *Ibid.*, 12 and 18.

40 Mao Tse-tung & Liu Shao-chi, *Lessons of the Chinese Revolution* (Bombay, 1950) 30.

41 "No material aid in the form of arms, ammunition or reinforcements was reaching them from China, Indo-China or elsewhere in Southeast Asia." Statement by Malcolm MacDonald, British High Commissioner General for Southeast Asia, 11 May 1950. *The Hindu*, 12 May 1950.

42 Reinforcements that arrived in Malaya from Hong Kong in March and July 1950 were made possible by the "easing of local tension following the peaceful Communist occupation of the Hong Kong border." *Ibid.*, 15 Mar 1950.

43 Kenneth Younger, "Western Policy in Asia," *Pacific Affairs* (Jun 1952) 127.

44 Terrorist activity did certainly increase in January and February 1950. It was however, debatable how far that was due to the act of British recognition. In the opinion of the British Government it was "due to the success of Communist armies in China than to the effect of recognition." Statement by Minister of State Younger, 29 March 1950. *H. C. Deb.*, 473 (1950) 391-2.

45 Statement by Younger, 24 May 1950. *Ibid.*, 475 (1950) 2187.
46 *Annual Report of the Federation of Malaya* 1949 (London, 1950) 203-4.
47 *Annual Report of the Federation of Malaya* 1950 (Kaula Lumpur, 1951) 1 and 9.
48 "Some Communist Governments do meddle in their neighbour's business. Tyrants in Moscow, for instance, regard themselves as leaders of a movement to bring the whole human race under Communist rule. This is the danger which now threatens the Chinese. The Communists in the Kremlin would dearly love to dominate China. They are attempting to do so, exploiting Manchuria's resources to increase not China's but Russia's power....The Russians would like to extend their threat to Southern Asia. They will not succeed." Malcolm MacDonald, 6 January 1950. *The Hindu*, 8 Jan 1950.
49 *The Times*, 7 Jan 1950.
50 Thus, *People's China* accused Britain of continuing "murder and mass imprisonment of Chinese" in Malaya where the British authorities "have banned 150 Chinese books and have taken repressive measures against Chinese journalists." *PC* (1 Jun 1950) 2.
51 *WWCC* : 1949-50, 154-5.
52 *Ibid.*, 194.
53 Statement on 6 April 1951. *H. C. Deb.* 486 (1950-51) 31. Written Answers.
54 Thus the Report of a Government mission on Chinese education in Malaya recommended the setting up of a Committee for "Revision and Preparation of Text books for Use in Chinese Schools." *Chinese Schools and the Education of Chinese Malayans.* The Report of a Mission invited by the Federation Government to study the problem of education of the Chinese in Malaya (Kaula Lumpur, 1951) 40-1.
55 British authorities did all they could to deprive the rebels of their food resources. They did not hesitate to take recourse even to chemical warfare.
56 See *The Times*, 1 Dec 1952.
57 Chou En-lai's interview with Rt. Hon. Harold Wilson, M. P., at Geneva. *Ceylon Daily News*, 10 Jun 1954.
58 *Labour Monthly* (London) (Aug 1955) 376-8.
59 *PC* (1 Feb 1956) 40-2.
60 J. H. Brimmel, *Communism in Southeast Asia* (London, 1959) 335. The Malayan Communist Party's December 1955 communique was published in full by the *New China News Agency* on 6 January 1956 and was later carried by the Cominform Journal. *Ibid.*, 332.
61 *PC* (1 Nov 1956) 44.
62 *JMJP*, 4 and 5 Oct 1956.
63 *CT*, 25 Jul 1957.
64 *WWCC* : 1956-57 (Peking, 1958) 364-5.
65 *PR* (12 May 1959) 26.
66 See Joint Communique of the Governments of China and Malaysia,

31 May 1974. *PR* (7 Jun 1974) 8.

67 Siamese trade, banking and teak have remained largely in British hands. H.C.K. Woddis, "Siam : Cock-pit of Anglo-American Interests." *EW* (Jan-Feb 1949) 7-9.

68 As early as February 1949 Marshal Pibul Songgram, Premier of Siam, announced that Thailand had agreed to take joint measures with the Government of Malaya to seal the Thailand-Malaya frontier in order to prevent the movement in either direction of Communist terrorists operating in Malaya, and to make possible coordinated police sweeps against them. Central Office of Information, *Thailand* : *R.* 4236 (London). In September 1949 an agreement was concluded between the Governments of Thailand and the Federation of Malaya providing reciprocal arrangements for the police of the respective territories to cross the frontier in pursuit of terrorists up to points in Thailand or Malaya specified in the agreement. *Annual Report of the Federation of Malaya: 1949* (London, 1950) 205. Large-scale combined operations against the terrorists were carried out in January 1955 by Thai and Malayan forces. *Thailand R.* 4236.

69 See Anthony Eden, *The Full Circle* (London, 1960) 101. British arms and equipment for the use of Thai infantry battalions were supplied as early as mid-1949 and later deliveries were made of Spitfire fighters and Chipmunk training aircraft to the Royal Thai Air Force. *Thailand* : *R.* 4236, n. 68.

70 See Eden, n. 69, 101. While Britain was not prepared to give any assurance in April 1954 about possible action on its part in the event of failure to reach an agreement at Geneva for a cessation of hostilities in Indo-China, it was quite willing to join the United States Government "in studying measures to ensure the defence of Siam and the rest of South-East Asia, including Malaya, in the event of all or part of Indo-China being lost." See Paper prepared by the Foreign Secretary, April 1954. *Cmnd.* 2834, 67.

71 Maclean, n. 10, 321.

72 Eden, n. 69, 123.

73 See Maclean, n. 10, 315.

74 William Haytor, "Need the West Still 'Contain' Communism?" *The Observer*, 6 Nov 1966.

75 Military opinion was that "if the Communists were victorious in Indo-China, the British forces would have to be quadrupled to hold down the guerillas in Malaya, who would receive arms across the Gulf of Siam." *Jerusalem Post*, 11 Jun 1954.

76 "It costs France now some £450 million a year, about a third of her defence budget. By tying up her regular army on the other side of the world it prevents France from playing her necessary part in the defence and the diplomacy of Europe.... This makes it of deep concern to the western world." *The Times*, 29 Aug 1953. "Indo-China," Eden said, "had become the key to European problems" and "the fate of E.D.C. was in part dependent upon its solution."

Eden, n. 69, 84.

77　Kenneth Younger, "A British View of the Far East," *Pacific Affairs*, (Jun 1954) 104.

78　"We are in close touch with Indo-China, there is close association both militarily and politically." Griffiths on 27 February 1951. *H.C. Deb.*, 484 (1950-1) 2035.

79　See Eden, n. 69, 79-81.

80　Communist China recognized the Democratic Republic of Vietnam (proclaimed by Ho Chi Minh on 14 January 1950) on 18 January 1950 and the Soviet Union on 31 January 1950. On 2 February 1950 the East German Government offered a free return voyage and suitable jobs at home to all Germans fighting with the French Foreign Legion in Vietnam who desert to the Vietnamese People's Army. *CWR* (11 Feb 1950) 175-6.

81　*The Times*, 1 Feb 1950.

82　Statement on 24 May 1950. *H.C. Deb.*, 475 (1950) 2189.

83　"The new head of State was neither a popular nor an inspiring figure.... But the choice lay between him and Ho Chi Minh. There was no third force in Vietnam." Eden, n. 69, 80. Foreign Secretary Bevin justified British recognition of Bao Dai but he wanted the French to give "more independence" to him. *H.C. Deb.*, 475 (1950) 2089. Minister of State Younger agreed with Wyatt that Britain should press the French "to develop the present state of considerable independence into a state of full independence." See statement in the House of Commons, 14 April 1950. *Cmnd.* 2834, 63.

84　*The Times*, 1 Feb 1950. The words in the parenthesis are those of the author.

85　Both Britain and the USA recognized the Bao Dai regime on 7 February 1950.

86　Eden, n. 69, 80.

87　*The Hindu*, 14 May 1950.

88　Eden, n. 69, 83.

89　Lorna Morley, "Menaced Laos," *Editorial Research Reports* (Washington) (23 Sep 1959) 723.

90　Article by A. Guber in *Voprosy Istorii*, Oct 1949 as translated in *SPT* (1 Apr 1950) 206.

91　"It was not until July 1950...that organized Chinese aid (in the form of training camps across the border in China) began. In the autumn, the Vietminh capture of all the French-held frontier posts on the Chinese border was the first serious military loss to the French, and also the necessary preliminary to further Chinese aid...Chinese aid continued on a modest scale." *The Times*, 9 Apr 1954.

92　This was admitted even by the US Government. See US Department of State, *Background : Indo-China : the War in Viet-Nam, Cambodia, and Laos* (Washington, 1953) 2.

93　An article in *Jen-min Jih-pao* of 11 December 1950 accused USA of planning to invade China "from three sides, namely: Korea, Taiwan and Indo-China." *SPT* (1 Jan 1951) 27-8.

94 The gap in the Hankow-Canton Railway, which runs to the Indo-China border, was not filled till the end of 1951. See Wilfred Ryder, "China's Policy in South-East Asia," *EW* (Aug 1954) 13-4.

95 *PC* (1 Sep 1950) 25.

96 *NB* (23 Jan 1953).

97 In their joint communique (issued on 29 March 1951), the Presidents of the USA and the French Republic spoke of French forces and the forces of the Associated States as "successfully opposing Communist aggression." *AFP*, 1672. The British Commissioner General in Southeast Asia, Malcolm MacDonald, thought that the appointment of Commander-in-Chief, the reinforcements sent and the great financial aid from America, on top of what went before should give to our "friends in Indo-China within a year or two a decisive military ascendancy over the Viet-minh." Address to the Singapore Union of Journalists, 16 November 1953. Regional Information Office, *The Asian Revolution* (Singapore, undated).

98 See *Background : Indo-China: the War in Viet-Nam, Cambodia, and Laos*, n. 92, 2.

99 *The Times*, 4 May 1953. The latest Vietminh drive towards Laos was the cause of much anxiety to the West as it appeared a "part of a long planned campaign which politically is led by the so-called Free Thai Movement." *Ibid.*, 11 Apr 1953.

100 In April 1954 Vietminh forces invaded Cambodia. These "aggressive acts" of Vietminh forces in Laos and Cambodia, Eden stated at the Geneva Conference on 8 June 1954, "cause concern far beyond the confines of the states concerned." *Cmd.* 9186, 152.

101 As early as 11 January 1952 Anthony Eden, speaking at Columbia University, said: "It should be understood that an intervention in force by Chinese Communists in Southeast Asia—even if they were called 'volunteers'—would create a situation no less menacing than that which the United Nations met and faced in Korea." Office of the UK High Commissioner in India, *Cambodia, Laos and Viet Nam*, R. 3143 (New Delhi, undated) 7. On 12 January 1954 Secretary of State Dulles proclaimed the doctrine of massive retaliation and warned that Chinese intervention would have "grave consequences which might not be confined to Indo-China." *DSB* (25 Jan 1954) 108.

102 Joint Statement by the US Secretary of State and the British Foreign Secretary, 13 April 1954. *AFP*, 1705.

103 See J.P. Jain, *A Documentary Study of the Warsaw Pact* (Bombay, 1973) Introduction.

104 *WWCC*: 1951-1953 (Peking, 1958) 136.

105 *The Hindu*, 21 Feb 1954.

106 Eden, n. 69, 83.

107 Statement by Foreign Secretary Eden, 5 February 1952. *H.C. Deb.*, 495 (1951-2) 833-4.

108 Eden, n. 69, 102, 113, 91 and 124.

109 Younger, n. 31, 108. On 28 April 1954, the National Executive

Committee of the British Labour Party passed a resolution almost unanimously opposing any steps that might involve Britain in military action to help "imperialist policies." *The Statesman,* 30 Apr 1954.

110 Eden, n. 69, 142 and 83.

111 See *Cmnd.* 2834 66-7.

112 "America could not at that time be reached by bombs from Soviet Russia.... The same was not true either of Soviet Russia or of ourselves, for we were sharply conscious of what the spread of an Indo-China conflict must mean. Soviet Russia would have the grim choice of leaving her ally to her fate, and half the communist world to its destruction, or plunging herself into the abyss of nuclear conflict. We can argue as to which would have been her choice had she been compelled to make it. It was certain that she would at least consider a compromise arrangement to avoid it." Eden, n. 69, 124. See also Royal Institute of International Affairs, *Collective Defence in South-East Asia* (London, 1956) 154-5.

113 This was discernible from the speech of Pham Van Dong, Foreign Minister of the Democratic Republic of Vietnam, on 3 August 1954, in which he expressed dissatisfaction with the Geneva Agreements. He said: "The Geneva Conference is for us a victory, but is only the first phase of the victory. We still have to consolidate and develop this victory." *NB* (11 Aug 1954) 8. See also H.C. Hinton, *China's Relations with Burma and Vietnam* (New York, 1954) 19.

114 China could have desired to see the US and the UK heavily committed in Europe. However, Peking was also aware that in case Russia was involved in a global war, it might not get all the supplies it needed for waging a successful fight from the Soviet Union.

115 Eden refers to it in his *Memoirs.* See Eden, n. 69, 123.

116 *Ibid.,* 122-3.

117 *NB* (14 Apr 1954) 2-4.

118 "Our purpose," Eden stated, "is to reach a settlement." "There exists," Chou En-lai responded, "the possibility of reaching agreement in this Conference." *Cmd.* 9186, 122 and 126.

119 Statement by Chou En-lai at the Geneva Conference, 9 June 1954. *Ibid.,* 157 and 159.

120 Statement at the Geneva Conference, 8 May 1954. *Ibid.,* 114. Molotov repeated this view again on 8 June 1954 when he stated that "the events in all three Indo-Chinese States—Vietnam, Cambodia and Laos—have the same basic causes." *Ibid.,* 146.

121 Eden, n. 69, 113. "What we were being asked to do was to assist in misleading Congress into approving a military operation, which would in itself be ineffective, and might well bring the world to the verge of a major war." *Ibid.,* 105.

122 *The Times,* 17 May 1954.

123 In thinking of a settlement in Indo-China, Eden stated, "my chief concern was for Malaya." Eden, n. 69, 87.

124 Encouraged by the Chinese gestures of goodwill, such as the agree-

ment on the dispatch of a Chinese *charge d' affaires* to London, the relaxation of exit controls on British nationals in China and the offers of increased trade (see Chapter Eight), the British began to take more interest in the "improvement in Anglo-Chinese relations" (which, as Eden stated, "have already proved of benefit to this country.") than in continuing or enlarging the fighting in Indo-China or prejudicing in any way the chances of arriving at a negotiated settlement at Geneva. See statement by Foreign Secretary Eden, 23 June 1954. *H.C. Deb.*, 529 (1953-4) 440. Clement Davies, M.P., called the formal and legal Chinese representation in the UK as "a most important step" which China had taken "towards a better understanding," while C.R. Attlee, the Opposition Leader, described the "contacts" established between the British and the Chinese delegations at Geneva as "the most important part of the Conference." *Ibid.*, 442 and 445.

125 Eden, n. 69, 91.
126 *Ibid.*, 91, 123 and 92.
127 Younger, n. 31, 110. As early as 1952 Younger believed that the partition of Vietnam was a probable solution which "might produce a relatively bloodless breathing-space." Kenneth Younger, "Western Policy in Asia," *Pacific Affairs* (Jun 1952) 127. By the beginning of 1954 Foreign Secretary Eden's thoughts "began to turn to the possibility of some form of partition as a solution which might bring hostilities to an end and effect a settlement which would hold." Eden, n. 69, 87.
128 *Ibid.*, 142 and 140.
129 In his statement before the Geneva Conference on 9 June 1954, Chou En-lai laid stress on the "cessation of the entry into [all the three states of] Indo-China from outside of all kinds of fresh troops and military personnel and all types of arms and ammunition simultaneously with the cessation of hostilities in the whole of Indo-China" for otherwise there was every possibility of these states becoming "military bases for foreign interventionists." *Cmd.* 9186, 159-60. Under the Geneva Agreements, both the Governments of Laos and Cambodia undertook not to enter into a military alliance or to agree to the establishment of bases on their territories for the military forces of foreign Powers. See *Cmd.* 9239, 10 and 41-2.
130 Eden, n. 69, 122.
131 *Ibid.*, 143. The Geneva Agreements, Eden stated on 21 July 1954, "are the best that our hands could devise. All will now depend upon the spirit in which those agreements are observed and carried out." *Cmd.* 9239, 8. For the text of the Agreements see *Ibid.*, 5-42.
132 *JMJP* Editorial, 22 Jul 1954. See NCNA, 23 Jul 1954. The Chinese paper added: "This major victory is helpful to the promotion of collective peace and security in Asia and to the further easing of international tension. It is an achievement of immense, historic significance, bringing joy and inspiration to all mankind."
133 Eden, n. 69, 143.

134 *Cmd.* 9239, 21-2.

135 Statement by the Parliamentary Under-Secretary for Foreign Affairs, R. H. Turton, 6 July 1955. *H. C. Deb.*, 543 (1955) 95. Written Answers.

136 Statement by the British Foreign Secretary, 13 July 1955. *Ibid.*, 1916.

137 See *DSB* (13 May 1957) 771-2.

138 See Central Office of Information, *Laos: Political Developments* 1958-60, supplement to R. 3706 (London, 1960) 1-4.

139 See Statement by Chen Yi, 25 May 1959. *Cmnd.*, 2834, 139.

140 Selwyn Llyod's note to Gromyko, 9 June 1959. *Ibid.*, 143-6.

141 *Ibid.*, 153-4.

142 UN Doc. S/PV 848 (7 Sep 1959) 14-5.

143 *Cmnd.* 2834, 152-3.

144 *Ibid.*, 155-6.

145 See Maclean, n. 10, 320-1.

146 Declaration on the Neutrality of Laos, signed in Geneva, 23 July 1962. *Cmd.* 1828, 17. For the text of the Declaration and Protocol to the Declaration on the Neutrality of Laos, see *Ibid.*, 15-24.

147 See *Cmnd.* 2834, 31-2

148 See SEATO Council Communique, 5 May 1965. *Ibid.*, 259.

149 *JMJP* editorials, 26 Jun 1955, 16 Aug 1955 and 18 Sep 1955. For English translations, see *NB* (2 Jul 1955) 5-6; *Ibid.*, (24 Aug 1955) 11-3; and *Ibid.*, (28 Sep 1955) 7-8. See also Chou En-lai's letter to British Foreign Secretary, 31 October 1955. *Cmnd.* 2834, 113-4.

150 *NB* (24 Aug 1955) 11-3.

151 *H.C. Deb.*, 578 (17 Apr 1957) 18. Britain "understood" Saigon's viewpoint that "the absence of all freedom" in North Vietnam constituted an obstacle to holding all-Vietnam elections. See *Cmnd.* 2834, 127.

152 See *Ibid.*, 193.

153 W. Averell Harriman, "Leadership in World Affairs," *Foreign Affairs* (Jul 1954) 528-9.

154 Address by Secretary of State Dulles, 15 September 1954. *AFP*, 919.

155 Eden, n. 69, 93. "By the beginning of May, the rains would be starting in Indo-China and extensive campaigning by either side would be impossible for several months." *Ibid.*, 93. A pact for Southeast Asia, Eden said on 23 June 1954, "could be a future safeguard, but it is not a panacea." *H.C. Deb.*, 529 (1953-4) 433.

156 Eden, n. 69, 96.

157 "It was doubtful whether the situation in Indo-China could be solved by purely military means and we must at least see what proposals, if any, the communists had to make at Geneva." *Ibid.*, 96.

158 See statement by Foreign Secretary Eden on 13 April 1954 and by Premier Churchill on 27 April 1954. *H.C. Deb.*, 526 (1953-4) 972 and 1456. When Dulles sought to convene a meeting on 20 April 1954 in Washington of the Ambassadors of the UK, Australia, New

Zealand, France, the Philippines, Thailand and the three Associated states with the object of setting up "an informal working group to study the collective defence of South East Asia," Britain opposed the idea. London feared that not only "the countries invited would be regarded as already constituting the proposed organization" and thereby prejudging the question of membership at the outset, but would also prove "harmful in its effects on the Geneva Conference." Eden, therefore, instructed the British Ambassador in Washington "not to participate in such a meeting." A serious rift between the UK and the USA was averted only when Dulles agreed "to convert it into a general briefing conference on the coming negotiations at Geneva." However, Eden, still felt unhappy "about the impression which the Washington 'get-together' might create." Eden, n. 69, 98-9. If on 28 June 1954 Premier Churchill, together with the President of the USA, stated that "We will press forward with plans for collective defence" (*AFP*, 1706), its sole purpose seemed to be to quicken the pace of settlement at Geneva by the use of pressure tactics. That it was so was evident from the communique issued by ANZUS Powers (the USA, Australia and New Zealand) on 30 June 1954 (See *The Times*, 1 Jul 1954) and the slow progress of the Anglo-American talks, of an exploratory nature, following the Churchill-Eisenhower statement.

159 *H.C. Deb.*, 527 (1953-4) 1693.
160 *Ibid.*, 528 (1953-4) 208-9.
161 *Ibid.*, 527 (17 May 1954) 1693.
162 *Ibid.*, 529 (1953-4) 435.
163 The main effect of the Locarno treaty of 1925 was to guarantee the post-war settlement in Western Europe, especially the frontiers between Germany, France and Belgium as established at Versailles. The Locarno analogy could hardly fit in the conditions of Southeast Asia in 1954. In the words of *The Times*, there was "nobody available in Southeast Asia to play the part assigned by Locarno to Britain and Italy, that of guarantor against any breach of the agreement by either side." The uncommitted Asian Powers, the paper said, lacked the strength for the task "even if these Powers had the will to hold the balance in southeast Asia." "In essentials, therefore," the paper added, "any pact with the Communists in Southeast Asia would be one of simple non-aggression, and in view of the past history of such pacts and modern Communist teachniques of synthetic aggression, this is not a prospect to inspire enthusiasm. The Locarno analogy is not one that can be pushed very far. Probably Mr. Eden did not intend that it should be." *The Times*, 26 Jan 1954.
164 *H.C. Deb.*, 529 (1953-4) 551.
165 Eden, n. 69, 133.
166 Twelve of the 30 members of the House of Representatives Foreign Affairs Committee, in a letter to the White House, advised President Eisenhower to reject the British plan for a non-aggression pact in

Asia since that would adversely affect "the whole mutual security concept and programme." *The Statesman*, 28 Jun 1954.
167 *H.C. Deb.*, 532 (1953-4) 934.
168 *Ibid.*, 935.
169 *Ibid.*, 1003.
1 70 *Cmd.* 9239, 11. The USA refused to sign the Geneva Agreements or "to join" in the Declaration. It, however, declared that "it will refrain from the threat or the use of force to disturb them." *Ibid.*, 7.
171 Statement by Foreign Secretary Selwyn Llyod, 27 February 1956. *H.C. Deb.*, 549 (1955-6) 859.
172 Statement by Secretary of State Dulles, 8 March 1955. US Department of State, *The Bangkok Conference of the Manila Pact Powers* (Washington, 1955) 5.
173 See Article IV of the Treaty. *DSB* (20 Sep 1954) 394.
174 Statement by Dulles at the Manila Conference, *The Statesman*, 7 Sep 1954.
175 *DSB*, n. 173.
176 *Collective Defence in South-East Asia*, n. 112, 150.
177 *The Bangkok Conference of the Manila Pact Powers*, n. 172, 26.
178 *NB* (18 Aug 1954) 5-6.
179 Foreign Languages Press, *Important Documents Concerniug the Question of Taiwan* (Peking, 1955) 139.
180 See *JMJP* editorial, 2 Dec 1954, as translated in *NB* (8 Dec 1954) 8.
181 *Ibid.* (9 Mar 1955).
182 *Ibid.* (16 Mar 1955) 7.
183 See *Cmnd.* 2834, 96-9.
184 See *H.C. Deb.*, 19 Feb 1962 and 26 Mar 1963 as reproduced in *Cmnd.* 2834, 186-95.
185 *Ibid.*, 32.
186 See statement by the British Premier, 6 August 1964. *Ibid.*, 209.
187 See *Ibid.*, 250-5.
188 See *Ibid.*, 257-60.
189 *Ibid.*, 260.
190 Press conference at the United Nations, 7 October 1965. See UK Mission to UN, Press Release No. 84.
191 *NYT*, 15 Jun 1971.
192 *The Washington Post*, 18 Jun 1971.
193 See Maclean, n. 10, 316.
194 See *Ibid.*, 325.
195 *Ibid.*, 324.
196 See *Cmnd.* 2834, 260.
197 *NYT*, 21 Jun 1965.
198 Many prominent Labourites became critics of US policies. In a letter to *The Times*, Philip Noel Baker, John Menielson and Shinwell considered that the American bombings, whi ch caused extensive civilian damage in Vietnam, was a further escalation "more dangerous than the attacks on oil installations near Hanoi and Haiphong,

against which our Government made its public protest at the time."
The mounting criticism led to Labour and Liberal M.P.s presenting
a memoranda in their individual capacities to the British Premier.
They urged the British government to dissociate from the American
actions and asked the President of the USA to stop bombing permanently.

199   *PR* (8 Oct 1965) 8.
200   *PR* (4 Feb 1966) 17-22.
201   *PR* (25 Feb 1966) 11-2.
202   *PR* (11 Mar 1966) 5-7.
203   *PR* (5 Aug 1966) 28.
204   *PR* (12 Feb 1967) 30.
205   *PR* (12 May 1967) 31.
206   *PR* (23 Feb 1968) 31.
207   *H.C. Deb.*, 801 (5 May 1970) 208-66.
208   *H.C. Deb.*, 838 (12 June 1972) 994.
209   *Ibid.*, 849 (24 Jan 1973) 461-5.
210   *Ibid.*, 852 (5 Mar 1973) 32-6.
211   *Ibid.*

Chapter Six : Hong Kong

1   Lewis Gen, "Will the Chinese Communists Attack Hong Kong,"
    EW (Oct 1949) 7.
2   Evan Luard, *Britain and China* (London, 1962) 198.
3   The closure of the naval dockyard at Hong Kong, the recognition
    of the Mao regime, the continuance of trade with China within the
    permissible limits of embargo and the exclusion of Hong Kong from
    the protection of the SEATO are cases in point. "Hong Kong's
    own demeanor," Lionel Gelber states, "has...been studiously in-
    offensive; where other offshore islands had been fortified for assault
    on the Chinese mainland, the Crown Colony remained as circum-
    spect as possible." Lionel Gelber, *America in Britain's Place* (New
    York, 1961) 160.
4   R.L. Walker, *The Continuing Struggle* (New York, 1958) 42.
5   See Hong Kong Government Press, *Hong Kong 1960* (Hong Kong,
    1961) 4, 5, 24, 26-7 and 74.
6   The colony's prosperity was originally founded on the entrepot
    trade in goods passing into and out of China. In 1890, 55% of
    China's imports and 37% of its exports passed through the colony
    and in 1900 the corresponding figures were 42% and 40%. G. B.
    Endacott, *A History of Hong Kong* (London, 1958) 253. In the post-
    World War II period also China occupied a prominent place in
    Hong Kong's trade. Thus, in 1954 imports from and exports to

China still headed the list, being 20.2% and 16.2% respectively of the Hong Kong totals. Edward Szczepanik, *The Economic Growth of Hong Kong* (London, 1958) 158 and 179-80. Tables 14 and 45.

7 See Godfrey E.P. Hertslet, *Hertslet's China Treaties* Vol. 1 (London, 1908) 8.

8 See *Ibid.*, 50-1.

9 *Ibid.*, 121. "News of the cession came on 11 June 1898, and caused great jubilation in the colony, but when *The Times* summarized the terms there was disappointment over the Kowloon City reservation." Endacott, n. 6, 262.

10 The British colony succumbed to the Japanese invasion in December 1941 and remained in Japanese hands for over three and a half years. The Japanese could not, however, subdue the Chinese guerrillas, who remained in control of parts of the New Territories, "in spite of vigorous punitive measures taken against them." *Ibid.*, 316. In these circumstances, it was extremely doubtful if Hong Kong could withstand the onslaught from Communist China.

11 Hong Kong Government Press, *Hong Kong* 1960 (Hong Kong, 1961) 314.

12 C.P. Fitzgerald, *Revolution in China* (London, 1953) 53.

13 In November 1941, Morgenthau, Secretary of the Treasury, proposed that the United States should try to induce the British to sell Hong Kong to China, the price being loaned by the United States. In the discussions over the Atlantic Charter in March 1943, Roosevelt felt that clause 3 in the Charter, urging the liberation of all people, applied as much to those of the British colonies as to those peoples overrun by the Germans and the Japanese, and the President "once or twice urged the British to give up Hong Kong as a gesture of goodwill....At the Yalta Conference...he urged in private conversations with Stalin that Hong Kong should be given back to the Chinese or internationalized as a free port. Churchill was excluded from that part of the negotiations relating to the Far East—as was the Chinese representative—and we are told he 'exploded' at a resolution on the subject of trusteeship which he thought questioned the British control over her colonies." Endacott, n. 6, 300-1.

14 *H.C. Deb.*, 416 (1945) 705. "Hong Kong has become more important in relation to China than it was before the war. It always had a special contribution of its own to make towards the affairs of China, quite apart from its independent existence for itself as a British colony; and that special contribution continues, but is enhanced by the fact that Hong Kong has in part assumed also some of the former functions of Shanghai. Now that there are no longer any foreign concessions left in Shanghai, it is the nearest place to the main centres of population and of trade in China where there is a system of law and administration on Western lines with political, economic and financial stability. There is hardly a British firm in Shanghai which has not since the war transferred its principal office

in that part of the world from Shanghai to Hong Kong. Many Chinese foreign firms have done the same, and this movement is not confined to commerce but applies also, though with less force, to industry." Board of Trade, *Report of United Kingdom Trade Mission to China* (London, 1948) 151.

15 Endacott, n. 6, 304. "The stridently nationalistic Kuomintang naturally eyed the colony jealously, and its representative in Hong Kong assumed an influential position among a local population which was anxious to prepare for any contingency." *Ibid.*, 304 and 301.

16 *Ibid.*, 302. In his lecture delivered on 13 November 1946 before the Royal Central Asian Society, Sir Harcourt observed : "Before we went into Hong Kong there were a good number of people in China who, I believe, confidently hoped and expected that they would go and occupy Hong Hong, and when we went in before they were able to do so, they were very upset." In the surrender terms which he signed "on behalf of both the British Government and General Chiang Kai-shek as the Commander of the armies in the China area," he noticed that "they carefully left out all mention of Kowloon." The surrender terms, he added, "had been negotiated at Chungking, and I know that there are a number of Chinese who think they will get it back." He agreed with Admiral Kelly that it would be "impossible to hold Hong Kong without Kowloon and without considerable rights over the leased territory." Cecil Harcourt, "The Military Administration of Hong Kong," *JRCAS* (Jan 1947) 12 and 16. See also Evan Luard, n. 2, 182.

17 See Endacott, n. 6, 303.

18 Evan Luard, n. 2, 182.

19 *China Handbook* : 1950 (New York, 1950) 320.

20 The Chinese Government formulated a plan in 1946 for resuming its administration in Kowloon city. It was "temporarily shelved only out of consideration of the friendly relations between our two countries." Reply note from Ching Tien-hsi, Chinese Ambassador in London, to Foreign Secretary Ernest Bevin, 5 February 1948. *Ibid.*, 321. In 1900, a Colonial Office official minuted : "We have definitely decided not to allow the city to fall under Chinese jurisdiction, and have told the Chinese Government so, and have passed an Order in Council including it in the new territory, and the matter is at an end." Evan Luard, n. 2, 180. See also *The Times*, 24 Jan 1948.

21 *China Handbook* : 1950, n. 19, 320-1. Chinese Government regretted that the incident had occurred and offered to give protection to British subjects in future but attempts to secure compensation for the damage (estimated at about £300,000) and an inquiry into the incident proved fruitless, despite lengthy negotiations. "In spite of the arguments at the Hong Kong courts, claiming British sovereignty and jurisdiction over the area, the special status of the walled city of Kowloon is still in force. Thus, no resident there has to pay taxes to the Hong Kong Government. Furthermore, it is only in

connection with serious crimes that the police enter the area and make arrests." *EW* (Mar 1961) 26.

22 UK Colonial Office, Annual Reports, *Hong Kong* : 1948 (London, 1949) 1-3.

23 See *Report of United Kingdom Trade Mission to China,* n. 14, 172-3, 152 and 46.

24 See *Hong Kong* : 1948, n. 22, 36-8.

25 Hong Kong had been carrying on unofficial and indirect trade with the Communists for quite some time. Hong Kong's imports from North China increased from HK $63.7 million in 1947 to 135-6 million in 1948, to 233.9 million in 1949 and 355.7 million in 1950. Hong Kong's exports to North China increased from HK $55 million in 1947 to 118.4 million in 1948, to 287.5 million in 1949 and 677.2 million in 1950. Colonial Office, Annual Report, *Hong Kong* : 1949 (London, 1950) 35 and *Hong Kong* : 1950 (Hong Kong, 1951) 39. It is significant to note that the Communists permitted the British to continue operations at the Kailan mines and its subsidiary enterprise in North China.

26 *Hong Kong* : 1948, n. 22, 38.

27 *Hong Kong* : 1949, n. 25, 32-4. By 1949 trade was already running at over £35 million in each direction, besides a fairly large invisible trade in shipping, insurance and banking. Luard, n. 2, 195.

28 See *Ta Kung Pao* editorial, 27 Feb 1950, as translated in *CPS* (Mar 1950) 128-9.

29 While discussing the Formosan problem with Premier Chou En-lai, Edgar Faure referred in passing to Hong Kong. Thereupon, Chou En-lai observed : "That is not the same thing. There has been a treaty about Hong Kong, which creates a special situation. I do not say the same as far as the New Territories are concerned." Edgar Faure, *The Serpent and the Tortoise* (London, 1958) 21.

30 The Communists, it was believed, must give first priority to mopping up operations, *i.e.* the liquidation of remaining Kuomintang bases, and consolidation of what they have gained must weigh seriously the hazards of war with Britain that "would inevitably involve the United States," and must think of the adverse effects that attack on Hong Kong would have on the supply of materials and equipment from the Western countries. The closure of Shanghai, Tientsin & C., forced practically all China's ocean-borne foreign trade through Hong Kong and as such the moment the colony fell to the Communists, the blockade would have been "rendered doubly effective." Lewis Gen, n. 1, 7-8. "There can be no doubt," a Conservative Party Research Paper stated, "that the Chinese Communists will use every weapon to try to force the British out of Hong Kong. Direct military attack is perhaps the least likely method to be employed. Mao Tse-tung still has the really resistent half of China to subdue; he has no air force and no really first class troops. Unless, therefore, Moscow should dictate his course of action and supply him with much greater military aid than hitherto,

he is unlikely to go out of his way to attack Hong Kong and risk defeat." Conservative Research Department, *A Monthly Survey of Foreign Affairs* (London) No. 13 (Aug 1949) 2. Thus, armed conflict with Britain entailed militarily—diversion of resources from the Kuomintang front; politically—postponing, if not prejudicing, any possible recognition of Peking regime by Britain and some Western and Commonwealth nations; and economically—retarding the economic development of the country. It was for these concrete reasons that Peking desisted from the risky venture of forcibly taking Hong Kong.

31 *H.C. Deb.*, 464 (1949) 1255.

32 During the year, *i.e.* from May 1949 to May 1950, the Legislative Council of the Colony passed 16 emergency regulations. See *CWR* (13 May 1950) 190.

33 With a view to prevent Hong Kong from becoming a scene of "political quarrels" of the Kuomintang and the Communists and to preserve law and order in the colony, Hong Kong Briäish authorities passed a Societies Ordinance in May 1949 "declaring illegal all societies or organizations which had affiliations with political parties outside the Colony." *Hong Kong* : 1949, n. 25, 2-3.

34 As a prelude to immigration control, registration of the people and the issue of identity cards was introduced in 1949. From 28 April 1950 onwards the British Government withdrew "previous exemptions to citizens of the Chinese Republic" in regard to entry into the colony "in view of the very serious overcrowding of the colony, with consequent danger to public health and to food and water supplies." Statement by the Minister of State for Colonial Affairs, Dugdale, 24 May 1950. *H.C. Deb.*, 475 (1950) 2054. This measure was considered necessary by the British in the interests of the Colony's economy and health but invited an immediate protest from Peking. See statement by Vice-Foreign Minister Chang Han-fu in *CMR* (Oct 1950) Supplement, 9-10. In 1953 the long tradition of free access for the Chinese came to an end when legal Chinese immigration was virtually stopped. As a trial, all restrictions on Chinese immigration were relaxed in February 1956, but in September 1956 the quota system had to be imposed again. UK, Colonial Annual Report, *Hong Kong* : 1956 (London, 1957) 5.

35 Lewis Gen, n. 1, 8.

36 *H.C. Deb.*, 464 (1948-9) 1340.

37 *Ibid.*, 473 (1950) 780.

38 H.J. Collar, "Recent Developments of British Commercial Relations with China," *JRCAS* (Jan 1954) 33.

39 "Indeed, during the first three years of the new regime in China the Hong Kong trade was running at the remarkable level of £123 million per annum more than twelve times that of the direct trade." "Britiain, Hong Kong and the China Trade," By a Peking Observer, *FEER* (15 Nov 1956) 628.

40 *Hong Kong* : 1956, n. 34, 10.

41 *The Times*, 9 Jan 1950.

42 *Ibid.*, 26 Sep 1950.

43 See Szczepanik, n. 6, 158.

44 See "China's Foreign Trade and Prospects for Hong Kong & Britain," Editorial in *FEER* (26 Aug 1954) 261.

45 Chinese imports from Hong Kong increased sharply in the second half of 1950 and the first half of 1951 mainly because of heavy purchases in anticipation of commodity scarcity in international markets and of the extension of trade control in Hong Kong. In the second half of 1951, however, on account of Hong Kong's embargo on exports of strategic materials, imports from Hong Kong were sharply reduced by about two-thirds. UN, Department of Economic Affairs, *Economic Survey of Asia and the Far East*, 1951 (New York, 1952) 162-3.

46 In January 1951 the export figures stood at HK $235 million, by December 1951 they dwindled to 52 million and further dropped to 18 million by February 1952. It was computed that had Hong Kong continued to send goods to China during these 14 months at approximately the same rate as it did in January 1951 (*i.e.* at the rate of $235 million per month) it would have exported $1648 million worth of additional goods more than it actually did. From a purely business point of view, the loss of so much of export trade "to local traders is tremendous." Mercator, "Hong Kong's Trading Relations with People's China," *FEER* (8 May 1952) 602. In 1951 exports to China constituted 36.2 per cent of the Colony's total exports; in 1952, 18.3 per cent; in 1953, 19.7 per cent; in 1954, 16.2 per cent; in 1955, 7.2 per cent; and in 1956, 4.2 per cent. Thereafter, up to 1960 it had remained at about 4 per cent level. Szczepanik, n. 6, 158.

47 Statements on 7 and 10 May 1951. *H.C. Deb.*, 487 (1950-1) 1599, 2179 and 2182-5.

48 Colonial Reports, *Hong Kong* 1951 (London, 1952) 7-8. "In the initial application of the American restrictions furthermore practically no distinction was made between Hong Kong and China."

49 Between 1951 and 1952 earnings from the entrepot trade, the traditional source of the colony's income, fell from HK $644 million to HK $421 million, that is by about 35 per cent. Szczepanik, n. 6, 48.

50 See Chapter Eight.

51 *FEER* (20 Mar 1952) 386.

52 Yuan-Li Wu, *An Economic Survey of Communist China* (New York, 1956) 485.

53 *The Statesman*, 31 Oct 1953.

54 Both these movements were launched towards the end of 1951 and brought to conclusion in the first half of 1952. See Chapter Eight. As a result of these drives all purchases from Hong Kong by Chinese government agencies were suspended. This further aggravated the economic situation of the colony. Mercator, n. 46, 601-2.

55 See *H. C. Deb.*, 501 (1951-2) 267. See also *The Times,* 5 Mar 1953.
56 *H. C. Deb.*, 521 (1953-4) 43. Written Answers.
57 *Ibid.* "British exports to China mainland passing through Hong Kong showed a 17-time increase in January and February 1953, over the first two months in the previous year." *Ceylon Daily News,* 10 Jun 1953
58 *The Times,* 5 Mar 1953. "It is open to doubt," P. S. Cassidy, Chairman of the Hong Kong General Chamber of Commerce stated on 31 March 1952, "whether China is getting the value of her exports" to Communist countries of Europe. If this is the case, the *Far Eastern Economic Review* editorial remarked : "China must soon discover the disadvantages of her position and should react accordingly, given peace in Korea, a definite return to normalcy should ensue and with it a more normal flow of trade towards which both Hong Kong and China are looking." "Hope for Hong Kong's Future," Editorial in *FEER* (24 Apr 1952) 541.
59 *H. C. Deb.*, 521 (1953-4) 44. Written Answers.
60 Statement by Lord Mancroft. Quoted in *FEER* (1 Jan 1954) 97.
61 While export restrictions were considerably eased in case of the USSR in 1954, no changes were made in relation to China. The Colonial Report for 1956, therefore, stated : "Export controls over strategic items...remained unchanged, except that reasonable shipments of particular items of relatively low strategic value were permitted to the China Mainland in cases where the civilian end-use of the commodities was satisfactorily established." *Hong Kong* 1956, n. 34, 79-80.
62 Colonial Reports, *Hong Kong* 1955 (London, 1956) 4.
63 "Prospects for Hong Kong's Prosperity," Editorial in *FEER* (17 Jun 1954) 751-2. The purchase by the Chinese Government of a number of ships that trade direct between European and Chinese ports and the development of the former French concession port of Kwangchow, now renamed Tsam Kong, also affected the position of Hong Kong *vis-a-vis* China. Luard, n. 2, 197.
64 Yuan-Li Wu, n. 52, 499.
65 There had been a steady increase in the export of Chinese goods to the Southeast Asian countries via Hong Kong. By 1957, although Hong Kong's trade with Peking had risen to $220 million, its exports to Communist China reached a new low of $22 million, while Peking's exports to Hong Kong—roughly one-third of which were re-exported—reached a new high of $198 million. A. Doak Barnett, *Communist China and Asia* (New York, 1960) 239.
66 G. F. Hudson, "British Relations with China," *Current History* (Dec 1957) 329.
67 UK, Colonial Reports, *Hong Kong* 1953 (London, 1954) 6.
68 UK, Colonial Reports, *Hong Kong* 1952 (London, 1953) 4; and *Hong Kong* 1954 (London, 1955) 2.
69 See *Hong Kong* 1951, n. 48, 9-10.
70 *WWCC* : 1949-50, 135.

71 *The Times*, 5 Sep 1950.
72 *PC* (16 Oct 1950) 6.
73 *NB* (5 Mar 1953) 8-9.
74 *PC* (1 Feb 1952) 27. In its note to Peking on 26 May, Britain rejected as "completely without foundation," Chinese allegations about the persecution of Chinese inhabitants in Hong Kong. *FEER* (12 Jun 1952) 749.
75 *The Mainichi*, 4 Mar 1952. The Hong Kong Government blamed the Colony's strongest labour group, the pro-communist Federation of Trade Unions, for the riots. *Singapore Standard*, 3 Mar 1952. Peking Radio and newspapers accused Hong Kong authorities of plotting to turn the island into an advance base for the invasion of China and asserted that Hong Kong was harbouring ' Chiang Kai-shek's gangsters and shielding their infiltration into China to create disturbance and loot." *The Hindu*, 3 Mar 1952.
76 *Hong Kong* 1953, n. 67, 6. Seven people were killed and five wounded in the incident.
77 *Hong Kong* 1954, n. 68, 13.
78 *PC* (1 May 1955) 40. For this "grave political conspiracy," *People's Daily* stated on 15 April 1955, "the responsibility of British authorities was "inescapable." *NB* (22 Apr 1955) 5.
79 The first note dated 31 January 1956 demanded that the Chiang plane be detained. The second note, submitted on 4 February 1956, expressed the belief that the British authorities would not allow Hong Kong to be used as a base and a refuge for carrying out destructive military activities against China. The third note, delivered on 16 March 1956, characterized the British action in permitting the personnel of the aircraft to return to Taiwan as "an unfriendly action towards China." The note concluded with the following words : "The Chinese Government cannot tolerate the activities of the Chiang Kai-shek clique making use of Hong Kong to endanger China's security being connived at." *NB* (31 Mar 1956) 6. On 28 March 1956 the Secretary of State for Colonies explained the circumstances in which the pilot was allowed to leave in the following words : "In this case we do not recognise a state of belligerency between Chinese Nationalists and Chinese Communists and I therefore think that our action in this matter was right." *H. C. Deb.*, 550 (1955-6) 2161.
80 "Disturbances took place after a Government official removed Nationalist flags which, contrary to regulations, had been posted on the walls of Government buildings. Crowds began to set fire to cars, schools and other buildings, to loot shops and to attack Europeans in the streets." Evan Luard, n. 2, 190-1. The *People's Daily* called it "the most serious riots of this century." *JMJP*, 24 Oct 1956. In the riots, 56 people were killed and 3,500 arrested. *The Statesman*, 18 Oct 1956.
81 *JMJP*, 14 Oct 1956. See also *The Times*, 15 Oct 1956.
82 *PC* (16 Nov 1956) 44.

83 *Ibid.*, 44. See also *JMJP*, 24 Oct 1956.
84 Foreign Languages Press, *Oppose U. S. Occupation of Taiwan and "Two Chinas" Plot* (Peking, 1958) 105.
85 *CT* (25 Apr 1958) 10.
86 Chinese Note to Britain, 10 June 1958. *CT* (25 Jun 1958) 2.
87 *PR* (2 Sep 1958) 3, 15-6 and 2.
88 *Ibid.*, 16. It is significant to note that the shelling of Quemoy began on 26 August 1958. *People's Daily* Editorial of 28 August 1958 stated : "Of late, in coordination with the efforts of the U.S. and its Chiang Kai-shek hirelings to create tension in the Far East and the Taiwan Straits, Britain has not only allowed U. S. troops to land at Singapore but has turned Hong Kong into a haunt for them. It has even sent its military aircraft stationed in Hong Kong to intrude over our territorial air, for reconnaissance and harassment. It was in these very serious circumstances that the Hong Kong British authorities set their armed police on to brutally attack totally unarmed Chinese teachers, students and newspapermen...Up to this moment, the Chinese people have shown the greatest tolerance over the whole series of hostile actions of the British Government and the Hong Kong British authorities. However, the tolerance of the Chinese people cannot be limitless." Quoted in R. L. Walker, n. 4, 146-7.
89 E. Lauterpacht, "The Contemporary Practice of the United Kingdom in the field of International Law—Survey and Comment, VII," *International and Comparative Law Quarterly* (London) (Jan 1959) 182.
90 *PR* (8 Dec 1967) 38.
91 *PR* (11 Aug 1967) 30.
92 *PR* (26 May 1967) 51.
93 *PR* (28 Jul 1967) 23. *Hsinhna* Correspondent Hsueh Ping was arrested on 11 Jul 1967 and released on 16 November 1968.
94 *PR* (8 Sep 1967) 29.
95 *PR* (19 May 1967) 14-5.
96 *PR* (7 Jul 1967) 37.
97 *PR* (14 Jul 1967) 35.
98 *PR* (25 Aug 1967) 22.
99 *PR* (20 Oct 1967) 35 and 37.
100 *PR* (1 Mar 1968) 28-9.
101 *PR* (22 Mar 1968) 13 and 39.
102 *PR* (31 May 1968) 30-1.
103 *PR* (2 Aug 1968) 31; and *PR* (23 Aug 1968) 8 and 30-1.
104 *PR* (30 Aug 1968) 29-30.
105 Luard, n. 2, 193.
106 Richard Hughes, "Peking's Tolerance Based on Mutual Gain," *The Times*, 21 Oct 1972.
107 Gary Catron, "Hong Kong and Chinese Foreign Policy," *China Quarterly* (Jul-Sep 1972) 409.
108 "This proposal," Selwyn Lloyd observed, "raises a number of

issues which are still under consideration....What has to be thought about very carefully is whether it would improve our relations with the Chinese People's Republic or otherwise." *H. C. Deb.*, 553 (1955-6) 1083 and 556 (1955-6) 21. It is worth recalling that in 1883 the Hong Kong Government opposed the suggestion about the Chinese Imperial government being represented in Hong Kong by a consul on the grounds that the Chinese population might begin to look to the Chinese consul rather than the colonial government as the source of authority. Luard, n. 2, 193.

109 Hong Kong had shown considerable resilience and resourcefulness and had passed the critical phase in its economy created by the embargo. Hong Kong did not exclusively depend upon China; "it is also the entrepot to the countries of the Far East in general, and its extensive banking and insurance activities contribute much both to the prosperity and surviving power of this colony." Lewis Gen, "Hong Kong Today," *EW* (Nov 1952) 16.

110 Without the New Territories the British colony of Hong Kong, possessing no raw-materials, no local coal, oil or other sources of power, lacking adequate food or water supply, could hardly remain a viable economic unit.

111 Barnett, n. 65, 202

112 *JMJP* Editorial, 26 Oct 1955, as reproduced in *NB* (2 Nov 1955) 4-5.

113 *Times of India*, 8 Nov 1972.

Chapter Seven : Chinese Representation in the UN

1 Statement by Foreign Secretary Bevin, 14 December 1950. *H. C. Deb.*, 482 (1950-1) 1462.

2 Between 19 January 1950 and 26 August 1950 Peking appointed delegates to 21 international bodies. *CMR* (Oct 1950), Supplement, 5-6.

3 Statement by Bevin, 29 November 1950. *H. C. Deb.*, 481 1950-1) 1167.

4 *CMR*, n. 2, 2.

5 UN Doc. S/PV 458 (29 Dec 1949) 2.

6. *CMR*, n. 2, 2.

7 UN Doc. S/PV 459 (10 Jan 1950) 2-3.

8 *Ibid.*, 5-6.

9 *Ibid.*, S/PV 460 (12 Jan 1950) 12-3.

10 Malik was obviously referring to the British vote on President's ruling. The voting on the question of Chinese representation had not yet taken place.

11 *Ibid.*, 14-5

12 *Ibid.*, S/PV 461 (13 Jan 1950) 10.

13 Statement on 14 December 1950. *H. C. Deb.*, 482 (1950-1) 1458.

14 See *The Economist* (24 Jun 1950) 1375.

15 Statement by Premier Attlee, 12 September 1950. *H. C. Deb.*, 478 (1950) 953.

16 Nehru addressed this appeal to Stalin and US Secretary of State Dean Acheson on 13 July 1950. See *DSB* (31 Jul 1950) 170.

17 Acheson's reply to Nehru's letter, 18 July 1950. *Ibid.*, 170-1.

18 *CMR*, n. 2, 4.

19 *WWCC* : 1949-50, 135.

20 *PC* (1 Oct 1950) 27.

21 *H. C. Deb.*, 482 (1950-1) 1458.

22 Bevin instructed His Majesty's *charge d'affaires* in Peking to give that assurance on his behalf personally to Chinese authorities. Britain was quite aware that any attack on Manchuria was bound to produce a world war "almost immediately." *Ibid.*, 1461.

23 Thereafter, the UK cast its affirmative vote in favour of Peking in the Economic and Social Council. The Under-Secretary of State for Foreign Affairs, Ernest Davies, asserted on 1 November 1950 that Britain had taken the "lead" in bringing about "the change-over from Chinese Naionalist to People's Government" in the UN. He, however, regretted that "so far it has not been possible to obtain the necessary majority to bring about the change." *Ibid.*, 480 (1950) 241-2.

24 While the Indian resolution was defeated, the Canadian resolution, which set up a seven-nation Committee to study the question of Chinese representation and report back to the Assembly with recommendations, was adopted by the General Assembly. Of the seven nations on the Committee, only two (India and Poland) had recognized Peking. The Committee held several meetings in 1950 but was unable to agree on any recommendations after China became involved in the Korean War, and reported *impasse* on 8 October 1951.

25 UN Doc. A/PV 283 (25 Sep 1950) 88.

26 So long as Nationalist China continued to be represented in the UN, the West could take action under the UN Charter for the defence of Formosa against any Chinese Communist attack on Formosa. In the event of the Kuomintang being denied this privi-lege, the West would have been deprived of this legal basis of defending Formosa. "Chinese Communist attack on Formosa," Earl of Perth observed on 26 July 1950, "will be classed as 'aggres-sion,' since that Government would be attacking territory which the majority of the members of the Security Council recognize as being legitimately administered by the Nationalist Government of China." *H. L. Deb.*, 168 (1950) 782.

27 Statement on 14 December 1950. *H. C. Deb.*, 482 (1950-1) 1354-5. Emphasis added.

28 Although the British Government tried to demonstrate that they were taking the lead and pressing the matter before the General

Assembly, the fact remained that ever since the beginning of the Korean War, they had, in reality, no desire to see the decision taken on this issue until a satisfactory solution of the Korean problem had been reached. See Foreign Secretary Eden's statement, 19 November 1951. *Ibid.*, 494 (1951-2) 102.

29 *WWCC* : 1949-50, 151.
30 See Statement by Foreign Secretary Bevin, 14 December 1950. *H. C. Deb.*, 482 (1950-1) 1458.
31 Statement by Lord Strabolgi, Labour Whip in the House of Lords. *H. L. Deb.*, 168 (1950) 777-8.
32 Statement by Parliamentary Under-Secretary of State for Foreign Affairs, Lord Henderson, 14 December 1950. *H. L. Deb.*, 169 (1950) 984-6. After referring to the "difference of view" between the UK and the USA over the question of China's seat in the UN, Premier Attlee and President Truman, in their Joint Communique on 8 December 1950, observed : "We are determined to prevent it from interfering with our united effort in support of our common objectives." *DSB* (18 Dec 1950) 960.
33 *H. C. Deb.*, 482 (1950-1) 1458.
34 Statement by Bevin, 14 December 1950. *Ibid.*
35 "During all that time," the British delegate, Sir Alan Burns, stated in the UN Trusteeship Council, "his delegation had been hoping that the People's Republic of China, which claimed a seat in the United Nations, would recognize the obligations of Member States of the United Nations, in particular the obligation to settle its disputes by peaceful means." Burns was pointing to the British desire that Peking refrain from intervention in Korea. UN Doc., Trusteeship Council, 346th Meeting (5 Jun 1951) 2. For the first time since September 1950, Burns voted in favour of postponement of any discussion of the question of Chinese representation.
36 Statement by Sir Alan Burns. *Ibid.*, 2.
37 *H. C. Deb.*, 489 (1950-1) 1380-1. Emphasis added.
38 Donald Maclean, *British Foreign Policy Since Suez 1956-1968* (London, 1970) 308.
39 On 18 June 1952 Foreign Secretary Eden expressed his "complete agreement" with Morrison's statement of 27 June 1951 because the conditions "which the previous Government found unaccepable for the support of China's membership at that time applies now; that is, the fact that she is, actually breaking the rules of the club that she desires to join." *H. C. Deb.*, 502 (1951-2) 1183-4.
40 "All the other questions," including that of Peking's admission in the UN, Lord Chancellor, Viscount Jowitt, stated on 2 May 1951, "which I agree are exceedingly difficult—Formosa and the like—are questions which will arise only if and when we get our cease-fire" in Korea. *H. L. Deb.*, 171 (1951) 682-5. In his speech before the UN General Assembly on 11 November 1952 Foreign Secretary Eden referred to Italy, Portugal and Ceylon, which he said "are still

excluded from their rightful place in this organization," but he did not say a word about Communist China. UN Doc. A/PV 393 (11 Nov 1952) 209.

41 UN Doc. A/BUR/SR 77 (10 Nov 1951) 17. See also A/PV 542 (13 Nov 1951) 103.

42 In reply to a question on 2 July 1952 Minister of State Selwyn Lloyd observed : "I think that when an armistice is concluded there [Korea] we may hope to make some progress over this difficult matter." *H. C. Deb.*, 503 (1951-2) 403.

43 *H. C. Deb.*, 512 (1952-3) 2078.

44 On 21 January 1953 Eden simply said that the UK was not "prepared to take any initiative in this matter," so long as Peking participated in aggression in Korea. *Ibid.*, 510 (1952-3) 201.

45 *PC* (16 Apr 1953) 5-7.

46 *H. C. Deb.*, 513 (1952-3) 1077.

47 *Ibid.*, 518 (1952-3) 213.

48 *DSB* (27 Jul 1953) 105.

49 *H. C. Deb.*, 518 (30 Jul 1953) 1557-8.

50 *Ibid.*, 1604-6.

51 UN Doc. A/PV 432 (15 Sep 1953) 5.

52 In the beginning of 1950, the United States regarded the question of China's admission in the UN as "a procedural question involving the credentials of a representative of a member." But now it was determined to "invoke the veto if necessary," in the Security Council and to regard it as an "important matter," requiring two-thirds vote in the General Assembly. Statement by Dulles, 8 July 1954. *DSB* (19 Jul 1954) 87. William F. Knowland, majority leader in the Senate, threatened US withdrawal from the world organization in case "Communist China is voted into membership into the United Nations." *NYT*, 2 Jul 1954.

53 Statement by Premier Churchill, 14 July 1954. *H. C. Deb.*, 530 (1954-5) 494.

54 *Ibid.*, 494.

55 This was evident from C. R. Attlee's remark that "unless we have in contemplation a long-term policy towards China" regarding Formosa and seat at UNO "we shall not get a settlement, easily, if at all, of these immediate matters," *i. e.* Indo-China and Korea. *H. C. Deb.*, 530 (1953-4) 488.

56 Statement by Premier Churchill, 14 July 1954. *Ibid.*, 495, 492 and 494.

57 *Ibid.*, 545.

58 *Ibid.*, 587-9.

59 See Eden's statement in the House of Commons, 26 July 1954. *H. C. Deb.*, 531 (1953-4) 26.

60 *NYT*, 1 Sep 1954.

61 Votes cast in favour of Peking were 7 in 1954 as compared to 10 in 1953. Abstentions were 5 in 1954 as against 2 in 1953.

62 Council on Foreign Relations, *The United States in World Affairs* :

1954 (New York, 1956) 265-6.

63 UN Doc. A/PV 473 (21 Sep 1954) 6-7.

64 *Notes et etudes Documentaires* (Paris) No. 1977 (3 Feb 1955) 12.

65 See UN Doc. S/3354, 27.

66 UN Doc. S/3355, 27.

67 Royal Institute of International Affairs, *Documents on International Affairs* : 1955 (London, 1958) 449-50. Commenting on Chou's cable Foreign Secretary Eden stated on 7 Februaıy 1955 : "I do not consider that the tone and content of the reply of the Chinese People's Republic to the invitation to the Security Council is calculated to promote a settlement of this question" of China's entry in the UN. *H. C. Deb.*, 536 (1954-5) 169. Written Answers.

68 *NB* (6 Jul 1955) 10-1.

69 *JMJP* Editorial, 24 Sep 1955, as translated in *NB* (10 Oct 1955).

70 *JMJP* Editorial, 21 Sep 1955, as translated in *NB* (28 Sep 1955).

71 UN Doc. A/PV 516 (20 Sep 1955) 6, 8 and 4.

72 UN Doc. A/PV 529 (30 Sep 1955) 165-6.

73 *NB* (10 Oct 1955).

74 *NB* (30 Nov 1955).

75 Another large-scale influx of new members to the UN occurred at the 15th session of the UN General Assembly in 1960 when 13 newly-independent countries of Africa were admitted. This again swelled the votes in favour of Peking. The US resolution was adopted by 42 votes for, 34 against and 22 abstentions. If the 12 African countries under French influence had not abstained, but had supported China, then a majority of the UN members would have voted in favour of Peking.

76 During his visit to Washington in 1956, Eden, not for the first time, sounded Eisenhower and Dulles on the pɔssibility of reopening the question. Against his hosts' contention that, owing to the state of American opinion, "a move to get China into the United Nations now...would be fatal," he still argued, as he had often done before, the case for seating the People's Republic. There was now a truce in the Far East, he said, and the United Nations was a universal organisation in which one must expect to have unpleasant people. But he came away empty-handed. See Anthony Eden *The Full Circle* (London 1960) 333. See also Donald Maclean, n. 38, 308-9.

77 UN Doc. A/PV 684 (23 Sep 1957) 90. Exactly similar words were used by the British delegate Beeley at the 15th session. See UN Doc. A/PV 884 (3 Oct 1960) 361.

78 UN Doc. A/BUR/SR 108 (14 Nov 1956) 12.

79 UN Doc. A/BUR/SR 112 (19 Sep 1957) 9.

80 UN Doc. A/BUR/SR 118 (19 Sep 1958) 10-1.

81 UN Doc. A/BUR/SR 121 (16 Sep 1959) 3.

82 UN Doc. A/PV 753 (22 Sep 1958) 76.

83 UN Doc. A/PV 580 (16 Nov 1956) 75-6.

84 UN Doc. A/PV 755 (23 Sep 1958) 101.

85 UN Doc. A/PV 754 (23 Sep 1958) 95. Commenting on the statement

of Selwyn Lloyd that the discussion of the subject would "spilt the organization up the middle," one British writer observed : "This is a curious argument to use. If no subject were ᴛo be discussed except those on which agreement was assured, it is difficult to know what the organization could effectively achieve." Evan Luard, *Britain and China* (London, 1962) 244.

86 UN Doc. A/PV 754 (23 Sep 1958) 85.
87 UN Doc. A/PV 803 (22 Sep 1959) 92.
88 *Ibid.*, 93.
89 *JMJP* Editorial, 10 Oct 1960, as translated in *CT* (25 Oct 1960).
90 *Ibid.*
91 *The Observer* (London), as reproduced in *Hindustan Times*, 31 Oct 1960.
92 *H. C. Deb.* (Weekly) No. 443 (7-9 February 1961) 438.
93 *Hindustan Times*, 13 Nov 1960.
94 *Times of India*, 28 Jan 1961.
95 *DSB* (10 Apr 1961) 523.
96 See *JMJP* Editorial, 14 July 1961, as reproduced in *PR* (21 Jul 1961) 5-6. It was obvious that Peking was not inclined to surrender its rights on Taiwan, which the separate ɪepresentation of Nationalist China in the UN seemed to imply, for the dubious advantage of becoming a member of the World Organization.
97 UN Doc. A/PV 1069 (1 Dec 1961) 905-6.
98 Statement by the British Minister of State. UN Doc. A/PV 1079 (14 Dec 1961) 1045.
99 UN Doc. A/L. 360 and A/L. 375.
100 UN Doc. A/PV 1080 (15 Dec 1961) 1070. In voting for the Soviet draft resolution during the Seventeenth session (UN Doc. A/L 395) Godber offered the same explanation of his vote as in 1961. See UN Doc. A/PV 1162 (30 Oct 1962). Replying to a question in the House of Commons on 13 December 1965, Minister of State George Thomson stated that the Security Council and the General Assembly were separate organs of the UN and the decisions of the former were not binding on the latter. Nevertheless, he thought it was the right view of the relations between the Assembly and the Security Council that the General Assembly should remain the appropriate organ of the United Nations for reaching decisions of principle about changes in China's representation. *H. C. Deb.*, 722 (1965-66) 908. If Peking occupied "China seat in the United Nations," Minister of State Mrs. White observed on 28 June 1966, it would naturally involve the acceptance by China of the obligations imposed upon members by the Charter. *Ibid.*, 730 (1966-67) 217. Written Answers,
101 According to Evan Luard, Formosa could be given representation in the UN on a "temporary" basis and as an "exceptional" case in the special circumstances following civil war in China. Although this solution would not be acceptable to either Peking or Taipeh, "it would be at least a first step towards the rationalization of

existing absurdity." Luard, n. 85, 245.
102 UN Doc. A/PV 1801.
103 *H. C. Deb.*, 801 (29 May 1970) 605. Written Answers.
104 UN Doc. A/PV 1848.
105 *H. C. Deb.*, 822 (2 Aug 1971) 1068-9.
106 UN Doc. A/PV 1973 (21 Oct 1971) 67-70.
107 *H. C. Deb.*, 825 (4 Nov 1971) 480-1.
108 Statement by Foreign Secretary Alec Douglas-Home. *Ibid.*, 345.
109 *Ibid.*, 482.

Chapter Eight : Trade

1 UK, Board of Trade, *Report of the United Kingdom Trade Mission to China, October to December* 1946 (London, 1948) 171.
2 In early 1949, the Central Committee of the Chinese Communist Party resolved that within the next 3-5 years national production, both agricultural and industrial, should be restored to pre-war levels, and that within the next 10-15 years the relative weight of industrial production in national economy should be raised from about 10% to 30%—40% so that China could be gradually transformed from an agricultural into an industrial country. J.C. Tsao, "Science and Industry in New China," *CD* (28 Jun 1949) 15-6.
3 *Report of the United Kingdom Trade Mission to China*, n. 1.
4 Article by O.M. Green. See *The Globe News*, 28 Jun 1949. See also C.F. Fang, "Industrial Policy in Liberated China," *CD* (7 Sep 1948) 8-9.
5 O.M. Green, "British Trade with China," *EW* (Feb 1951) 34-5. British ships were permitted, as they had not been under the Nationalists, to transport goods and passengers between Chinese ports. Moreover, it was reported that as a result of the telegram addressed to Mao Tse-tung taxation imposed on a large British company was reduced by 30%. Evan Luard, *Britain and China* (London, 1962) 132.
6 The heavy air raid by Kuomintang planes on the Shanghai Power Company's works on 6 February 1950 was especially serious as it brought most of the big industries of the city to a standstill and inflicted serious losses on British commercial concerns. See O.M. Green, "Shanghai Faces Ruin," *EW* (May 1950) 16-7.
7 *H.C. Deb.*, 475 (1950) 2086.
8 See O.M. Green, n. 5, 34-5.
9 While in 1950 only four Communist countries traded with China, their number increased to 11 in 1954. China's trade with the Soviet Union and the People's Democracies constituted 26% of the total value of its trade in 1950, 61% in 1951, 70% in 1952, 75% in 1953 and 80% in 1954. C.F. Remer, ed., *Three Essays on the*

International Economies of Communist China (Mishigan, 1959) 210-1.

10 The five-Anti movement against bribery, tax evasion, fraud, theft of state assets and leakage of state secrets was officially launched in November 1951 and continued until the end of May 1952.

11 Chinese Committee for the Promotion of International Trade, *New China's Economic Achievements* : 1949-1952 (Peking, 1952) 158 and 281.

12 Choh-ming Li, *Economic Development of Communist China* (California, 1959) 6. See also Yuan-Li Wu, *An Economic Survey of Communist China* (New York, 1956) 381.

13 Choh-ming Li, n. 12, 175. According to Yuan-Li Wu, the share of state trading in foreign trade rose from 70% of imports and 53.5% of exports in 1950 to 92% of total imports and exports in 1953. Yuan-Li Wu, n. 12, 461.

14 Chou En-lai, *Report on the Work of the Government* (Peking, 1954) 18-9.

15 See Raja Hutheesing, *The Great Peace* (New York, 1953) 167, 149, 151 and 165.

16 G.E. Mitchell, "China and Britain: Their Commercial and Industrial Relations," *JRCAS* (Jul-Oct 1952) 251.

17 Established in 1889, the China Association has been a very old and influential organisation of British businessmen specially concerned with the Chinese market. The objects for which it "exists," E. Nathan observed, "are to endeavour to keep Her Majesty's Foreign Office straight in dealing with China affairs." *Ibid.*, 246.

18 *Ibid.*, 251. See also H.J. Collar, "Recent Developments of British Commercial Relations with China," *JRCAS* (Jan 1954) 26.

19 See Hutheesing, n. 15, 134.

20 See Collar, n. 18, 27 and 29.

21 See *Ibid.*, 36. How the managers, etc. of foreign firms came to be harassed by their Chinese employees is aptly described by Mitchell in the following words: "One of the more distinguished and reputable of our British merchants in Shanghai was recently stopped within two hours of the time he was due to leave, by a claim for £600 advanced by a coolie who had left his employment several years previously, and he only just managed to catch his train and thus snatch at the opportunity to leave, which might not present itself again for a very long time, by paying £300. Only one word can be applied to this kind of thing, and it is 'blackmail'." Mitchell, n. 16, 251.

22 Statement by Lord Reading, Minister of State in the Foreign Office, 18 February 1953 *H.L. Deb.*, 180 (1952-3) 507-8.

23 Lord Reading agreed that this process had probably reduced the value of the assets of British firms in Shanghai alone from £300 million to less than £40 million, that is about one-tenth of that sum. *Ibid.*, 189 (20 Oct 1954) 503-4.

24 *H.C. Deb.*, 505 (1951-2) 194.

25 *The Times*, 9 Oct 1952.
26 Royal Institute of International Affairs, *Survey of International Affairs* 1952 (London, 1955) 348.
27 *H.C. Deb.*, 577 (1957-8) 47-9. Written Answers.
28 *NB* (5 Mar 1953) 9-10.
29 Collar, n. 18, 28.
30 "Theoretically a firm may wind up on paying its employees three months wages and settling its liabilities. In practice this entails paying in addition a month's bonus for each year of service to every employee, plus about another month's wages to enable him to go home. This may total a lump sum payment of over two years wages apart from income tax and other imposts. These additional imposts include commodity taxes and business turn-over taxes, the former averaging 16 per cent of the manufacturing price. Even then, the Government may delay the issue of an exit permit. Conversely, some British businessmen who have temporarily left the country are finding it difficult, if not impossible, to obtain re-entry visas." *The Times*, 16 Jul 1952.
31 *The Times*, 11 Sep 1951.
32 *Cmd.* 8639, 2-4. British firms were being squeezed into bankruptcy and British managers and their assistants lived in China "as virtual prisoners, unable to do business, unable to leave, with all the privileges of their old life disappearing round them." See H. Trevelyan, *Worlds Apart : China 1953-55 Soviet Union 1962-65* (London, 1971) 54.
33 *Ibid.*, 7. By winding up their businesses, the British washed their hands off millions of pounds worth of their investments. They also faced a recurring loss of income which the UK derived by way of interest, profits and dividends, payments for use of British ships and "earnings from thousand and one financial services of the city of London." The income from invisible exports had considerably helped Britain in balancing its foreign trade for over a century. *The Times*, 12 Jun 1961.
34 *PC* (1 Aug 1952) 34-5.
35 *Survey of International Affairs*, n. 26, 347.
36 *H.C. Deb.*, 510 (1952-3) 107-8. Written Answers. See also statement by Chairman C. Blaker at the ordinary yearly general meeting of the Hong Kong and Shanghai Banking Corporation, 5 March 1954. *EW* (Mar 1954) 52.
37 *H.C. Deb.*, No. 44, 107-8. Written Answers.
38 See *H.L. Deb.*, 180 (1952-3) 668-70 and 507-8.
39 *H.C. Deb.*, 518 (1953-4) 1606.
40 *Ibid.*, 524 (1953-4) 18.
41 "After a delay of three years, 12 exit permits have now been granted to British businessmen in China, who will now be able to leave the country." *The Times*, 4 Jun 1954.
42 *H.L. Deb.*, 189 (1953-4) 504.
43 *The Times*, 27 Jul 1955. In December 1959 the Shanghai correspondent of the *Far Eastern Economic Review* reported the closure of the

last remaining British import-export firm in Shanghai, the China Engineers Ltd. *FEER* (24 Dec 1959) 1008.

44 *H.C. Deb.*, 581 (1957-8) 24.

45 H. Trevelyan, n. 32, 58-9.

46 Mitchell, n. 16, 246.

47 "We have not been trading in China", Collar observed on 30 September 1953, "but trade with China has continued at a fair volume, and in fact the volume is higher than that we would have anticipated." Collar, n. 18, 32-3.

48 The obvious reference here is to the speeches of Nan Han-chen and Lei Jen-min, leader and member of the Chinese delegation, to the International Economic Conference, Moscow, 4-12 April 1952. On 7 April 1952, Lei Jen-min stated: "Trade relations between China and Britain go back over 270 years....Under appropriate conditions, with artificial barriers removed...it is estimated...that in another two or three years, quite apart from the trade with the Soviet Union and People's Democracies, trade between China and private enterprise countries can reach between 15,000 million and 19,000 million roubles." *PC* (16 May 1952) 33-4. See also *PC* (1 May 1952) 27-32.

49 *Cmd.* 8639, 3.

50 *Ibid.*, 4. "Both Her Majesty's Government and the firms themselves remain convinced of the need and desirability for British trade with China to be continued." Statement by Foreign Secretary Eden in the House of Commons, 20 May 1952. *Ibid.*, 7.

51 On 29 July 1952, however, it was stated in the House of Commons that the value of orders definitely placed with Great Britain as a result of the Moscow Conference amounted to only £70,000 worth of chemicals and £500,000 worth of wooltops. *H.C. Deb.*, 504 (1951-2) 1255-6. The Secretary for Overseas Trade, Mockeson, said that he had no knowledge of the contracts to the value of £6 million. *Ibid.*, 1256.

52 *PC* (1 Aug 1952) 34-5.

53 C.M. Woodhouse, *British Foreign Policy since the Second World War* (London, 1961) 126.

54 "In 1950, our total trade with the capitalist countries exceeded the record of the pre-war year of 1936. Especially our trade with Great Britain showed marked increase, this trade in 1950 registering an increase of 220 per cent over 1948." Article by Kao Ping-shu in *World Culture*, 5 Oct 1954 as translated in *Current Background* (Hong Kong) No. 307 (6 Dec 1954) 13. In the first half of 1951 "Free World" exports to China were at US $314 million. They dropped to about $130 million in the second half. W.W. Rostow, *The Prospects for Communist China* (New York, 1954) 250.

55 Donald Maclean, *British Foreign Policy Since Suez* 1956-1968 (London, 1970) 309.

56 See Collar, n. 18, 32.

57 Statement by the Secretary for Overseas Trade, Mockeson, 28 April 1953. *H.C. Deb.*, 514 (1952-3) 1940. British exports to China during

January-March 1952 were £0.197 million while its imports from China were £0.981 million. Statement by the President of the Board of Trade, 1 May 1952. *Ibid.*, 499 (1951-2) 1653.

58 A Sino-British Trade Agreement for 1952 was signed in Moscow on 12 April 1952 by Nan Han-chen, Head of the Chinese Communist Delegation to the Moscow International Economic Conference and Lord John Boyd Orr, Head of the British Delegation. The agreement provided for exchange of goods worth £20 million, that is, £10 million each way.

59 A British trade delegation under the auspices of the British Council for the Promotion of International Trade, which was established after the Moscow Conference, visited Peking in June-July 1953 and concluded a Commercial Agreement to the value of £30 million.

60 "We have never neglected any possibility of developing trade with any country....Some people think that the expansion of our trade with the Soviet Union and the People's Democracies will adversely affect our trade with the Western countries. This is utterly wrong," Yeh Chi-chuang, Minister of Foreign Trade, said on 30 September 1952. *New China's Economic Achievements*, n. 11, 242. On 4 February 1953 Chou En-lai stated: "We do not discriminate against any capitalist country that is willing to develop trade relations with us on terms of equality and mutual benefit." *PC* (16 Feb 1953) Supplement 3-8.

61 Harold Davies, "The Moscow Economic Conference," *EW* (May 1952) 28.

62 Statement on 22 April 1952. *H.C. Deb.*, 499 (1951-2) 365.

63 See *NYT*, 21 May 1953 and *H.C. Deb.*, 514 (1952-3) 1940. For the total Sino-British trade in 1952 and 1953 see Appendix 3.

64 See *Quarterly Economic Review of China and Hong Kong* (Mar 1954) 7.

65 *Cmd.* 8800, 6, 12-3, 15 and 45.

66 The British Council for the Promotion of International Trade, "a Communist front organisation," sponsored a trade delegation to China for the purpose of studying trade possibilities. This group concluded a Commercial Agreement with the China Import and Export Corporation on 6 July 1953 up to the value of £15 million each way. See Fa-li Ch'u-pan-hsie, *Chung-hua Jen-min Kung-he-kuo T'iao-yueh Chi* 1952-1953 (Peking, 1957) II, 380.

67 Statement on 18 June 1953. *H.C. Deb.*, 516 (1952-3) 1163.

68 See Report of the Senate Sub-Committee issued on 18 July 1953. *NYT*, 19 Jul 1953. See also statement of Senator Joseph R. McCarthy, 24 November 1953. *Ibid.*, 25 Nov 1953.

69 *BTJ* (12 Jun 1954) 1271.

70 *Ibid.* (17 Jul 1954) 54.

71 *Ibid.*, 104. At a press conference following the London talks, Harry Pilkington, President of the Federation of British Industries, described those discussions "a good first step towards the re-establishment of Sino-British trade on a more normal basis."

72 *Quarterly Economic Review of China and Hong Kong* (Mar 1955) 7. The mission consisted of 28 businessmen representing 30 British firms and was in China from 22 November 1954 to 2 December 1954. The joint statement issued at the end of the visit stated : "There is ample scope for further development of Sino-British trade. particularly when normal relations are restored." *FEER* (29 Sep 1955) 399.

73 *Quarterly Economic Review of China and Hong Kong*, n. 72, 7.

74 *H.L. Deb.*, 185 (1953-4) 277.

75 A. James, "U.K. Trade with China," *EW* (Dec 1954) 47. In an interview granted to Morgan Phillips, Secretary of the British Labour Party at Geneva on 19 July 1954, Premier Chou En-lai stated: "It is both possible and necessary to promote and expand industrial and commercial cooperation between the two countries on the basis of equality and mutual benefit. Such cooperation would help to improve the living conditions of the peoples of our two countries. The Government of the People's Republic of China attaches great importance to developing and expanding industrial and commercial connections with Britain. The Chinese *Charge d' Affaires* to be appointed to London will do his best in this respect." *NB* (28 Jul 1954) 2-3.

76 *Ibid.* (2 Mar 1955) 10-1.

77 Kayser Sung, "The China Trade Riddle," *FEER* (1 Sep 1960) 505.

78 *NB* (27 Apr 1955) 8-9.

79 Tsao Chung-shu, "More Trade with Britain," *China Reconstructs* (Apr 1955) 27-8.

80 Lu Hsu-chang, "Foreign Trade Expands," *Ibid.* (Jul-Aug 1954) 2-3.

81 "In 1954, capital goods made up 93.5 per cent of all commodities shipped from fraternal countries (in the case of the Soviet Union it was 97 per cent). Most of these are goods 'banned' for export to China by the United States government." Li Che-jen, "Fraternal Economic Cooperation," *Ibid.* (Aug 1955) 7.

82 Tsao Chung-shu, "The Embargo and China Trade," *EW* (Sep 1956) 44 and 60.

83 In September 1949 itself, the British and American Governments had already banned the export to China of machine tools, heavy lorries, aircraft parts, telephone and signal equipments and other items. Luard, n. 5, 141. In July 1950 Britain announced ban on the export of oil to China. *H.C. Deb.*, 477 (1950) 2256.

84 *Cmd.* 8366, 61-2.

85 See Statements in the United Nations, 25 January, 30 January and 1 February 1951. *Cmd.* 8159, 12-4, 16 and 20.

86 Statement by the British delegate, 17 May 1951. UN Doc. A/C. 1/ PV 443, 633.

87 Statement by H. Shawcross, President of the Board of Trade. *H.C. Deb.*, 487 (1950-1) 2176. Shawcross added : "We considered that it would reduce the chances of confining the conflict to Korea and reaching, at the end of the day, a reasonable settlement of that kind if we were to stop all trade with her." *Ibid.*, 2177.

88 *H.C. Deb.*, 489 (1950-1) 247-52.
89 C.M. Woodhouse, n. 53, 117.
90 Under the Control of Trade by Sea (China and North Korea) Order 1953, which was laid before Parliament on 16 March 1953 by the Minister of Transport, any British ship registered in the UK or colonies of 500 gross tons or more carrying any item of the strategic cargo to China or North Korea on or after 31 March 1953 was liable to a maximum penalty of £500 or two years imprisonment or both. *BTJ* (28 Mar 1953) 24.
91 *H.C. Deb.*, 546 (1955-6) 2094.
92 *H L. Deb.*, 181 (1952-3) 242-4.
93 *H.C. Deb.*, 514 (1952-3) 2102. On 23 April 1953 the Parliamentary Under Secretary of State for Foreign Affairs, Lord Reading, observed: "The time may come, sooner or later, when these restrictions will no longer enter into people's calculations at all. That will be blessed and most welcome day. Until that day we must look at this trade with these two parts of the world with some caution." *H.L. Deb.*, 181 (1952-3) 1215.
94 *H.C. Deb.*, 516 (1952-3) 1163.
95 *Ibid.*, 518 (1952-3) 2141. Emphasis added.
96 *H.L. Deb.*, 182 (1952-3) 50.
97 *H.C. Deb.*, 529 (1953-4) 1775-6.
98 *Ibid.*, 528 (24 May 1954) 17.
99 Statement by Earl of Gosford, Joint Parliamentary Under-Secretary of State for Foreign Affairs, 21 May 1958. *H.L. Deb.*, 209 (1957-8) 544.
100 Statement by Lord Mancroft, Joint Parliamentary Under-Secretary of State for Home Department, 20 January 1954. *Ibid.*, 185 (1953-4) 298.
101 *Ibid.*, 182 (1953-4) 40.
102 On 25 February 1955 P. Thorneycroft, President of the Board of Trade, told the House of Commons that the embargo list for China covered 480 items of industrial equipment compared with 250 such items in case of the USSR. *H.C. Deb.*, 524 (1953-4) 55. Written Answers. On 26 July 1954 he announced the revision of strategic controls on exports to the Soviet bloc, as distinct from exports to China, effective from 16 August 1954. He said: "The present embargo list will be reduced by one-third from about 250 to 170 items and the quantitative control list will be drastically cut from 90 to 20....The overall result will be substantial increase in the area of permitted trade." *Ibid.*, 531 (1953-4) 39-42.
103 Statement by Viscount Elibank, 21 October 1954. *H.L. Deb.*, 189 (1953-4) 565-6.
104 F.C. Jones in Royal Institute of International Affairs, *Survey of International Affairs: 1951* (London, 1954) 365.
105 Statement by Eden. *H.C. Deb.*, 531 (1953-4) 1599.
106 "There is no question whatever of our unilaterally altering the China list," Minister of State, Board of Trade, stated on 6 July 1954. *Ibid.*,

529 (1953-4) 1967.

107 Statement in UN General Assembly by Macmillan, 30 September 1955. UN Doc. A/PV 529, 165-6.

108 *FEER* (22 Mar 1956) 357.

109 Donald Maclean, n. 55, 310-1.

110 Anthony Eden, *The Full Circle* (London, 1960) 332 and 337-8.

111 Statement by Nutting, 11 April 1956. *H.C. Deb.*, 551 (1955-6) 202. To British businessmen, the tractor deal was "an indication of Chinese readiness to purchase essential equipment for development outside the Soviet bloc, than as a breach of the embargo." *TMER* (May 1956) 11.

112 On 13 April 1956, China sent its reply to the British notes of 23 February 1955 and 25 January 1956 to the effect that it was ready to consider registration of trade marks on each other's country on the conditions similar to those accorded by one nation to the other. While expressing satisfaction about Peking's decision in the matter, London inquired about the "names and addresses of the organisations to which the British companies should apply for the registration of trade marks" and expressed the hope that the British trade marks sent to the Chinese Foreign Ministry during the last two years would be recognised and given protection. *Chung-hua Jen-min Kung-he-kuo Tiao-yueh Chi*, n. 66, Vol. V: 1956 (Peking, 1958) 68-9.

113 *H.L. Deb.*, 202 (1956-7) 351.

114 Statement by Selwyn Lloyd, 28 January 1957. *H.C. Deb.*, 563 (1956-7) 111. Written Answers.

115 Statement by Lloyd, 19 December 1956. *Ibid.*, 562 (1956-7) 1263. The relaxation of controls, Lloyd stated on 28 January 1957, "is better dealt with on the basis of individual cases rather than general principles." *Ibid.*, 563 (1956-7) 671.

116 Editorial in *Eastern World*. See *EW* (Apr 1957) 9-10.

117 Chen Ming, Vice-Director, Ministry of Foreign Trade, welcomed the application of the exception rule by the British Government in connection with the embargo and was glad to see other countries following this example. "But this," he added, "is only the first step in the right direction. Our trade cannot be established on such a basis." *EW* (Sep 1956) 36.

118 Statement by D. Eccles, 30 January 1957. *H.C. Deb.*, 563 (1956-7) 202. Written Answers.

119 D. Eccles, 21 March 1957. *Ibid.*, 567 (1956-7) 528.

120 See Statement by Selwyn Lloyd, 19 December 1956. *Ibid.*, 562 (1956-7) 1264.

121 According to the statement of Swingler, M.P., the Paris Consultative Group met 50 times in the last 12 months to discuss the relaxation of controls on China trade. *Ibid.*, 568 (14 Apr 1957) 1903.

122 Remer, n. 9, 135-6. See also Choh-ming Li, n. 12, 186-8.

123 "The supply of capital goods from Russia being reduced," Remer observed, "Communist China is having to build up her trade with the West for that purpose," if Peking wanted to keep the pace of

its industrialization. Remer, n. 9, 145, 143 and 137. In his speech before the National People's Congress on 11 July 1957, Yeh Chi-chuang, Minister of Foreign Trade, pointed out that while "the Soviet Union has endeavoured to satisfy our demand for superior quality steel products," China was forced to buy in 1956 "some nickle from the capitalist nations." at a high price—"more than two times the price." *Current Background*, No. 468 (22 Jul 1957) 7.

124 Remer, n. 9, 97. Speaking about the proposals for the Second Plan before the 8th National Congress of the Communist Party of China on 16 September 1956, Chou En-lai disclosed that, during the Second Plan period, at least 30% of the needed machinery and equipment still could not be supplied domestically and would have to be imported, if China was to keep "a fairly high tempo for development of the national economy." Chou En-lai, *Report on the Proposals for the Second Five-year Plan for Development of the National Economy* (Peking, 1956) 66 and 51.

125 "The total volume of our foreign trade in 1953 was six times greater than in 1949." Lu Hsu-chang, n. 80, 2. As compared to $2739 million in 1952 China's foreign trade amounted to $4613 million in 1956. *Contemporary Japan* (Tokyo) 25 (1957-8) 215.

126 Peking was in a better position to trade with the West than with the Soviet bloc. Throughout 1950-56, China had a favourable trade balance with the former and an unfavourable one with the latter. Remer, n. 9, 150. See also *FEER* (15 Nov 1956) 628.

127 *TMER* (Jun 1957) 10.

128 *EW* (Apr 1957) 10.

129 *H.C. Deb.*, 567 (1956-7) 528.

130 *Ibid.*, 570 (1956-7) 37. Written Answers.

131 *Ibid.*, 568 (1956-7) 167.

132 Statement by Selwyn Lloyd, 30 May 1957. *Ibid.*, 571 (1956-7) 618. As a result of this decision some 270 items were released from the China embargo list. *H.L. Deb.*, 205 (1956-7) 399.

133 *H.C. Deb.*, 571 (1956-7) 618-9. For American reaction see *DSB* (13 May 1957) 722-3.

134 *Keesing's Contemporary Archives*: 1957-8, 15607.

135 At the meeting of China's National People's Congress in June 1957, it was disclosed that the total planned volume of exports and imports in 1957 would drop by 8.4% as compared with the high 1956 level. *TMER* (Aug' 1957) 7.

136 *Keesing's*, n. 134, 15608.

137 *BTJ* (7 Mar 1958) 528.

138 *Ibid.*, 528. The Mission arrived in England in two parties on 5 September and 22 October and left London on 6 December 1957. Brisk preparations were made for its reception. The SBTC reconstituted itself into a top-level council to receive the Mission and a special Liaison Office was opened. The Mission was also given a cocktail reception by the Federation of British Industries. *Ibid.*, 528.

139 Even though the Mission was not expected to place immediate

orders it nevertheless concluded contracts worth more than £700,000 before its departure. This was regarded by the Sino-British Trade Council as "a matter for gratification." *Ibid.*, 528. The Chinese Mission showed keen interest in the embargoed items.

140 Kayser Sung, n. 77, 511.

141 *H.C. Deb.*, 579 (1957-8) 342, 346 and 348. Although Eroll found no evidence of a Chinese desire to obtain goods on credit terms, he nevertheless believed that it might "change as the need for imports to fulfil the second five-year plan increases" He disclosed that a new post of Commercial Secretary had been set up in the British Embassy in Peking, which would greatly help in providing information and advice to would-be British exporters to China. *Ibid.*, 347-8.

142 *H.L. Deb.*, 221 (1957-58) 481. The revised list effective from 15 August 1958 was published in the *Board of Trade Journal*. See *BTJ* (15 Aug 1958) 314-20. As a result of this major relaxation of embargo on export to the Soviet bloc and China, most types of machine tools, motor cars and lorries not built to military specification, civil aircraft, aero engines, diesel engines, electrical equipment, most forms of petrol and most types of ships were freed.

143 Following the flag incident in Nagasaki, Peking cut its trade ties with Japan in May 1958. Trade, between the two countries was running at $50 million each way in the first half of 1958. It came down to $1 million or so in the "intervening two years." *The Times*, 24 Mar 1961.

144 By spending its sterling reserves on the goods it needed, China sought to avoid the risk of its foreign currency being frozen (Chinese assets in the USA were frozen in December 1950) and to avoid big losses through devaluation or depreciation of sterling. "For all these reasons," Tsou Szu-yee, Assistant Director in the Ministry of Foreign Trade, observed, "China regards a constant excess of either imports or exports as unsound, and is a firm advocate of balance in foreign trade...with any country with which she trades." Tsou Szu-yee, "A Balanced Foreign Trade," *China Reconstructs* (Sep 1956) 10-1.

145 "Our exports to China in 1958," the Earl of Dundee, Minister without Portfolio stated, "totalled £26,700,000. That compares with £12,100,000 for 1957." *H.L. Deb.*, 213 (1958-9) 1187.

146 Luard, n. 5, 146.

147 *WWCC*: 1951-53, 27.

148 Statement of 28 June 1956. See *PC* (16 Jul 1956) Supplement 10.

149 *JMJP*, 2 Jun 1957.

150 Chi Chao-ting, "The Embargo—breaking up," *China Reconstructs* (Sep 1957) 9-11.

151 Yeh Chi-chuang, "China's Foreign Trade," *EW* (Oct 1957) 35.

152 *JMJP*, 16 Aug 1958.

153 *Ibid.*

154 *JMJP*, 22 Sep 1959.

155 "According to the Soviet Minister of Foreign Trade, Sino-Soviet

trade in 1959'was 35 per cent higher than in 1958....Much of the impetus for the expansion in trade was probably provided by the agreement of February 1959 under which the Soviet Union undertook to provide China with medium term aid totalling 5,000 million roubles." *TMER* (Jun 1960) 9.

156 "Trade ties between Japan and China were servered in May 1958, but at the end of October this year the Japanese Ministry of International Trade accepted applications for the import af mainland Chinese goods *via* Hong Kong under a barter system." *TMER* (Dec 1959) 7.

157 From 1953 to 1957, the balance of payments situation was favourable to China. Since 1958 this trend in Sino-British trade was reversed. See Appendix 3.

158 While removing nearly all quota restrictions on imports from the so-called Relaxation and Dollar Areas, the British Government transferred China from the Relaxation Area to the "Eastern Area," with the result that few items could be imported under open general licence. Specific quotas were set up for some goods—notably silk piece goods, imports of which were limited to £250,000 in 1960. For details of the quotas thus fixed vide Notice to Importers No. 921 dated 5 November 1959 see *BTJ* (6 Nov 1959) 697.

159 Statement by Lord Mills, Pay Master General, 25 November 1959. *H.L. Deb.*, 219 (1959-60) 921.

160 In March 1960, sixteen new quotas were established and four of the original twelve were increased by a total of £450,000. Subsequently, in April, 22 further new quotas were set up, with a total value of £1,350,000 and 20 of the existing quotas were increased by a combined total of £3.5 million. Altogether, quotas for Chinese goods in 1960 totalled nearly £9 million as compared with only £3.6 million initially. *TMER* (Jun 1960) 9.

161 See *H.L. Deb.*, 216 (1958-9) 486.

162 UN Department of Economic Affairs, *Economic Survey of Asia and the Far East*: 1950 (New York, 1951) 172.

163 *H.L. Deb*, 203 (1956-7) 546.

164 Collar, n. 18, 33.

165 See John Keswick, "The British Exhibition in Peking November 1964," *JRCAS* (July-Oct 1965) 278-9.

166 *PR* (22 Jan 1965) 7-10.

167 Maclean, n. 55, 311.

168 See Keswick, n. 165, 275-7.

169 *Ibid.*, 277.

170 C.P. Fitzgerald, "Present Trends in China," *JRCAS* (Feb 1967) 32.

171 *H.C. Deb*, 791 (12 Nov 1969) 829-30.

172 *Ibid.*, 806 (16 Nov 1970) 851.

173 *H.C. Deb.*, 834 (10 Apr 1972) 841-2.

174 *Ibid.*, (11 Apr 1972) 1025.

175 *H.C. Deb.*, 838 (12 Jun 1973) 994.

176 *Ibid.*, (5 Jun 1972) 13. Written Answers.

177 *Ibid.* 846 (20 Nov 1972) 886-8.
178 *H.C. Deb.*, 854 (9 Apr 1973) 923-6. See also *Ibid.*, 860 (24 Jul 1973) 386. Written Answers.

Chapter Nine : Conclusion

1 *The Times*, 10 Mar 1948.
2 See *Saturday Evening Post* (16 Jan 1954) 28-9.
3 *The Times*, 6 Jan 1950.
4 Statement by Bevin, 15 September 1948. *H.C. Deb.*, 456 (1948)97.
5 Statement by Bevin, 25 September 1950. UN Doc. A/PV 283 (25 Sep 1950) 88.
6 Kenneth Younger, "Western Policy in Asia," *Pacific Affairs*, 25 (Jun 1952) 118.
7 A.S.B. Olver, *Outline of British Policy in East and Southeast Asia 1945-May* 1950 (London, 1950) 22.
8 Oliver Franks quoted by Ronald Farquharson, "China—Past, Present, and Future," *JRCAS* (Apr 1952) 111.
9 Clement R. Attlee, "Britain and America: Common Aims, Different Opinions," *Foreign Affairs*, 32 (Jan 1954) 199.
10 Statement by Kenneth Younger, 20 November 1951. *H.C. Deb.*, 494 (1951-2) 332.
11 Statement by Philip Noel Baker, 11 May 1953. *Ibid*, 515 (1952-3) 902.
12 *H C. Deb.*, 482 (1950) 1464.
13 *Cmd.* 8159, 12.
14 Statement on 5 November 1953. *H.C. Deb.*, 520 (1953-4) 311.
15 One might recall here the signing of the Sino-Indonesian Treaty concerning the question of dual nationality; the announcement made by Premier Chou En-lai to hold bilateral diplomatic negotiations with the USA to ease tension in the Taiwan area; and the release of four American pilots on 30 May 1955, etc.
16 H. Trevelyan, *Worlds Apart: China 1953-55 Soviet Union 1962-65* (London, 1971) 82-3 and 110-1.
17 During 1953-4 the terms of trade turned in Britain's favour and the two years showed a surplus of £188 million and £228 million in the balance of payments. C.M. Woodhouse, *British Foreign Policy Since the Second World War* (London, 1961) 117.
18 Anthony Eden, *The Full Circle* (London, 1960) 99.
19 Editorial in the *Far Eastern Economic Review*. See *FEER* (10 Jun 1954) 714.
20 *Ibid.*
21 "We cannot survive if we are to be restricted, unable to trade effectively with United States, cut off from China and with all the

difficulties of the Iron Curtain." Statement by Attlee, 12 May 1953. *H.C. Deb.*, 515 (1952-3) 1067.

22 The ideological debate in the early 1960s revealed some important differences in viewpoints of the USSR and Communist China in regard to their attitudes towards war and peace, the nature of imperialism, the role of the national *bourgeoisie* and of national liberation movements and the forms of transition from capitalism to socialism. The Chinese believed in the inevitability of war and the use of force to solve international disputes. They were against peaceful coexistence, disarmament and peaceful transition from capitalism to socialism.

23 In the three-year period ending 1961, the volume of China's trade with the Communist world went down by as much as 40 per cent as against a fall of only 8 per cent during the same period in China's trade with the rest of the world. *Times of India*, 31 Mar 1960. See also A. Boone, "The Foreign Trade of China," *China Quarterly* (Jul-Sep 1962) 182.

24 Washington disliked the contract which was signed on 1 December 1961 at a probable cost of about £2 million. London, however, regarded it "a worthwhile commercial transaction" and "a matter which Governments must ultimately decide for themselves." See *The Times*, 5 Dec 1961.

25 Choh-ming Li, *Economic Development of Communist China* (California, 1959) 194-5.

26 The United States, Dulles stated, had "heavy security commitments in the China area" and "carries the primary responsibility for peace in the area." Therefore, it could not allow Britain to "build up the military power of its potential enemy." See *DSB* (1 Jul 1957) 14 and *DSB* (15 Jul 1957) 93.

27 *PR* (17 Nov 1961) 19-20.

28 Quoted in Donald Maclean, *British Foreign Policy Since Suez 1956-1968* (London, 1970) 233.

29 See Richard Hughes, "Peking's Tolerance Based on Mutual Gain," *The Times*, 21 Oct 1972.

30 Kenneth Younger, *Changing Perspectives in British Foreign Policy* (London, 1964) 28.

31 See articles by W.A.C. Adie, a former Foreign Office specialist on Far Eastern Affairs, in *International Affairs* (London) Apr 1966 and Jul 1967.

32 See Yao Nien-keng, "British Strategy East of Suez," *PR* (4 Mar 1966) 19-21.

33 P. B. Harris, "An Assessment of Sino-British Relations in the 1970's," *Pacific Community* (Jul 1972) 733.

34 *PR* (31 May 1974) 8.

35 *Ibid.*, 9.

36 Quoted in *Asia Research Bulletin* (30 Jun 1974) 2769.

37 See UN Doc. A/2200 (10 Apr 1974) 71-95.

APPENDIX 1

Communique of the Agreement between the Government of the People's Republic of China and the Government of the United Kingdom of Great Britain and Northern Ireland on the Exchange of Ambassadors, 13 March 1972

Both confirming the principles of mutual respect for sovereignty and territorial integrity, non-interference in each other's internal affairs and equality and mutual benefit, the Government of the People's Republic of China and the Government of the United Kingdom have decided to raise the level of their respective Diplomatic Representatives in each other's capitals from *Charges d'Affaires* to Ambassadors as from 13th March 1972.

The Government of the United Kingdom, acknowledging the position of the Chinese Government that Taiwan is a province of the People's Republic of China, have decided to remove their official representation in Taiwan on 13th March 1972.

The Government of the United Kingdom recognise the Government of the People's Republic of China as the sole legal Government of China.

The Government of the People's Republic of China appreciates the above stand of the Government of the United Kingdom.

APPENDIX 2

Trade Between China and Hong Kong

(\$ HK Million)

Year	Hong Kong Imports	Hong Kong Exports
1946	333	305
1947	464	338
1948	520	417
1949	671	853
1950	962	1670
1951	863	1604
1952	830	520
1953	857	540
1954	692	391
1955	898	182
1956	1038	136
1957	1131	123
1958	1397	156
1959	1034	114
1960	1186	107
1961	1028	91
1962	1213	77
1963	1487	62
1964	1970	47
1965	2322	54
1966	2769	54
1967	2282	42
1968	2429	36
1969	2700	30
1970	2830	34
1971	3330	43
1972	3847	82
1973	5634	226
1974	—	196

Source : U.K., Board of Trade, *Report of the United Kingdom Trade Mission to China* (London, 1948) 155; and *Colonial Reports for Hong Kong* for the years 1948 to 1974.

APPENDIX 3

Trade Between China and Britain

($ US Million)

Year	British Imports	British Exports
1938	17.1	21.1
1946	7.0	36.0
1947	15.0	33.0
1948	33.2	35.3
1949	14.8	9.7
1950	30.1	10.1
1951	23.7	7.9
1952	8.3	12.8
1953	28.6	17.5
1954	25.1	19.4
1955	34.4	22.2
1956	35.2	30.2
1957	39.8	34.1
1958	51.9	76.3
1959	55.2	69.4
1960	69.7	89.8
1961	86.4	36.5
1962	64.8	24.1
1963	51.9	37.4
1964	68.9	49.9
1965	83.2	72.4
1966	94.7	93.6
1967	82.8	105.6
1968	82.8	69.3
1969	91.2	130.8
1970	80.4	106.8
1971	76.8	69.3
1972	88.8	78.0
1973	117.4	207.0
1974	156.2	167.5

Source : *Far Eastern Economic Review; China Trade Reports; Quarterly Economic Review: China, Hong Kong, North Korea;* Supplemented by other sources.

Bibliography

PRIMARY SOURCES

Australia, Department of External Affairs. *Select Documents on International Affairs: Korea Part I.* Canberra, 1950 and *Part II.* Sydney, 1951.

BOYCE, SIR L. *Report of the United Kingdom Trade Mission to China, 1946.* London, 1948.

British Labour Party. *Reports of the Annual Conference of the Labour Party,* 1950-1974.

Carnegie Endowment for International Peace. *Treaties and Agreements with and concerning China:* 1919-1929. Washington, 1929.

CHEN, YIN CHING. *Treaties and Agreements Between the Republic of China and Other Powers:* 1929-1954. Washington, 1957.

CHIANG KAI-SHEK. *China's Destiny and Chinese Economic Theory,* Notes and Commentary by Philip Jaffe. New York, 1947.

Chinese Committee for the Promotion of International Trade. *New China's Economic Achievements,* 1949-1952. Peking, 1952.

Chinese Embassy in India. *Causes of Tension in Taiwan Area.* New Delhi, 1955

———. *China Will Liberate Taiwan.* New Delhi, 1955.

Chinese People's Institute of Foreign Affairs, comp. *Oppose U.S. Occupation of Taiwan and "Two Chinas" Plot.* Peking, 1958.

COLE, A. B. AND ASSOCIATES. *Conflict in Indo-China and International Repercussions: A Documentary History 1945-1955.* New York, 1956.

Council on Foreign Relations. *Documents on American Foreign Relations: 1952 to 1974.* New York.

DEGRAS, JANE, ED. *The Communist International 1919-1943: Documents vol.* 1 (1919-22). London, 1956.

Fa-li Chu'-pan-hsie. *Chung-hua Jen-min Kung-he-Kuo T'iao Yueh Chi (Collection of Treaties of the People's Republic of China with Foreign Powers)* Volumes I to V. Peking, 1952-58.

Foreign Languages Press. *Eight Years of the Chinese Peoples' Volunteers' Resistance to American Aggression and Aiding of Korea.* Peking, 1958.

————. *Imperialism and All Reactionaries Are Paper Tigers.* Peking, 1958.

————. *Important Documents Concerning the Question of Taiwan.* Peking, 1955.

————. *Oppose U.S. Military Provocations in the Taiwan Straits Area.* Peking, 1958.

Foreign Languages Publishing House. *Everlasting Friendship Between Korean, Chinese and Vietnamese Peoples.* Pyongyang, 1959.

————. *For the Peaceful Unification of the Country.* Pyongyang, 1958.

Great Britain, Colonial Office. *Annual Reports of the Federation of Malaya:* 1949 and 1950.

————. *Annual Reports on Hong Kong,* 1948 to 1974.

————. *British Dependencies in the Far East:* 1945-1949. *Cmd.* 7709, May 1949.

Great Britain, Foreign Office, British Involvement in the Indo-China Conflict 1945-65 (Documents). *Cmnd.* 2834, 1965.

————. Correspondence between the Government of the United Kingdom of Great Britain and Northern Ireland and the Central People's Government of China on British Trade in China, Peking, 12th April-5th July 1952 (China No. 1, 1952) *Cmd.* 8639, Aug 1952.

————. Declaration of Washington: Joint Declaration by the President of the United States of America and the Prime Minister of United Kingdom, with accompanying communique. *Cmd.* 9700, Feb 1956.

————. Documents relating to the discussion of Korea and Indo-China at the Geneva Conference (Miscellaneous No. 16, 1954). *Cmd.* 9186, Jun 1954.

————. Further Documents relating to the discussion of Indo-China at the Geneva Conference (Miscellaneous No. 20, 1954). *Cmd.* 9239, Aug 1954.

————. *Summary* of Events: 1950 (Korea No. 1, 1950). *Cmd.* 8078, Oct 1950.

————. Korea: United Nations Resolution on Chinese Intervention in Korea (Korea No. 1, 1951). *Cmd.* 8159, 1951.

————. Further Summary of Events relating to Korea (Korea No. 2, 1951). *Cmd.* 8366, Sep 1951.

————. Korea: A Summary of Developments in the Armistice Negotiations and the Prisioner of War Camps (Korea No. 1, 1952). *Cmd.* 8596, Jun 1952.

————. Korea: The Indian Proposal for resolving the Prisioners of War Problem (Korea No. 2, 1952). *Cmd.* 8716, Dec 1952.

————. Korea: A Summary of Further Developments in the Military Situation, Armistice Negotiations and Prisioner of War Camps up to January 1953 (Korea No. 1, 1953). *Cmd.* 8793, Mar 1953.

————. Special Report of the Unified Command on the Korean Armistice Agreement (Korea No. 2, 1953). *Cmd.* 8938, Sep 1953.

————. Visit of the Prime Minister to the United States: Communique of 8th December 1950, and Extract from House of Commons Debate of 12th December 1950. *Cmd.* 8110, 1950.

HERTSLET, GODERY E.P. *Treaties etc. Between Great Britain and China:* Vol. I. London, 1908.

MANSERGH, NICHOLAS, ED. *Documents and Speeches on British Commonwealth Affairs:* 1939-52. London, 1953.

MAO TSE-TUNG. *On Coalition Government.* Peking, 1955.

————. *On People's Democratic Dictatorship.* Peking, 1952

————. *Selected Works of Mao Tse-tung,* 4 vols. Peking, 1961.

MAO TSE-TUNG AND LIU SHAO-CHI. *Lessons of Chinese Revolution.* Bombay, 1950.

People's Publishing House. *Working Class in the Struggle for National Liberation,* Reports and Resolutions of Trade Union Conference of Asian and Australian Countries called by World Federation of Trade Unions. Peking, Nov-Dec 1949; Bombay, 1950

Report by the Chief Minister of the Federation of Malaya on the Bailing Talks. Kaula Lumpur, 1956.

Royal Institute of International Affairs. *Documents on International Affairs,* 1947 to 1970.

Shih-chieh Chih-shih Ch'u-pan-hsie. *Chung-hua Jen-min Kung-he-Kuo tui-wai Kuan-hsi Wen-Chien Chi (Selection of Documents Concerning Diplomatic Relations of the People's Republic of China)* Vol. I, 1949-1950, Peking, 1957; Vol. II, 1951-1953, Peking, 1958; Vol. III, 1954-1955, Peking, 1958; and Vol. IV, 1956-1957, Peking, 1958.

UK, House of Commons. Parliamentary Debates (Hansard) 1946 to 1975.

UK, House of Lords. Parliamentary Debates (Hansard)

1943 to 1975.

US, Department of State. *A Decade of American Foreign Policy 1941-1949*. Washington, 1950.

————. *American Foreign Policy 1950-1955 Basic Documents* 2 vols. Washington, 1957.

————. *Background: Indo-China: The War in Viet-Nam, Cambodia and Laos*. Washington, 1953.

————. *Background: South East Asia, Area of Challenge, Change and Progress*. Washington, 1959.

———— *Korea, 1945 to 1948*. Washington, 1948.

————. *Malaya: Trouble Spot in Southeast Asia*. Washington, 1953.

————. *Nazi-Soviet Relations: 1939-41*. Washington, 1948.

————. *The Bangkok Conference of the Manila Pact Powers*. Washington, 1955.

————. *The Record on Korean Unification, 1943-1960: Narrative Summary with Principal Documents*. Washington, 1960.

————. *United States Policy in Korean Conflict*, Jul 1950-Feb 1951. Washington, 1951.

————. *United States Relations with China*. Washington, 1949.

US Foreign Operations Administration. *Country Series: Formosa*. Washington, undated.

US International Cooperation Administration. *Reports to Congress on Mutual Defense Assistance Control Act of 1951* (Battle Act.)

US Senate. *The United States and the Korean Problem, Documents 1943-1953*. Washington, 1953.

————. *Military Situation in the Far East*, Hearings before the Committee on Armed Services and the Committee on Foreign Relations, US Senate, 82nd Congress, 1st Session, Parts I-V.

World Peace Foundation. *Documents on American Foreign Relations*, Vols. IX to XIII, 1947 to 1951. Princeton, N.J.

Memoirs and Biographies

ACHESON, DEAN. *Sketches from Life*. London, 1961.

ATTLEE, C. R. *As It Happened*. London, 1955.

DULLES, JOHN FOSTER. *War or Peace*. New York, 1955.

EDEN, ANTHONY. *Memoirs: The Full Circle*. London, 1960.

EISENHOWER, DWIGHT D. *The White House Years: 1956-1961*. London, 1966.

HOME, ALEC-DOUGLAS. *Great Britain's Foreign Policy*. London,

1961.

MACMILLAN, HAROLD. *Winds of Change*. London, 1966.

———. *The Blast of War*. London, 1967.

MORRISON, HERBERT. *An Autobiography*. London, 1960.

TREVELYAN, H. *Worlds Apart: China 1953-55, Soviet Union 1962-65*. London, 1971.

TRUMAN, HARRY S. *Memoirs*, 2 Vols. New York, 1955.

WILLIAMS, FRANCIS, *A Prime Minister Remembers: The War and Post-War Memoirs of the Rt. Hon. Earl of Attlee*. London, 1961.

SECONDARY SOURCES

Books

ALLEN, H.C. *The Anglo-American Relationships Since* 1783. London, 1959.

Alliance Platform for the Federal Elections. *Menuju Kearan Kemerdekaan. (The Road to Independence)*. Kuala Lumpur, 1955.

ATTLEE, CLEMENT AND BEVIN, ERNEST. *Britain's Foreign Policy*. London, 1946.

BALLANTINE, JOHN. *Formosa*. Washington, 1952.

BARNETT, A. DOAK. *Communist China and Asia*. New York, 1960.

BAU, MINGCHIEN JOSHUA. *The Foreign Relations of China*. London, 1922.

———. *The Open Door Doctrine in Relation to China*. New York, 1923.

BELDEN, JACK. *China Shakes the World*. New York, 1949.

BELL, CORAL. *The Debatable Alliance*. London, 1964.

BELOFF, MAX. *Soviet Policy in the Far East*. London, 1953.

BETTLEHEM, CHARLES. *China Shakes the World Again*. New York, 1950.

BEVAN, ANEURIN. *In Place of Fear*. London, 1952.

BEVIN, ERNEST. *The Labour Party's Policy on Foreign Affairs*. London, 1946.

BODDE, DERK. *Peking Diary*. New York, 1950.

BRANDT, CONRAD AND OTHERS. *A Documentary History of the Chinese Communism*. Harvard, 1952.

BRIMMEL, J. H. *Communism in Southeast Asia*. London, 1959.

BROOK, David. *The U.N. and the China Dilemma*. New York,

1956.

CAMPS, M. *Britain and the European Community:* 1955-1963. London, 1964.

Carnegie Endowment for International Peace. *China and the United Nations.* New York, 1959.

CHANG, CARSUN. *The Third Force in China.* New York, 1952.

CHURCHILL, SIR WINSTON. *Triumph and Tragedy.* New York, 1954.

CLARK, GERALD. *Impatient Giant: Red China Today,* London, 1960.

CLARK, GROVER. *Economic Rivalries in China.* New Haven, 1932.

COLLINS, CHARLES. *Public Administration in Hong Kong.* London, 1951.

Conference of Asian Countries, New Delhi, 6-10 April 1955. New Delhi, 1955.

Council on Foreign Relations. *The US in World Affairs: 1954.* New York, 1956.

COSTIN, W.C. *Great Britain and China 1833-1860.* London, 1968.

CROSSMAN, R.H.S. AND YOUNGER, KENNETH. *Socialist Foreign Policy.* London, 1951.

DONNELLY, DESMOND. *Speak For Britain: No War with China.* London, 1953.

DONOVAN, ROBERT J. *Eisenhower: The Inside Story.* New York, 1956.

Economist Intelligence Unit. *An Economic Geography of the Commonwealth.* London, 1957.

ELEGANT, ROBERT S. *The Dragon's Seed, Peking and the Overseas Chinese.* New York, 1959.

ENDACOTT, G.B. *A History of Hong Kong.* London, 1958.

EPENSTEIN, LEON D. *Britain—Uneasy Ally.* Chicago, 1955.

FAIRBANK, JOHN KING. *The United States and China.* Harvard, 1958.

FALCONER, ALUN. *New China: Friend or Foe.* London, 1950.

FALL, BERNARD B. *The International Position of South Viet-Nam 1954-58.* New York, 1958

FAURE, EDGAR. *The Serpent and the Tortoise.* London, 1958.

FEIS, HERBERT. *The China Tangle.* Princeton, N.J., 1953.

FIFIELD, RUSSELL H. *The Diplomacy of Southeast Asia: 1945-58.* New York, 1958.

FITZGERALD, CHARLES P. *Flood Tide in China.* London, 1958.

———. *Revolution in China.* London, 1952.

FITZSIMONS, M.A. *The Foreign Policy of the British Labour*

Government, 1945-51. Indiana, 1953.

FORMAN, HARRISON. *Blunder in Asia.* New York, 1950.

————. *Changing China.* New York, 1948.

————. *Report from Red China.* New York, 1945.

FRANKS, OLIVER S. *Britain and the Tide of World Affairs.* London, 1955.

FRIEDMAN, IRVING S. *British Relations with China:* 1931-9. New York, 1940.

GANGULEE, N., COMPILED. *The Teachings of Sun Yat-sen, Selections from His Writings.* London, 1945.

GELBER, LIONEL. *America in Britain's Place.* New York, 1961.

GOODWIN, GEOFFREY L. *Britain and the United Nations.* London, 1957.

GORDENKER, LEON. *The U.N. and the Peaceful Unification of Korea.* Hague, 1959.

GORDON, MICHAEL R. *Conflict and Consensus in Labour's Foreign Policy* 1914-1965. Stanford, Calif., 1969.

Handbook to Malaya and the Emergency. Singapore, 1952.

HANRAHAN, GENE Z. *The Communist Struggle in Malaya.* New York, 1954.

HIGGINS, TRUMBULL. *Korea and the Fall of MacArthur.* New York, 1960.

HINTON, H.C. *China's Relations with Burma and Vietnam.* New York, 1958.

————. *Communist China in World Politics.* New York, 1966.

HO KAN-CHIH. *A History of the Modern Chinese Revolution.* Peking, 1959.

HUBBARD, G.E. *British Far Eastern Policy.* New York, 1943.

HUDSON, G.F. *Questions of East and West.* London, 1953.

————. *The Far East in World Politics.* London 1939.

HUGHES, T.J. AND LUARD, D.E.T. *The Economic Development of Communist China,* 1949-58. London, 1959.

HU SHENG. *Imperialism and Chinese Politics.* Peking, 1955.

HUTHEESING, GUNOTTAM PURUSHOTTAM. *Window on China.* London, 1953.

HUTHEESING, RAJA. *The Great Peace.* New York, 1953.

INGRAM, KENNETH. *History of the Cold War.* London, 1955.

JAIN, J.P. *China Pakistan and Bangladesh.* New Delhi, 1974.

————. *A Documentary Study of the Warsaw Pact.* Bombay, 1973.

————. *After Mao What? Army Party and Group Rivalries in China.* New Delhi, 1975.

JAY, DOUGLAS. *After the Common Market.* London, 1968.

JONES, F.C. *Manchuria Since* 1931. London, 1949.

JOSEPH, PHILIP. *Foreign Diplomacy in China* 1894-1900. London, 1928.

KEETON, GEORGE W. *China, The Far East and the Future*. London, 1949.

KIRBY, E. STUART. *Contemporary China*. Hong Kong, 1956.

LANDMAN, LYNN AND AMOS. *Profile of Red China*. New York, 1951.

LATOURETTE, KENNETH SCOT. *The American Record in the Far East*, 1945-51. New York, 1952.

LEVI, WERNER. *Modern China's Foreign Policy*. Minneapolis, 1953.

LI CHANG TAO. *Why China Helps Korea*. Bombay, 1951.

LI CHOH-MING. *Economic Development of Communist China*. California, 1959.

LINDSAY, MICHAEL. *China and the Cold War*. New York, 1955.

LOK Sabha Secretariat. *Brochure on Formosa, Pescadores and Other Islands*. New Delhi, 1955.

LUARD, EVAN. *Britain and China*. London, 1962.

―――. *Chinese Foreign Policy*. New York, 1957.

MACKENZIE, NORMAN. *Conspiracy for War: The China Lobby*. London, 1952.

MACLEAN, DONALD. *British Foreign Policy Since Suez*: 1956-1968. London, 1970.

MAYHEW, CHRISTOPHER. *Britain's Role Tomorrow*. London, 1967.

MCBEY, RUTH T. *The Calcutta Conference and the Southeast Asian Uprisings*. New York, 1958.

MCDERMOTT, GEOFFREY. *The Eden Legacy and the Decline of British Diplomacy*. London, 1969.

MCKITTERICK, T.E. AND YOUNGER, KENNETH. *Fabian International Essays* (Chap. V, The Far East by Kenneth Younger). London, 1957.

MEDLICOTT, W.N. *British Foreign Policy Since Versailles:* 1919-1963. London, 1968.

MILLS, LENNOX A. AND ASSOCIATES. *The New World of South East Asia*. Minnesota, 1949.

MORAN, LORD. *Winston Churchill: The Struggle for Survival*, 1940-1965. London, 1966.

MORRISON, HERBERT. *Government and Parliament*. London, 1959.

MORSE, HOSEA BALLOU. *The International Relations of the Chinese Empire*. London, 1910.

NICHOLAS, H.G. *Britain and the United States*. London, 1963.

NORTH, ROBERT C. *Moscow and Chinese Communists.* Stanford, 1953.

NORTHEDGE, F.S. *British Foreign Policy: The Process of Readjustment,* 1945-1961. London, 1962.

OLVER, A.S.B. *Outline of British Policy in East and South East Asia,* 1945-May 1950. London, 1950.

PELLING, H.M. *America and the British Left: From Bright to Bevan.* London, 1956.

PORTER, BRIAN. *Britain and the Rise of Communist China: A Study of British Attitudes* 1945-1954. London, 1967.

PRATT, JOHN T. *Korea: The Lie that Led to War.* London, 1951.

———. *The Expansion of Europe into the Far East.* London, 1947.

———. *War and Politics in China.* London, 1943.

PRITT, D.N. *New Light on Korea.* London, 1951.

PRITT, D.N., S.O. DAVIES, R. PALME DUTT, ETC. *Korea Handbook.* London, 1950.

PURCELL, VICTOR. *The Chinese in Malaya.* London, 1948.

———. *The Chinese in South East Asia.* London, 1951.

———. *The Position of the Chinese in South East Asia.* New York, 1950.

———. *War or Settlement in the Far East?* London, 1952.

READ, COLLINS, NICHOLAS. *Report on the War in Indo-China.* London, 1953.

REES, DAVID. *Korea: The Limited War.* London, 1964.

Regional Information Office. *The Asian Revolution.* Singapore, undated.

———. *Malaya: The Road to Independence.* Singapore, 1957.

REISCHAUER, EDWIN O. *Wanted: An Asian Policy.* New York, 1955.

REMER, C.F. *Three Essays on the International Economics of Communist China.* Michigan, 1959.

———. *Foreign Investments in China.* New York, 1933.

ROBERTS, HENRY L. and WILSON, PAUL A. *Britain and the United States: Problems in Cooperation.* London, 1953.

ROSE, SAUL. *Britain and South-East Asia.* London, 1962.

ROSINGER, LAWRENCE K. AND ASSOCIATES. *The State of Asia.* New York, 1951.

ROSTOW, W.W. *The Prospects for Communist China.* New York, 1954.

———. *The United States in the World Arena.* New York, 1960.

ROWE, DAVID NELSON. *China Among the Powers.* New York, 1945.

Royal Institute of International Affairs. *Collective Defence in South East Asia.* London, 1956.

————. *Survey of International Affairs,* 1939-46, *The Far East* 1942-46. London, 1956.

————.*Survey of International Affairs,* 1947-48. London, 1952.

SARDESAI, D.R. *Indian Foreign Policy in Cambodia, Laos and Vietnam* 1947-1964. California, 1968.

SARGENT, A.J. *Anglo-Chinese Commerce and Diplomacy.* London, 1907.

SCHWARTZ, BENJAMIN. *Chinese Communism and the Rise of Mao.* Harvard, 1952.

SETON-WATSON, HUGH. *Neither War Nor Peace.* New York, 1960.

SNYDER, WILLIAM P. *The Politics of British Defence Policy,* 1945-1962. London, 1964.

SOOTHILL, W.E. *A History of China.* New York, 1951.

SPANIER, JOHN W. *The Truman MacArthur Controversy and the Korean War.* Harvard, 1959.

SPRENKEL, OTTO B. VAN DER, AND OTHERS. *New China, Three Views.* London, 1950

STEBBING, RICHARD P. *The United States in World Affairs* 1958. New York, 1959.

STEINER, ARTHUR H. *Maoism: A Sourcebook.* Los Angeles, 1952.

————. *The International Position of Communist China.* New York, 1958.

————, ed. *Report on China.* Philadelphia, 1951.

STRANG, WILLIAM. *Britain in World Affairs.* New York, 1961.

SUN FO. *China Looks Forward.* London, 1945.

SUNDER LAL. *China Today.* Allahabad, 1952.

SZCZEPANIK, EDWARD. *The Economic Growth of Hong Kong.* London, 1958.

TANG, PETER S.H. *Communist China Today.* New York, 1957.

TEWKESBURY, DONALD G. *Source Materials on Korean Politics and Ideologies.* New York, 1950.

TOWNSEND, PETER. *In China Now.* London, 1953.

TSOU, TANG. *America's Failure in China,* 1941-50. Chicago, 1963.

WALKER, RICHARD LOUIS. *China Under Communism: The First Five Years.* New Haven, 1955.

————. *The Continuing Struggle: Communist China and the Free World.* New York, 1958.

WEEMS, CLARENCE NORWOOD. *Korea: Dilemma of Under-developed Country.* New York, 1960.

WHITING, ALLEN S. *China Crosses the Yalu.* New York, 1960.

WHITNEY, COURTNEY. *MacArthur: His Rendezvous With History.* New York, 1956.

WHYTE, SIR FREDERICK. *China and Foreign Powers.* London, 1928.

WILSON, P.A. *The Political, Strategic and Economic Interests of United Kingdom*, Pt. I. London, 1954.

WINDRICH, ELAINE. *British Labour's Foreign Policy.* London, 1952.

WOODHOUSE, C.M. *British Foreign Policy Since the Second World War.* London, 1961.

WU, YUAN-LI. *An Economic Survey of Communist China.* New York, 1956.

YOUNG, L.K. *British Policy in China* 1895-1902. London, 1970.

YOUNGER, KENNETH. *Changing Perspectives in British Foreign Policy.* London, 1964.

————. *Three Public Addresses.* Melbourne, 1955.

Articles

ACHESON, DEAN G. "Crisis in Asia: An Examination of U.S. Policy." *Department of State Bulletin* (3 Jan 1950) 111-8.

————. "The Premises of American Policy." *Orbis* (Fall, 1959) 269-81.

ALLEN, G G. "Western Enterprise in the Far East." *International Affairs* (London) (Jul 1954) 294-303.

AMERY, JULIAN. "The Inexcusable War." *Nineteenth Century and After* (Jan 1950).

ARISTEIDES. "The Chinese Aircraft in Hong Kong." *The International Law Quarterly* (Apr 1951) 159-77.

ATTLEE, CLEMENT R. "Britain and America: Common Aims, Different Opinions." *Foreign Affairs* (Jan 1954) 190-202.

BEVAN, ANEURIN. "Britain and America at Loggerheads." *Foreign Affairs Quarterly* (5 Oct 1957).

BOWLES, CHESTER. "The 'China Problem' Reconsidered." *Foreign Affairs* (Jun 1954) 146-51

BUTWELL, RICHARD. "Communist Liaison in Southeast Asia." *United Asia* (Jun 1954) 146-51.

C.P.F. "The Chinese Revolution." *The World Today* (Jun 1950) 237-48.

CHEN MING. "China's Foreign Trade Policy." *Eastern World* (Sep 1956) 36-7.

CHEN, THEODORE H.E. "Relations between Britain and Communist China." *Current History* (Nov 1952) 295-303.

CHEN, THEODOR HSIE-EN AND CHEN WEN-HUI. "The Thre-Anti and Five-Anti Movements in Communist China." *Pacific Affairs* (Mar 1953) 3-23.

CHI CHAO-TING. "Growing Interest in China Trade." *China Reconstructs* (Nov-Dec 1953) 2-5.

————. "The 'Embargo'—Breaking Up." *China Reconstructs* (Sep 1957) 9-11.

CHUAN, LENG SHAO. "Communist China's Economic Relations with Southeast Asia." *Far Eastern Survey* (Jan 1959) 1-11.

CLUBB, O. EDMUND. "Chinese Communist Strategy in Foreign Relations." *The Annals of the American Academy of Political and Social Science* (Sep 1951) 156-66.

————. "Communist Strategy in Asia." *Eastern World* (Oct 1952) 10-1.

COLLAR, H. J. "Recent Developments of British Commercial Relations with China." *Journal of the Royal Central Asian Society* (Jan 1954) 26-36.

————. "British Commercial Relations with China." *International Affairs* (London) (Oct 1953) 418-28.

————. "China and Hong Kong." *Asian Review* (Apr 1954) 64-5.

CONSTANTINE, LEONARD. "Inside Communist China." *New Republic* (8 Jan 1951) 10-4 and (18 Jan 1951) 25-7.

DAVIES, HAROLD. "The Moscow Economic Conference." *Eastern World* (May 1952) 28-9

DEAN, ARTHUR. "United States Foreign Policy and Formosa." *Foreign Affairs* (Apr 1955) 360-75.

DEAN, VERA MICHELES. "Korean Crisis Exposes Changes in Balance of Power." *Foreign Policy Bulletin* (15 Dec 1950).

"Debate on China Continues: Views of Frank Altschul, Stanley K. Hornbeck, Thomas K. Finletter and Thomas E. Dewey." *Foreign Policy Bulletin* (15 Nov 1958) 37-9.

D.E.T.L. "The Foreign Policy of the Chinese People's Republic." *The World Today* (Apr 1957) 162-73.

DULLES, J.F. "Dulles Talks to the British About Red China." *U.S. News and World Report* (31 Oct 1958) 78-81.

EPSTEIN, LEON D. "The British Labour Left and U.S. Foreign Policy." *American Political Science Review* (Dec 1951).

FAIRBANK, JOHN K. "Formosa Through China's Eyes." *New Republic* (13 Oct 1958) 9-10.

FANG, C.F. "Industrial Policy in Liberated China." *China Digest* (Sep 1948) 8-9.

FARQUHARSON, RONALD. "China—Past, Present and Future." *Journal of the Royal Central Asian Society* (Apr 1952) 104-17.

FITZERALD, C. P. "The Chinese Revolution and the West."

Pacific Affairs (Mar 1951) 3-17.

————. "Peace or War with China." *Pacific Affairs* (Dec 1951) 339-51.

————. "Should Asians Fight Asians." *Eastern World* (Jul 1953) 9-10.

FITZMAURICE, G. G. "Chinese Representation in the United Nations." *Yearbook of World Affairs*, 1952.

"Five Views on Formosa." *Foreign Policy Bulletin* (15 May 1955) 132-4.

FLEMING, D. F. "Our Brink of War Diplomacy in Formosa Strait." *The Western Political Quarterly* (Sep 1956) 535-52.

GAITSKELL, HUGH. "The Search for Anglo-American Policy." *Foreign Affairs* (Jul 1954).

GEN, LEWIS. "General Review of Hong Kong." *Eastern World* (Feb 1955) 18-20.

————. "Will the Chinese Communists Attack Hong Kong?" *Eastern World* (Oct 1949) 7-8.

————. "Towards the Understanding of New China." *Eastern World* (Feb 1953) 10-2.

————. "Hong Kong Today." *Eastern World* (Nov 1952) 16-7.

————. "China's Merchants in Transformation." *Eastern World* (Feb 1956) 19-21.

GHERSON, RANDOLPH. "British Recognition of China: Some Issues Examined." *New Commonwealth* (Mar 1950).

GOOLD-ADAMS, R. "Formosa—The British View." *English-Speaking World* (Mar 1955).

GOULD, RANDALL. "Shanghai during the take over 1949." *Annals of the American Academy of Political and Social Science* (Sep 1951) 182-92.

————. "China Outlook: A Business View." *Far Eastern Survey* (20 Apr 1949) 90-2.

GREEN, MARC T. "Danger Point in Hong Kong." *Eastern World* (May 1950) 16-7.

GREEN, O.M. "Shanghai Faces Ruin." *Eastern World* (May 1950) 16-7.

————. "Russia in China." *Eastern World* (Apr 1953) 19-20.

————. "British Trade with China." *Eastern World* (Feb 1951) 34-5.

GREGORY, JOHN S. "British Intervention Against the Taiping Rebellion." *The Journal of Asian Studies* (Nov 1959) 11-24.

HAFFNER, SEBASTIAN. "The Anglo-American Quarrel: Another View." *Twentieth Century* (Oct 1953).

HARRIMAN, W. AVERELL. "Leadership in World Affairs." *Foreign Affairs* (Jul 1954) 525-40.

HARTWELL, J.N. "The Korean War and Indo-China." *Eastern World* (Nov 1952) 11-2.

HEATON, WILLIAM. "Maoist Revolutionary Strategy and Modern Colonialism: The Cultural Revolution in Hong Kong." *Asian Survey* (Sep 1970) 840-57.

HSIA, RONALD. "Private Enterprise in Communist China." *Pacific Affairs* (4 Dec 1953) 329-34.

———. "The Chinese Economy under Communist Planning." *Pacific Affairs* (2 Jun 1954) 112-23.

HSU TI-HSIN. "Transforming Capitalist Industry and Commerce: A New Stage." *People's China* (1 Feb 1956) 4-11.

HSU TSAI-TAN. "Northeast China sets the Pace." *People's China* (1 Apr 1950) 8-9.

HU SHIH. "China in Stalin's Grand Strategy." *Foreign Affairs* (Oct 1950) 11-40.

HUAN HSIN-YI. "The Foreign Policy of the People's Republic of China During the Last Two Years." *Soviet Press Translations* (15 Dec 1951) 667-77.

HUDSON, G.F. "British Relations with China." *Current History* (Dec 1957) 327-31.

———. "Korea and Asia." *International Affairs* (London) (Jan 1951) 18-24.

———. "Present Position of Hong Kong." *Far Eastern Economic Review* (17 Dec 1953) 779.

———. "Privileged Sanctuary." *Twentieth Century* (Jan 1951).

———. "The Anglo-American Quarrel." *Twentieth Century* (Oct 1953).

———. "The Problem of China." *United Empire* (May-Jun 1954).

———. "The Two Chinas." *Current History* (Jul 1956) 1-6.

———. "Will Britain and America Split in Asia ?" *Foreign Affairs* (Jul 1953) 536-47.

"Is China Policy Changing ?" *Foreign Policy Bulletin* (1 Nov 1958) 28.

JAIN, J.P. "Chinese Reaction to British Recognition of the People's Republic of China." *International Studies* (Jul 1962) 24-55.

———. "The Legal Status of Formosa: A Study of British, Chinese and Indian Views." *The American Journal of International Law* (Jan 1963) 25-45.

———. "La Gran Bretana Y China en las Naciones Unidas" ("Great Britain and China in the United Nations"). *Foro Internacional* (Mexico) (Jan-Mar 1963) 403-36.

JAMES, A. "British Trade with China." *Eastern World* (Jun

1954) 49.

———. "Chinese Trade Mission Visits Britain." *Eastern World* (Aug 1954) 48.

———. "U.K. Trade with China." *Eastern World* (Dec 1954) 47-9.

———. "Britain's Trade with China." *Eastern World* (Feb 1955) 46-7.

———. "U.K. Trade with China." *Eastern World* (May 1955) 40-1.

———. "China's Foreign Trade." *Eastern World* (Jun 1955) 43.

———. "China's Trade With Communist Countries." *Eastern World* (Sep 1956) 42-3.

J.B.P.R. "The Emergency in Malaya—Some Reflections." *The World Today* (Nov 1954) 477-87.

JESSUP, PHILIP C. "The Two Chinas and U.S. Recognition." *Reporter* (6 Jul 1954) 21-4.

JOSEY, ALEX. "Is China Expansionist?" *Eastern World* (Oct 1955) 18-9.

KAIM, J. R. "Trade Prospects in China." *Far Eastern Survey* (1 Jun 1949) 121-4.

KE CHIA-LUNG. "Manchuria's Economic Victories." *People's China* (1 Jun 1950) 7-9.

KESWICK, JOHN. "The British Exhibition in Peking, November 1964." *Journal of the Royal Central Asian Society* (Jul-Oct 1965) 275-80.

KHAN, MOHAMED SAMIN. "Legal Aspects of the Problem of China's Representation in the U.N." *Pakistan Horizon* (1957) 134-43.

KING, FRANK H.H. "British Trade with Nationalist China." *Far Eastern Economic Review* (17 Jun 1954) 747.

KIRBY, E. STUART. "The British and the Chinese." *Far Eastern Survey* (18 Apr 1951) 74-6

———. "Hong Kong Today." *Far Eastern Economic Review* (20 Aug 1953) 225-6.

———. "Hong Kong in the World Today." *Far Eastern Economic Review* (27 Mar 1952) 399-401.

———. "Hong Kong and the British Position in China." *Annals of the American Academy of Political and Social Science* (Sep 1951) 193-202.

KNOWLAND, WILLIAM F. "Should U.S. Recognize Peiping?" *Foreign Policy Bulletin* (15 Feb 1955) 84-5.

KOVALYOV, E. "The Agrarian Policy of the Chinese Communist Party." *Soviet Press Translations* (1 Apr 1951) 163-72.

LAUTERPACHT, E. "The Contemporary Practice of the United Kingdom in the Field of International Law—Survey and Comment VII." *International and Comparative Law Quarterly* (Jan 1959) 146-212.

————. "The Contemporary Practice of the United Kingdom in the Field of International Law—Survey and Comment IV." *International and Comparative Law Quarterly* (Jul 1957) 506-32.

LI CHE-JEN. "Fraternal Economic Cooperation." *China Reconstructs* (Aug 1955) 6-9.

LI THIAN-HOK. "The China Impasse : A Formosan View." *Foreign Affairs* (Apr 1958) 437-48.

LINDSAY, MICHAEL. "Chinese Puzzle: Mao's Foreign Policy." *New Republic*, 139 (6 Oct 1958) 8-11.

————. "China: Report of a Visit." *International Affairs* (London) (Jan 1950) 22-31.

LINEBARGER, PAUL M.A. "Taipei and Peking: the Confronting Republics." *Journal of International Affairs* (No. 2, 1957) 135-42.

LITTLEJOHN, JUSTIN. "China and Communism." *International Affairs* (London) (Apr 1951) 137-50.

LU HSU-CHANG. "China's Foreign Trade Expands " *Eastern World* (Jul 1954) 40.

————. "Foreign Trade Expands." *China Reconstructs* (Jul-Aug 1954) 2-3.

MACGILLIVRAY, SIR DONALD. "Malaya—The New Nations." *International Affairs* (London) (Apr 1958) 157-63.

MAYHEW, CHRISTOPHER. "British Foreign Policy Since 1945." *International Affairs* (London) (Oct 1950) 477-86.

MERCATOR. "Hong Kong's Trading Relations with People's China." *Far Eastern Economic Review* (8 May 1952) 601-3.

MITCHELL, G.E. "China and Britain: Their Commercial and Industrial Relations." *Journal of the Royal Central Asian Society* (Jul-Oct 1952) 246-58.

New Statesman and *Nation* Editorial. "How to Defend Hong Kong." *New Statesman* and *Nation* (14 May 1949) 489.

NOLDE, JOHN J. "The U.S. and the Chinese Blockade." *Far Eastern Survey* (22 Mar 1950) 57-61.

NORTH, R.C. "Nep and the New Democracy." *Pacific Affairs* (Mar 1951) 52-60.

O. E. C. "Titoism and the Chinese Communist Regime: An American View." *The World Today* (Dec 1952) 521-32.

O. R. "British Trade with Communist China." *The World Today* (Dec 1951) 537-43.

PEFFER, NATHANIEL. "Our Asian Policy: Part Blunder, Part Thunder." *Nation* (11 Dec 1954) 504-5.

People's China Editorial. "Realism and Duplicity." *People's China* (1 Jun 1950) 4.

PRATT, JOHN. "Korea, China and Formosa." *Eastern World* (Mar 1955) 16-9.

———. "China, U.N. and the Korean War." *Eastern World* (May 1953) 20-1.

———. "Korea and the Comity of Nations." *Eastern World* (Oct 1953) 11-4.

PURCELL, V. "Overseas Chinese and People's Republic." *Far Eastern Survey* (25 Oct 1950) 194-6.

P. W. "East-West Trade, Current Prospects." *The World Today* (Jan 1954) 19-31.

RATNAM, P. "The Economy of New Democracy." *India Quarterly* (Oct-Dec 1950) 331-41.

RAVENHOLT, ALBERT. "Formosa—The Test." *The Reporter* (12 Sep 1950) 6-9.

ROSE, SAUL. "Formosa—For Whom?" *Eastern World* (Dec 1953) 20-1.

Round Table Editorial. "Britain, America and China—Divergence of Policy." *Round Table* (Dec 1958) 7-16.

RUCKER, SIR ARTHUR. "Korea—The Next Stage." *International Affairs* (London) (Jul 1954) 313-9.

RYDER, WILFRED. "China—A New Military Power." *Eastern World* (Apr 1952) 15-6.

———. "China Builds for War." *Eastern World* (Jan 1953) 14-5.

SCHWARZENBERGER, GEORG. "Title to Territory: Response to a Challenge." *The American Journal of International Law* (Apr 1957) 308-24.

SCOTT, D. E. "Hong Kong." *New Statesman* and *Nation* (21 May 1949) 530.

SCOTT, JOHN. "The Case for two Chinas." *The New Leader* (6 Oct 1958) 3-6.

STANDFORD, NEAL. "Tug of War of Two Chinas." *Foreign Policy Bulletin* (15 Oct 1958) 19.

STEINER, A. H. "Mainsprings of Chinese Communist Foreign Policy." *The American Journal of International Law* (Jan 1950) 69-99.

———. "United States and the two Chinas." *Far Eastern Survey* (May 1953) 57-61.

———. "Maoism or Stalinism for Asia." *Far Eastern Survey* (14 Jan 1953) 1-5.

———. "China's Development Programme." *Eastern World* (Jul 1953) 17-8.

STEVENSON, ADLAI E. Radio Speech on April 11, 1955. *Foreign Policy Bulletin* (15 May 1955) 133.

STEWART, NEIL. "China at the Leipzig Fair." *Eastern World* (Oct 1953) 42-4.

STRONG, ANNA LOUISE. "World's Eye View from a Yennan Cave: An Interview with Mao Tse-tung." *Amerasia* (Apr 1947) 122-6.

――――. "The Thought of Mao Tse-tung." *Amerasia* (Jun 1947) 161-74.

SU YU. "The Liberation of Taiwan in Sight." *People's China* (16 Feb 1950) 8-9.

SUN DOUGLAS. "The Trend of China's Foreign Trade." *Eastern World* (Aug 1958) 34.

SUNG, KAYSER. "The China Trade Riddle." *Far Eastern Economic Review* (1 Sep 1960) 504-13.

TAN, T. H. "The Chinese in Malaya." *Eastern World* (Nov 1953) 13-6.

THOMAS, S. B. "Sino-Korean Economic and Cultural Agreement." *Pacific Affairs* (Mar 1954) 61-5.

TSAO, CHUNG-SHU. "Sino-British Trade Relations." *Eastern World* (Apr 1955) 51-60.

――――. "More Trade with Britain." *China Reconstructs* (Apr 1955) 27-8.

――――. "The Embargo and China Trade." *Eastern World* (Sep 1956) 44 and 60.

TSAI, YING-PING. "The Road to Final Victory." *People's China* (16 Feb 1950) 6-7.

TSAO, J. C. "Science and Industry in New China." *China Digest* (28 Jun 1949) 15-6.

TSIAO, KUAN-HUA. "The Chinese People's Republic. A Bulwark of Peace." *International Affairs* (Moscow) (Jun 1955) 27-38.

TSOU, SZU-YEE. "A Balanced Foreign Trade." *China Reconstructs* (Sep 1956) 10-2.

TSOU, TANG. "Mao's Limited War in the Taiwan Strait." *Orbis* (Oct 1959) 332-50.

"What is Formosa." *Foreign Policy Bulletin* (15 Oct 1954) 19.

"What Should U.S. Do About China? Views of John Foster Dulles and Dean Acheson." *Foreign Policy Bulletin* (15 Oct 1958) 20-2.

WHITING, ALLEN S. "Communist China and 'Big Brother'." *Far Eastern Survey* (Oct 1955) 145-51.

――――. "Formosa's Future: Neither China?" *Foreign Policy Bulletin* (15 Sep 1956) 1-2 and 7-8.

WODDIS, H. C. K. "Siam: Cockpit of Anglo-American Interests." *Eastern World* (Jan-Feb 1949) 7-9.
WOLPERT, V. "China's Trade with Non-Communist Countries." *Eastern World* (Sep 1956) 38-40.
WOOLSEY, L. H. "Closure of Ports by Chinese Nationalists." *The American Journal of International Law* (Apr 1950) 350-6.
WRIGHT, QUINCY. "The Status of Communist China." *Journal of International Affairs* (No. 2, 1957) 171-86.
————. "The Chinese Recognition Problem." *The American Journal of International Law* (Jul 1955) 320-38.
————. "Non-recognition of China and International Tensions." *Current History* (Apr 1958) 152-7.
YEH, CHI-CHUANG. "China's Foreign Trade." *Eastern World* (Oct 1957) 34-5.
————. "China's Foreign Trade During Her First Five Year Plan." *People's China* (1 Dec 1957) 9-11.
YOUNGER, KENNETH. "An Analysis of British and U.S. Policies in the Far East." *Eastern World* (Mar 1953) 10-2.
————. "Western Policy in Asia." *Pacific Affairs* (Jun 1952) 115-29.
————. "A British View of the Far East." *Pacific Affairs* (Jun 1954) 99-111.
————. "The Dyason Lectures." *Australian Outlook* (Dec 1955) 201-30.

Newspapers and Periodicals

Board of Trade Journal, London.
China Digest, Hong Kong.
China Monthly Review, Shanghai.
China Today, New Delhi (Chinese Embassy in India).
China Weekly Review, Shanghai.
Chinese Press Survey, Shanghai.
Current Background, Hong Kong (US Consulate-General).
Department of State Bulletin, Washington.
Eastern World, London.
Far Eastern Economic Review, Hong Kong.
Hsin-hua Pan-yueh-kan (*New China Fortnightly*).
Hsin-hua Yueh-pao (*New China Monthly*), Peking.
Hung Chi (*Red Flag*), Peking.
Jen-min Jih-pao (*People's Daily*), Peking.
Journal of the Royal Central Asian Society, London.

New Times, Moscow.

New York Times, New York.

News Bulletin, New Delhi (Chinese Embassy in India).

Peking Review, Peking.

People's China, Peking.

Quarterly Economic Review of China and Hong Kong, London, (Economist Intelligence Unit).

Soviet Press Translations, Washington.

Survey of the China Mainland Press, Hong Kong (US Consulate General).

The Times, London.

Three Monthly Economic Review of China, Hong Kong and North Korea, London (Economist Intelligence Unit).

Vietnam Information, Rangoon.

Index

A bomb, 60-1
Afternoon News, 179
Albania, 210-1
Aleutian Islands, 82
All-China Federation of Trade
  Unions, 177
All-China Journalists Association,
  179
Amery, 246
Amoy, 11, 82
Ando, 89
Anglo-American relations, 34-5,
  107, 149, 250, 260, 266
Anglo-Japanese Alliance, 4-5
Anti-British Movement of 1925-7, 7
ANZUS Pact, 144
Association of British Chambers of
  Commerce, 243
Attlee, Clement (Earl), 50, 58, 60-1,
  64, 66, 88-9, 94, 120, 191
Australia, 82, 110, 112, 243

Bandung Conference, 101, 173, 201
Bank of China, 123
Bao Dai, 126
Beamish, 88
Belgium, 243, 263
Berlin, 227
Bevin, Ernest, 14, 37, 41, 112, 189,
  215, 253, 260
BOAC, 246
Borneo (North), 173
Boxer Protocol, 7, 11
Boxer rebellion, 6
Brandt, Willy, 264
Britain
    and Indo-China War, 129-33,
      149, 254
    and Korea   50-4, 95-9, 68,

74-6
    on Chinese intervention, 56-9
    on political settlement, 70-1
    support to USA, 51, 192
  and Laos, 137, 139
  and Marshall Plan, 249
  and Middle East, 148
  and nationalist movement in
      China, 7-12
  and SEATO, 143-6
  and Vietnam conflict, 151
  and Washington Conference, 9
  and West Europe, 28, 257, 261
  establishment of diplomatic
      relations with China, 24, 36,
      42-3, 45-7, 72, 109, 156,
      229, 252
  on Formosa, 85-9, 97, 102,
      104, 111
  on offshore islands, 106
  on representation of China in
      UN, 37, 41, 46, 156, 184-5,
      195, 199
  predominance in China, 2-3, 6
  protests to China, 219, 221
  relations with EEC, 257, 261
  relations with Formosa, 47,
      110
  relations with Japan, 4-5
  relations with Soviet Union,
      4, 46
  relations with USA, 30, 51, 192
  restrictions on Chinese in, 44
  role in Chinese Civil War, 6,
      25
  seizure of Weihaiwei and
      Kowloon, 3, 5
  trade with China, 1, 36, 43,
      163-4, 215-48
  on embargo, 232-8

sale of aircraft, 244, 246, 255
trade with Formosa, 98
see also British recognition of China, British business in China etc.
Britain-China Conference, 36
British business in China, 168, 217-24, 229
  Chinese attitude towards, 223
  decision to withdraw, 222-3, 259
  difficulties under communists, 217-24
  difficulties under Nationalists, 15
  representations and protests on behalf of, 219, 221
British-China Campaign Committee, 35
British-China Friendship Association, 43
British Council, 39
British Council for the Promotion of International Trade, 229, 243
British Industrial Exhibitions in China, 243, 245, 247-8
British investments in China, 23, 28, 32, 259
British Memorandum of Dec 1926, 9-10
British recognition of China, 23-9, 251
  assumptions behind, 24-9
  Chinese reaction to, 29-37, 120
  Indian influence on, 259
  Soviet attitude to, 37-41
British trade missions to China, 20-1, 215
British trade with China, 28, 163-4, 215-48
  competition with USA, 19-22
  prospects after World War II, 15-6, 17-22
Brown, George, 150-1
Burma, 100, 112, 117, 128, 130, 198
Butler, R.A., 165, 194

Cadogan, Alexander, 186

Cairo Declaration (1943), 13, 85-6, 88-90, 92, 94, 109-11, 191
Calcutta Conference of Asian Communist Parties (1948), 115-6
Cambodia, 79, 128, 131, 133-4, 143-4, 146, 154-5
  neutrality of, 155
  withdrawal of foreign forces from, 156
Canada, 45, 97, 189, 243
Canton, 22, 117
Caradon, Lord, 210
Castle, Mrs., 198
CENTO (Central Treaty Organization), 112
Ceylon, 40, 100, 205, 234
Chang Han-fu, 101, 122, 174, 222, 225
Chang Po-chun, 35
Chartered Bank of India, Australia and China, 168
Chen Yi, 151
Chennault, 34
Cheung Chou, 160
Chi Chao-ting, 237, 239
Chi Peng-fei, 245
Chiang Kai-shek, 6-7, 12-3, 16, 19, 21-2, 30, 39, 82, 84-5, 87, 89, 91, 93-4, 97, 100, 102, 105, 161, 173, 175-6, 199-200, 215
Chiao Kuan-hua, 245
Chien Lung, 31
Chin Chang, 122
China
  aid to Malayan insurgents, 118
  aid to Vietminh, 127, 130
  and Africa, 260
  and EEC, 246, 262, 264-5
  and Indo-China, 132, 151-4, 254
  and Korean Crisis
    military intervention, 42, 50, 54-9, 88
    on cease-fire, 62, 64
    on political settlement, 70-1
    on withdrawal of UN troops, 76-8
  and Laos, 136-7
  and Malaya, 116-8, 123

and North Korea, 54-5, 79-81, 258

and unequal treaties, 1-2, 12

anti-British movement in, 7, 22, 27

attitude towards Hong Kong, 158, 172-4, 178, 181-3, 188

burning of British mission, 44

criticism of British policy towards Formosa, 99

detention of British citizens, 220, 244-5

diplomatic relations with Britain, 36, 42-3, 45-7, 72, 109, 141, 229, 252

establishment of People's Republic of, 33-4, 49, 116, 164-5, 258

industrialization of, 16, 31, 38, 164

isolation from Western world, 35

Maritime Customs Administration of, 3

Nationalist movement in, 7-10

Nixon's visit to, 46, 72, 109, 185, 211, 256-7

possible Soviet intervention in, 17-9, 27, 33, 35

possibility of becoming a Soviet satellite, 27-8, 38, 49

reaction to British proposals on Vietnam, 151-4

reaction to British recognition, 29-37, 120

reaction to SEATO, 145-6

recognition of Ho Chi Minh regime, 40, 126

recovery of tariff autonomy, 1, 9, 11

relations with EEC, 246, 262, 264-5

relations with France, 262

relations with Soviet Union, 33, 35, 49, 251-2, 258, 261

relations with USA, 46, 72, 80, 101, 109, 185, 191, 201, 211, 213, 245, 256-8, 261-2

representation in UN, 30, 39, 41, 46, 156, 184-214

Three World concept, 265

trade with Britain, 36, 43, 163-4, 244, 246, 254-5

trade with Hong Kong, 42, 160-1, 164-8

trade with Soviet bloc, 236

trade with Western nations, 38, 236, 242-5

China and the Cold War, 30

China Association, 217, 228, 243

China Committee for the Promotion of International Trade, 227, 237

China Democratic League, 35

China Digest, 36

China National Import and Export Corporation, 229

Chinese Aeronautical Society, 245

Chinese and Russian Communism, 25-7

Chinese Civil War (1945-49), 16-9, 39, 93, 215

American intervention in, 17-9

British attitude to, 16-9

possible Soviet intervention in, 17-9, 27, 33, 35

Chinese Communist Party, 9

and the Shanghai Incident, 9

establishment of, 9

Manifesto of, 9

on tariffs, 9

Chinese Mechanical Engineering Society, 245

Chinese Oceanography Society, 245

Chinese Peoples' Consultative Conference, 33

Chinese People's Volunteers, 193

Chinese ports, blockade of, 22-3, 30

American attitude, 23

British attitude, 22-3

Soviet attitude, 23

Chinkiang, 11

Chorley, Lord, 233

Chou En-lai, 36-7, 43, 46-7, 55-7,

61-4, 66, 68, 70, 92, 96, 98-9, 101,105, 123, 153, 156, 172, 181, 185, 198-200, 211, 216, 223, 232, 247, 259
and Geneva Conference, 133
on Chinese representation in UN, 188
on Commonwealth Peace Mission, 150
on embargo, 238
on Formosa, 102
on Korean armistice, 194
on Malaya, 121
on SEATO, 145
on talks with USA on Formosa, 101
on US-Chiang military pact, 99
visit to Soviet Union, 37
Chousan Islands, 216
Chung-hua Middle School, 175
Chungking, 12
Churchill, Winston S., 51, 89, 95-6, 197-8
on Chinese entry in UN, 198
on Formosa, 83, 95
on offshore islands, 104-5
Cold War, 33, 251
Collar, H.J., 241, 245
Cominform, 118
Comintern, 7-8, 10
Common Market, *see* EEC
Common Programme, 36
Commonwealth, 34, 36, 40, 98, 112, 126, 150, 250, 261
Communist Party of Britain, 43
Concessions, leases and settlements in China, 3
rivalry of Powers for, 3-5
Conference of Asian and Australasian Countries (Peking, 1949), 117-8
and Malayan insurgency, 117-8
manifesto of, 117-8
Connolly, 37
Conservative Party of Great Britain, 12
Convention of Peking (1860), 160

Convention of 1898, 162
Crosthwaite, 204
Crowe, Colin, 212-3
Cuba, 190, 206
Cultural Revolution, 44, 47, 176-81, 244, 261
Czechoslovakia, 17, 134

Davies, Ernest, 88
Davies, Harold, 227
Deep Bay, 160, 163
Denmark, 199, 242, 263
Denson John, 46
Dictatorship of the Proletariat, 25-6
Diego Garcia, 154, 261
Dixon, Pierson, 199, 204
Douglas-Home, Sir Alec, 47, 110-1, 137, 183, 207, 209-12, 241, 245
Dulles, John Foster, 90, 107, 131, 144, 196, 203, 256

Eastern Europe, 25, 27
Eccles, D., 236
Economic Survey for 1953, 227
Eden, Anthony, 43, 71, 96, 105, 126, 143, 197-8, 234-5, 259
Locarno idea of, 140-3, 145, 255
memoirs of, 141
on British enterprises in China, 218, 222
on China's admission in UN, 194
on Formosa and offshore islands, 103-4
on Indo-China, 126, 131, 133-4, 148
on Korea, 68, 70, 72
on SEATO, 145
on US-Chiang Treaty, 104
Eisenhower, Dwight D., 106, 108, 148, 234
Elizabeth, Queen, 183
Embargo, 42, 67, 166-7, 169, 193, 216, 226, 230-2, 253
Chinese reaction to, 238-40

relaxation of, 232, 234-7, 255
Enterprise, 180
Errol, Frederick J., 238
European Defence Community (EDC), 129
European Economic Community (EEC), 46, 246, 263-4, 266
  British membership of, 257, 261
  Chinese attitude towards, 246, 262
  establishment of Chinese relations with, 264-5
Extraterritorial rights, 2, 12

Fairbank, J.K., 5
Far Eastern Economic Review, 169
Farquharsan, Ronald, 7
Federation of British Industries, 228, 243
Finland, 204
Fitzerald, C.P., 29, 31, 38, 117
Five-Anti campaign, 168, 216-7
Foochow, 82
Formosa (Taiwan), 39, 45, 51, 53, 72, 82, 174, 209
  British attitude on, 85-9, 97, 102, 104, 111
  British consulate in, 110
  Chinese attitude towards, 98-103
  expulsion from UN, 46, 184, 188, 209, 211, 213
  legal aspects of the problem of, 84-92
  neutralization of, 51, 88, 95
  political aspects of the problem of, 92-103
  proposal to convene a conference on, 100-1
  sovereignty over, 91
  strategic importance of, 83
  treaty of mutual defence with USA, 84-5, 104
  "two-China" solution, 96, 205, 209-10, 212-4
  UN trusteeship over, 89, 91-2, 95, 253

US attitude towards, 33, 83, 87-8, 91, 93, 102, 108-9, 182, 197
France, 40, 100, 136, 190, 195, 242
  recognition of China, 40
  relations with China, 262
  relations with Soviet Union, 262
  seizure of Kuang-chou, 3
Frank, Oliver, 27
Fu Chi, 180
Fukien, 82, 174

Gaitskell, Hugh, 107
Gen, Lewis, 158
Geneva Agreements on Indo-China (1954), 134, 139 142-3, 146, 153, 198-9
  Chinese attitude, 135
Geneva Conference, 43 69, 95, 99, 131, 140, 146, 201, 233, 254, 259
  impact on Sino-British relations, 255
Geneva Convention on POWs, 68
George III, 31
Germany (West), 3-5, 8, 16, 19-20, 109, 130, 242
Ghana, 150
Godber, 209, 213-4
Grantham, Alexander, 168, 181
Grantham, Vincent Alpe, 168
Great Britain-China Committee, 245
Great Wall of China, 4
Greece, 126
Grey, Anthony, 44, 178
Griffith, James, 120

Hainan, 93, 216, 254
Hanifah, 201
Hankow, 3, 11
Harbin, 11
Harcourt, Cecil, 161
Harriman, Averell, 140
Harvey, Ian, 224
Hay, 5
Haytor, William, 125

Heath, Edward, 263-4
Henderson (Lord), 66
Hewitt, P.M., 178
Ho Chi Minh, 40, 125-6, 132
Ho Hsiang-ning, 120
Holland, 243, 263
Home Lord, *see* Douglas-Home, Sir Alec
Hong Kong, 19, 28-30, 34, 36, 44, 48, 51, 59, 83, 98, 109, 116-7, 152-3, 234, 250-1, 256
  acquisition of, 1
  and Cultural Revolution in China, 45
  as a security threat to China, 171
  as an entrepot, 253
  British investments in, 159
  British military reinforcements in, 165
  Chinese attitude towards, 158, 172-4, 178, 181-3, 188
  Chinese immigration into, 40, 165
  Chinese representation in, 181
  defence of, 162
  dependence on China, 148
  disturbances in, 176, 179
  future of, 182-4
  its effect on Communist Asia, 29
  its utility for China, 170-2, 181-3, 257
  possible invasion by China, 28, 31
  question of 71 Chinese aircraft in, 34, 40-2, 219, 252
  trade with China, 42, 160-1, 164-8
  US attitude towards, 161
Hong Kong Evening News, 179
Hopkinson, 227
Hopson, D.C., 44, 178, 180
House of Commons, 50, 67
House of Lords, 137
Hsiao Chien, 37
Hsiao Tien-lai, 173
Hsien T'ai Daily, 120

Hsueh-hsi, 31
Huang Hua, 77-8
Hudson, G.F., 117, 249
Hutchinson, 36

Iceland, 199
Inchon, 52
India, 130
  resolution on China's admission in the UN, 189
  resolution on POWs, 68,
  Sino-Indian conflict, 260
Indian Ocean, 112, 124, 154, 261
Indo-China, 79, 253-4
  Anglo-American intervention in, 130
  British attitude, 124-5
  Chinese attitude, 40, 126-7, 132, 151-4, 254
  communist victory in, 125
  French attitude, 124
  Soviet interest in, 129
Indo-China War, 125-6, 197
  and Britain, 129-33, 149, 254
  and China, 126-30
  and France, 125
  and question of Chinese representation in UN, 197-9
  possible Chinese military involvement in, 128-9
  Western Powers' intervention in, 132
Indonesia, 100, 117, 130, 149, 234
International Court of Justice, 92
International Settlements and Concessions in China, 13-4
Italy, 45, 243
Izvestia, 40, 150

Japan, 19-20, 34, 55-6. 80, 83-4, 98, 243, 265
  acquisition of German rights, 5
  aggression in Manchuria, 12
  alliance with Britain, 5
  and Korea, 48-9
  and Washington Conference, 8

competition with Britain, 16
economic resurgence of, 34
Treaty of Peace with Republic
   of China, 84
Twenty-one Demands on China,
   4
victory over Russia, 7
Japanese Peace Treaty, 84-5
Jardine, Matheson, 223
Jay, Douglas, 243
Jebb, Gladwyn, 62-3, 65, 67, 196
Johnson, Lyndon B., 148-9, 151-4
Jones, F.C., 18
Jordan, 107
Jowitt, Viscount, 50

Karakhan, 8
"Kashmir Princess," 174
Kelly, David, 52
Kennedy, J.F., 138, 206, 256
Kenya, 130
Keswick, John, 244
Khmer Rouge, 133, 157
Khrushchov, N.S., 176, 181
Kiao-chou, 3-4
Killearn, Lord, 112
Kim Il Sung, 79-81
Kissinger, Henry A., 46
Kiukiang, 11
Knowland, 37
Ko Pai-nien, 31
Kohl, Helmut, 264
Kong Lae, 137-8
Korea, 48-81, 130
   All-Korean Commission, 70
   ceasefire negotiations, 95
   elections in, 70-1
   North-South Korea dialogue, 74
   partition of, 72
   political settlement of, 69-71,
      197
   recent developments in, 73-81
   reunification of, 59, 69, 74, 77,
      81, 95
   strategic importance of, 48-9,
      95
   UN Command in, 66-8, 76-9

dissolution of, 78
withdrawal of foreign troops
   from, 71, 77-8, 80
withdrawal of UN troops from,
   73, 76, 79
Korea, North (Democratic People's
   Republic of Korea), 69, 74,
   78, 188, 231, 256, 258
   admission into WHO, 74
   ambition to unify Korea, 80-1
   observer status at UN, 74
   relations with China, 54-5,
      79-81, 258
Korea, South (Republic of Korea),
   55, 69, 74, 78-9, 98
   withdrawal of UN troops from,
      73, 76, 79
Korean Armistice, 169, 195, 228,
   230, 232
Korean War, 42, 99, 120, 127-8,
   130, 172, 187, 233, 253, 258,
   260
   and Britain, 50-4, 56-9, 69-72
   and Sino-British trade, 216-7
   and Truman's threat to use
      atom bomb in, 60-1
   armistice agreement, 67-9, 75-9
   armistice and its aftermath, 43
   Chinese conditions for cease-
      fire, 62
   Chinese intervention in, 42, 50,
      54-6, 58, 88, 167, 190-2, 253
   efforts to reach a political
      settlement, 69-71
   Good Offices Committee, 65
   Group on Ceasefire, 63-4
   impact on Sino-British rela-
      tions, 71-2
   outbreak of, 47, 72, 80, 85
   quest for a ceasefire, 59-69
   question of POWs, 67-8
   UN Command in, 66-8, 76-9
   UN objectives in, 53, 61, 71,
      94, 233
   war aims of Western Powers,
      57
Kosygin, A.N., 153-4
Kowloon, 2-3, 5, 22, 159, 173, 175-7

Incident of 1948 in, 162-3
riots in, 160
Kuangchow, 3
Kuo Mo-jo, 200
Kuomintang, 9, 11, 15, 18-9, 22,
30, 32, 34, 36, 51, 165, 174, 185,
208, 215
Kwangtung, 172-4, 188

Lai-chou, 128
Lamma, 160
Lancashire, 34
Landsdowne, Lord, 4
Lantou, 160
Laos, 124, 128, 131, 133-4, 143, 146,
149, 205
abortive coup of 1964, 138
agreement of Nov 1957, 136
agreement on the cessation of
hostilities in, 135
and Britain, 137, 139
and China, 136-7
and international conference on
settlement of Laotian question, 138
and international supervisory
commission, 135
and Soviet Union, 136-7
civil war situation in, 131
coalition government in, 138
crisis of 1960-61, 137
elections in, 136
invasion by Vietminh, 128, 131
neutralization of, 138
political settlement in, 135
uprising of Kong Lae, 137-8
US military intervention in, 137
withdrawal of Vietminh forces
from, 133
"Lean-to-one" side policy, 33, 249,
252
Lebanon, 107
Lei Jen-min, 228
Li Chi-sen, 35
Li, S.K., 36
Lin Hai-yun, 242
Lindsay, Michael, 30-1

Listowel, Lord, 15
Liu Shao-chi, 32
on aggressive Chinese policy,
117
on liberation struggles in
Southeast Asia, 117
on socialism in China, 117
Lloyd, Selwyn, 107, 139, 194-5,
198, 223, 233, 236-7
Lo Kuei-po, 180
Lome Convention, 265
London Chamber of Commerce,
243
Luang Prabang, 128

Ma Shu-lun, 35
Macao, 158, 177, 182-3
MacArthur, Douglas, 56, 59-60
Macdonald, Malcolm, 112
Maclean, Donald, 107, 124, 149
Macmillan, Harold, 201
Malacca Straits, 112
Malaya, 36, 40, 83, 98, 112, 123,
128, 130, 133-4, 234-5, 259
aim of communist insurgents
in, 121
and China, 116-8, 123
British stake in, 113
change in tactics of communist
insurgents in, 121-3
impact of British recognition of
China on, 118
military uprising in, 113-6
possible presence of Chinese
consuls in, 119-20, 259
trade with China, 122
Malayan Communist Party (MCP),
114-6, 122
Malayan People's Anti-Japanese
Army (MPAJA), 114
Malaysia, 149
confrontation with Indonesia,
149
relations with China, 123
Malik, Jacob, 67, 185-7
Man Kam To, 177
Manchuria, 18, 33, 48, 55, 58, 84,

189
Manchurian War, 4
Mancroft, 232-3
Mao Tse-tung, 25-6, 31, 33-6, 38, 80, 102, 123, 215, 251, 263
  and "lean-to-one" side policy, 33, 249, 252
  and "new democracy", 33
  and Stalin, 33
Maritime Customs Administration, 2-3
Marshall Plan, 21, 28, 37, 115, 249
Marxism, 27
  and nationalism, 27
Matsu, 82, 97, 106, 108
"May 4th Movement," 8-9
Mei Ju-ao, 90
Menon, Krishna, 201, 204-5
Mirs Bay, 160, 163
Mitchell, G.E., 217
Molotov, V.M., 133
Morrison, Herbert, 88, 193
Moscow Declaration of Dec 1945, 17-8
Moscow International Economic Conference, 226-7
  and Britain, 227
Murray, 78

Nan Chiao Daily, 120
Nanking, 36, 161
  treaty of, 159
Na-sam, 128
National Liberation Front (NLF)
  formation of, 146
National People's Congress, 102
NATO, 129, 141, 171, 251, 261-2, 264
Nehru, Jawaharlal, 37, 188
New China News Agency, 176, 178, 240
"New Democracy", 33
New Democratic Youth League, 114
New Territories, 159-60, 182
  expiration of lease of, 257
New Zealand, 112

Ng Heng, 121
Ngo Dinh Diem, 139, 147
Nigeria, 150
Nixon, Richard M., 212
  visit to China, 46, 72, 109, 185, 211, 256-7
North Altantic Treaty Organization, *see* NATO
Northern Island, 258
Norway, 243
Nosavan Phoumi, 136
Nutting, Anthony, 96, 232

O' Neill, 174
"Open Door" Policy in China, 5-6
  and Britain, 5
  Hay's Notes on, 5
Overseas Chinese, 36, 120, 171
Oxford University, 44

Pakistan, 100
Palmerston, Lord, 6
Pan Malayan Federation of Trade Unions, 114
Parallel, 38th, 51-2, 61, 67, 172
  crossing of, 53, 58, 62
Parker, Douglas Dodds, 198
Parker, Tu, 175
Pathet Lao, 127, 133, 135-6, 157
  integration in Royal Army, 136
Peking Review, 175
Penghu, *see* Pescadores Islands
Pentagon Papers, 147
People's Daily, 90, 99-102, 112, 118, 127, 132-3, 135, 139, 145-6, 152, 174, 176, 182, 200, 202-3, 206, 239
People's Democracy, 25
People's Liberation Army (PLA), 55
People's Republic of China, *see* China
Pescadores Islands, 84, 92, 107
Philippines, 83, 98, 117, 123
Phong Saly, 135-6
Phouma Souvanna, 138

Pierson, Lester, 205
Pishan, 108
Pompidou, George, 263
Port Arthur, 3
Portugal, 158
Pospelov, 26
Potsdam Declaration, 84-5, 88-90, 92, 111
Pratt, Sir John, 1, 3
Pravda, 25-6
proletarian internationalism, 27
Pyongyang, 54

Quemoy, 82, 97, 106-8, 199

Rahaman, Tengku Abdul, 123
Rahaman, Tuanku Abdul, 123
Reading, Lord, 96, 218, 223
Red Guards, 44, 177
"Relief Committee for Overseas Refugees from Malaya," 120
Rhee, Syngman, 55
Robinson, John, 243
Romulo, Carlos P., 185
Royal Central Asian Society, 241
Royle, Anthony, 47, 157, 246
    visit to China, 246, 257
Rusk, Dean, 208
Russia, *see* Soviet Union
Russo-Japanese War (1904-5), 7

Saillant, Louis, 117
Sam Neua, 128, 135-6
San Francisco Peace Treaty with Japan, 84-5
Sananikone, Phoui, 136
Sarawak, 173
Schwarzenberger, Georg, 87
SEATO, 43, 112, 139-40, 143-6, 148, 256-8
    and Britain, 143-5
    and China, 145-6
    Bangkok Conference of, 145-6
    provisions of, 144
Sha Tau Kok, 179

Shanghai, 2, 8-9, 23, 32, 34, 100, 161, 163, 178, 215, 219, 225, 248
Shanghai Incident of 30th May 1925, 7, 9
Shantung, 4-5, 8
Shawcross, Sir Hartley, 166, 231
Shen Chun-ju, 35
Shih Hui, 180
Shimoneseki Treaty, 90-1
Shumchun Reservoir, 178
Singapore, 112, 122-3, 234-5
Sino-British Trade Committee (SBTC), 229, 236
    formation of, 228
    activities of, 228
Sino-British Trade Council, 243
Sino-Indian conflict (1962), 260
    Britain's aid to India in, 260
Sino-Soviet rift, 28, 43, 245, 247, 251, 261
Soames, Christopher, 263
Society for Anglo-Chinese Understanding, 43
Southeast Asia, 28, 40, 93, 112
    British interests in, 112, 123-4, 130
    formation of a defence organization in, 140, 199
    possible Chinese intervention in, 129
    strategic importance of, 112
    see also SEATO, Malaya, Laos, Indo-China, Vietnam, etc.
Soviet Union, 84, 108, 142, 249
    abrogation of unequal treaties with China, 7-8
    alliance with China, 29, 37, 130
    and Formosa, 99-100
    and Indo-China conflict, 132
    and Korea, 48, 51, 76, 81, 192
    and Laos, 136
    and military uprising in Malaya, 116
    and Sino-British relations, 38, 186
    and Southeast Asia, 119
    attitude towards Calcutta Conference of Asian Communist

Parties, 115-6
collaboration with Chinese nationalism, 6-9
on Washington Conference (1921-22), 8
possible intervention in China, 17-9, 27, 33, 35
relations with Britain, 4, 46
relations with China, 28, 33-5, 37-41, 43, 49, 245, 247, 251-2, 258, 261-2, 266
relations with France, 262
rupture of relations with Kuomintang, 11
seizure of Port Arthur, 3
supply of industrial equipment to China, 226, 242
trade with China, 236
Ssu, Mu, 37
Stalin, J.V., 33, 50, 68, 129, 194
China policy of, 26
Stevenson, Adlai, 207-8
Stewart, Michael, 152, 155
Stonecutters Island, 160
Strauss, Franz Josef, 263-4
Suez Canal, 130
Suez War, 236
Sun Yat-sen, 6-8, 174
Sunday Times, 223
Sweden, 242
Switzerland, 242

Tachen, 108
Taipei, 82, 92, 103
"Taiping" rebellion, 6
Taiwan, *see* Formosa
Taiwan Straits Crises
First (1954-55), 103-6, 200
Second (1958), 103, 106-8
Tariff, 1-2, 6, 9
Tass, 39
Teng Hsiao-ping, 263, 265
Tennant, Peter, 228
Thailand, 123-4, 128
British interests in, 124
Thompson, R.G.K., 147
Thorneycroft, Peter, 228, 232

Three-Anti Campaign, 168
Three World Concept, 265
Tibet, 205
Tientsin, 2
Times, The, 16-8, 21-2, 47, 95, 113, 126, 166
Tin Fung Daily News, 179
Tito, Marshal, 35, 38
Titoism, 29, 33
Tonkin Gulf Incident, 147
Treaties
Convention of Peking (1860), 160
Convention of 1898, 162
Nanking Treaty (1842), 1, 159
Portsmouth Treaty (1905), 4
San Francisco Peace Treaty, 84-5
Sino-British Commercial Treaty, 15
Sino-US Commercial Treaty (1946), 15
Tientsin Treaties, 2, 244
Treaty of 1943, 12-5, 161
Treaty of Shimoneseki, 90-1
Trevelyan, H., 93, 105, 224
Trevor-Roper, Hughes, 44
Trinidad and Tobago, 150
Truman, Harry S., 60-1, 85, 88, 93
Trygve, Lie, 188
Tsao Chung-shu, 229-30
Tsao Jo-ming, 219
Tsiang, T.F., 185
Tsingtao, 41
Tsuen Wan, 175
Tumen River, 48
Tung Fang-hsiang, 151-2
Turton, R.H., 86-7, 91, 143
"Two-China" solution, 96, 206, 209-10, 212-4

United Nations, 53, 156, 182, 235
admission of China in, 211-4
admission of 16 States in, 203
Charter of, 88, 91, 106, 147, 163, 200, 212

condemnation of China as an aggressor, 62, 65-6, 252
embargo resolution, 166-7, 216, 226, 230
expulsion of Taiwan, 46, 184, 188, 209, 211, 213
General Assembly, 42, 65, 67-8, 74, 88, 166, 189, 192, 199, 201, 204, 208-9, 213, 230
question of Chinese representation in, 39, 41, 156, 184-214
Security Council, 39-40, 51, 57, 76, 78, 89, 185-7, 189-90, 200, 209, 213
trusteeship over Formosa, 89, 91-2, 95, 253
UNCURK (United Nations Commission for Unification and Rehabilitation of Korea), 73, 75
UNRRA (United Nations Relief and Rehabilitation Association), 20
Universal Postal Union, 193
USA, 84, 91, 142
and Britain, 30
and Indo-China War, 26, 130
and Japan, 34
and Korea, 51, 70-1
and offshore islands, 107
and Tonkin Gulf Incident, 147
assistance to Chiang Kai-shek, 21
attitude towards Hong Kong, 16
bilateral talks with China, 100-1, 201
bombing of N. Vietnam, 147, 150-1, 153
Commercial Treaty with China (1946), 15
Defence Treaty with Chiang, 96, 99, 102, 109
military presence in East Asia, 261
on China's seat in UN, 190, 197
policy towards Formosa, 33, 87-8, 91, 93, 102, 108-9, 197
relations with China, 46, 72, 80,

101, 109, 185, 191, 211, 213, 245, 256-8, 261-2
threat to use A-bomb in Korea, 60-1
withdrawal of forces from Vietnam, 148, 153
withdrawal of troops from Europe, 262

Vietcong, 139
Vietminh, 40, 125-7, 132
Chinese aid to, 127, 130
withdrawal from Laos, 133
Vietnam, 115, 117, 124, 133
coalition government in, 134
partition of, 134, 139
reunification of, 135, 139, 146, 157
use of poison gas in, 152
withdrawal of American forces from, 148, 153
Vietnam Conflict, 146-51, 258
and British proposals, 151
Chinese reaction to, 151-4
and Paris Agreements of 1973, 156-7
and Paris peace talks, 155
extension of, 154
victory of Communists in 1975, 157
Vietnamisation of, 155
Vietnam, North (Democratic Republic of Vietnam), 142, 147-8, 154
Communist Party of, 146
US bombing of, 147, 150-1, 155
Vietnam, South (Republic of Vietnam), 79, 131, 139, 146-8, 151, 153, 155
victory of Communists in, 157
withdrawal of American troops from, 148, 153
Voprosy Istorii, 115, 126
Vyshinsky, A., 68

Walker, Gordon, 150

Walker, Peter, 247
Wang Min-chih, 34, 36
Washington Conference (1921-22), 8-9, 255
Wedemeyer, A.C., 48
Weihaiwei, 3, 5, 11
Wilson, Harold, 147-8, 150, 152-5, 264
World Culture, 34, 37, 256
World Federation of Trade Unions (WFTU), 117
World Health Organization (WHO), 74
World War I, 2, 4-5
World War II, 12, 15, 54, 83, 249
Wright, Quincy, 85

Wu, 145
Wu Hsiu-chuan, 60-2, 89

Yalu River, 48, 50, 129
Yang Kuang, 177
Yangtse, 2-6, 11, 18
Yeh Chi-chuang, 228, 240
Yeh Chien-ying, 172-3, 188
Younger, Kenneth, 61, 86, 119, 131, 258
Yuan Li-wu, 170
Yuan Shih-kai, 6-7
Yugoslavia, 27, 33, 188
Yunnan, 129
Yushan, 108